WA

POCKET HANDBOOK

2012

WATTS · PEOPLE WITH A PASSION FOR BUILDINGS

First published in 1983, the *Watts Pocket Handbook* is an annual publication.

The editors wish to express their indebtedness to previous editors of the handbook, who laid the foundations on which this 28th edition has been built.

The editors would also like to acknowledge with thanks the contributions of individuals in the property market and construction industry who send suggestions and comments. Such contributions are always welcome and should be sent to the Marketing Department. T: +44 (0)20 7280 8000. Email: marketing@watts.co.uk

Acknowledgments

The project stages and descriptions from the *RIBA Outline Plan of Work 2007* (as amended), copyright Royal Institute of British Architects, are reproduced here with the permission of the RIBA.

BRE material is reproduced with permission from Building Research Establishment Ltd.

Crown copyright material is reproduced under the Open Government Licence v1.0 for public sector information: www.nationalarchives.gov.uk/doc/open-government-licence/

ISBN 978 1 84219 725 7

Published by the Royal Institution of Chartered Surveyors (RICS)

Typeset by Columns Design XML Ltd, Reading, Berks

Cover design work by Art & Industry (UK) Ltd, Clerkenwell, London

Printed by Page Bros, Norwich

Contents

Contents

Design 241

Contents

Introduction

It has been a stormy year for the property industry and with no immediate prospect of relief it's good to know that you can continue to rely on a familiar guide. Now in its 28th year, the *Watts Pocket Handbook* brings together the considered thoughts, comments and guidance of over 40 contributors from within Watts and from other luminaries in the legal and insurance industries.

I am immensely proud of the handbook, and in my travels up and down the country I am always reassured by the number of positive and unsolicited comments from readers in many branches of the profession. We strive to keep the content topical, relevant and concise but inevitably changes in legislation and good practice occur throughout the year – subscribers to our regular bulletins can also benefit from regular updates so if you would like to receive these please send an email to wattsbulletin@watts.co.uk

The handbook continues to grow and this year we have added whole new sections on property and construction insurances as well as building information modelling (BIM), knowledge management and office relocation and fit-out. All chapters have been reviewed and some heavily modified to reflect the current state of play.

I'm confident that you will find this handbook useful and that if this is your first copy it will become a valued and dog-eared first-point of reference. We'd love to hear from you if you have any comments or suggestions for future editions.

Trevor Rushton

Technical Director, Watts Group PLC

Technical due diligence

Property investment and ownership

Best practice in building surveys

Conceptually, there is little difference between the inspection and method of reporting upon commercial and industrial property compared with surveys of residential or other property. Many of the principles of setting up, confirming the instruction and report writing are identical, as is of course the process of reflective thought that is a key ingredient in any survey for investment or occupation.

Of course, it is the form of construction and style of building that is often different (although not exclusively so) and surveyors must be familiar with both of these and common defects and things to watch out for before accepting instructions; it is far better to decline an instruction if the scope of the survey would be beyond your expertise than to muddle through and potentially miss an important issue.

Commercial and industrial property

Commercial and industrial buildings take many forms, but just as importantly, purchasers and occupiers have many different requirements. The form of reporting on an identical building for an investor could require a different emphasis from that needed for an occupier or indeed that needed to be included in a vendor's pack. Flexibility and professionalism is the key, both for providing an appropriate level of service and for maintaining the quality of professional advice. There is a risk of allowing quality standards to drop in favour of fiercely competitive fee quotations and timescales that are unrealistic. However, a brief report need not be a 'lightweight' report if it is prepared properly and based upon proper consideration of the evidence.

In 2010, the Royal Instiution of Chartered Surveyors (RICS) updated its guidance note *Building surveys and technical due diligence of commercial property* (hereafter referred to as the 'Commercial/Industrial GN'). As with the 2005 version, the 2010 edition provides comprehensive guidance and advice for surveyors and engineers involved in building surveys of commercial property. It is written to apply in England and Wales, although its content is equally applicable elsewhere. The document is important for RICS members. They are not obliged to follow the advice and recommendations given and are free to make their own mind up when it comes to what to include or how to present the information, and as long as the advice given is properly thought through with the correct level of skill and care there should be no need for concern. However, in cases where professional negligence is being considered, adherence to the guidance note would at least give partial defence by virtue of having followed recognised practice.

Taking instructions

Experience has shown that managing client expectation is the key to ensuring that the client is satisfied with the service and the quality of the report. The instruction stage is often botched or not recorded properly – in many cases this is where a job will start to go wrong. It is very important to take the time to understand the client's exact requirements, the purpose of the survey, the scope and limitations, specialist inspections, etc.

The guidance note sets out in some detail the issues to be resolved at this stage including:

- ❖ the identity of the client (this is sometimes unknown until completion);
- ❖ the scope of service;
- ❖ timescales;
- ❖ the fee;
- ❖ terms and conditions of business; and
- ❖ limitations.

At this stage it will be apparent whether or not specialist subconsultants will be required. Commonly this will include mechanical, electrical, public health and lift engineers, cladding consultants, environmental engineers or structural engineers. Are these consultants to be paid direct by the client (preferable) or by the surveyor? In the latter case, make sure that these appointments are tied down – preferably with back-to-back agreements – and that Professional Indemnity Insurance (PII) levels are matched.

Time pressures are usually acute and purchasers often make optimistic promises in order to secure preferred bidder status. This often places unreasonable pressure on the surveyor. Whereas at one time quick 'walk-around' surveys were frowned upon, the Commercial/Industrial GN acknowledges that it may be necessary to accept this type of instruction, but points out that surveyors must ensure that the client is under no illusion that compromising on time will reduce the quality of the report. Under these circumstances you should take great care to explain the limitations of such an approach. Preferably, demands to compromise should be resisted, but as an alternative spend the same time on site and reduce the time reporting by focusing on key issues only. Composing a short report is as much of an art as writing a full one: in many respects the task is more difficult.

Health and safety

'Time spent in reconnaissance is seldom wasted' is a maxim that surveyors should remember. Aside from giving the opportunity to plan resources, assess the fee and determine the need for specialist investigations, it also enables time for a proper risk assessment to be prepared.

Regrettably, too few surveyors treat health and safety as seriously as they should; it is criminal law and penalties for non-compliance are severe. Employers have a duty to protect the safety of their staff – one of the key issues being a proper risk assessment. The risk assessment should be appropriate for the particular circumstances, but it should be recorded in writing.

Key points are:

- ❖ risk assessment – can be in any appropriate form but it should be recorded and filed;
- ❖ the employer has a duty not to put the surveyor at risk;
- ❖ the surveyor must bring limitations to the employer's notice;
- ❖ wear appropriate dress; and
- ❖ use appropriate equipment and maintain it in good order.

You must also ensure that:

- ❖ the places in which you work are safe;
- ❖ safe working practices are clearly defined;
- ❖ first aid equipment is available;
- ❖ you do not endanger yourself or others;
- ❖ you protect anyone who uses your services;
- ❖ you protect the people that work for you; and
- ❖ you protect anyone affected by your work.

Perfect Planning Prevents Poor Performance – make sure that your team is properly briefed as to their roles and responsibilities, the purpose of the survey and the extent of the instruction. Furthermore, it is vital to arrange proper access with the tenant/occupier.

Preparation is essential, it gives the opportunity to seek out relevant documents – as-built drawings, certificates, previous reports, etc. It also establishes any particular working practices on site that could impinge upon the survey and any particular health and safety issues that may be relevant. Arranging for a hydraulic platform to attend site to facilitate a roof inspection is fine, but not if the tenant is not expecting it and has, say, a 24-hour operation with lorries coming and going all the time. Frequently, working arrangements on large industrial or distribution sites are such that the operators demand full risk assessments before using access equipment – trying to sort these out at 10:00 on the morning of the survey with the team on site is not the most productive use of time.

When surveying a property – especially an empty one – practitioners ought to conform to the procedures outlined under 'Practical Procedures' in *Health and safety at work* on page 154.

See also *Surveying Safely* published by RICS.

Equipment and note taking

Unlike the equivalent residential survey guidance, the Commercial/Industrial GN is not specific as to the equipment that you must use when conducting a survey – it merely lists a range of basics that a survey kit 'may' include. Clearly, one should expect to take the equipment that would be necessary to undertake the task properly – it would not be very sensible, for example, to turn up without a measuring tape if you had specifically been asked to prepare a reinstatement valuation.

Many surveyors prefer to use digital recording equipment to take comprehensive notes – there is no problem with that but:

- ❖ beware of things like wind and background noise;
- ❖ keep checking to make sure that you are actually recording;
- ❖ beware that sometimes you can record things you don't intend; and
- ❖ consider whether it is productive to have secretarial staff typing notes all day before you can write the report.

The key issue is to take good, legible notes and to retain these on file. Do not expect to dictate the final version of the report on site – this does not allow time for reflective thought.

The inspection

Different survey types demand different levels of inspection, and this should be agreed with the client at the outset. In the event that physical restrictions are more onerous than expected, this needs to be communicated back to the client as soon as possible and certainly not left to a short line in the completed report.

Making friends with the occupier is a good move; often there will be issues with site security and the need to be accompanied (although this can often be worked around by diplomacy – and weight of numbers). A team of five or six cannot do their job properly if one security guard has been allocated, but patience and compromise can often work well in achieving proper access.

Surveyors will each have their own methodology for dealing with surveys and the guidance notes do not dictate how inspections should be carried out. However, a methodical approach is the key, and this would normally mean that an elemental approach is to be preferred.

Conducting a good building inspection and preparing a good report should not be treated lightly. Taking a graduate with you and then asking him or her to 'do the insides' while you examine the exterior – or the interesting parts – is not very good training and certainly runs the risk that small pieces of evidence that relate to a bigger picture may not be assimilated. Technical knowledge is all too often taken for granted – but if you don't know what can go wrong how can you possibly be expected to look for it? It is very easy to look at something and to describe it, but does this necessarily address the real issues?

Surveyors are not infallible, but it is imperative that you do not fall into the trap of simply describing what you see without thinking about the job that the element is doing and how it interrelates with other components or elements – think behind the surface – consider the building in its underpants.

The guidance note sets out many of the types of issue that ought to be identified during an inspection; some of the more important are summarised below:

❖ In a large building it is not anticipated that the surveyor will check each and every unit/window or feature where there is a lot of repetition.

❖ Comment on fire resistance, compartmentation, thermal and insulation standards.

❖ Assess the effectiveness and condition of structural frames.

❖ Check the degree of flatness along with surface defects (particularly important for industrial and storage buildings).

❖ Inspect ceiling and floor voids. Check space for services/crossovers as well as fixity of pedestals/suspension systems.

❖ Inspect roof voids where they are accessible.

❖ Efforts should be made to inspect ducts and similar enclosed areas where this is possible.

❖ Check staircase width, handrail height, etc. and general compliance with Building Regulations.

❖ Check provision of sanitary facilities for DDA and Workplace Regulations.

❖ Disability considerations should include different textures to wall and floor finishes.

Services installations

In complex buildings, mechanical, electrical and public health (MEP) installations are usually inspected by specialists, often under the direction of the surveyor. However, in certain circumstances this will not occur and a surveyor may be commissioned to provide general advice. The object here is to carry out a general visual inspection and to form a view as to the type of installation, the materials used and the need for more detailed investigations. RICS cautions against direct appointments and payment of subconsultant's fees for fear of assuming a liability for parts of the report.

One point to watch is the services engineers' tendency to rely upon Chartered Institution of Building Services Engineers (CIBSE) tables of life expectancy. Too frequently we find observations like 'the installation is 25 years old and therefore at the end of its life' without comment upon the standard of maintenance and use of the particular component, when in reality a longer life can be anticipated. It is the surveyor's role to challenge such observations and make sure that the advice given is sensible and practicable.

Surveyors will be expected to provide general advice on issues such as compliance with relevant lighting standards under the Workplace Regulations. The position of gas service intakes as well as the condition of appliances and pipe runs should also be identified. Any smell of gas should be reported immediately.

Surveyors are advised to note and report on the nature of the installation including pipework, point of entry, stopcocks, etc. as well as compliance with water by-laws, visual corrosion and leaks. The guidance note suggests a representative number of taps be turned on.

Hot water and heating installations should be checked for operation and general condition.

Underground drainage is often an area that fails to be mentioned properly – either through lack of access for visual inspection (reasonable) or because the surveyor forgot to bring drain cover keys or could not be bothered to lift lightweight covers (unreasonable). Be clear about the extent of the inspection and whether or not covers are to be lifted. The guidance note advises surveyors to:

❖ open all reasonably accessible lightweight inspection chamber covers within the curtilage of the property;

❖ record assumed drainage runs; and

❖ report their general condition.

CCTV inspections might be commissioned, but beware of the limitations of these – it is not always possible, within the time available, to inspect and plot all runs. Furthermore, silting and encrustation may mean that an element of jetting and cleaning is needed before a survey can be undertaken. It is worth being very clear about the scope of work in these circumstances and agreeing this with the client at the outset. For example, if a fixed sum is required, agree that this be limited to what can be achieved with this equipment for a fixed time.

Another point worth checking is the direction that drainage runs take when they leave site – for example, do they cross adjoining land?

External areas

The scope of the external inspection depends upon instructions, but remember to be alert for boundary issues, tree growth, Japanese Knotweed, Giant Hogweed, power lines, etc. as well as any particular topographical points of concern.

Health and safety legislation

A detailed analysis of the property for compliance is not normally undertaken unless specifically agreed with the client at the outset. Surveyors should be aware of relevant legislation that might affect health and safety in the building and advise accordingly. The following are important:

❖ protection against falling;

❖ sanitary provision;

❖ lighting;

❖ floors and traffic routes;

❖ glazing;

❖ working at height;

❖ fire precautions – resistance, means of escape and protection; and

❖ ventilation and cleanliness.

For more detail on these aspects, see page 154 onwards.

Security

With increased terrorist threats, security issues have become more important and should command some attention to detail in an inspection and report.

One of the points recommended for attention is the existence and condition of window film – a word of caution though – to be effective, the film must transfer explosion loads back to the structure of a building where it is more likely that they can be dissipated safely by the inertia of the building. This can only be achieved with physical connection to glazing beads with silicone at the perimeter. Furthermore, providing film on laminated glass alters the properties of the glass and can give rise to a greater propensity for the glass to rupture around the edge – and so form a large and lethal projectile.

The guidance note recommends reference to guides like *Secured by design* which may help a surveyor comment on security aspects.

Within the UK, crime mapping has now become established and via local police websites the surveyor can interrogate data down to sub-ward level. Such material can provide useful background information when assessing risks.

Social inclusion

Unless otherwise instructed, a surveyor would not be expected to carry out a detailed audit of the premises. However, the identification of key barriers to access and any other significant points of concern ought to be mentioned, not forgetting that there is much more to social inclusion than simply the provision of ramps and disabled toilets. See also the social inclusion section on page 164 onwards.

Environmental issues and sustainability

Investors and funders are sensitive to environmental issues. More often than not an investment purchase will involve the preparation of a suitable Phase I (and sometimes a Phase II) environmental audit by appropriately qualified specialists. In these circumstances (and assuming that the process includes a site visit) it is important to establish exactly where responsibility stops to avoid duplication and, more importantly, conflicting information.

If an audit is not being undertaken, the surveyor should be alert to the usual environmental risks and comment accordingly. In the UK, several valuable sources of information (such as the Environment Agency and the Scottish Environment Protection Agency) have accessible postcode-search facilities to allow detailed advice on matters such as flooding risk. However, take care to understand the limitations of the material that is provided and in particular what is meant by the risk assessments themselves.

Knowledge of gas protection measures – membranes and passive venting – is also useful. Sometimes solicitors turn up a requirement for gas protection in planning documents or past environmental reports – and it will be useful to be able to reply that indeed measures were in place.

Sustainability should now be a key component of a building survey. RICS publishes guidance on sustainability with reference to the property lifecycle. Examination of that guidance will reveal that many of the topics listed above fall neatly into the sustainability heading – it is not simply a matter of carbon reduction and 'green' materials, but more an all-encompassing assessment of the building and its impact on the people who use it, as well as its impact on the environment. Matters such as biodiversity, water management, waste management, health and welfare are all relevant and should be considered.

The *impact* of orientation (not just the orientation) of the building should be clearly stated as this affects the performance of materials used in the construction of the building as much as thermal performance.

With the impact of climate change becoming ever more topical, it is to be expected that surveyors will need to take a more active role in the analysis of the performance of buildings. At present, surveyors are advised to:

❖   describe the thermal shell taking into account orientation;

❖   consider the nature of the heating and cooling systems;

❖   consider the nature of artificial lighting; and

❖   provide advice on practical methods of upgrading insulation and measures to reduce associated condensation risk.

In many circumstances, an Energy Performance Certificate (EPC) is required and should be presented by the vendor. It is worth checking to see if the certificate is in place before the inspection to see if additional work is likely to be required. Data collection for an EPC needs to be methodical and careful; a knowledge of the modeling systems is useful as most systems rely upon simplified models as opposed to detailed CAD drawings of the building. There can be a tendency to collect too much data if you are unfamiliar with the procedure.

Noise and disturbance issues to note would include:

❖   the effects of noise from external sources;

❖   sound insulation of party structures; and

❖   other possible nuisances.

For more detail on the *Energy Performance of Buildings Directive* see page 387, for *Flooding* see page 355 onwards.

Deleterious materials

While testing for deleterious materials may be outside the scope of the survey (at least to begin with), surveyors should be aware of the key issues and materials and provide reasoned advice accordingly. Typically, the list of materials normally considered would include:

❖ high alumina cement (HAC);

❖ calcium chloride additive;

❖ asbestos;

❖ lead in plumbing and paint;

❖ woodwool as permanent shuttering;

❖ toughened glass, particularly in overhead situations; and

❖ Mundic (mainly in the south-west of England).

Some clients may have particular concerns with, for example, glass reinforced concrete (GRC), reinforced autoclaved aerated concrete (RAAC) planks, machine made mineral fibre (MMMF), etc. In Scandanavian countries, the use of mastic containing polychlorinated biphenyls (PCBs) has been viewed with concern, and owners can go to great lengths to decontaminate their buildings of this material. For more on PCBs see page 290.

For buildings constructed up until 1974, it is common to consider tests for High Alumia Cement (HAC). Calcium chloride was effectively banned from 1978, so buildings constructed later than this should be free of those materials in construction (although, of course, chloride contamination can still occur as a result of atmospheric conditions or exposure to de-icing salts). For more detail on HAC see page 291.

Asbestos merits a specific section in the report owing to the special considerations that this material warrants. Ask to see a copy of the asbestos register and consider its adequacy. For more detail on asbestos see page 281.

For industrial and retail buildings, particularly those constructed in the last ten years or so, the likelihood is that composite cladding materials will have been used. Since 2000, insurers have been wary of panels that contain combustible cores – expanded polystyrene (EPS), polyurethane (PUR) and some types of polyisocyanurate (PIR). Of these, EPS is of most concern as this will be found in cold stores and self-supporting panels. Some insurers may significantly increase premiums or deductibles where there is uncertainty as to the nature of the core and whether or not it is Loss Prevention Standard (LPS) approved. While the industry has taken a slightly more robust view of late, it is important to take steps to try and identify the nature of the core and if it is of an approved type. If it is not, provide advice on the thickness and location and particular fire risks – arson, cardboard storage, battery charging, etc. to facilitate a proper risk assessment.

Warning of the existence of deleterious and hazardous materials is one thing – but their existence needs to be placed in perspective and straightforward advice given. For more information see *Investigating Hazardous and Deleterious Building Materials*, published by RICS Books. See also *Materials and defects* later in this handbook, starting at page 277.

Further enquiries

During the course of the inspection, various technical and legal issues might arise. It is appropriate to draw attention to these points with the client and the client's legal adviser. However, questions and referrals should be relevant and sensible – not issues that are readily within the ambit of a surveyor to establish (for example, contacting the manufacturer of a composite panel to find out if it complies with Loss Prevention Standards).

Recommendations to do something inappropriate – like check the warranty package on a 12-year-old building – may cast the surveyor in poor light and should be considered carefully rather than added as a 'throw-away' line.

Always make it clear whether or not the enquiries and investigations need to be concluded before proceeding to completion.

The report

However competent and experienced the surveyor, he or she will be let down by a badly-presented, ill-prepared report, particularly if it contains errors in presentation and spelling or if it appears 'lightweight' in the quality of the advice. Remember:

> 'The difficulty', said Robert Louis Stevenson, 'is not to write, but to write what you mean, not to affect your reader, but to affect him precisely as you wish.'

Clarity of thought and clarity of advice are vital ingredients – a few hours spent reviewing material from the Plain English campaign will be worthwhile – even if you think that you know how to do it.

The Commercial/Industrial GN sets out a 'coat hanger' for successful presentation:

- ❖ What is wrong with it?
- ❖ Why it is wrong.
- ❖ What damage has occurred?
- ❖ How serious this is.
- ❖ What is needed to put it right?
- ❖ How much?
- ❖ When?

By the time the client has read the report, he or she should have been informed and influenced in precisely the way in which the surveyor wished.

Some tips for clearer writing

- ❖ Think of your reader, not yourself.
- ❖ Do not try to impress people by using your language and technical knowledge to show off: keep it as straightforward as possible. Use everyday words, avoid Latin or foreign phrases.
- ❖ Use sentences of 15–20 words. Use shorter ones for 'punch'. Longer ones should not have more than three items of information; otherwise they become difficult to follow.
- ❖ Be careful with jargon. It is only useful if people are familiar with it. Be prepared to explain your jargon words and acronyms – will your audience know them?
- ❖ Use 'active' verbs mainly, not 'passive' ones. For example, 'John Smith inspected the property' (active) is better than 'The property was inspected by John Smith' (passive).
- ❖ Use lower case bold for emphasis. Don't underline or use block capitals (these are harder to read).
- ❖ Put complex information into bullet points.
- ❖ Plan and draft your writing. Break it into short steps that follow a logical sequence and are easy to understand.
- ❖ In text, write numbers one to ten as words; with 11 and upwards, put the figure. Do not add 'No.' after a figure (for example, '5 toilets', not '5 No. toilets').
- ❖ Use the 'personal touch'. For example, 'A flood helpline is also operated by Surveys R Us for the convenience of our clients' becomes 'We also operate a flood helpline for your convenience'.

The above points are derived from the Plain English campaign. See also their guide to writing reports: www.plainenglish.co.uk/free-guides.html

Content of the report

The Commercial/Industrial GN suggests that an executive summary be provided: this should include recommendations for further tests, budgets, programme, etc. – main items of concern. A number of possible inclusions are suggested, but exercise care here and avoid the summary simply becoming an abridged version of the main body of the report – keep it to a page or two at most. And don't simply cut and paste text from the main body of the report into the summary.

The introduction should include a résumé of the instructions, the limitations that apply, the date of inspection and by whom, weather conditions and the names of persons providing information. Make it clear in the introduction that, in view of the complexity of most buildings, the surveyor does not guarantee to have seen each and every defect/deficiency that may exist at the property, but that he or she expects to have seen all the major items relating to the brief and many/most of the lesser ones.

A description of the property and its locality should follow the introduction. If floor areas are included, make it clear who has provided them or if they have been derived from site measurements. The elemental condition of the building is the main section of the report, with each element being described under separate headings.

Given the importance of legislative issues, health and safety, deleterious materials, asbestos and means of escape, these topics demand separate sections in their own right.

Budget costs are a useful way of giving weight to your observations, but make clear the basis upon which they are produced. Similarly, it is worth drawing a distinction between essential repairs and improvements.

Finally, give thought to the presentation of a risk assessment for the building; this need not be a stand-alone section, as suitable comments can be given in the main body of the report. A clear indication of the relative importance of each defect, together with a statement as to how that risk can be mitigated, will enable a balanced and informative report to be produced.

Residential surveys

Most of the comments on commercial surveys apply equally to surveys of residential buildings. In this case the most appropriate guidance for RICS members is *Building Surveys of Residential Property* (2nd edition), published in 2004 (hereafter referred to as the 'Residential GN').

While the essentials of taking instructions, setting up the job, agreeing a fee and limitations are equally as important as with commercial and industrial surveys, in many cases clients will not be experienced in property and the different levels of service that can be provided. It is very important therefore to explain the differences and limitations of types of survey so that the client is in no doubt as to the scope of the instruction and that the contract between the parties is properly set up and documented.

Prior to visiting the site, the surveyor is encouraged to undertake a desk top study wherever possible. The study should include such matters as:

- ❖ property sale particulars;
- ❖ relevant site information;
- ❖ particular exposure to environmental factors;
- ❖ statutory consents for previous work to the building;
- ❖ relevant guarantees, etc.;
- ❖ conservation area or listed building status; and
- ❖ lease details if relevant.

Readers are urged to follow the advice of the Residential GN, which covers taking and giving instructions, preparing for the survey, the inspection, and the report. 'Example Terms and Conditions of Engagement' are also included.

The Residential GN makes specific recommendations regarding the nature of the inspection and the report; they are too numerous to mention here, but among the most important are the following:

❖ Allow time for reflective thought.

❖ Be wary of making recommendations for further investigations to be carried out by persons who have a financial interest in the implementation of their own advice or recommendations.

❖ Provide a clear statement of the limitations posed by the building or its occupation.

Suggested pre-survey checklist for surveyors

❖ Confirm instructions:
  – nature of the instructions;
  – date and time of the survey;
  – access arrangements, particularly occupied premises;
  – statement of surveyor's intentions; and
  – limitations.

❖ Bear in mind:
  – *Unfair Contract Terms Act* 1977;
  – liability in negligence and contract; and
  – 'requirements of reasonableness'.

Suggested outline of report

Introduction
  – brief;
  – limitations;
  – general description of property and situation; and
  – present accommodation.

Structural condition and state of repair

❖ *External*:
  – roofs;
  – other defects at roof level;
  – eaves;
  – flashings;
  – external walls;
  – likelihood of cavity wall tie failure;
  – airbricks (provision and adequacy);
  – damp-proof course;
  – foundations and settlement/subsidence/heave;
  – rainwater goods;
  – soil/waste stacks, gullies;
  – other external comments; and
  – external decorations.

❖ *Internal*:
  – roof spaces;
  – partitions;
  – plasterwork;
  – windows;
  – doors;
  – joinery;
  – ceilings;
  – other internal defects; and
  – internal decorations.

❖ *Services*:
  – plumbing/wiring;
  – heating;
  – electricity/gas;
  – sanitary fittings; and
  – drainage.

❖ *Outside*:
  - boundaries, pavings, fences, gates and outbuildings;
  - noise, contamination and other environmental factors;
  - adjoining properties;
  - garden/trees – risk of ground movements/mining subsidence;
  - garage/car parking; and
  - probability of flooding.

❖ *General*:
  - compliance with statutory regulations;
  - planning situation;
  - energy consumption;
  - any responsibilities under a lease;
  - limitations of report;
  - any appropriate approximate costings;
  - presence/condition of toxic materials, e.g. asbestos;
  - general condition and conclusion;
  - risk and likelihood of fungal decay, insect infestation or conditions that could give rise to these attacks;
  - possible existence of protected species;
  - risk of contaminated land;
  - risk of radon emissions, power lines, etc.; and
  - any other relevant information.

Golden rules

When drafting the report, endeavour to avoid technical jargon and take care to communicate precisely.

Avoid assumptions and ill-thought out statements.

When describing elements answer the following questions:

❖ What is it?

❖ What is wrong with it?

❖ What will need to be done to put it right?

❖ What are the consequences of not putting it right?

Home Condition Reports

In England and Wales a home condition report (HCR) was a voluntary document which could be contained within a Home Information Pack (HIP). Unlike a formal survey report it does not contain advice as such but should identify the physical condition of various common elements; these are usually categorised in terms of needing no repair, routine repair or urgent repair. Following the 2010 general election, the government announced the suspension of HIPs and changes to the requirements for Energy Performance Certificates.

Homebuyer Survey and Valuation Reports and HomeBuyer Reports

The RICS *Homebuyer Survey and Valuation Report* (HSV) was replaced, in July 2009, by the RICS HomeBuyer Service. Detailed guidance for members for the use of the HomeBuyer Reports (HBR) may be found at www.rics.org/site/scripts/documents_info.aspx?categoryID=493&documentID=422

Further information

❖ *Building surveys and technical due diligence of commercial property* (4th edition), RICS guidance note, 2010

- ❖ *Building surveys of residential property* (2nd edition), RICS guidance note, 2004
- ❖ *Surveying safely*, RICS, 2006: www.rics.org/surveyingsafely
- ❖ *Sustainability and the RICS property lifecycle*, RICS guidance note, 2009

Contributed by Trevor Rushton, trevor.rushton@watts.co.uk

Vendor surveys

The traditional approach to selling investment grade property is to release details to the market, consider offers and reach heads of terms which are often subject to survey and legal enquiries. This due diligence process may give the prospective purchaser cause to renegotiate terms with a risk to the vendor in terms of cost and time. If matters proceed smoothly, exchange of contracts and completion can then take place.

The process is time consuming and fraught with risk. To streamline the procedure and manage risks, vendors are increasingly procuring full survey reports prior to sale. A vendor survey can be defined as a building and other surveys commissioned by a vendor but primarily for the benefit of a purchaser.

Normally, the vendor's sale pack will include a building survey, a Phase 1 environmental report or land quality statement, test reports on deleterious materials or specialist areas such as cladding (where relevant), and probably a report on the building's services installations.

Whereas a conventional report may often make recommendations for further investigation, a vendor survey must not invite further questions. Thus, it is very important to either make a judgment and express an opinion based upon the evidence, or commission additional tests and inspections where it is relevant to do so. Similarly, questions that would normally be referred to the legal team should be addressed in advance of the production of the final report. In other words, every effort must be made to 'close' particular issues or observations.

Traditionally, building and other surveys include a number of limitations. The third party clause (where the report can only be relied upon by the client) clearly needs variation with vendor surveys. There is always some scope for discussion, but the usual basis is that the client (or vendor) can rely upon vendor survey reports as well as the first purchaser. A duty is often extended to the first purchaser's financiers. Furthermore, there should be no change of use, as this may have impacts on the building that the surveyor cannot foresee. The purchaser must also accept that the building's condition may have changed since the date of the report. Assignment of the report to the first purchaser is traditionally done by exchange of letters but can also be executed as a deed.

Often, the surveyor is asked to readdress the report to the successful purchaser. Readdressing is inadvisable. A better and more reliable course is to issue a letter of reliance to the purchaser, see page 90.

An advantage of a vendor survey is making information on the condition of the property available to the vendor, which is essential for good asset management. Such surveys also take technical due diligence off the critical path, because they are prepared before the property is marketed. Heads of terms can be entered into without being subject to survey.

This approach may also give less scope to prospective purchasers who are not sincere in proceeding on the basis of their original offer.

Contributed by Trevor Rushton, trevor.rushton@watts.co.uk

Identifying the age of buildings

This section cannot pretend to be a comprehensive dissertation on the architectural and construction history of Britain. It is a concise yet wide-ranging guide to clues and explains where to look when seeking to assess the age of a building and fully and properly understand its forms and materials of construction. Almost without exception, any building, unless of very recent construction, will, at some time in its life, have undergone some form of change, modernisation or conversion that may well hide the age and materials of the original construction.

Archival research

If you have the time and opportunity, always seek to consult such archival sources as are immediately available. Indeed, it is important to impress upon the client the value of such research. Even if the building is not a historic building, some records of the original date of construction will exist somewhere in the files of the local administration.

If the building is listed as being of Special Architectural or Historic Interest or a Scheduled Ancient Monument, the listing description or entry in the Scheduled Monuments Register will provide some indication of the believed age of the building or monument. A word of caution here though, these believed ages are based in most cases on external inspections only and even the most experienced inspectors of historic buildings and ancient monuments have been known to have been deceived. Usually a more recent age is attributed to the structure based on external elevations that are the result of, say, a late Victorian refronting of a Georgian building, or an early 18th century brick refronting of a Tudor or earlier timber-framed building. The latter is often referred to as a Queen Anne front on a Mary Anne back, so always ensure that you look at the back of the property as well as the front. The Heritage Authorities are very gradually bringing in 'Statements of Significance', either as stand-alone documents or integrated into more comprehensive listing descriptions. However, with over 580,000 listed buildings across the UK and offshore islands, this is a mammoth task. Even when a 'Statement of Significance' exists, while this will assist in archival research to identify the true age of a building, it will not be a substitute for it. Eventually the local authority Historic Environment Record (HER) for the property will be of use but the paucity of resources being made available for the compilation of HERs is such that many years will elapse before HER data is anything other than sketchy.

Where to go to find records

Every county in Britain has a County Archivist who can be contacted through the local authority of the area in which the building is situated. Alternatively contact can be made via the relevant heritage authority – English Heritage, Scottish Heritage, Welsh Heritage (CADW) or the Heritage Department of the Department of Environment of Northern Ireland. Alternatively the local authority Conservation Officer will be able to put you in touch and indeed the relevant conservation or heritage authority or office could be useful sources in their own right. Do ask for the HER for the property – you may be lucky and get one of the few properties for which there is some information in HERs.

Archives, be they county, district or more local, even down to parish level, may include one or more of the following:

- ❖ maps, especially tithe maps, showing (down to considerable detail) ownerships and the building in outline on each site or plot;
- ❖ sale documents, especially auction details, that may give indications of believed age(s) of the building;
- ❖ newspaper and other articles indicating the believed age(s) of the building;
- ❖ deeds registers, which can be particularly useful in establishing exact dates for the original building lease from the lord of the

> manor or landed estate owner, granting the right to the construction of the building being considered;

❖ local authority building by-law and drainage permissions or approvals for the construction of the building and subsequent alterations. This last one usually only reaches back to the mid-19th century but the equivalent landed estate or manorial records can reach back much further. If the building is still held in freehold or equivalent by the landed estate or manorial estate then such records may still be held by them. However, some such estate records have been transferred to the county or district archives; and

❖ the National Monuments Records Office in Swindon via their website at www.english-heritage.org.uk will link you into 'Research & Conservation' and 'Learning & Resources' with various sites via 'Online Resources' including Images of England and Access to Archives, the United Kingdom strand of the A2A Archives database – at www.nationalarchives.gov.uk/a2a which links into over 400 record offices. English Heritage has undertaken trials of revisions to their in-house websites, which this author has participated in, but so far they have not been implemented. When and if implemented, these should give greater and easier access to their databases. At present the Heritage Gateway scheme with links into Local Authority HERs at www.heritagegateway.org.uk/gateway/ offers the best available research tool. Welsh Heritage (CADW) has 'Coflein' and other free to use, no need to register, databases on www.rcahmw.gov.uk. For Scotland use www.historic-scotland.gov.uk under the category 'Looking after our heritage' and subcategory 'How to search for a listed building' to get to their 'FASTMAP' system. This is a comprehensive integrated search system across all categories – from listed buildings and Scheduled Monuments through wreck sites, RCAHMS (Royal Commission on the Ancient and Historical Monuments of Wales) records, gardens and landscapes to local authority historic environment records. For Northern Ireland try www.ni-environment.gov.uk

Published and unpublished archival research

The *Victoria County Histories*, which should be available in the county or district central reference library, may contain a reference to your building. These are increasingly available online at www.british-history.ac.uk. Search by either 'local history' or by 'region'.

London has the Survey of London volumes now produced by the Survey of London branch of English Heritage. Those started in the late 19th century only cover a part of the historic areas of London and are available in principal reference libraries online at www.british-history.ac.uk (link to 'Survey of London'). The British History site has numerous additional online sources covering London and the UK, including records and documents back to the 13th century.

Other public and private publications may exist for your particular building. The Dr Nikolaus Pevsner *Buildings of England/Britain* series may well assist. Local history librarians are a mine of information in such a search. They and the county or district archivists may also be able to assist in pointing you towards unpublished works held by them or produced by local historians.

Research in specialist public archives can also be extremely positive in producing plans and documentation. For any building that is or has been in government or Crown ownership, including the Crown Estates, the Public Record Office at Kew can be invaluable, with large parts of their catalogues available online. See www.nationalarchives.gov.uk and enquiry@nationalarchives.gov.uk

For a building by an important architect, the *V&A/RIBA Drawings Collection* at the Victoria and Albert Museum can produce drawings back to the 17th century. See www.vam.ac.uk/collections/architecture/va_riba/index.html

For London, the Metropolitan Archives (T: 020 7332 3820) hold papers dating back to the 16th century. See www.cityoflondon.gov.uk/Corporation/LGNL_Services/Leisure_and_culture/Records_and_archives/

For any building that has at any point in its life been in the direct ownership of (or occupation by) the Monarchy, the Royal Archives at Windsor Castle can produce vital details unobtainable elsewhere.

The building

Once you have understood the types and forms, and materials of construction used in particular periods, as you inspect or survey a building the less altered areas of the building can be very revealing. This is particularly true of roof spaces, basements, rear elevations, back or rear additions or anywhere else that has escaped the previous owners' 'improvements'. As you crawl around the building look out for such unaltered places. 'Above-ground archaeology' is the increasingly common term for such on-the-property investigations.

What to look for – the ages of architecture and their clues

Remember that every building will have been altered and changed over the decades so each is an amalgam of various periods. It is crucial to seek to ascertain in the first instance the original building date of the first part of the building in question.

For example, a major country mansion attributed in the listing description to Edmund Blore as of 1834-1838 in Tudor style turns out to be a major Elizabethan house of the 1500s, badly damaged by fire in 1836, and rebuilt in Mock Gothic style incorporating the Elizabethan chimneys and cellars.

So what do we look for in the periods of architecture in Britain and where might we refer to for assistance? Knowledge gained over decades helps but if you are starting out you might carry the following with you as an aide-memoire.

The table below gives a brief description of the key ages of architecture in Britain. Even if the original windows and doors have been replaced, the form, shape and materials and forms of construction of the openings (especially the head arch, lintel, bressumer or beam over) is least likely to have changed.

A brief list of the ages of architecture in Britain

Form of architecture	Approximate period	Characteristics
Romanesque	500 to 1200 AD	The spread of the classical architecture of Rome adapted to incorporate the heavy, stocky squat Romanesque architecture characterised by rounded arches.
Gothic	1100 to 1450 AD	Pinnacles reaching for the sky, characterised by the creation of the great cathedrals.
Renaissance	1400 to 1600 AD	The return from Gothic to the classical precise rules of the 'Golden Section' of the Graeco-Roman architecture of 850 BC to 476 AD. Influenced by the 'Age of the Awakening and the Enlightment' from the Grand Tours of Europe and the rediscovery of Roman and Greek architecture. Remember Andreas Palladio and Palladian architecture.

Form of architecture	Approximate period	Characteristics
Baroque	1600 to 1830 AD	While in such places as Italy Baroque is characterised by opulent and dramatic churches with very extravagant decorations, Britain followed more of a restrained French form of highly-ornamented Baroque style combined with classical features.
Rococo	1650 to 1790 AD	In essence the latter phase of Baroque, with graceful white buildings incorporating sweeping curves.
Georgian	1720 to 1800 AD	This stately symmetrical style predominates in British and Irish towns and cities, from London to Bath to Edinburgh to Dublin – the age of Jane Austen so frequently portrayed on screen.
Neoclassical	1730 to 1925 AD	Renewed interest in Palladio and Palladianism brought a return to classical shapes and forms.
Greek revival	1790 to 1850 AD	Major classical mansions and buildings featuring columns, pediments and details inspired by Greek architecture of 850 BC to 50 AD.
Victorian	1840 to 1900 AD	The Industrial Age with its greater use of iron brought many innovations in the use of new materials and a flurry of architectural styles – Gothic Revival, Italianate, Queen Anne and Romanesque, all using previous styles and sometimes intermixing them.
Arts and Crafts Movement	1860 to 1900 AD	The backlash against Victorian industrialisation, with renewed interest in simplistic handicraft forms being applied to architecture.
Art Nouveau	1890 to 1914 AD	Originally patterns in fabrics, this spread rapidly to architecture and is characterised by assymetrical shapes, arches and decorations incorporating curved – often plant-inspired – designs.
Beaux Arts	1895 to 1925 AD	Also known as Classical Revival, this incorporates formal orders, symmetry and elaborate ornamentation.
Neo-Gothic	1905 to 1930 AD	Here Medieval Gothic forms were applied to the new breed of tall office blocks and skyscrapers.
Art Deco	1925 to 1939 AD	The jazz age, when zig-zag patterns and vertical lines created dramatic stage-like effects on facades.

Form of architecture	Approximate period	Characteristics
20th century extending into 21st century	1900 to the present day	Confusion of forms from Walter Gropius and Bauhaus through Modernism, Brutalism (functionalist blocks of concrete and steel) to Post-Modernism, the last of which represents some return to classical and true forms of architecture, However, it is best described as where styles collide and seek exuberance in building techniques and stylistic references, e.g. a skyscraper with a crowning over-sized Chippendale pediment.

The best way to get used to identifying styles, and ages and matters on site is to carry an easy-to-use pocket-sized illustrated reference book such as:

❖ *The Observer's Book of Architecture*, Number 13 in a series of most useful reference books, ISBN-10 0 72320 055 6 or ISBN-13 978 0 72320 055 0 (the best by far – sadly out of print but may be available through second-hand booksellers/websites); or

❖ *British Architectural Styles: An Easy Reference Guide*, ISBN 978 1 84674 082 4.

Contributed by Allen Gilham, allen.gilham@watts.co.uk

Site archaeology

While the UK Government, including associated Scottish Parliament, Welsh Assembly and Northern Irish Authorities, have consulted on changes to Heritage, Scheduled Ancient Monuments and Archaeological Protection legislation, including the production of Unified Lists covering all categories, no final decisions have yet been made. The previous government's abandonment of the draft *Heritage Protection Bill* means change in England and Wales is unlikely now before 2012 or 2013. Scotland, however, has the *Historic Environment (Amendment) (Scotland) Act* 2011.

The sole positive move in England and Wales has been the issue of *Planning Policy Statement 5: Planning for the Historic Environment* (PPS5) effective from 23 March 2010. This, together with the accompanying *Historic Environment Planning Practice Guide*, replaced PPG16 in matters of archaeology. Accordingly at present in England, Wales, Scotland and Northern Ireland, current statutes remain presently in place.

For England and Wales, PPS5 sets out the relevant government policy on archaeological remains on land and how they should be preserved or recorded, both in an urban setting and in the countryside. The key reference points in PPS5 are paragraphs HE6.1 (relating to Statements of Significance and requirements for desk-based or field evaluations for archaeological sites) and HE9.6 (regarding undesignated archaeological assets). Paragraphs 99–109 of the Practice Guide accompanying PPS5 are also key reference points. The government announced in October 2011 that it aims to finalise the National Planning Policy Framework for England by March 2012. There are presently no indications as to what might replace PPS5 if the NPPF abolishes it.

Scotland has the useful NPPG5 *Archaeology and Planning*. At the time of going to print, the link www.scotland.gov.uk/Publications/1998/10/nppg5 takes you to NPPG5 – but you may anticipate redirection when the link is established to a replacement website. Northern Ireland has the equally useful PPS6 *Planning, Archaeology and the Built Heritage* (March 1999). Go to www.doeni.gov.uk and search under 'Planning' for PPS6, or try www.planningni.gov.uk/index/policy.htm. NPPG5 and PPS6 are recent integrated documents.

How does archaeology affect construction?

Traditional dictionary definitions of archaeology focus on the study of history through excavation (usually implicitly below ground) and the analysis of the remains.

Not everyone will realise that in the construction world we have to deal with two types of archaeology:

❖ the traditional excavation of what lies hidden below ground; and

❖ the archaeology of standing buildings or 'above-ground archaeology'.

Archaeology affects construction primarily through the way that the planning process limits and controls development. Both above and below-ground archaeology can easily be applicable to the same site.

Planning permission is required for works of development – the carrying out of building, engineering, mining or other operations in, on, over or under land or the making of any material change in the use of any buildings or other land.

The first port of call for any planning application is the local planning office and the published documentation in either the Development Plan or the Unitary Development Plan.

If the Local Development Plan and/or the local planning office identifies a site as one with Scheduled Ancient Monuments or locations where archaeological remains are believed to exist then it is vital to engage in the earliest possible consultation with the county archaeologists or their equivalents at English Heritage, Historic Scotland, Welsh Heritage (CADW) and the Environment and Heritage Service in Northern Ireland.

This consultation will identify the archaeological sensitivity of the site.

Following discussions with the county or national archaeologists the next step for the developer is to research exactly what is or might be there and how it will or could impinge on the proposed development.

This is a development cost that the developer will have to pay for in the same way as any other site investigation prior to a development being undertaken.

Options for archaeological investigations are potentially twofold; desktop study and field evaluation.

Desktop studies

These draw on the archaeological records of the site itself and those of neighbouring sites. They are relatively quick and easy. Crucially they must be done by a trained archaeologist. The handbook of the Institute of Field Archaeologists (IFA) will help in locating the right archaeologist or archaeological unit to undertake the study. The IFA website at www.archaeologists.net gives excellent advice. Alternatively, email admin@archaeologists.net or phone 0118 378 6446.

Discussions may, however, indicate that the next level of investigation is necessary.

Field evaluation

This is not a full archaeological evaluation or 'dig' but a ground survey and small-scale trial trenching.

The results from the desktop study and/or the field evaluation will inform the developer, the county archaeologist and the local planning officers, especially the conservation officer, as to the importance of the site in archaeological terms.

Draft model agreements (December 1986 editions) between developers and the appropriate archaeological body regulating archaeological site investigations and excavations can be obtained from the British Property Federation, www.bpf.org.uk (search under 'Who we are' and 'Publications') or phone 020 7828 0111.

Current statutory protection for archaeological sites

Where Scheduled Ancient Monuments have been identified under the *Ancient Monuments and Archaeological Areas Act* 1979, these are sites of national importance and as such rank as the equivalent of Grade I (Grade A in Scotland) or Grade II* (Grade B in Scotland) buildings of special architectural or historic interest.

The protection of Scheduled Ancient Monuments is based on the requirement that scheduled monument consent has to be obtained from the Secretary of State (of the Department for Culture, Media and Sport: www.culture.gov.uk) or CADW, Historic Scotland or the Department of Environment (DoE) Northern Ireland.

Application has to be made to the Secretary of State for any works that would have the effect of demolishing, destroying, damaging, removing, repairing, altering, adding to, flooding or covering up a monument.

If you find a Scheduled Ancient Monument standing on or lying below your site, take great care. Ensure your professional advisers fully appreciate the implications before an application is made. If in doubt, enter into the earliest possible discussions with the relevant heritage and conservation authorities covering the site. These will include the local authority conservation officer, the county archaeologist, and the Inspectors of Ancient Monuments at English Heritage, Historic Scotland, CADW and the Environment and Heritage Service in Northern Ireland.

Above-ground archaeology

A Scheduled Ancient Monument is usually, although not exclusively, an unoccupied structure and can be either remains below ground and/or a standing structure above ground.

Above-ground Scheduled Ancient Monuments will require Scheduled Ancient Monuments Consent for works to the structure. The need to fully understand what a structure's contribution is to understanding 'ancient peoples by the study of their physical remains' led to the concept of above-ground archaeology.

Above-ground archaeology can involve physically digging into the structure above ground, or completing a 'desktop study', bringing together the known archive or history of the structure to fully understand what is important in the remains and what is less important.

This is because as structures are added to and/or changed over time there may well be pieces or parts of what is now extant that can well be removed or modified to benefit the scheduled monument.

Another purpose of exploring the archaeology in standing structures is the extrapolation of the 'desktop study' for above-ground Scheduled Ancient Monuments into conservation plans for all types of listed historic buildings.

Conservation plans and their near cousins Statements of Significance under PPS5 are increasingly required by heritage and listed building authorities, particularly for the more important Grade I (Scottish A) and Grade II* (Scottish B) buildings as listed as being of Special Architectural and Historic Interest. This is incorporated as part of the application process for Listed Building Consent for works that will affect the special architectural or historic interest of these listed buildings. Indeed it is reasonable now for heritage authorities to expect that any professional adviser dealing with an application for these grades of listed buildings will automatically have executed a conservation plan and Statement of Significance for the scheme and cross-related it to any Statement of Significance that the listing authorities may have previously undertaken for the property.

Surveyors of historic buildings must become able to execute conservation plans and Statements of Significance incorporating above-ground archaeological assessments on behalf of their clients and the property.

Conservation plans have a number of practical and financial advantages for the developer/renovator of historic buildings. The key ones are:

❖ certainty for the design team in formulating what can or cannot be done to the building and site before they formulate details for the listed building consent and planning permission applications; and

❖ certainty for the developer/renovator that the scheme will not be stopped in its tracks by the heritage authorities discovering that the building contains important previously unknown historic elements in the structure that precludes all or part of the development going forward.

Contributed by Allen Gilham, allen.gilham@watts.co.uk

Development monitoring

The need for development monitoring

Development monitors are appointed to oversee a third party's interest in a development. Development monitoring involves identifying, advising on and monitoring construction-related risks which are not under the client's direct control. There is a need for the monitor to actively protect the client's interest during the lifetime of the development. This is particularly important where the client takes a more risk-averse approach to the project than the developer.

A key element of the role is that advice is provided to the client from a party that is independent and not associated with the development or the development team.

The need for development monitoring is diverse and each instruction will reflect the requirements of the client and its relationship to a particular development. Development monitoring is typically undertaken on behalf of investment funds, banks and future occupiers, as summarised in the following table.

Development monitors are also commonly referred to as project monitors, fund surveyors, construction monitors and monitoring surveyors.

Typical clients

Type of organisation	Examples of organisation	Interest in development
Fund	Property investment fund, pension fund, private equity fund, joint venture partner	Will purchase the scheme as an investment on completion, or will acquire the land and fund the development during construction as an investment
Funder/ lender	Clearing banks, investment banks	Will earn interest on a loan for the land purchase and/or the building during construction, as well as a pre-agreed arrangement fee and possibly an exit fee
Prospective occupier	Various tenants	Will acquire a leasehold interest in the completed development, which may include full repairing and insuring obligations

The monitoring service

The development monitoring service will depend on the nature of the client's interest in the development and the risks associated with this interest. Therefore, there is no standard service to suit all schemes. The client and the monitor must work closely together to ensure the monitor's brief fully meets the specific project requirements.

Where a funder is providing debt finance, the principal focus is likely to relate to the value of the works undertaken and the completion of the works within the agreed budget. Progress of the works during construction will also be an important aspect to monitor. However, where the loan is secured against the property, it is prudent for the funder to ensure that the quality of the works is also considered.

Banking clients often have pre-qualified 'panels' of monitoring surveyors, who work in accordance with defined terms of bank appointments.

In situations where the client has purchased, or has agreed to purchase, the development, a quality focus is more prevalent. The client will want to ensure that the completed development is of a quality suitable as an investment asset. Where the fund is financing the works, it is common for development and purchase agreements between funds and developers to include maximum cost limits for the fund, or developer profit erosion provisions, which protect the fund from cost overruns.

Progress of the works may be critical if there is an agreement for lease with a future tenant, or tenants. In this instance, close monitoring of the likelihood of achieving the access date(s) for the tenant's fit-out works will be required. This can be undertaken on behalf of the fund, funder or future occupier.

In general terms, the monitor will comment on the cost, programme, quality and statutory compliance of the proposed development, from the initial concept to full design, throughout the construction period, and into the defects liability period.

The key skills and competencies that should be sought in a development monitor are:

- ❖ diverse technical knowledge of construction;
- ❖ thorough understanding of the client's interest in the development, including the development/purchase/finance agreement and the conditions precedent;
- ❖ project management and procurement expertise;
- ❖ cost management knowledge;
- ❖ risk awareness;
- ❖ independence from the development team;
- ❖ reporting and appraisal skills; and
- ❖ being proactive and a good communicator.

Development monitoring is usually carried out in four stages:

- ❖ Appraisal and risk assessment.
- ❖ Construction and finance monitoring during the works.
- ❖ Advice at practical completion.
- ❖ Advice at end of the defects liability period.

Appraisal and risk assessment

The development monitor will request and then review a wide range of information on the proposed development, including the programme, construction cost, design quality, future maintenance requirements, procurement route, selection of consultants and contractors, building contract, provision of warranties, insurances, statutory requirements, neighbourly matters, and land contamination issues. This review is summarised in an appraisal report, or initial report, which will highlight any potential risks associated with the project.

This stage is a critical part of the due diligence process for the client and impacts on their decision to proceed with the deal.

The focus of the appraisal will reflect the needs of the client and its interest in the particular development. This should be defined in the legal documentation, such as the development/purchase/finance agreement or the agreement for lease. Where possible, it is advantageous for the development monitor to provide technical advice to the client on the construction-related matters at the pre-agreement stage. Such advice would relate to any potential significant risks associated with undertaking the development that may have an adverse effect on value.

Construction and finance monitoring during the works

Following the appraisal stage and agreement to proceed with the development, monitoring is undertaken during the construction works. This involves periodic site inspections and attendance at site progress meetings, typically on a monthly basis. A formal report will be prepared that comments on a variety of construction issues, including:

- construction costs, cash flow and expenditure against budget;
- progress of the works against programme;
- quality of workmanship on site;
- development of the design;
- status of any statutory approvals and other compliance issues;
- status of appointment documents and warranties; and
- status of insurances.

It should be noted that the monitor will undertake an audit of the construction costs, however, they are independent from the developer's team and do not certify payments under the building contract.

The monitor may also be required to oversee expenditure of all development costs against the agreed budget. This can include expenditure such as legal fees, marketing costs and professional fees. These monthly requests for payments are typically referred to as drawdowns.

In recent times, clients, particularly banks, have become increasingly interested in payments made to contractors, consultants and subcontractors. The monitor can also track these payments as an additional service.

The exact extent of the services will depend on the client's specific requirements.

Practical completion and the end of the defects liability period

The role of the development monitor at practical completion and at the end of the defects liability period is usually set out in the development/purchase/finance agreement or in the agreement for lease. A robust role may be specified involving inspection of the completed development and advising the client on whether it should accept the development as complete, or that the end of the defects liability period has been achieved.

Practical completion is particularly critical where a prospective tenant is in place, as practical completion is likely to trigger rent commencement. Furthermore, practical completion is likely to result in payment for the building to the developer (projects which are not interim funded), or payment of the developer's profit.

The monitor can help to ensure that all the necessary handover documentation is in place, such as the health and safety file, as-built drawings, the operation and maintenance manuals and warranties.

See also the section *Practical completion* at page 95.

Further information

- *Project monitoring*, RICS guidance note, 2007.

Contributed by Rebecca Jermy, rebecca.jermy@watts.co.uk

Housing and residential property

Property investment and ownership

Housing Health and Safety Rating System

The Housing Health and Safety Rating System (HHSRS) was introduced under the *Housing Act* 2004. It also superseded the Fitness Standard as an element of the Decent Homes Standard.

Local authorities' obligations

Under the *Housing Act* 2004, a local authority is obliged to keep housing conditions under review and take any enforcement action needed to ensure that housing conditions meet the requirements of the HHSRS.

Local authorities are also obliged to investigate any official complaints regarding the condition of any residential premises. This includes homeowners and private sector landlords.

The regulations are designed to ensure that any residential premises and their environs provide a safe and healthy environment for occupiers and their visitors. The HHSRS works by assessing the risk associated with particular hazards that may be encountered in the home. If there is a significant chance that they could cause harm, a local authority may take action to ensure that the risk is removed or reduced.

Unlike the former Fitness Standard, the HHSRS assessment is not designed to set a standard but to provide objective information which will determine and inform enforcement decisions made by local authorities. The assessment sets out 29 categories of housing hazard, including factors not covered (or considered to be covered inadequately) by the former Housing Fitness Standard.

The hazards

Under HHSRS the hazards given priority are:

1. Damp and mould growth
2. Excess cold
3. Excess heat
4. Asbestos and MMF (machine-made mineral fibre)
5. Biocides
6. Carbon monoxide and fuel combustion products
7. Lead
8. Radiation
9. Uncombusted fuel gas
10. Volatile organic compounds
11. Crowding and space
12. Entry by intruders
13. Lighting
14. Noise
15. Domestic hygiene, pests and refuse
16. Food safety
17. Personal hygiene, sanitation and drainage
18. Water supply
19. Falls associated with baths, etc.
20. Falling on level surfaces, etc.

21. Falling on stairs, etc.

22. Falling between levels

23. Electrical hazards

24. Fire

25. Flames, hot surfaces, etc.

26. Collision and entrapment

27. Explosions

28. Position and operability of amenities, etc.

29. Structural collapse and falling elements

The list of hazards can be found in Schedule 1 of the *Housing Health and Safety Rating System (England) Regulations* 2005 (SI 2005/3208). © *Crown copyright material is reproduced under the Open Government Licence v1.0 for public sector information: www.nationalarchives.gov.uk/doc/open-government-licence/*

Scoring the hazards

Each of the 29 hazards is provided with a risk rating for an average property. This risk rating is based upon statistics, gathered by the government, on the likelihood of that hazard occurring to an occupant and the level of harm that will occur as a result of the hazard occurring.

Likelihood x harm = risk

In undertaking an HHSRS inspection of a property, it is the inspector's role to establish whether the likelihood and the level of harm associated with each hazard is above the national average provided by the government guidance. Alterations to the likelihood and harm will result in a change in the hazard band rating.

A rating is given for each hazard, rather than for the dwelling as a whole or, in the case of dwellings in multiple occupation, for the building as a whole. Hazard ratings use a numerical score which falls within one of ten bands. Scores in Bands A to C are Category 1 hazards. Scores in Bands D to J are Category 2 hazards.

According to Department for Communities and Local Government (DCLG) guidance, 'the HHSRS assessment is based on the risk to the potential occupant who is most vulnerable to that hazard'. For example, when rating stairs, these 'constitute a greater risk to the elderly, so for assessing hazards relating to stairs they are considered the most vulnerable'. A dwelling that is safe for those most vulnerable to a hazard is safe for all, says the DCLG.

Enforcement

Any action taken by the local authority as a result of an HHSRS assessment will be based on a three-stage test:

❖ the hazard rating given;

❖ whether the authority has a duty or power to act; and

❖ that authority's judgment as to the most appropriate course of action to be taken.

New enforcement options are now available to local authorities, taking into account the statutory enforcement guidance.

Authorities can:

❖ serve an improvement notice requiring remedial works;

❖ make a prohibition order, which closes the whole or part of a dwelling or restricts the number of permitted occupants;

❖ suspend these types of notice;

❖ take emergency action;

❖ serve a hazard awareness notice;

❖ make a demolition order*; and

❖ declare a clearance area*.

(* not available for Category 2 hazards, i.e. scores in bands D–J as described above)

Further information

❖ www.communities.gov.uk/publications/housing/hhsrsoperatingguidance

Contributed by Tom Kibblewhite, tom.kibblewhite@watts.co.uk

Affordable housing schemes

Right to buy (RTB)

This scheme allows established **council tenants** to purchase their rental property at a discounted price depending on how long they have been tenants.

To be eligible for the scheme, a tenant must have been a **secure council tenant** living in public sector accommodation for two years if they were tenants before 18 January 2005, or five years after that date.

If a property purchased under the right to buy is repossessed or sold within five years, then some, or all, of the discount has to be repaid to the council.

Tenants that have the ownership of their home transferred to a housing association may be eligible for a Preserved Right to Buy (PRTB), if they were the tenants during the transfer.

Right to acquire (RTA)

The right to acquire is similar to the right to buy in that you need to have been a tenant for two years, however, it is for eligible **secure or assured tenants** of **registered social landlords** (RSLs) and the discount is based on where you live, not on the length of tenure.

It is only covered under this scheme if the property was built or acquired by the housing association from 1 April 1997 onwards.

Properties which are exempt from the scheme include some special needs housing and dwellings in certain rural areas.

Homebuy

The government's range of ownership schemes are called HomeBuy (in London, HomeBuy is known as 'First Steps'), and they come in a number of different forms:

❖ **FirstBuy**: equity loan funding of up to 20% of the purchase price is split equally between the Homes and Communities Agency (HCA) and a housebuilder, with purchasers being required to raise funding (a mortgage plus deposit) of at least 80% of the purchase price.

❖ **Shared Ownership**: tenants share ownership of their home with a housing association, paying a mortgage on the part they own plus affordable rent on the portion they don't own. In addition to the standard New Build HomeBuy product, the Agency also offers two specific versions; Home Ownership for People with Long Term Disabilities (HOLD) and Older Persons Shared Ownership (OPSO).

❖ **Equity Loans**: some providers will offer homes for sale where purchasers buy with the assistance of an equity loan, to top up what they can afford on their own.

❖ **Rent to HomeBuy**: individuals pay reduced rent on a new build home for up to five years, to help them save for a deposit and purchase the property.

❖ **HomeBuy Direct**: purchasers buy a selected newly-built property with the assistance of an equity loan.

❖ **Social HomeBuy**: housing association and local authority tenants buy their home on a shared ownership basis or outright, with a discount on the share being purchased.

❖ **Armed Forces Home Ownership Scheme**: purchasers take out a mortgage which, together with any cash contribution, must cover a minimum of 50% of the purchase price. This is topped up with an equity loan covering between 15% and 50% of the remaining purchase price. The maximum value of a home purchased through the Armed Forces Home Ownership Scheme is £300,000.

Renting (through councils or housing associations)

Renting is the most prominent form of affordable housing and what councils usually use to meet their statutory responsibility to meet homelessness.

Rented properties are normally provided by RSLs, who work in partnership with councils to provide homes which meet councils needs, and as determined via the Housing Need Assessment. Nominations are offered to the host borough and wider subregion where a grant is provided by the HCA. Prospective tenants get placed on waiting lists according to a number of criteria, and are then allocated a suitable property when one is available. The alternative is Choice Based Lettings (CBL), where people can apply for available council/RSL accommodation which is openly advertised.

The HCA has started a programme called 'Affordable Rent' which changes the way that renting is offered – the method of allocation is the same, however. Affordable Rent homes will be made available to tenants at up to a maximum of 80% of market rent. Properties will be able to be relet using the same principles.

Further information

❖ www.direct.gov.uk/en/HomeAndCommunity/BuyingAndSellingYour Home/HomeBuyingSchemes/DG_4001347

❖ www.homesandcommunities.co.uk/ourwork/affordable-rent

Contributed by Cullum Alexander, cullum.alexander@watts.co.uk

Property insurance

Property investment and ownership

Post-completion insurance policies

Buildings insurance

- ❖ **Who is protected**: the owner or occupier of a property, after practical completion.

- ❖ **The cover**: all risks of physical loss/damage in respect of the reinstatement of the structure, out buildings, walls, gates, walk ways including removal of debris, professional fees, etc. Rental income can also be included as can property owner's liability.

- ❖ **What is not covered**: maintenance issues, gradual deteriorations, defective workmanship, wear and tear and building design defect.

- ❖ **Typical policy exclusions**: liability assumed under contract, financial loss, products supplied.

- ❖ **Duration of cover**: for the life of the structure, policies are usually arranged on an annually renewable basis; however, occasionally long-term agreements can be made to secure a premium rate for a limited number of years.

- ❖ **Important points**: financial institutions are increasingly taking an interest in the insurance arrangements and may ask to be included as a co-insured, which grants them the benefit from the policy in place. Most policies will contain a noted interest clause, which automatically includes any parties with a financial interest.

Loss of rent derived from the property can also be covered under a property owner's policy. Rental income and/or costs for alternative accommodation is protected following an interruption or interference with the business as a result of damage caused by an insured peril. It is important to note that a loss of rent claim must follow a valid material damage claim (with a limited number of exceptions, e.g. denial of access).

All policies exclude cover for terrorism as standard, this can, however, be 'bought-back' for an additional premium. Therefore, if this cover is required, it is important to specifically ask for it to be included.

It is vital that the correct sums insured are provided when taking out a policy. All too often, the purchase price or constructions costs are used. These are usually too high (meaning that a higher premium is paid) or too low (which means that average will apply – a claim will be reduced by the percentage that the overall amount has been underinsured). The sum insured should be based upon an insurance valuation for the reinstatement of the entire structure following a total loss. This should include the building, any surrounding walls, pathways, costs for debris removal and professional fees (VAT should also be added for residential buildings or where the owner is not VAT registered).

Insurers will usually look to restrict the insured perils on an unoccupied property (these are normally: fire, lightning, explosion, earthquake and aircraft) as it is perceived that this presents a greater risk. Cover on an all risk basis can be arranged, but the premiums are likely to be much greater and there will be additional implications imposed on the owner. Usually they include regular inspections (which must be recorded), and removal of waste and combustible material on a regular basis. Most insurers would also expect an increased level of security including boarding windows and sealing letter boxes, and the disconnection and drainage of utilities.

Engineering insurance and inspection

- ❖ **Who is covered**: the contractor during the build phase and the owner of the property thereafter.

❖ **The cover**: Statutory inspection of various items of plant and/or machinery, the costs involved following breakdown, collapse, sudden and unforeseen damage and explosion of plant. Expendable items.

❖ **What is not covered**: liability arising out of the use of plant or machinery, wear and tear.

❖ **Typical policy exclusions**: damage caused if no maintenance or inspection agreement is in place, fire, storm and associated perils, theft, defective workmanship, installation and testing.

❖ **Duration of cover**: policies are usually arranged on an annually renewable basis, allowing for more frequent inspections throughout the year.

❖ **Important points**: due to various health and safety regulations, the frequency at which the various types of plant and equipment must be inspected differs depending on which regulations they fall under.

Type of plant	Legislation	Inspection frequency
Portable appliance testing	EAW (Electricity At Work)	12 months
Steam boiler	PSSR (Pressure Systems Safety Regulations)	14 months
Pressure vessel	PSSR	14-60 months*
LEV dust/fume/vapour extraction	COSHH (Control of Substances Hazardous to Health)	14 months
LEV metal working	COSHH	6 months
Power press fixed guard	PUWER (Provision and Use of Work Equipment Regulations)	12 months
Power press interlock guard	PUWER	6 months
General work equipment	PUWER	6-12 months*
Racking	PUWER	12 months
Escalators	PUWER	6 months
Roller shutter doors	PUWER	12 months
Fixed wiring	EAW	3-60 months*
Fork lift trucks	LOLER (Lifting Operations and Lifting Equipment Regulations)	6 or 12 months*
Passenger lift	LOLER	6 months
Other equipment lifting people	LOLER	6 months
Cranes	LOLER	12 months
Other lifting equipment	LOLER	12 months
Lifting accessories	LOLER	6 months
Vehicle lifting table	LOLER	6 months

* Frequency can vary between types of plant/industry and is subject to suitable risk assessment.

Latent defects and building warranties

❖ **Who is protected**: the owners of the structure and any predecessors to the title.

❖ **The cover**: inherent faults within the structure of the building which do not become apparent until after practical completion. Cover can be extended to include machinery and equipment.

❖ **What is not covered**: Accidental damage, fire, subsidence, earthquake, theft and snagging works.

❖ **Typical policy exclusions**: indirect or economic loss, ingress of water within the first 12 months, maintenance, structural changes.

❖ **Duration of cover**: policies are usually taken out for a period of 10 years from the date of practical completion; however, 12-year policies are available.

❖ **Important points**: ideally this policy should be arranged before the building phase of the project as insurers will require a survey of the structure and the methods being implemented in order to produce a quotation.

It is usual for a non-refundable fee to be charged for the pre-quotation survey. This must be paid in advance of any cover being granted. Depending on the insurer, this fee may be refunded by way of premium reductions.

Latent defect policies are becoming more popular due to the protection they provide against first party property damage, even if the contractor becomes insolvent. There is also no reliance on professional indemnity cover being maintained.

The policy is usually assignable to any future purchasers (during the policy period), therefore making this a good marketing tool for newly-built properties.

Latent defects insurance policies differ from the building warranties very slightly. The main difference is that a building warranty will cover the insolvency of the main contractors appointed to the project by providing a surety bond for any amount of deposit (which cannot be recovered) which has been paid in advance, should the contractor not start work. If works have started and cannot be completed, the warranty will pay the amount that was paid to the builder under the contract and that cannot be recovered; or the extra cost above the original purchase price for work necessary to complete the contract substantially. It is important to note however that the contractor must be registered with the required trade organisation in order for this type of warranty to take any effect and the latent defect cover attaching to this to be in effect after completion. Latent defect insurance, however, is attached solely to the building and not the contractor and therefore will pay any costs to put right defects which may occur regardless of who the contractors were.

Contributed by Peter Morse, 020 7280 3460, peter.morse@ thecleargroup.com and Grant Pye Cert CII, 020 7280 3467, grant.pye@thecleargroup.com of Clear Insurance Management Ltd, 10 Eastcheap, London EC3M 1AJ, www.thecleargroup.com

Legal indemnity insurance

The ownership of property often involves the acceptance of risks that may be difficult to eliminate entirely but which nevertheless demand some measure of protection. This section gives a brief outline of the main insurance policy covers which can be obtained. It is, however, recommended that advice is sought from an insurance broker or adviser before cover is arranged.

Duration of cover: For legal indemnity policies, most insurers will provide cover in perpetuity and also permit transfer of the cover to successors in title.

Indemnity name/type	Cover
Absence of easement	Policy protects against interference with the use of the property (the easement) due to a lack of legal grant for access and/or services to a property
Absent landlord	Policy protects against forfeiture of the lease of a property for non-compliance with covenants in this lease (and loss caused by an inability to enforce other parties' maintenance obligations contained in this lease – this is really maisonette indemnity)
Adverse possession	Policy protects against a challenge to occupation of land that forms part of the insured's property, but is not included in the documentary title to the property
Breach of planning, or building regulations or listed buildings consent	Policy protects against enforcement action by a local authority in respect of lack of appropriate consents for alterations to or use of the insured's property
Breach of restrictive covenant	Policy protects against the financial consequences of a person successfully enforcing through legal proceedings a covenant burdening the insured's land
Building over sewer	Policy protects against increased costs of construction works under a build-over agreement with the local water authority and/or a sewer authority's requirement for demolition/alteration of the insured's property to allow access to the sewer
Chancel repair	Policy protects against a liability to contribute towards the repair of the chancel of a church
Contaminated land	Policy protects against financial costs should any historical contamination be discovered
Contingent buildings insurance	Policy protects against uncertain or inadequate insurance arrangements for the building of which the property forms part
Defective title	Policy protects against a third party attempting to: ❖ enforce an estate right or interest adverse to or in derogation of the insured's title to the property; ❖ prevent the insured's use of any right of way or easement necessary for the enjoyment of the property.
Enforcement of (known/unknown) adverse third party rights	Policy protects against the exercise of rights or easements over or under the property
Enlargement of lease indemnity	Policy protects against the exercise of historic rights, easements or other interests over the property contained or reserved in the original lease of the property
Flat/maisonette indemnity	Policy protects against uncertain or inadequate arrangements for maintenance of the building of which the property forms part
Flying/creeping freehold	Policy protects against uncertain or inadequate arrangements for maintenance of a flying/creeping freehold element of the property

Forfeiture of lease – bankruptcy/insolvency	Policy protects a mortgagee against forfeiture of their borrower's lease due to borrower's bankruptcy
Forfeiture of lease – breach of covenant	Policy protects a mortgagee against forfeiture of their borrower's lease due to breach of covenant
Freehold rent charge coverage	Policy protects against re-entry by a rent-charge holder due to non-payment of a rent-charge
Good leasehold	Policy protects against a challenge to the property's title and unknown covenants
Insolvency Act	Policy protects a mortgagee or successor in title to the transfer in the event the transfer of the property is set aside pursuant to the Insolvency Act
Judicial Review	Policy protects in the event that a planning permission is quashed
Mining/mineral rights indemnity	Policy protects against financial loss as a result of the future exercise of rights to extract mineral reserves underneath the property
Missing deeds	Policy protects in the event that ownership of the property is challenged and cannot be substantiated by reference to original title deeds
Possessory title indemnity (residential)	Policy protects against a challenge to the property's title
Search insurance	Policy protects against financial loss caused by a matter that would have been revealed to the owner of a property by a search conducted by the local authority relating to mining, drainage, village green
Town and village green	Policy protects against damages or compensation, costs of altering/demolishing, diminution in value, and abortive costs, where any third party (including any corporation) applies to the relevant statutory authority for the registration of the property or any part thereof as a town or village green after the policy date

Contributed by Rob Cooke ACII, 020 7280 3466, rob.cooke@thecleargroup.com and Grant Pye Cert CII, 020 7280 3467, grant.pye@thecleargroup.com of Clear Insurance Management Ltd, 10 Eastcheap, London EC3M 1AJ, www.thecleargroup.com

Maintenance management

Primary objectives of maintenance management

It is essential that property owners and managers allocate sufficient time and resources to maintenance. This is reinforced by the introduction of legislation such as the *Corporate Manslaughter and Corporate Homicide Act* 2007, facilitating prosecution of cases where poor maintenance manifests itself with fatal results. Managers need to be aware of the full extent of maintenance liabilities and how much money should be spent and when. Maintenance management requires a systematic approach to ensure high standards, value for money and management control.

Buildings comprise a number of elements. Their constituent materials and components have a range of life expectancies that in most cases will be shorter than the life of the building as a whole. Maintenance is therefore inevitable and arises from failure at this component level.

The primary objectives of maintenance are:

❖ **Protection of the investment to ensure high utilisation of the building and its long life:** Maintenance affects the profitability of a commercial organisation in a number of ways. First there are the direct costs of labour, plant, materials, and management. The second category is indirect, where inadequate maintenance of buildings prevents the organisation from functioning properly.

❖ **Safeguarding the return on the investment:** Poorly maintained commercial buildings fare unfavourably in the market when compared with their well-maintained equivalents. The run down of an investment from lack of maintenance will discourage tenants from wishing to remain in occupation. This will have an effect on rent levels and encourage assignments and vacations on termination of leases.

❖ **The control of costs:** Timely, planned maintenance enables efficient use of resources.

❖ **Establishing a safe working environment:** The safety of the building and establishing a safe working environment must be the first priority of the maintenance manager.

Maintenance closes the gap between the actual state of the building and the acceptable standard. The acceptable standard will be dependent upon a number of factors, which may include:

❖ statutory requirements (health and safety, and waste management);

❖ tenant or occupant satisfaction;

❖ minimising loss of production;

❖ morale of users, employers and customers;

❖ public image; and

❖ carbon footprint.

Contributed by Steve Brewer, steve.brewer@watts.co.uk

A systematic approach to maintenance management

A systematic approach to maintenance management has a number of elements: policy, measurement, planning and organising, procuring works, and monitoring.

Policy

A building may be an asset to an investor or a resource to the user. The maintenance policy defines the objectives that maintenance of the building sets out to achieve. It is a dynamic concept, subject to change, just as the plans and objectives of the user or organisation will change.

Standards have to be defined. The use of 'normal standard' is inadequate. The acceptable range of performance of any element of a building will depend upon the relationship between each of its functional requirements and the use of the building as a whole.

The policy must therefore contain objective criteria to define what constitutes failure or non-conformance in each category. The policy must identify those activities that are sensitive to the physical condition of the building and those building elements that play a significant role in providing the necessary conditions.

Once these components are identified, the acceptable delay time in correcting any failure can be assessed.

The statement of policy constitutes the brief for the maintenance manager. It should cover future requirements of the buildings, changes of use, statutory and legal conditions, maintenance cycles, required standards and acceptable response times for breakdown or failure.

The policy must be regularly reviewed and amended as necessary. Consideration of a maintenance policy often shows that there may be some conflict between parties with different interests, for example, between landlord and tenant.

Survey and data gathering

In order to measure how the buildings compare against the policy, and how to close the gap, it is essential to review all existing maintenance information and to undertake regular condition surveys. These identify the condition of the asset and record the status of the building at any one time. A condition survey has the specific purpose of:

- ❖ identifying maintenance needs;
- ❖ recording the priority of the need;
- ❖ recording proposed remedies and quantities of items requiring attention before the next survey; and
- ❖ predicting the scale of items requiring attention after the next survey.

Planning of work

Having agreed a policy for the organisation and identified work to be done, the first function of the maintenance manager is to formulate a maintenance plan. The objective of planning is to ensure that work is carried out with maximum economy. A key function of maintenance management is to achieve positive control over the work and to avoid overloading or inefficient utilisation of resources. Planned maintenance consists of preventive and corrective work.

- ❖ **Preventive maintenance:** that which is carried out at predetermined intervals and is intended to reduce the probability of failure.

❖ **Corrective maintenance:** that which is carried out after failure has occurred and is intended to restore an item to a state in which it can perform its required function.

Generally speaking, the most economic plan in direct cost terms would be the one that maximises preventive maintenance. However, by definition, this form of maintenance takes place before failure has occurred and some degree of useable life has been wasted. This wasted life has a value that can be costed and must be added to the direct cost of the maintenance resource used. The split of work between preventive and corrective maintenance is a management decision. The actual proportion of each will be determined by reference to the maintenance policy.

Plans must take into account practical considerations and the availability of resources. They are prepared with different time horizons for different purposes:

❖ **Long term:** for strategy, to establish general expenditure levels and to profile the maintenance demands of a property or portfolio over an extended time horizon.

❖ **Medium term:** addressing demands that are predicted within the next five years and to refine budgeting and the assessment of workload.

❖ **Annual:** for work and resource allocations.

Organising

This is the construction of an organisation and a control system capable of ensuring the implementation of the plan.

The main constituents of a maintenance organisation are:

❖ **Resources:** i.e. labour, materials, plant and management. These may be either directly employed or obtained through contracts with outside contractors.

❖ **Administration:** a staff structure for coordinating and directing resources.

❖ **Work planning and control:** the system for work, budget, cost and condition control. At its heart lies a documentation procedure, an information base to support effective decision-making.

The documentation system will include a number of elements, such as an asset register, a property information base, and preventive maintenance documentation together with a system for initiating and controlling works: works orders, work request forms, etc. These systems are generally computerised. There are a number of proprietary computer programs available. Such programs revolve around relational databases that can be tailored for strategic work, planning and budgeting right through to processing of day-to-day orders for reactive maintenance.

Procuring

A contract and procurement strategy must be established. The strategy will be driven by the nature of anticipated and known workloads, and the need to achieve maximum efficiency of operation.

The workload may include the need to provide reactive maintenance cover for unforeseen or accidental repairs, 24-hour emergency call-out cover, planned maintenance contracts and small items of maintenance work packaged into cost-effective contracts.

The decision about which contract and procurement strategy to adopt will depend on a number of factors, including the geographic spread of the portfolio in question; the preferred type of model arrangements to be implemented; and the number and type of resources available to the maintenance manager.

Monitoring

Monitoring and auditing is essential to ensure that the maintenance management system is functioning properly and achieving the requirements of the policy statement and, if not, to record deficiencies and initiate corrective action.

The maintenance manager needs to monitor the system and organisation to ensure that quality and value for money is being achieved. The audit is a post examination of maintenance work and procedures, not dissimilar to a financial audit. The audit can be condition, technical, systems or design based or a combination of all these.

The condition audit involves the checking of planned maintenance schedules against the actual condition of the building.

The aim of the technical audit is to examine a sample of maintenance activities to investigate how each task has been approached and dealt with.

The systems audit will analyse maintenance management practices. It will establish the true nature and extent of the database being used and how this is stored and accessed. It will look at overall policy and whether or not there are realistic plans and programmes in existence, and at the method used for budget preparation, budget control, and for feedback of information to assist managers in future decision-making.

The design audit concentrates on the interaction between design and building performance. In most cases it is a question of lessons to be learned for the future.

Contributed by Steve Brewer, steve.brewer@watts.co.uk

'Best value' in local authorities

What is 'best value'?

The government has defined best value as:

> 'A duty to deliver services to clear standards – covering both cost and quality – by the most economic, efficient and effective means available.'

This clearly has a direct bearing on construction-related services provided by local authorities. The government will require local authorities to publish an annual best value performance plan (BVPP) covering the entire range of the authorities' services. This is intended to be a public document and will include an assessment of the authorities' past and current performance against nationally and locally defined standards.

The performance plan will be the main instrument by which local authorities will be held accountable to the local community for delivering best value.

How are best value studies carried out?

The Audit Commission appoint an external auditor to undertake an audit of the authorities' BVPP. In the case of construction-related services this is likely to be a professional consultant in the relevant field. The audit will cover:

- ❖ compliance with legislation and guidance;
- ❖ performance information; and
- ❖ continuous improvement strategies (the '4 Cs' – see below).

The '4 Cs'

Authorities are required to carry out a Best Value Review as part of the BVPP. This includes putting in place strategy for continuous improvement implementing the '4 Cs':

- ❖ **Challenge**: why and how the service is being provided.

❖ **Compare**: with others' performance (including organisations in the private sector) across a range of relevant indicators.

❖ **Consult**: with local taxpayers and service users with the view to setting new performance targets.

❖ **Compete**: as a means of securing efficient and effective services.

More detail regarding the methods of inspection can be seen on the Audit Commission website: www.audit-commission.gov.uk

Continuous improvement for construction and property services

A Service Improvement Plan (SIP) is one which identifies areas of potential improvement from:

❖ those services already subjected to a Best Value Review;

❖ advice from the Audit Commission inspection service; or

❖ advice from an external consultant by way of a best value 'healthcheck' (commonly termed a 'critical friend').

Depending on the particular service, the following core issues will be included in the SIP:

❖ **Description of action**: to be taken to improve service.

❖ **Target**: either qualitative or quantitative.

❖ **Target and timescales**: timescale for achieving the improvement(s).

❖ **Likely effect**: impact of the improvement identified.

Other issues which are likely to be included in construction-related services could be:

❖ current performance;

❖ national benchmarks;

❖ resource requirements; and

❖ monitoring and review strategies.

This overview of best value is intended to give some insight into government efforts in improving services to the taxpayer. When considering the detail of SIPs for construction- and property-related services it is recommended that consultancy advice be sought.

Contributed by Stuart Russell, stuart.russell@watts.co.uk

Sources of information in maintenance management

Building Maintenance Indices/Building Cost Information Service (BMI/ BCIS): www.bcis.co.uk

❖ *Building Maintenance Price Book*, published annually

❖ SR 361 *Review of Maintenance Costs 2007*

❖ SR 362 *Review of Occupancy Costs 2007*

❖ *Building Running Cost Indices online*

❖ *Life Expectancy of Building Components August 2006*

The Building Services Research and Information Association (BSRIA): www.bsria.co.uk

❖ AG24/97 *Operation and Maintenance Audits 1997*

- ❖ AG1/98 *Maintenance Programme Set-up 1998*
- ❖ AG20/99 *CD Cost Benchmarks for the Installation of Building Services* Parts 1–3 1999
- ❖ AG4/2000 *Condition Survey of Building Services 2000*
- ❖ AG1/2003 *Condition-based Maintenance: Using Non-destructive Testing 2003*
- ❖ AG5/2001 *Condition-based Maintenance – an evaluation guide for building services 2001*
- ❖ BG1/2007 *Handover, O & M Manuals, and Project Feedback*
- ❖ BG2/2004 *Computer-based Operating and Maintenance Manuals – Options and Procurement Guidance 2004*
- ❖ BG7/2004 *Business-focused Maintenance Toolkit 2005*
- ❖ BG3/2004 *Business-focused Maintenance Sample Schedules 2004*
- ❖ BG3/2008 *Maintenance for Building Services*
- ❖ BG 26/2011 *Building manuals user guides – Guidance and worked examples*
- ❖ MS4 *Facilities and Maintenance Set,* (Set of 3), July 2009

National Joint Consultative Committee for Building (NJCC)

- ❖ Procedure Note 16, *Record Drawings and Operating and Maintenance Instructions and the health and safety file* (2nd edition), June 1996, RIBA Publications

Note: NJCC is no longer in existence, but guidance notes are still in general use.

Miscellaneous

- ❖ RICS, *Building Maintenance: Strategy, Planning and Procurement* (2nd edition), RICS guidance note, May 2009
- ❖ BRE, *Building Services: Performance, Diagnosis, Maintenance, Repair and the Avoidance of Defects*, BR404, August 2000, BRE
- ❖ B. Chanter, *Building Maintenance Management* (2nd edition), August 2007, Blackwell Publishing
- ❖ P. Wordsworth, *Lee's Building Maintenance Management* (4th edition), November 2000, Blackwell Science
- ❖ CIBSE Guide M, *Maintenance Engineering and Management*, CIBSE, 2008

British Standards in maintenance management

Standard number	Standard title	Year
BS 3811	*Glossary of Terms in Terotechnology*	1993
BS 3843	*Pt 1 Guide to Terotechnology*	1992
	Pt 2 Introduction to techniques and applications	1992
	Pt 3 Guide to the available techniques	1992
BS 6150	*Code of Practice for Painting Buildings*	2006
BS 6270	*Code of Practice for Cleaning and Surface Repair of Buildings Pt 3 metals (cleaning)*	1991
BS 7543	*Guide to Durability of Buildings and Building Elements Products and Components*	2003

Standard number	Standard title	Year
BS ISO 15686	*Pt1 Buildings and constructed assets. Service life planning. General principles and framework*	2011
	Pt 2 Service Life Prediction Procedures	2001
	Pt 3 Performance Audits and Reviews	2002
	Pt 5 Life cycle costing	2008
	Pt 6 Procedures for considering environmental impacts	2004
	Pt 7 Performance evaluation for feedback of service life data from practice	2006
	Pt 8 Reference service life and service life estimation	2008
BS 8210	*Guide to Building Maintenance Management*	1986
BS 8221	*Code of Practice for Cleaning and Surface Repair of Buildings*	
	Pt 1 Cleaning of natural stones, brick, terracotta and concrete	2000
	Pt 2 Surface repair of natural stones, brick and terracotta	2000

Contributed by Angela Dawson, angela.dawson@watts.co.uk

Asset management

Organisations, be they commercial, not-for-profit or social, will rely on buildings for many of their functions. Often planned preventative maintenance is relegated to the bottom of the list of priorities for many organisations, perhaps under the misconception that maintenance can usually be deferred until absolutely necessary or ignored completely. Buildings comprise many physical assets which have differing maintenance requirements and 'asset management' is a definable system by which maintenance and renewal is controlled throughout the life of the organisation's use of any building or structure, whether in part or whole.

In successful and profitable organisations the constant awareness of the condition and life expectancy of physical assets plays a key role in the control of costs and being able to extract best value from the building. Asset management can be employed to make informed management decisions on levels of expenditure and to optimise the whole-life costs of assets while maintaining business continuity.

At its most basic level, an asset management plan should logically record all the elements and components of a building and its support engineering systems, and should determine the lifecycle programme for each element and each component from initial provision to end-of-life replacement. From this most basic information a diary of maintenance tasks and inspections can be prepared over the full lifecycle and an estimate of cost can be prepared for such tasks. Much of this cost would, of course be revenue expenditure and as such will consume financial resources progressively. Having such a plan in place enables the organisation to monitor costs and ensure that waiting repairs do not get out of hand. There is also a further benefit by planning revenue expenditure; it becomes possible to predict optimum capital reinvestment in the property many years ahead and for the organisation to prepare itself for these outlays, potentially avoiding costly financial bridging to handle these events.

While not solely intended for property, PAS 55 (Publicly Available Specification), published by the British Standards Institution, has been establishing itself as a recognised whole-life management system that can be applied to property assets.

The standard was originally produced in 2004 under the leadership of the Institute of Asset Management. PAS 55:2008 was released in December 2008 along with a toolkit for self-assessment against the specification.

PAS 55 can be used to help establish a system of asset management. It gives the key requirements of good practice but it does not specify how these must be met. The 'plan-act-do' methodology is a key approach to designing a compliant system.

Whatever format is chosen, modern organisations are becoming familiar with planned maintenance requirements and the need to control expenditure. While it is sometimes daunting to consider whole life costs, knowing the forward costs for the buildings and structures used by an organisation is a valuable advantage. It can avoid unnecessary expenditure and optimise the point at which assets are replaced or renovated.

Contributed by Adrian Singleton, adrian.singleton@watts.co.uk

Development

Development and procurement

Achieving excellence in construction

'Through the Achieving Excellence initiative, central government clients commit to maximise, by continuous improvement, the efficiency, effectiveness and value for money of their procurement of new works, maintenance and refurbishment.'

With this statement, the Office of Government Commerce (OGC) launched 'Achieving Excellence' in 1999 – a programme which aims to incorporate the recommendations of the Latham (*Constructing the Team*, 1994) and Egan (*Rethinking Construction*, 1998) reports into new ways of working for a construction industry that is notoriously resistant to change.

The initiative prescribes best practice for construction procurement in the public sector. Principal themes that run through the guidance are:

 ❖ long-term relationships, encouraging shared learning as a route to improving performance;

 ❖ crisper decision-making;

 ❖ investment in people through skills development then empowering them to take ownership and make decisions;

 ❖ development of 'metrics' so that performance can be measured and compared; and

 ❖ active management of value and risk across the whole life of a built asset – from construction to operation.

Certain factors are seen as critical to success

 ❖ **Leadership and commitment**: the successful project starts at the top with 'ownership' by a senior competent individual and the correct commitment of his or her time. This is seen as absolutely crucial but frequently neglected.

 ❖ **Stakeholder involvement throughout**: 'stakeholders' are all those parties with an interest in the project and who will influence its outcome. This may range from bosses to staff to neighbours to the general public. These parties will each have a different perspective on the project. These perspectives need to be understood and reconciled as far as is possible. The successful project aims to exceed the expectations of all these parties.

 ❖ **Roles and responsibilities**: each player should know their place in the team and what is expected of them.

 ❖ **Integrated teams**: the 'design team' or 'construction team' should be subsumed within the greater group of client, designers, constructors, specialist suppliers and even facilities managers, operating as a single development team with common overriding goals and objectives. This means investment in bringing the parties together and building the team ethos.

 ❖ **Integrated processes**: in which design, construction, operation and maintenance are considered as parts of a whole rather than separate activities.

 ❖ **Design quality**: that which achieves whole-life value by combining functionality with serviceability while respecting the environment. Design Quality Indicators (DQIs) have been developed as tools to give measurability to this multi-faceted dimension of individual projects.

 ❖ **Health and safety**: a commitment to excellence, because it is ethical, shows respect to the team and community and makes business sense.

❖ **Procurement strategies**: adopting those that ensure an integrated team and process approach. The Private Finance Initiative, Prime Contracting, and Design and Build are those preferred by the government for this reason. Traditional routes of procurement should only be used if they can be fully justified by business case.

❖ **Risk and value management**: These are interrelated activities that should involve the integrated team in constructive collaboration to deliver best value throughout the project. The independent key stage, or 'gateway' review process has an important role to play here.

❖ **Whole-life business perspective**: business decisions should be made based on the balanced long-term costs of site acquisition, design, development and operation, rather than short-term costs only. This is consistent with the integrated process approach.

❖ **Continuous improvement**: this requires a genuine commitment allied to schemes of measurement, key performance indicators (KPIs) and benchmarks so that levels of performance can be established and trends tracked.

❖ **Sustainability**: Construction has a major impact on the environment and project teams have an important responsibility in this respect in areas such as quality of life, flexibility, creating desirable environments and ensuring efficient use of resources.

The Achieving Excellence initiative is supported by a suite of publications and a web-based toolkit. They jointly comprise perhaps the most comprehensive best practice 'manual' in the history of the industry. As of 15 June 2010, OGC (and the achieving excellence agenda) were moved to the Cabinet Office and now form part of the new Efficiency and Reform Group intended to drive through recent government spending cuts.

The Cabinet Office document, *Government Construction Strategy*, May 2011, sets out the current model for public sector procurement in the UK. To access it, visit www.cabinetoffice.gov.uk

Contributed by Steve Brewer, steve.brewer@watts.co.uk

Project management

Project management can be defined as the direction of any complex of activities that have a defined beginning and an end. This process has a direct application to all industries and particularly to the construction process. The application of project management techniques in construction has developed rapidly over the past 40 years in response to the growing complexity of projects and the need to coordinate an increasingly fragmented and specialised industry.

The first task of a project manager is to define precisely the scope of the project, including gaining an appreciation of the fundamentals of the client's business plan for the anticipated scheme.

The second task is to gain an understanding of the client's objectives in terms of time, cost, quality and perceived risk. These objectives should be specified by means of a precise brief and schedule of target dates, a master budget, a risk register and specification standards. The relative priority that the client gives to each of these measures should also be understood. For example, a client may have an overriding need to complete by a certain date, so requiring the expenditure of additional funds to make this event a greater certainty. The project manager needs to reflect these factors in a strategy and plan for the project, usually termed the Project Execution Plan (PEP).

The third task is to assemble a competent team to deliver the project. The team needs to be briefed on the client's objectives and their precise role in such delivery. Coordination and reporting routines should be clearly defined at this point.

An effective project manager will be skilled in leading and directing a team drawn together specifically for the duration of the project. This requires personal, managerial, presentational and, above all, communication techniques. Stimulation of coordination in the project team and control of time, cost and quality requires the establishment of master control documents, such as the PEP, information flow tracking tools, risk registers, project master budgets and programmes. These are invaluable tools to enable the project manager to promote coordination, monitor progress, evaluate status and manage delivery.

Successful construction project management entails:

- ❖ strong balanced leadership;
- ❖ an empowered client project sponsor;
- ❖ project team focus on client's objectives;
- ❖ strong team relationships and motivation;
- ❖ a strong business case;
- ❖ a clear and developed brief and schedule;
- ❖ identification of measurable time, cost and quality objectives;
- ❖ defining roles and communicating objectives throughout the team;
- ❖ establishment of strategic as well as detailed controls;
- ❖ recognition that only the remaining time, cost and performance can be managed;
- ❖ management apportionment of risk;
- ❖ awareness of opportunity;
- ❖ robust project management practice – alive to risks and opportunities;
- ❖ an appropriate procurement and delivery methodology;
- ❖ an appropriate project contractual matrix;
- ❖ balanced risk apportionment;
- ❖ early established use of project control documentation;
- ❖ dynamic programme management;
- ❖ use of gateway review techniques;
- ❖ open, truthful and transparent lines of communication;
- ❖ continual challenge to ensure best quality, long-term value and programme;
- ❖ active management; and
- ❖ regular review to ensure long-term value.

Contributed by Daniel Webb, daniel.webb@watts.co.uk

Quality management and professional construction services

Quality management is a continual process that does not just happen but evolves over time and through experience. As clients' needs change and their expectations grow, it is essential that businesses continually improve so that they can carry on providing high quality products and services that continue to meet changing requirements. Organisations can help secure their future in an effective and efficient way by introducing a quality management system (QMS), which includes a commitment to continual improvement.

The ISO 9000 family of standards listed below provide the basis for many organisations to develop, implement, operate and maintain an effective QMS:

❖ ISO 9000:2005 *Quality management systems – Fundamentals and vocabulary*

❖ ISO 9001:2008 *Quality management systems – Requirements*

❖ ISO 9004:2009 *Managing for the sustained success of an organization – A quality management approach*

❖ ISO 19011:2011 *Guidelines for auditing management systems.*

The ISO 9000 documents were developed around the following quality management principles:

❖ customer focus;

❖ leadership;

❖ involvement of people;

❖ process approach;

❖ system approach to management;

❖ continual improvement;

❖ factual approach to decision making; and

❖ mutually beneficial supplier relationships.

ISO 9001: 2008 is the only auditable standard within the series and, although there is no legal requirement to adopt it, many client organisations make third party ISO 9001 certification a prerequisite for their suppliers. This is especially true for clients operating in the public sector.

ISO 9001 promotes a 'process approach' and looks to integrate quality management with business management. The content has been arranged into five main sections as follows:

❖ quality management system;

❖ management responsibility;

❖ resource management;

❖ product realisation; and

❖ measurement, analysis and improvement.

In addition, ISO 9001 supports the methodology known as Plan-Do-Check-Act, which can briefly be described as follows:

❖ **Plan**: establish the objectives and processes necessary to deliver results in accordance with client requirements and the organisation's policies.

❖ **Do**: implement the processes.

❖ **Check**: monitor and measure processes and product/services against policies, objectives and requirements for the product/services and report the results.

❖ **Act**: continually improve process performance.

ISO 9004: 2009 is designed to complement ISO 9001 but can also be used independently. It provides guidelines on a wider range of objectives associated with a QMS that go beyond the requirements set out in ISO 9001. In fact ISO 9004 clearly states that 'It is not intended for certification, regulatory or contractual use'.

ISO 9004 aims to help organisations achieve sustained success by a quality management approach. It encourages organisations to self-assess their own strengths and weaknesses, to determine their level of maturity, and to identify opportunities for improvement and innovation.

With the development and introduction of ISO 14001:2004 (*Environmental management systems – Requirements with guidance for use*) and BS OHSAS 18001:2007 (*Occupational health and safety management systems – Requirements*), organisations are increasingly looking to develop more integrated management systems that build on the common elements shared with ISO 9001. Once again, there is no legal requirement to adopt ISO 14001 or OHSAS 18001. However, some clients and organisations at the head of supply chains are looking to make third party certification to these standards a benchmark measure of competence for their providers.

As well as providing guidance on the conduct of quality and/or environmental audits, ISO 19011:2002 is also designed to facilitate this integration of quality and environmental management systems. It replaces six older standards in the ISO 9000 (quality) and ISO 14000 (environment) families and aims to help organisations optimise their management systems. In particular, by promoting single audits of both systems, it is designed to decrease disruption and should allow organisations to save time and money during internal and external audits.

Contributed by Dave Dorrington, dave.dorrington@watts.co.uk

Insurance policies pre-/during construction

This section gives a brief outline of the main policy covers which can be obtained. However, it is recommended that advice is sought from an insurance broker or adviser before cover is arranged.

Professional indemnity insurance (PII)

- ❖ **Who is protected**: architects; engineers; surveyors; project managers; designers and other professionals.

- ❖ **The cover**: losses resulting from professional negligence, errors and/or omissions which cause financial loss to a third party.

- ❖ **What is not covered**: material damage, theft, personal injury, and damage to third party property.

- ❖ **Typical policy exclusions**: work carried out prior to the inception of the policy, insured v insured claims (i.e where the board of a company will seek damages against an employee for their professional negligence which causes a loss to the company), and insolvency.

- ❖ **Duration of cover**: one year – annually renewable contracts are usually arranged. Policies are placed in to run-off should the consultant cease trading.

- ❖ **Important points**: professional indemnity is usually underwritten on a claim made basis. This means that it is the policy at the time a claim is made which will respond and not the policy in place at the time of the initial error or omission. It is also essential to ensure that the cover provided under this policy extends to include collateral warranties.

Depending on the contract, cover should usually be maintained for at least 6 (usually 12) years after the completion of the contract.

Collateral warranties are frequently executed under seal which increases the limitation period from 6 to 12 years. Contractors may also find themselves responsible for their specialist subcontractors (e.g. plumbers, electricians, roofers, scaffolders, and piling contractors).

Most professional indemnity insurers accept that collateral warranties are used quite regularly and some have taken positive steps to accept certain warranties and to give helpful advice.

Employer's liability (EL)

- ❖ **Who is protected**: building/engineering contractors, including any bona fide subcontractors.

- ❖ **The cover**: death, injury or illness to employees as a result of the employer's negligence.

- ❖ **What is not covered**: people on sick leave or action brought at an Employment Tribunal.

- ❖ **Typical policy exclusions**: none, however restrictions as to the type of work that is covered may apply.

- ❖ **Duration of cover**: one year – this type of policy is usually arranged on an annually renewable basis.

- ❖ **Important points**: EL is a compulsory insurance under statute. The minimum legal requirement is a limit of indemnity of £5m however, and most insurers provide £10m as a standard. Even a limited company with only one employee is required to have employer's liability insurance.

Cover of employees is extended to include, volunteers, labour-only subcontractors, working principals, apprentices and young people on work experience.

Under new legislation it is now a requirement of EL policies to be registered with the Employers' Liability Tracing Office (ELTO, www.elto.org.uk) in order to be able to identify the correct insurer in the event of any claims being made a few years down the line. Additionally, due to the ELTO regulations, Employee Reference Numbers (ERN) must be supplied to insurers at the inception or renewal of the policy, this includes the ERN of all subsidiary companies.

Public/products liability insurance

- ❖ **Who is protected**: building/engineering contractors.

- ❖ **The cover**: third party property damage or injury, resulting from negligent acts or omissions or caused by the supply of faulty or defective products.

- ❖ **What is not covered**: material damage, theft, and pure financial loss suffered by third parties.

- ❖ **Typical policy exclusions**: injury to employees, work involving explosives, defective workmanship.

- ❖ **Duration of cover**: at all times during the contract. Annually renewable contracts are usually arranged.

- ❖ **Important points**: products liability is usually provided on an aggregate basis and not for each and every claim. This means that the limit of indemnity provided will be for all claims occurring during the policy period and not for each claim. It is therefore important to set the correct limit from the outset in order to ensure there is adequate cover for any potential claims.

Most policies will also contain a bona fide subcontractors clause (BFSC); this means that any BFSC must carry the same limit of indemnity as the main contractor in order of the policy to respond.

Cover will automatically extend to include acts of labour only subcontractors and indemnity to principals, together with any costs relating to legal fees, expenses and hospital treatment, including ambulance costs that the NHS may claim.

Non-negligent liability insurance

- ❖ **Who is protected**: building/engineering contractors and their employers in joint names.

- ❖ **The cover**: damage to third party property as a result of collapse, subsidence, heave vibration, weakening or removal of support, or lowering of ground water in the normal course of the works being carried out and for which no party can be found to be negligent.

❖ **What is not covered**: any damage or injury for which negligence can be established, damage to the works or materials.

❖ **Typical policy exclusions**: defective design or workmanship, inevitable damage.

❖ **Duration of cover**: at all times during the contract, cover arranged on a project specific basis.

❖ **Important points**: this type of cover is sometimes referred to by the reference in the JCT standard contract as 21.2.1 or 6.5.1 cover.

Because of the nature of the work, it is possible that adjoining properties to the contract site may be damaged following the activities of the contractor. However, the contractor may not have carried out the work negligently. The contractor's public liability insurance policy deals with allegations of negligence only and without evidence from the third party that the contractor had been negligent, their claim may well fail.

However, the employer (developer) may still be liable, as it will be seen as the party that brought the contractor to site (*Gold v Patman & Fotheringham* 1958), hence the need for this more specific insurance cover.

It is the employer's responsibility to ensure cover is taken out but it is usually easier for the contractors to arrange this as an extension to their public liability insurance and charge the premium back to the employer. This prevents an argument between the public liability and non-negligent liability insurers in the event of a claim.

This cover is usually arranged on a project-by-project basis. However, a limited number of insurers will offer an annual policy (usually based on declarations from the contractor).

Contract works/contractors all risk/erection all risks policies

❖ **Who is protected**: building/engineering contractors and their employers in joint names.

❖ **The cover**: 'all risks' of loss to the works and/or contractors' plant, materials and the existing structure being worked upon (if applicable).

❖ **What is not covered**: injury to employees or third parties, third party property damage, defective workmanship or defective materials.

❖ **Typical policy exclusions**: disappearance and shortages, damage occurring after practical completion and after the maintenance period.

❖ **Duration of cover**: one year – renewable annually. At all times during the contract and any maintenance period after practical completion.

❖ **Important points**: attention should be paid to the selected clauses within the contract. Under JCT (or similar) contacts, several options are available in terms of who becomes responsible for insuring the works and existing structures (sometimes referred to as Clause 22 or 6.7):
  – *Option A*: for new builds, the contractor is responsible for arranging an all risks policy in joint names to cover the works and professional fees.
  – *Option B*: for new builds, the employer is responsible for arranging an all risks policy in joint names to cover the works and professional fees.

> – *Option C*: for refurbishment/renovation, the employer is responsible for arranging an all risks policy in joint names to cover the works, and professional fees and a specified perils policy, again in joint names for the existing buildings.

Joint names policies contain subrogation waivers, which means that the insurer cannot recover their costs from the party responsible for the damage caused.

When selecting the contract sum insured, various factors should be taken into consideration, not just the value of the materials used. Cover should be arranged to include professional fees, costs of removing debris and VAT.

Contractors will be responsible for insuring their own or hired-in plant against theft or other types of loss. It should also be arranged that contractors are responsible for insuring against their own risks of employer's and public liability and that all BFSC carry adequate levels of insurance.

Cover can be arranged on a project specific basis, which is usually the case if a joint names policy is required or for a larger contract that would normally fall outside of the contractor's usual activities or would be extended beyond the policy period and therefore would not be covered under an annual contractors all risks policy.

Environmental impairment liability insurance

- ❖ **Who is protected**: property owners and developers; environmental engineers and consultants; plastics manufacturers; businesses with own oil tanks or diesel supplies; businesses involving hazardous chemicals; general manufacturing.

- ❖ **The cover**: environmental damage and/or prevention and remediation whether from gradual or sudden and accidental events. It includes covers such as first party (own site) clean-up costs (resulting from gradual and sudden and accidental pollution), third party (off site) clean-up costs (resulting from gradual and sudden and accidental pollution), third party nuisance claims, transportation, biodiversity damage, (Environmental Damage Regulations) coverage, business interruption, mitigation expense, defence costs.

- ❖ **What is not covered**: known conditions, microbial matter, abandoned property, asbestos and lead (but covers clean up), intended or expected loss, identified underground storage tanks (unless specified with insurers), intentional non-compliance with legislation, insured v insured, prior knowledge and non-disclosure.

- ❖ **Typical policy exclusions**: employer's liability, contractual liability, fines and penalties.

- ❖ **How long should cover be maintained**: annually renewable policies are available for operational business risks and for property owners. Special requirements policies with periods of three, five and ten years are the norm.

- ❖ **Important points**: under Environmental Damage Regulations, operators (property owners, business operators, etc.), are strictly liable whether or not the operator intended to cause damage or was negligent. The basic principle is that the polluter pays. The Environment Agency has powers to rectify pollution damage and then recover the costs from the polluter.

Conventional public liability policies carry a standard exclusion in respect of gradual pollution and contamination; the policy only indemnifies against pollution claims as a result of sudden and unforeseen events. Gradual pollution losses are excluded so a specific environmental impairment liability policy is needed.

Right of light indemnity insurance

Right of light (RoL) policies are considered when a developer has commissioned a specialist rights of light survey/report that has identified that rights of light exist benefitting neighbouring property, primarily through prescription or through title. Developers have the option of negotiating a deed of release with the 'injured' neighbour, or remaining silent on the subject and arranging insurance.

❖ **Who is protected**: The principal, the developer, the financier of the project lessees, and any subsequent successors in title to the developed property.

❖ **What is covered**:
  – damages or compensation (including costs and expenses) awarded against the insured;
  – costs of alteration or demolition of the development to comply with an injunction;
  – diminution in market value following an injunction; and
  – costs of development, commenced or contracted, prior to an injunction.

❖ **What is not covered/excluded**:
  – developer profit;
  – any claim following any communication with an affected third party without the insurer's consent.

❖ **Important points**: One of the basic conditions is that once insurance is in place, the developer or any of his agents/advisers must not enter into conversation with any third party without the consent of insurers, regarding the existence of the policy.

  RoL policies are generally bespoke to the needs of each development. This may involve discussions between the developer, the surveyor, the insurance broker and legal representatives.

❖ **Extensions of cover** are available for such items as:
  – increased loan interest payments in the event of a temporary injunction; and
  – contractual penalties incurred as a result of delay.

  In the event of a claim, the insured must immediately advise insurers who will work with the insured and surveyor in order to resolve the issue to best advantage.

  Such polices are written in perpetuity and effectively attach to the development, as such the policy automatically transfers to successors in title.

❖ **Availability of cover**: the case of *HKRUK II (CHC) Ltd v Heaney* [2010] 44 EG 126 affirmed that injury to commercial property is injunctable, not just injury to residential property and as such insurers have become more cautious in their approach to providing cover.

In inner city cases (London in particular), because of a greater knowledge now of rights of light, neighbours are more likely to be aware of their potential rights. Some insurers encourage developers to be 'open' with the neighbour under an 'agreed conduct' wording. The policy can then be written on the basis of an excess to cover compensation plus associated costs. The policy would then cover the 'doomsday' scenario where a neighbour will not negotiate and still pursues an injunction – the policy would meet all costs over and above the excess.

There is a very limited market for this insurance (four to five insurers) and those interested should approach a specialist broker for advice and guidance.

Contributed by Rob Cooke ACII, 020 7280 3466, rob.cooke@thecleargroup.com

Performance and other bonding facilities

❖ **Who is protected**: owner of a project (obligee) or principal contractor (see below).

❖ **The cover**: a performance bond is the promise by a third party (the bonding company) to pay – or sometimes perform – if a contractor fails to complete a contract. A labour and material payment bond can also help protect an owner from liens against the owner's property if the contractor fails to pay workers, subcontractors and suppliers. Maintenance bonds are often required to guarantee the contractor's performance of certain maintenance over a fixed period of time after completion of the work.

❖ A bond is a three-way contract between the contractor (the principal), the owner (the obligee), and the bonding company (the surety). The contractor is called the principal because the contract is his or her primary responsibility. The surety and principal promise, in the bond, that the contract will be performed according to its terms. Essentially, the surety promises that if the contract is not performed, it will pay damages if the principal cannot. The principal may also require any subcontractors he appoints to provide a bond with him as the obligee.

❖ **What is not covered**: any material damage to the works or any liability attaching to the contractor for death, injury or damage to persons or property. Some important limitations of surety bonds to keep in mind are:

- A bond is not an insurance policy. It is not a substitute for adequate insurance coverage, either for liability or property damage. A bond will not be liable for personal injuries or for property damage that results from a contractor's negligence.
- A bond will not protect the obligee from valid claims by a contractor. If a contractor sues the obligee, the surety has no obligation to defend the obligee. If a contractor prevails in a dispute with an obligee, the bond will not pay for what the obligee owes to the contractor.
- A surety is entitled to most of the same defences that the principal has. Thus, if the obligee's problem with a contractor is a legitimate dispute, the obligee can expect the surety to dispute the claim as well.
- A bond is liable only if the obligee has performed all its own obligations. This includes the obligation to pay the agreed price (including agreed extras) for the work. The bond is responsible only for excess cost to complete or correct after the obligee has spent what it has agreed to pay the principal to do the work.
- The surety's basic obligation is to pay money. In some circumstances the surety may agree to obtain bids for completion or correction and/or to take over the contract and see that it is completed. The surety may do this when it believes that it is the least expensive way for it to meet its obligations. In other circumstances the surety will simply reimburse the obligee, up to the bond value, for the obligee's excess costs.
- The obligee must act reasonably to minimise any damages. An obligee cannot, for example, let an uncompleted project simply sit so that weather damage increases the cost to complete. An obligee may jeopardise bond recovery, by paying the contractor funds which have not been earned, or amounts in dispute, or amounts which an obligee is entitled to withhold for delay or for damage correction. Because an obligee must at the same time be sure that failure to pay does not result in the obligee breaching the contract, it is important to consult a solicitor whenever an important dispute arises.
- A performance bond covers only completion or correction costs within the scope of the original contract. Therefore an obligee who hires a new contractor to finish or fix the work must be sure that either (a) the new contract covers only the original work or (b) that the obligees can segregate and prove

what costs went toward finishing the original contract work. Extras added with the new contractor will not be covered by the bond.

❖ **Typical policy exclusion**: The contract specific purpose of the bond and the conditions under which it can be called upon are expressly given in the wording of the bond.

❖ **Duration of cover**: the duration of a bond will usually be structured in one of four ways:
   - start of works contract until practical completion of subcontract/works contract.
   - start of works contract until making good defects of subcontract/works contract.
   - start of works contract until on practical completion of main contract.
   - start of works contract until making good defects of main contract.

❖ **Important points**: surety bonding is considered a part of the insurance industry, but it shares some characteristics with the bank credit industry.
   - The surety company's primary duty is not to lend the contractor money. Instead, the surety company uses its financial resources to stand behind, or back, the contractor's commitment and ability to complete a contract.
   - The surety bond is advantageous for the business owner because it assures that the contracted work will be completed, and protection will be provided if it is not.
   - Unlike insurance companies, surety companies do not apply excesses based on the probability of loss.

Contributed by Andrew Moses, 020 8329 4920, andrew.moses@ thecleargroup.com and Grant Pye Cert CII, 020 7280 3467, grant.pye@thecleargroup.com of Clear Insurance Management Ltd, 10 Eastcheap, London EC3M 1AJ, www.thecleargroup.com

How to appoint consultants

In order to appoint consultants, as with contractors, it is preferable that a transparent and competitive process is undertaken to ensure best practice and to demonstrate best value for the client and the client's project.

There are three steps undertaken in any appointment process of a consultant, be it either on a competitive or a negotiated basis:

❖ a request for fee proposal, commonly known as the RFP process or the provision of a fee bid;

❖ the selection of successful consultant; and

❖ a formal appointment of the consultant.

Once the need for consultancy advice has been identified, the first step is to draw up a list of consultants who are known to be competent, and may be available, to provide the required services.

Invitation for consultant to present a fee proposal

In order for the consultant to provide a fee proposal, on which the appointment will be based, the following matters should be **clearly defined**.

Brief

The brief should be as specific as possible. In some cases, it may be useful to make informal approaches to a number of consultants to discuss the project before finalising the brief.

The following items will be relevant in most cases:

- ❖ the required end product (plans, contract drawings, report, etc.) – this is crucial and needs to be identified as clearly and explicitly as possible;
- ❖ the context for the proposed work;
- ❖ a list and copies of the basic information already available;
- ❖ the parameters: financial limitations, previous commitments, physical limits, area of influence, established plans and policies, etc. indicate which parts of the brief are fixed and which are open to proposals by the tendering consultants on methodology, timetable or sequence;
- ❖ an indication of the likely project budget if available;
- ❖ proposed key members of the client team, including the project manager and the steering group key stakeholder;
- ❖ the anticipated number of meetings with the project manager, project team, and/or the client group;
- ❖ any confidentiality requirements;
- ❖ the evaluation criteria, especially the price/quality relationship;
- ❖ unique aspects of the project must be covered (so as to avoid surprises, e.g. requirements for warranties, specific levels of required PII, requirement for Novation of consultants), i.e. something that might make a consultant change the proposal; and
- ❖ additional conditions relating to the particular project and the specific requirements of the client should accompany each RFP.

Programme

The programme should include:

- ❖ the timescale for the work, with target start and completion dates and a programme for any intermediate stages; and
- ❖ the timetable for the selection process and the work.

Scopes of service

In order to enable consistency between the same type of consultants, including different consultant disciplines, to be engaged on the same project, it is preferable to generate a bespoke set of scopes of service to be used in conjunction with a matrix of responsibilities. This allows the demonstration of clear definitions where each of the consultants' responsibilities start and finish and ensures there are no gaps between the consultants' services.

In addition, the consultant should be asked to provide:

- ❖ the background experience of the firm;
- ❖ any special experience relevant to the project;
- ❖ the proposed technical approach and methodology – ideally this should comprise an itemised account of the tasks to be undertaken and factors to be examined in carrying out the work;
- ❖ details of the consultancy staff to be assigned to the work, including their individual responsibilities and past experience;
- ❖ a proposed work schedule – this could, for instance, be in the form of a bar chart, indicating the timescale and completion date for each part of the work;
- ❖ details of how the consultant proposes to organise and manage the work – this should cover any planned head office involvement, back-up support, and use of subcontractors for, say, survey work;

❖ a financial proposal, covering the basis of charging fees, reimbursable expenses, etc. and

❖ any exclusions, assumptions and/or clarifications on the financial proposal.

Criteria for selection of consultants

The selection of a consultant is based on a number of factors including the consultant's expertise and specialist knowledge of particular issues and projects, fee costs and past performance.

In order to do this the following should be carried out:

❖ Assess consultants' bids on a level playing field of consistent terms (this is established by the first step in the process described on page 60/61 – the brief) to ensure the bids are comparable and are assessed fairly.

❖ Ensure multiple bids (preferably a minimum of three) from the same type of consultants and ensure that the bids and other elements of the consultant team are aligned with each other.

When analysing the consultants' bids the following should be carried out:

❖ Assess the bids in the context of quality, cost and value. The intangible aspects (such as quality of services, unique ideas that the consultant is able to bring to the project, ability of consultant to work within a team) also need to be assessed.

❖ Proposals should demonstrate sufficient flexibility to accommodate modifications to the bid. Payment regimes should reflect the client's cash flow forecast requirements or motivational milestones on the project. (In the absence of specific guidance, this is commonly shown as a monthly draw down.)

❖ Take account of factors such as the consultant's experience of comparable work, the seniority and experience of individual staff, and the extent to which the consultant has understood the nature of the project and the client's priorities.

In addition, the following points should be taken into consideration:

❖ Has the consultant demonstrated a real insight into the needs of the client, or does the proposal read like a routine effort?

❖ Does the quality of presentation of the proposal indicate hasty and careless preparation, or does it give the confidence that the end product will be of a high professional standard?

An element of subjective judgment will need to be made on the consultant's ability to deliver a high quality and cost effective service within an agreed financial and performance framework.

Fees and expenses

The fee basis should be agreed in writing between the consultant and the client prior to the commencement of work. It may reflect:

❖ the importance of the project to the client;

❖ the cost or value of the project;

❖ the skills required; and

❖ special circumstances, such as the need for urgent action or the novelty of the matters raised.

Fees should preferably be determined on a lump sum basis, in which the consultant agrees a fixed price to cover all the time likely to be spent on the work and all expenses likely to be incurred. This mitigates the financial exposure to the client and contributes to providing a better level of cost certainty on the project.

Where percentages of the contract value are proposed by the consultant, this should be compared with industry standard rates for competitiveness. Given the variability in a known cost, up until such time as a main contract is awarded and the changing nature of projects, it is common for consultant fees to be based upon a percentage of the contract value. However, once a contract value is known and/or agreed for the project it should then be possible to agree a fixed fee with the consultant on the basis of the initial percentage rate offered.

The fee basis should also include:

- ❖ rates for principals and assistants involved in the work, calculated on an hourly basis, including where applicable a definition of what is deemed to be a day;

- ❖ prospective changes in hourly rates (e.g. reviewed annually in line with inflation);

- ❖ details of the method of payment. This may include payments on account, interim payments or staged payments. The consultant may stipulate that if such payments are called for and not met within the specified time, the consultant may suspend work on the project;

- ❖ estimates of:
  - – the total fee (subject to assumptions or exclusions);
  - – the amount of billable time anticipated to be required to complete the project (subject to limitations);

- ❖ where appropriate, the rate of interest to be charged on outstanding accounts;

- ❖ specific administration costs;

- ❖ travelling time, and how this is to be charged;

- ❖ disbursements;

- ❖ indemnity insurance and any increase to provide cover for a specific project;

- ❖ the appointment and payment of subconsultants; and

- ❖ the method of charging for, and arrangements for distribution of income from, any report or other publication (including plans).

When fees are based on time costs, the time spent on a project (including travelling time) is chargeable at the daily or hourly rate of the person doing the work.

Activities that are included in the time charge include:

- ❖ technical work as defined in the contract or by agreement with the client;

- ❖ survey work or data processing;

- ❖ meetings with the client, with any other consultants or advisers associated with the work, and with relevant external organisations;

- ❖ site visits;

- ❖ travelling in connection with the work;

- ❖ preparation and production of project drawings and other graphic material;

- ❖ writing, editing and processing reports;

- ❖ community involvement and consultation procedures; and

- ❖ presentation of reports and follow-up work.

Expenses which are incurred directly as a result of an assignment and which are properly recoverable from the client are charged separately from time costs, usually in the form of an itemised invoice. Such expenses may include travel, accommodation and subsistence, data processing, and the purchase of maps and other documentation. They will normally be subject to VAT.

The issue of expenses (or disbursements) is an area of consultant appointment which can sometimes get overlooked so extra careful attention is required. Make sure, where possible, that consultant expenses ('all reasonable disbursements') are included in the consultant's fee offer. It is problematic to resolve this inclusion after a fixed fee is agreed. If inclusion of the disbursement into the fixed fee is not possible, then capping the expenses exposure is the next best option.

Appointment of the consultant

In most instances, a simple exchange of letters will be sufficient to confirm the appointment of a consultant, although it is becoming more common to arrange formal appointments. Where a client prefers to have a formal contract agreed, especially on larger value projects, these should be prepared in draft by the client's legal advisers, preferably in advance of selection, and a copy forwarded to the consultant for comment prior to formal agreement.

The items that should be specified in any contract with a consultant should include:

❖ the services to be provided by the consultant;

❖ the timing, phasing and stages of the work;

❖ report schedules, including the submission of progress reports;

❖ the keeping of project accounts and records by the consultants;

❖ costs and payments;

❖ ownership of reports, copyright of documents and plans;

❖ levels of required professional indemnity insurance (PII) – this will vary depending on the value of the project and services offered; and

❖ requirements for consultant warranties. (See *Collateral warranties and reliance letters* on page 87.)

In drawing up either a formal contract or a simpler document of appointment, other specific points may need to be considered:

❖ the terms of appointment and the fee basis:
  - avoid terms or conditions that come from other consultants;
  - if the provision of a consistent set of appointment terms for all consultant agreements on a project is desired, it is preferable to create a bespoke appointment document and avoid the use of industry standard agreements;
  - where industry standard agreements are used for the appointment of consultants on a given project, the overlap and underlap between these types of agreements needs to be managed;
  - if there is no readily available format, use or adapt the nearest equivalent in preference to trying to devise one from scratch;

❖ if any office is to act 'in association', the financial arrangements for this should be determined;

❖ the individual to whom the consultant will be directly accountable;

❖ provision for any additional work which may prove necessary for the satisfactory completion of the project, or which the client may wish to commission for some other reason;

❖ default or release clauses to cover the eventuality of the work not proceeding to completion; and

❖ provision for handing over survey and analysis information in a useable form for updating and review, and compatibility of computer-based data.

For industry standard agreement documents for consultant appointments please refer to the following:

❖ **General Consultancy Agreement**: BPF Version 2, July 2007.

- ❖ **General Consultancy Agreement**: The NEC3 Professional Services Contract, and Adjudicator's Contract, 3rd edition, ICE, 2005. This is part of the New Engineering Contract.

- ❖ **Architects**: RIBA Standard Agreement 2010 – Architect.

- ❖ **Engineers**: ACE conditions of engagement 2009. A suite of conditions to accommodate particular engineering services, including a subconsultancy agreement.

- ❖ **Quantity/building surveyors**: RICS Standard Form of Consultant's Appointment and scopes of services, June 2008.

- ❖ **CDM co-ordinators**: The RIBA, RICS and ACE standard form appointments make provision for CDM co-ordinator services. It is common for the architect, quantity surveyor or engineer to also undertake the role of CDM co-ordinator. Sometimes an independent consultant is appointed to undertake the CDM co-ordinator role.

- ❖ **Project managers**: RICS Project Manager Services, May 2008 and RIBA Standard Agreement 2010 – Consultant.

Contributed by Sarah Park, sarah.park@watts.co.uk and Angela Dawson, angela.dawson@watts.co.uk

Contracts and procurement

Development and procurement

Public sector procurement

This section provides an overview of public sector procurement. Due to the complexity of this field, together with differences in interpretation and practice between contracting authorities, it should be regarded as a guide only and specific advice sought in appropriate cases.

Public procurement legislation

Public procurement in the UK and the rest of the EU is governed by a number of Directives and Regulations designed to ensure the free movement of supplies, services and works within the EU. These include:

- ❖ Directive 2004/18/EC, dated 31 March 2004, on the coordination of procedures for the award of public works contracts, public supply contracts and public service contracts;

- ❖ Directive 2004/17/EC, dated 31 March 2004, coordinating the procurement procedures of entities operating in the water, energy, transport and postal services sectors; and

- ❖ Directive 2009/81/EC, dated 13 July 2009, on the coordination of procedures for the award of certain works contracts, supply contracts and service contracts by contracting authorities or entities in the fields of defence and security, and amending Directives 2004/17/EC and 2004/18/EC.

These are then implemented in national legislation; in the UK this includes:

- ❖ the *Public Contracts Regulations* 2006 as amended by the *Public Contracts (Amendment) Regulations* 2009;

- ❖ the *Utilities Contracts Regulations* 2006 as amended by the *Utilities Contracts (Amendment) Regulations* 2009; and

- ❖ the *Defence and Security Public Contracts Regulations* 2011, which apply to procurement procedures which started on or after 21 August 2011.

The regulations require competition for public supplies, services and works above certain cost thresholds and prescribe detailed advertising and tendering procedures which must be followed. The cost thresholds are reviewed every two years; a summary of those applying from 1 January 2012 are shown below (Note: reference should be made to the current EU Regulations, which contain exceptions and additional categories).

	Supplies or Services	Works
Public Contracts Regulations		
Central government bodies (see note 1)	£113,057 (€130,000)	£4,348,350 (€5,000,000)
Other public sector	£173,934 (€200,000)	£4,348,350 (€5,000,000)
Indicative notices	£652,253 (€750,000)	£4,348,350 (€5,000,000)
Small lots	£69,574 (€80,000)	£869,670 (€1,000,000)
Utilities Contract Regulations/Defence and Security Public Contracts Regulations		
All sectors	£347,868 (€400,000)	£4,348,350 (€5,000,000)

	Supplies or Services	Works
Indicative notices	£652,253 (€750,000)	£4,348,350 (€5,000,000)
Small lots	£69,574 (€80,000)	£869,670 (€1,000,000)

Note 1: With the exception of the following services, which have a threshold of £173,934 (€200,000):
❖ Part B (residual) services;
❖ Research and development services (Category 8);
❖ The following telecommunications services in Category 5;

— CPC 7524 – Television and radio broadcast services

— CPC 7525 – Interconnection services

— CPC 7526 – Integrated telecommunications services.

Note 2: 'CPC' means Central Product Classification of the United Nations.

Note 3: All thresholds are net of VAT.

Type of scheme

There is a big difference between the threshold for supplies and services, and that for works. Contracting authorities must ensure that their requirements are considered against the correct threshold if they are to avoid legal challenge.

Interpretation and practice varies and simple definitions for the different types are not readily available. However, the *Public Contracts Regulations* 2006 list 'Activities constituting works' in Schedule 2 and 'Categories of services' in Schedule 3. The Service Desk at the Office of Government Commerce (OGC) provided the following definitions in 2010 (bold indicates this author's emphasis):

'A **supply contract** is the purchase or hire of goods and [their] installation. This could include buying stationery, installation of a lift into an existing lift shaft or renting a car.'

'A **service contract** … requires a service element. This could include requirements such as electrical testing, cleaning, facilities maintenance and parcel delivery.'

'A **works contract** would be any construction from scratch or any permanent change to an existing structure. This could include the building of a new office or road, resurfacing a car park, building an extension to an existing structure or the putting in [of] a lift shaft.'

© *Crown copyright material is reproduced under the Open Government Licence v1.0 for public sector information: www.nationalarchives.gov.uk/doc/open-government-licence/*

It is important to consider the whole task and the context of each element required. For example, a contract to routinely service a boiler would be a service contract, the removal and replacement of a boiler would be a supply contract, whereas the installation of a new boiler in an extension would form part of a works contract.

Types of procurement procedure

If the total value of the supplies, services or works required over the lifetime of the proposed contract is above the current threshold, the public sector contracting authority must place a notice in the Supplement to the Official Journal of the European Union (OJEU).

The Official Journal actually comprises three series:

❖ The **L Series** contains EU legislation, including regulations, directives, decisions, recommendations and opinions.

❖ The **C Series** contains EU information and notices, including the judgments of the European Courts, calls for expressions of interest for EU programmes and projects, public contracts for food aid, etc.

❖ The supplementary **S Series** contains invitations to tender which can be found on TED (Tenders Electronic Daily).

All three series of the OJEU are published every working day (five days a week). Production of a hard copy 'journal' ceased in 1997, so European public procurement opportunities are now published on TED, the single official source of public contracts in Europe (www.ted.europa.eu).

TED provides free access for all potential suppliers, but several tender information subscription services are also available, which help suppliers find appropriate OJEU notices for a fee; notices for large projects may also be published in the construction press.

In the UK, on 11 February 2011, the Prime Minister launched Contracts Finder, a free new service for businesses, central government buyers and the public. It now claims to be the main source of government procurement opportunities with a value greater than £10,000.

The *Public Contracts Regulations* 2006 include four types of procurement procedure; the basic approach for each is summarised in the following table.

Stage	Open	Restricted	Negotiated	Competitive dialogue
Advertisement	OJEU contract notice			
Pre-qualification	n/a	Requests to participate submitted		
		Pre-qualification of tenderers		
Tendering	n/a	Invitation to tender issued	Invitation to negotiate issued	Invitation to participate issued
			Negotiation phase	Dialogue phase
		Submission of tenders		
		Evaluation		
Award	Clarification with preferred bidder			
	OJEU award notice			
	Standstill period			
	Entry into contract			

The choice of tendering procedure is made by the contracting authority, having regard to the nature of the supplies, services or works, and the circumstances under which they are to be delivered. For example, the nature of the service may mean that a specification cannot be drawn up with sufficient precision to allow the use of the Open or Restricted procedure.

Pre-qualification

Some schemes will have supply markets with very large numbers of potential providers. In these situations, it is not sensible to invite tender submissions from all those who would like to participate; pre-qualification questionnaires (PQQs) are therefore used to select the most appropriate providers to invite to tender.

The PQQ process regularly leaves suppliers faced with the prospect of laboriously preparing slightly different submissions to answer a series of similar basic questions in a slightly different format.

There have been a lot of attempts to rationalise and standardise this stage, the latest one being PAS 91:2010 (*Construction related procurement – Prequalification questionnaires*). This Publicly Available Specification, first published on 1 October 2010, was developed by BSI in conjunction with representatives from the construction industry's clients, trade bodies and accreditation organisations.

Despite its voluntary status, the UK government has already announced that it wants all central government departments to adopt the PAS as a standard. Time will tell if other public procurement departments start to use it and it reduces the amount of time and cost suppliers are forced to expend, but cannot recoup, during this initial phase of most public sector procurement exercises.

Standstill (Alcatel) period

The requirement for a standstill period was introduced because of a European Court of Justice judgment in the 'Alcatel' case (ECJ reference C-81/98 *Alcatel Austria v Bundesministerium fuer Wissenshaft und Verkehr*), which clarified that there had to be sufficient period for an aggrieved provider to challenge the award decision before the contract commences. All purchasers therefore have to include a ten calendar day standstill period between the point when the decision to award the contract is made and the signature of the contract. This allows participants to seek additional debriefing from authorities which must be requested and provided within set periods.

New regulations were applied to the content of contract award letters on 20 December 2009. This is part of a range of measures introduced by the European Commission to toughen up the rules for procuring authorities and to increase the remedies available to dissatisfied bidders.

Minimum number of tenderers

Under the restricted, negotiated and competitive dialogue procedures there is a requirement for a sufficient number of participants to ensure genuine competition. Where the restricted procedure is used, the minimum is **five**; where the negotiated procedure and competitive dialogue is used, the minimum is **three**.

Types of notice

Various OJEU notices will be published during the procurement process. The three most common are:

❖ **Prior Information Notice (PIN):** this is an optional notice of intent to invite tenders or expressions of interest at a later date. It can be used to reduce the 'normal' procurement timescales, see below.

❖ **Contract Notice:** this compulsory notice is used by the contracting authority to advertise a requirement. It gives suppliers information about the project and lets them know how to pre-qualify or tender for the contract. A standard format is used for these notices, see below.

❖ **Contract Award Notice:** this notice must be published at the end of the process, once a supplier has been selected for the contract.

Content of contract notices

OJEU contract notices are published in a form prescribed by the EU and group information into the following sections:

i. Contracting authority.

ii. Object of the contract.

iii. Legal, economic, financial and technical information.

iv. Procedure.

v. [Spare number].

vi. Complementary information.

Certain information is mandatory within each section, but notices that contain more than the minimum specified may encourage a better quality and level of response from bidders.

Certain conventions are used in the notices, including Common Procurement Vocabulary (CPV) codes and geographical information in the form of 'Nomenclature of Statistical Territorial Units' or NUTS codes. They allow the type and location of the project to be identified by a series of standard codes, which allow suppliers to focus on appropriate notices – see the SIMAP website (www.simap.europa.eu) for further information about these codes and the public procurement process in Europe.

Minimum time periods

The Regulations identify the minimum time periods that should be allowed between an OJEU notice being published and the cut-off date by which suppliers can respond. The standard periods may be reduced if:

- ❖ a PIN is used;
- ❖ the OJEU notice is sent electronically; and/or
- ❖ the contracting authority provides online access to the contract documents.

The mandatory time periods are summarised in the table below.

Procedure	Normal limit (calendar days)		Reduced limit (calendar days)	
			Electronic notification to OJEU	Electronic access to contract documents
Open	Minimum time from sending notification until tender return date	52	45	40
	With PIN (usual)	36	29	
	With PIN (minimum)	22		
Restricted	Minimum time from despatch of notice to receipt of **requests to participate**	37	30	
	If urgent	15	10	
	Minimum time from despatch of invitation to tender until **tender return date**	40		35
	With PIN (usual)	36		31
	With PIN (minimum)	22		
	If urgent	10		
Negotiated Procedure	Minimum time from despatch of notice until receipt of requests to be invited to negotiate	37	30	
	If urgent	15	10	

Procedure	Normal limit (calendar days)	Reduced limit (calendar days)	
		Electronic notification to OJEU	Electronic access to contract documents
Competitive Dialogue	Minimum time from despatch of notice until receipt of requests to be selected to participate	37	30

Notwithstanding the above, contracting authorities should always take into account the complexity of the contract and the time required by potential suppliers to prepare meaningful submissions when fixing the time limits for the receipt of tenders and requests to participate.

Contributed by Dave Dorrington, dave.dorrington@watts.co.uk

Public private partnerships

This section provides an overview of public private partnerships. Due to the complexity of this field, together with differences in interpretation and practice between contracting authorities, it should be regarded as a guide only and specific advice sought in appropriate cases.

Public private partnerships (PPPs) are arrangements typified by joint working between the public and private sector. In the broadest sense, PPPs can cover all types of collaboration across the interface between the public and private sectors to deliver policies, services and infrastructure. Where delivery of public services involves private sector investment in infrastructure, the most common form of PPP is the Private Finance Initiative (PFI).

HM Treasury set up an Operational TaskForce (OTF) in 2006 to provide free expert advice and support to public sector managers of operational PFI projects. The OTF advises and provides guidance on a wide range of operational issues, including the development of contract management strategies, benchmarking, market testing, managing variations, refinancing and other issues that occur during the operational phase of a contract. For more information see www.partnershipsuk.org.uk/PUK-OTF.aspx

The Private Finance Initiative

The PFI can form part of a government's overall strategy for delivering high quality public services. It requires the private sector to put its own capital at risk and to deliver clear levels of service to the public over the long term. In turn, that helps deliver high quality public services and ensures that public assets are delivered on time and to budget.

The key features of PFI are that there is an underlying asset, often a building or a series of buildings, and that private finance is used to provide the facility and service. In return, the private sector receives a regular payment from the public sector over the life of the concession, typically 25–30 years.

Features of PFI/PPP

❖ The private sector contracts not only for the provision of the building or other asset, but also for maintenance and services over the life of the concession. This encourages the integration of construction and services provision and investment decisions based on whole life cost, rather than capital cost only.

❖ The public sector requirements are expressed as outputs (requirements to be met) rather than inputs (standards to be achieved). This allows the private sector to meet requirements by the most cost-effective route and encourages innovation.

❖ The private sector is incentivised to deliver the services by a penalty structure which reduces or suspends the regular payment (called the Unitary Payment). Payment reductions may arise from parts of the asset no longer being available (unavailability) or performance failures (e.g. failure to rectify a defect within a prescribed period of time).

❖ The public sector remains responsible for the core public service (teaching, healthcare, administration, etc.).

❖ The PFI is funded entirely by the private sector in return for the Unitary Payment. In some cases, the public sector may offer long stop guarantees to improve Value for Money (VfM).

❖ The design, construction, operating and maintenance risks are largely transferred to the private sector. For example, if the project costs more or takes longer than agreed at the outset, the private sector is responsible for the overrun. The assessment, allocation and management of risks is one of the key disciplines in PFI/PPP procurement.

❖ The transfer of risk enables public sector authorities to benefit from accounting treatment of the Unitary Payment as revenue expenditure, which does not count against their capital allocations.

❖ The PFI proposal must demonstrate VfM, meaning broadly that PFI has to offer a more cost-effective solution to requirements than conventional public procurement. This comparison is made via the construction of a Public Sector Comparator (PSC) financial model for the public sector alternative. A 'shadow bid' is often compiled by the public sector to test the overall value at bid stage.

Key advantages and disadvantages

Advantages

❖ Public service improvements are brought forward by using private capital to offset the shortage of public capital.

❖ Development and operational risk is transferred to the private sector, freeing the public sector to concentrate on the core service provision.

❖ The private sector is incentivised to provide good quality VfM buildings and services.

Disadvantages

❖ The cost of private finance is greater than that of public capital, meaning that the PFI must achieve efficiency improvements to offset this.

❖ Major changes in public sector requirements during the concession period may be difficult or expensive to accommodate within a PFI.

Projects and clients

Types of projects using PFI include headquarters offices, environmental and waste recycling, transport (road, rail and light railway), education, health care, prisons, defence, housing and regional projects. Public sector clients include government departments, local authorities, NHS Trusts, and government agencies such as Her Majesty's Revenue and Customs (HMRC).

Because of the long-term nature of the transaction and the cost of the tendering process, PFI is rarely used for projects with a value of less than £20 million. A feature of some PFI transactions is the grouping of smaller projects into a single PFI to achieve the appropriate minimum size.

Project inception

The first formal step in the PFI process is the production of an Outline Business Case by or on behalf of the public sector contracting authority. This sets out the project brief and business case for the proposal, and forms the basis for applications for PFI credits from central government where applicable. It is followed up with the output specification which sets out the requirements for the project in performance terms, and in due course this forms a key part of the tender documentation.

A key feature of the output specification is that it is expressed in terms of required outputs, rather than prescribed inputs. Within any constraints set by the public sector, the private sector is free to meet these requirements by means of its own choosing; these can sometimes depart significantly from those envisaged by the client at the outset.

Transaction structure

The parties to a PFI transaction typically comprise the following:

- ❖ **Public sector client**: The government department, local authority or other public sector authority contracting for the project.

- ❖ **Private sector partner**: Usually a consortium comprising a contractor or developer, a facilities manager or operator, and a bank or other financial institution.

- ❖ **Funders**: In addition to the consortium partners, external organisations will normally be involved in the provision of funding. These can include banks or other financial institutions, bond issuers, rating agencies and insurers.

A number of companies with an interest in the PFI market have formed specialist subsidiaries or consortia to participate in contracting, funding or operation, particularly in the field of health care.

The above parties to the PFI will normally be advised separately and a typical consultant team would include a financial adviser, legal adviser and one or more technical advisers.

The organisational structure of a typical PFI transaction would look like this:

PFI transaction structure

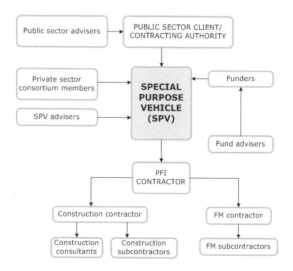

Project processes

The post-tender processes can vary widely depending on the project nature and external factors. Typically an Invitation to Negotiate (ITN) will be issued to a shortlist of bidders, and this may be followed by a further bidding round – Best and Final Offer (BAFO). In order to reduce bid periods and associated costs, current practice is to encourage the provision of full information by both parties at the outset, and the use of standard contract terms as far as possible.

At the conclusion of bidding and post-bid negotiations, a preferred bidder is selected, together with a reserve bidder. The parties then negotiate the remaining details of the project and confirm funding, legal and third party issues. During this period, development of the design and construction proposals continues, and planning permission may be sought. Once the terms are fully agreed and funding secured, contract award (or 'Financial Close') takes place, and the project can proceed.

Funding

PFI transactions are mainly debt financed, and senior debt is normally provided independently of the consortium partners. The main sources of PFI funds are:

❖ **Equity**: normally provided only in limited amounts by the private sector consortium partners.

❖ **Subordinated or mezzanine debt**: provided by consortium partners or other funding institutions.

❖ **Senior debt**: normally the bulk of the funding, provided by bank lending and/or via the capital markets.

The choice between bank and capital market options will depend on the nature and size of the project, and the market conditions at the time of placement. Bank debt is suitable for smaller, shorter life or higher risk projects, and the finance cost is generally higher than the capital markets option.

The capital markets option is particularly suitable for larger, lower risk projects for central government, where the covenant is perceived as strongest. This option requires the issue of an index-linked or fixed-rate bond which is typically taken up by other financial institutions and pension funds. Although the process of issuing a bond is more expensive than arranging bank debt, this will be recovered over the life of the bond in lower finance costs.

The bond issue is underwritten by a financial institution and may be credit-rated by an agency such as Standard and Poor's to improve marketability. As an alternative, or in addition, bonds may be enhanced by private or public sector guarantees, or by the use of credit risk insurance (called monoline insurance). A bond enhanced in this way is known as a wrapped bond.

PFI transactions may be refinanced during the concession period, typically by the renegotiation of debt finance once the development period is over and the project risk profile is reduced. Some PFI contractors have also begun to sell on their equity stakes, creating a secondary transaction market.

Value testing

Many PFIs have provisions in their contracts that require the value of certain soft services (e.g. catering, cleaning and security) to be tested at intervals, typically every five to seven years. Hard facilities management services such as building refits or life-cycle maintenance are not normally value tested.

Value testing is typically carried out by either:

- ❖ **benchmarking**: comparing information about the current service provider's provision with comparable sources; or
- ❖ **market testing**: inviting other suppliers to compete with the incumbent in an open competition.

Market testing allows the client a more flexible approach to soft service provision than benchmarking, because it ensures that the soft services can be reassessed to match public sector requirements at the time the exercise takes place.

Value testing should help the contracting authority ensure that value for money is achieved throughout the PFI contract. It is designed to ensure that both parties provide and receive services at a competitive market rate. However, it is sometimes perceived as a way for the public sector to cut costs, or for the private sector to increase prices for the next phase of the contract.

In addition to the financial aspects, the reviews provide an opportunity for the contracting authority to ensure that the existing services still meet their needs and, where necessary, redefine the requirements. They also provide an opportunity for service providers to introduce more innovative approaches and/or new technologies to improve efficiency and client satisfaction.

The current economic climate has put the spotlight firmly on testing VfM and HM Treasury published its report *Making savings in operational PFI contracts* in July 2011. This draws together the findings of four pilot cost-saving reviews and provides updated recommendations for savings measures to be pursued from the portfolio of UK operational PFI projects.

Success factors

Some PFI transactions are more successful than others, and some success or failure criteria are subjective. While it is difficult to draw general conclusions, research has identified the six most significant value for money drivers in PFI as:

- ❖ the level of risk transfer;
- ❖ linking the output specification requirements to payment;
- ❖ the length of the contract needed to recoup investment;

- ❖ appropriate performance measures and incentives;
- ❖ a competitive bidding process; and
- ❖ excellent management skills in the private sector.

The PFI model, which originated in the UK, has been taken up in several other countries, both in Europe and beyond. As long as there is a demand for better public services and a continuing shortage of public capital, it seems set to continue.

Contributed by Dave Dorrington, dave.dorrington@watts.co.uk

Procurement methods

Constructing Excellence led the development of BS 8534:2011 *Construction procurement policies, strategies and procedures – Code of practice* which was published in August 2011. It gives recommendations and guidance on the development of policies, strategies and procedures for the procurement of construction in the built environment. It is designed to allow public and private sector organisations to create a framework which allows a procurement system to be developed that facilitates fair competition, reduces the possibilities of abuse, improves predictability of outcome and allows the demonstration of best value.

All construction projects involve risk and the primary function of construction contracts is to assign risks to the respective participants to the building contract.

Risk is an inherent element of any construction project and therefore risk management is an essential part of contract strategy. The primary risks should be identified, and their likelihood and potential impact assessed.

This information should then be used, together with an understanding of the employer's priorities in terms of time, cost and quality, to decide upon the procurement method to be followed. The tendering procedure to obtain prices for the procurement route chosen can be single stage, two stage, or negotiated.

There are currently three main procurement methods used within the industry (other alternatives are Term Contracts and Partnering), which reflect various ways by which risk is balanced between the participants to the contract.

Traditional procurement (general contracting)

Under this method the contractor agrees to build the design that it is provided by the employer; the contractor has no responsibility for design.

This method is appropriate for projects where the employer's objectives have been clearly and comprehensively determined.

The financial outcome, responsibility and risk usually reside with the employer.

Advantages

- ❖ Most employers and contractors are familiar with this route;
- ❖ high degree of design and product control/selection;
- ❖ robust variation control; and
- ❖ direct employer relationship with designers.

Disadvantages

- ❖ Split responsibility between construction and design;
- ❖ limited risk transfer and increased economic uncertainty;
- ❖ limited opportunities to refine design and improve cost efficiency;
- ❖ potentially more likely to lead to disputes; and
- ❖ time – longer project delivery.

Design and build procurement

Design and build procurement can come in many forms, but the underlying basis is that the contractor takes on responsibility for both design and construction. This allows the contractor to have more flexibility on design and allows the employer to place the financial outcome responsibility and risk with the contractor.

Advantages

- ❖ Single point responsibility;
- ❖ time – potential to fast track projects by overlapping design and construction phases;
- ❖ contractor involvement in design and resolution of 'buildability' issues; and
- ❖ cost certainty.

Disadvantages

- ❖ Loss of design control;
- ❖ restricted scope for change post-contract (without paying a premium);
- ❖ possibility of increased cost – risk premium;
- ❖ quality – careful drafting of the employer's requirements is needed to ensure the required quality standards; and
- ❖ specification may be cost driven rather than quality driven.

Management procurement

The key feature of any management contract is that a 'manager' is appointed with the responsibility to manage a project on behalf of the employer. These contracts require the 'manager' to manage, procure and oversee the construction operations.

Advantages

- ❖ Less confrontational;
- ❖ contractor involvement to advise on buildability issues;
- ❖ time – can allow earlier start of physical works on site; and
- ❖ can provide flexibility to develop design while inviting tenders and letting packages.

Disadvantages

- ❖ Increased risk to employer – little contractual risk carried by the construction manager;
- ❖ out-turn cost is not defined until all packages are let – cost risk lies with the employer; and
- ❖ greater employer involvement may be required.

Under this procurement method there are two distinct routes that can be followed, either Management Contracting or Construction Management.

In Management Contracting the works contractors have direct contractual relationship with the Management Contractor, whereas in Construction Management the works contractors have direct contractual relationships with the employer.

Contributed by Dave Dorrington, dave.dorrington@watts.co.uk

Types of tendering route

Regardless of the form of contract, the method of tendering can impact on the successful outcome of a project. When appointing a main contractor, reference should be made to either the CIB *Code of Practice for the Selection of Main Contractors*, first published in 1997 or the *JCT Practice Note 6 (Series 2): Main Contract Tendering*. A summary of the three most commonly used appointment methods and an analysis of their merits follows.

Single stage selective tendering

Single stage selective tendering occurs when the client wishes to obtain the most competitive price for the project. This method will only be successful where the design is substantially complete for the type of contract being proposed, i.e. design and build or traditional, as any incomplete elements of the design will lead to post-contract variations and additional costs.

In using this method, the client usually seeks tenders from three to six preselected competent contractors issuing detailed tender information, whether it be performance specifications for a design and build route or full detailed bill of quantities for a traditional route. Tenders are returned and assessed under competition, with a contractor being selected on the basis of who best meets the evaluation criteria.

Advantages

- ❖ Most competitive price achieved;
- ❖ the client retains greater control of design; and
- ❖ increased cost certainty at signing of contract.

Disadvantages

- ❖ The contractor is not able to share its construction expertise at the design stage;
- ❖ increased programme requirements to produce the full design in advance of tender; and
- ❖ possible cost increases and variations are likely where the design is incomplete or errors have been made in design.

Two stage selective tendering

Two stage tendering is best suited where the client requires a competitive price but in particular requires early contractor involvement. The client will issue tenders with limited preliminary information (usually preliminaries, provisional sums, demolitions, earthworks) and a schedule of rates for the areas where the design is incomplete. Tenders are returned and assessed under competition, with the contractor being selected on the basis of who best meets the evaluation criteria. As the works progress, the schedule of rates is used to complete the pricing of the design.

Advantages

- ❖ Facilitates an earlier commencement on site;
- ❖ allows contractor input on specialist design areas during the construction phase; and
- ❖ allows for a degree of flexibility in design.

Disadvantages

❖ Greater cost risk as the contract is signed before the final cost is known;

and, if a large number of provisional items exist:

❖ risk to the programme, as design information needs to be completed during construction and in line with the contractor's programme.

Negotiated tendering

Negotiated tendering forms a hybrid of both the single and two stage routes. It allows the client to identify a contractor best suited for the project through tendering on limited information. The contractor then enters exclusively into negotiations with the client prior to agreeing a contract sum. This allows the design team to either:

❖ complete the design during the tender period and therefore, upon conclusion of the negotiations, the client has achieved a contract sum based on a full design; or

❖ provide the contractor with sufficient information at key stages to commence work earlier.

This method is often used where the number of contractors tendering is small or where the client has one or a small number of preferred partnering contractors for repeat projects.

Advantages

❖ Allows early site start;

❖ allows the contractor to have input into design and construction techniques;

❖ greater programme certainty as risks are identified early; and

❖ can build trust between client and contractor.

Disadvantages

❖ Possible increase in construction costs due to lack of competition on tendering;

❖ a risk to the programme if negotiations fail to meet targets; and

❖ less cost certainty if early site start is preferred.

Contributed by Dave Dorrington, dave.dorrington@watts.co.uk

Contractor appointment/tendering

There are a number of factors affecting the selection of contractors and their possible inclusion on a project shortlist.

Pre-tender/pre-qualification

The creation of a tender list will typically involve internal market intelligence from the project management and design team, based on previous performance in delivering key objectives matching those of the subject project.

Evaluation of any contractor shortlist should be based on agreement of the measurement criteria and thus the suitability of the selected group. The nature of the project will determine the most important criteria and thus assessment.

Typical pre-qualification submissions

- ❖ Company details including structure, financial standing and management systems, references from similar projects and Health and Safety policy.

- ❖ Specific details of the proposed project team – authority, experience, qualifications and resource, including design integration, control and coordination.

- ❖ Recent track record based on proposed project and procedure route.

- ❖ Project execution – programming approach, site logistics and snagging/completion strategy.

- ❖ In the public sector arena, submissions covering equality, diversity and environmental performance are increasingly required.

A weighted scoring system should be used to evaluate the information received and to prepare a shortlist of contractors to include on the tender list.

In most cases pre-tender interviews should take place to confirm the selected contractors' resources during the project period.

Quality and price assessment

- ❖ The objective of assessments is to select the one firm providing best value for money based on both quality and cost. A scoring format should be applied on both quality and cost – agreed prior to issuing tenders. Weighting of marks against criteria needs to be adjusted depending on project type. A 60:40, price:quality weighting is common.

- ❖ The design team should agree on a quality threshold (regardless of competitiveness) at which point any tenders below this level are discounted.

- ❖ Low price tenders should be thoroughly reviewed to ensure the full scope of the scheme is understood. Written explanations should be sought from contractors to test the robustness of any bid submitted.

Other factors

- ❖ Contractors should be aware of any specific provision in terms of appointment – i.e. variation to standard appointment contracts which they agree to as part of tender submission.

- ❖ Where contract amendments apply, it is worth ensuring that these are resolved and agreed as soon as possible. To avoid protracted contract negotiations interfering with project progress, it is wise to include a clause in contractors' terms of appointment relating to timely conclusion of any negotiations on contract amendments.

- ❖ Each project will have different drivers, be it time, cost or quality. Assessment of contractor shortlists and tender evaluation must be bespoke to ensure key drivers are met.

Contributed by Dave Dorrington, dave.dorrington@watts.co.uk

Letters of intent

Parties involved in construction works often find that it is not commercially feasible to delay the commencement of works until a full contract has been agreed and signed. Instead, they choose to proceed on the basis of a letter of intent (or a pre-construction services agreement as it is sometimes referred to these days) pending the completion of the full contract. 'Letters of intent' and 'pre-construction services agreements' are not legally defined terms and in practice, such documents vary widely in their legal effect.

It is important to understand that, depending on its terms, a letter of intent may or may not create a binding contract between the parties. A good example of the contractual uncertainty that letters of intent can create is the case of *RTS Flexible Systems Ltd v Molkerei Alois Muller GmbH & Co KG* [2010] 1 WLR 753, which was finally decided by the Supreme Court in March 2010. In that case the High Court, the Court of Appeal and the Supreme Court all had different interpretations of whether (and on what terms) a contract had been agreed at the expiry of the letter of intent. The case shows that even where a letter of intent does give rise to a binding contract, the effect is sometimes not what was anticipated by at least one of the parties! It is therefore important that the letter of intent covers certain minimum points.

When would you use a letter of intent?

In *Cunningham v Collett* [2006] EWHC 1771 (TCC), Judge Coulson QC (as he then was) acknowledged that letters of intent were sometimes the best way of ensuring that works can start promptly, but only in appropriate circumstances which he stated as follows:

❖ where contract workscope and price are either agreed, or there is a clear mechanism in place for such workscope and price to be agreed;

❖ where the terms and conditions are (or are very likely) to be agreed;

❖ where the start and finish dates and the programme are broadly agreed; and

❖ where there are good reasons for the works to be commenced in advance of the contract documents being finalised.

Judge Coulson did, however, comment that in his view, letters of intent are often used 'unthinkingly' in the construction industry and often simply to avoid difficult negotiations under the full contract. He observed that once a letter of intent was put in place and works started, there was a real risk that a full contract would never be put in place. It was therefore important that a letter should be drafted carefully so as to minimise the risk to both parties.

What provisions should go into a letter of intent from a developer's point of view?

Given the potential risk to the parties of entering into a letter of intent and a full contract materialising, the following provisions should be included as a bare minimum:

❖ **Limiting the scope of the letter**: By limiting the scope of the letter (either in time or money and ideally, both), the developer is not only encouraging the contractor to agree a full contract within a certain period of time or before a certain value of the works has been reached, but could also be limiting its exposure should a full contract not be agreed or signed. The letter must, however, state clearly what happens when the limit is reached.

In *RTS Flexible Systems* there was a dispute over whether the parties had intended a contract to come into existence after the termination of the letter of intent and if so what terms had been agreed. The High Court held that a contract on limited terms had come into existence on the basis of the parties' conduct. The Court of Appeal rejected that stating that no contract had been formed. The Supreme Court decided the matter finally by holding that a contract had come into existence but on wider terms than held by the High Court.

A letter of intent should therefore state whether or not the contractor is to stop working once the limit has been reached. If he is to continue working the terms and the basis on which he is to be paid should be made clear, e.g. by reference to an agreed rate or quantum meruit (an amount based on the value of the services provided calculated by reference to what is reasonable within the industry for such services).

❖ **Identify the works to be carried out under the letter of intent**: This can be used to limit the scope of the letter as mentioned above by authorising the contractor to carry out only a specified amount of work or place a specified number of orders.

❖ **Insurance**: If the contractor is to start works on site under the letter of intent, the letter should state the level of public and employer's liability insurance that must be taken out, as well as all risks insurance in respect of the works themselves. If the contractor is to carry out design services under the letter then the required level of professional indemnity insurance should be stated.

❖ **CDM Regulations**: There should be a contractual requirement for the contractor to comply with the requirements of the CDM Regulations and, if appropriate, act as Principal Contractor.

❖ **Warranties**: Depending on the level of works to be carried out under the letter of intent, third parties with an interest in the development may require a collateral warranty from the contractor and its design subcontractors. If so, the letter must provide for this in its terms.

❖ **Copyright**: If the contractor is carrying out any design services under the letter of intent, then it should provide for a licence to be given to the developer allowing it to use any design documents produced by the contractor in connection with the development. This is important, for example, in circumstances where the contractor's involvement in the development is terminated but the developer needs to use the design documents to appoint another contractor.

❖ **Termination**: The letter of intent must provide for the developer to terminate the contractor's engagement under the letter should it so wish. The letter should also make it clear that the developer is under no obligation to enter into a full contract with the contractor once the letter of intent has come to an end.

Summary

❖ Letters of intent should be treated with caution. As Lord Clarke said in *RTS Flexible Systems*, 'The moral of the story is agree first and start work later.'

❖ Parties should therefore give careful thought as to whether a letter of intent is appropriate, having regard to the circumstances suggested by Judge Coulson.

❖ A letter of intent depending on its terms and the conduct of the parties may or may not give rise to a binding contract.

❖ Therefore, if a letter of intent is deemed to be appropriate, it should be well drafted and precise, so that the parties are not left in a position of uncertainty prior to the execution of the full contract.

❖ If the letter is not drafted carefully, covering the main areas of risk, the parties may be unnecessarily exposed, both during the course of the works and when the letter comes to an end.

Contributed by Becky Johnson, 020 7395 3114, bjohnson@wedlakebell.com of Wedlake Bell, 52 Bedford Row, London WC1R 4LR, www.wedlakebell.com

Standard form contracts

Standard form contracts have always been a feature of the construction industry. There are many providers and types of building contract competing for use in the construction industry – all generally with a slightly different style and approach to clause drafting.

It is the lack of standardisation that is noticeable in the choice of contracts on offer.

Their use and popularity will often be determined by client familiarity/preference, industry trends (partnering, terrorist events, etc.), the intensity of their marketing and the ability of contract providers to support these trends.

The New Engineering Contract (NEC) form of contract, for example, was strongly endorsed by the Office of Government Commerce for use in public sector contracts in the early 2000s on the back of a trend in 'project partnering' and gained increasing popularity after use on some high profile jobs such as Heathrow Terminal 5.

The origins of many of the contracts go back to the bodies from which they were issued and intended to support. For example, the Royal Institution of British Architects and the National Federation of Building Trades Employers produced the standardised series of Joint Contracts Tribunal (JCT) contracts in 1931.

Changes to the *Housing Grants, Construction and Regeneration Act* 1996 ('the Construction Act') came into force in England and Wales on 1 October 2011 and in Scotland on 1 November 2011. In particular, the Construction Act included changes which related to the way in which payment and dispute resolution provisions are dealt with and operated.

Any contracts entered into after the Act came into force that have not been updated will be non-compliant. Procurers of construction contracts have two options for complying with the Act:

1   use an up-to-date contract such as listed in the table below; or

2   rely on the provisions of the Scheme for Construction Contracts, embodied under regulations made under the Act (SI No. 648 and 649 for the English and Welsh Scheme, SI No. 686 and 687 for the Scottish Scheme).

Option 1 should take precedence, but as these revised contract provisions have only been introduced recently, some further amendments may be required to the standard text to make them fully compliant with the Act. It is also important to note that there are a number of contracts used in the construction industry for both commercial and residential developments and therefore careful selection is required. The following table lists the more commonly used contracts for the three main procurement options, namely; traditional, design and build, and management.

Standard form contracts	Traditional	Design and build	Management
Large scale			
JCT Major Project Construction Contract 2011 (MP)	✔		
JCT Standard Building Contract Without Quantities 2011 (SBC/XQ)	✔		
NEC Engineering and Construction Contract	✔		
GC/Works/1 With Quantities (1998)	✔		
Simple content			
JCT Intermediate Building Contract 2011 (IC)	✔		
JCT Intermediate Building Contract with contractor's design 2011 (ICD)	✔		
JCT Minor Works Building Contract 2011 (MW)	✔		
JCT Minor Works Building Contract with contractor's design 2011 (MWD)		✔	
NEC3 Engineering and Construction Short Contract	✔		
ACA Form of Building Agreement 1982, 3rd edition 1998 (2003 revision)	✔		
CECA/ACE Infrastructure Conditions of Contract: Minor Works Version	✔		
GC/Works/2 (1998)	✔		
GC/Works/4 (1998)	✔		
Measurement			
JCT Measured Term Contract 2011 (MTC)	✔		
CECA/ACE Infrastructure Conditions of Contract: Measurement Version	✔		
Design and build			
JCT Design and Build Contract 2011 (DB)		✔	
CECA/ACE Infrastructure Conditions of Contract: Design and Construct Version		✔	
GC/Works/1 Single Stage Design and Build (1998)		✔	
GC/Works/1 Two Stage Design and Build (1999)		✔	
Management forms			
JCT Management Building Contract 2011 (MC)			✔
JCT Construction Management Trade Contract 2011 (CM/TC)			✔

Note: The Institution of Civil Engineers (ICE) officially withdrew from the ICE Conditions of Contract on 1 August 2011. ICE's part ownership of the contract was transferred to the Association for Consultancy and Engineering (ACE) and the Civil Engineering Contractors Association (CECA). The ICE Conditions of Contract have been rebranded as the Infrastructure Conditions of Contract (ICC). The suite will be managed entirely by ACE and CECA, and will incorporate relevant amendments to make them Construction Act compliant.

Further information

For further information on a range of construction contracts and supplementary guides please visit the following websites:

- ❖ www.jctcontracts.com/JCT/contracts/index.jsp
- ❖ www.ppc2000.co.uk
- ❖ www.cic.org.uk/services/publications.shtml

Contributed by Dave Dorrington, dave.dorrington@watts.co.uk

Collateral warranties and reliance letters

Collateral warranties

The doctrine of 'privity of contract' has for many years prevented someone who is not a party to a contract from enforcing that contract. As a consequence, third party reliance documents have been a feature of the property and construction industry for over 20 years and there is little sign of them dying out. Such documents commonly take the form of collateral warranties. These documents are also sometimes called 'duty of care deeds'.

What do they do?

Collateral warranties create a contract between two parties. The main purpose of the contract is to allow the recipient (**beneficiary**) of the collateral warranty to rely on the proper and competent performance of services by the giver (**warrantor**) of the collateral warranty when the services concerned have actually been provided originally to another party and not to the recipient.

Should the beneficiary discover that the services have not been provided properly and competently by the warrantor, the beneficiary has a contractual route of redress through the collateral warranty.

Who gives collateral warranties?

There is no general restriction in the UK property and construction industry on who can give collateral warranties. Literally any person providing professional services or supplying goods can give collateral warranties, but they are used more particularly by those responsible for design services, or responsible for construction activities, such as:

- ❖ project managers;
- ❖ architects (building, landscape);
- ❖ engineers (mechanical, electrical, structural, acoustic, geotechnical);
- ❖ cost consultants or quantity surveyors;
- ❖ main contractors; and
- ❖ specialist contractors with design obligations (lifts, cladding, steelwork, roofing).

The following diagram identifies, in simple form, how collateral warranties might come about.

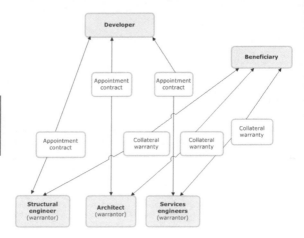

Who receives collateral warranties?

In the property and construction industry there are four basic parties who seek collateral warranties, namely:

❖ purchasers of freehold property (whether for investment or occupation);

❖ tenants of leasehold property (whether for investment or occupation);

❖ funders advancing loans for property acquisition and development; and

❖ employers under building contracts.

Are all warranties the same?

There is no single form of warranty wording adopted by the industry as a whole. Solicitors will have their own precedents, as might property owners and developers. Certain industry bodies have developed their own precedents for use, for example:

❖ British Property Federation;

❖ Joint Contracts Tribunal; and

❖ Construction Industry Council.

What are their common features?

Apart from identifying the beneficiary and the warrantor, warranties will normally contain clauses dealing with the warrantor's **primary obligation** to the beneficiary and **limits to the warrantor's liability**.

Primary obligation: This will normally be expressed in terms of use of reasonable skill and care, and the warrantor will acknowledge that it owes the beneficiary the same obligations as are owed to the warrantor's client/employer in return for consideration on the part of the beneficiary. The payment is nearly always a nominal sum (such as £1 or £10), but there is no reason why the sum should not be more substantial.

Limits on liability: Potential liabilities arising under the collateral warranty may be limited in terms of:

- ❖ type of loss for which the warrantor is to be liable;
- ❖ net contribution when other parties also giving warranties are considered equally or jointly liable for the loss;
- ❖ equivalent rights to defence allowing the warrantor to raise in defence rights equivalent to those available in respect of claims from the client or employer;
- ❖ prohibited (deleterious) materials;
- ❖ professional indemnity insurance required;
- ❖ copyright and use of documents by the beneficiary;
- ❖ assignment rights and restrictions;
- ❖ limitation periods for the bringing of an action; or
- ❖ exclusion of *Contracts (Rights of Third Parties) Act* 1999.

Collateral warranties given to purchasers and tenants are normally almost identical.

Collateral warranties given to funders contain many of the same provisions as purchaser or tenant warranties but they might also include 'step-in rights'. These are rights permitting a funder to replace the warrantor's client or employer, in order to ensure that a scheme or transaction being funded is completed in the event that the client or employer becomes insolvent or otherwise fails to properly discharge their obligations to the warrantor.

Collateral warranties will normally be completed as deeds rather than as simple contracts. This means that the limitation period (the period within which legal proceedings for breach of the terms of the warranty must be commenced) is 12 years. A warranty completed as a simple contract would impose a limitation period of 6 years only on the beneficiary (*Limitation Act* 1980).

What do collateral warranties cost?

It is common for warranties to be provided at little or no cost. However, there is no reason why a more substantial fee should not be charged for a warranty by the warrantor, if the circumstances merit the levying of such a charge. The beneficiary will normally be expected to pay the fee for the warranty. There is no industry-recognised scale for fees associated with the provision of a warranty. Reasonableness, the perceived commercial value of the warranty, and the bargaining positions of the parties are the drivers in respect of the fee sought and paid.

What about the Contracts (Rights of Third Parties) Act 1999?

In the late 1990s, in a move to offer an alternative to collateral warranties, parliament enacted the *Contracts (Rights of Third Parties) Act* 1999. This Act came into full force and effect on 11 May 2000. It allows one party entering into an agreement with another party to contract on behalf of a third party, which might be a specific person or a class of person. The Act has not abolished the doctrine of privity of contract – it still exists – but the 1999 Act provides parties with a means to modify the doctrine, for the purposes of individual contracts, if they so decide.

With the arrival of the *Contracts (Rights of Third Parties) Act* 1999, collateral warranties were expected to decline in importance and wither away. Collateral warranties were (and perhaps still are) viewed as difficult and costly to procure. The provisions of the 1999 Act have not fallen into common usage however, and remain largely untested in law. Collateral warranties still have the upper hand when it comes to extending the benefit of contractual obligations and rights to third parties. The operation of the *Contracts (Rights of Third Parties) Act* 1999 is usually expressly excluded from agreements, including collateral warranties.

Reliance letters

These are generally simpler documents than collateral warranties and, as the name suggests, they take the form of letters rather than more formal deeds or agreements. They are a recent appearance on the property and construction scene and tend to be encountered more frequently in relation to professional advisers' reports on properties as opposed to construction works.

Reliance letters tend to arise more commonly in relation to property transactions, as opposed to development work.

What do they do?

Reliance letters enable a third party to rely, for some purposes, on professional advice and opinion expressed in a report produced (normally) by a consultant for another party at an earlier point in time. This is particularly beneficial, for example, if the third party is seeking to purchase a property and wishes to rely on a report (or reports) produced in the recent past for the vendor.

Reliance letters can, but do not normally, result in the formation of a contractual relationship between the relying party and the party issuing the letter. The relying parties' redress is in the law of tort, specifically negligent misrepresentation following the House of Lords decision of *Hedley Byrne & Co Ltd v Heller and Partners Ltd* 1964.

Hedley were advertising agents who had provided substantial amounts of advertising on credit for Easipower. If Easipower did not pay for the advertising then Hedley would be responsible for such amounts. Hedley became concerned that Easipower would not be in a financial position to pay the debt and sought assurances from Easipower's bank (Heller and Partners Ltd) that Easipower could pay for the additional advertising which Hedley was proposing to give them on credit.

Heller gave a favourable report of Easipower's financial position, but stipulated that the report was given 'without responsibility'. On the strength of the report given by Heller, Hedley placed additional orders for Easipower. Easipower went into liquidation. Hedley lost £17,000 and commenced an action against Heller for damages under the tort of negligence.

The House of Lords held that a negligent, although honest, misrepresentation, may give rise to an action for damages for financial loss, even if there was **no contract** between the adviser and the advisee, and no fiduciary relationship. The law would imply a duty of care when the advisee seeks information from an adviser who has special skill and where the advisee trusts the adviser to exercise due care, and that the adviser knew or ought to have known that reliance was being placed upon his or her skill and judgment.

Fortunately for Heller, in this case, they expressly disclaimed responsibility and there was therefore no liability, as this effectively barred the claim. However, the decision established the doctrine of negligent misrepresentation.

Who gives reliance letters?

There is no general restriction in the UK property and construction industry on who can issue reliance letters. Literally, any professional person providing advice in the form of a report can allow a third party to rely on the report that he or she produces. There is no obligation in law on a professional to extend their liability in this manner: it is a commercial decision for the professional concerned and might well attract a fee.

Who seeks reliance letters?

Reliance letters are most commonly given to:

- ❖ purchasers of freehold property (whether for investment or occupation); or
- ❖ funders such as the banks.

There is no reason why a prospective tenant of property (whether for investment or occupation) could not seek a reliance letter, but this is less common.

It is for the party seeking reliance to determine whether they properly understand the context of the report and the circumstances surrounding its preparation. This might necessitate confirmation of the terms of reference and brief given to the professional originally, in order to be sure that the advice and opinions in the report itself are not taken out of context. The professional will not warrant that the report concerned is fit for the purposes of the relying party.

Are all reliance letters the same?

No – reliance letters vary widely in content. There is no single form of wording for such letters adopted by the industry as a whole. Solicitors will have their own precedents, as might professionals who issue reliance letters regularly.

What are the common features of a reliance letter?

Reliance letters are generally shorter than collateral warranties. For a reliance letter to be effectual, it is not necessary for it to record or evince the payment of a sum of money by the relying party to the professional. Reliance letters are addressed to the party seeking reliance. The letter should:

❖ state the reason why reliance is being sought – this will often, but not always, be linked to the purchase of a property, or funding of such a purchase;

❖ identify the document(s) on which reliance is being placed and expressly acknowledge that the relying party is entitled to and will rely on the documents;

❖ identify the specific instructions and brief pursuant to which the documents were originally produced; and

❖ set out any restrictions placed on the reliance including:
  – the financial limit of any liability that the professional is willing to assume;
  – a limit on the period of time over which the professional is willing to extend their liability (typically 6 or 12 years but sometimes less or more depending on the circumstances);
  – whether or not the benefit of the reliance can be assigned to any third party; and
  – confirmation that the advice in the document(s) concerned has not been updated.

What do reliance letters cost?

There are no recognised scales or rates in the property or construction industry relating to the provision of reliance letters.

It is more common to charge for reliance letters than for collateral warranties, as why should a professional extend their liability to others for nothing? A fee for each report relied upon is a reasonable starting point, as each report could potentially give rise to liability. The number of different parties to whom the letter is addressed is also a relevant consideration.

Reasonableness, the perceived commercial value of the letter, and the bargaining positions of the parties are factors to consider in the final agreement of a fee.

Conclusion

Depending on the precise manner of drafting, it can be possible for a reliance letter to comprise a collateral warranty. For this to be the case the letter needs to contain evidence of a payment by the relying party to the vendor and it needs to be signed and delivered as a deed rather than simply signed like a letter.

Further information

❖ www.cic.org.uk/services/publicationsCIC.shtml#Collateralwarranties

Contributed by Paul Lovelock, paul.lovelock@watts.co.uk

Contract management

Development and procurement

The contract administrator's role

It is a feature of most construction contracts that a person is appointed by the employer to administer the terms of the contract on the employer's behalf.

Although contracted by the employer, the contract administrator owes a duty of care to the contractor. Under the terms of the contract he or she must undertake a number of administrative functions including:

- ❖ managing the client/contractor;
- ❖ coordinating the pre-project, project and post-project phases;
- ❖ implementing client variations;
- ❖ agreeing interim payments; and
- ❖ issuing certificates, including payment certificates and practical completion.

The contract administrator has an important role in giving advice and information, and in monitoring the work. However, he or she must also remain unbiased in matters such as certification of payments and ensuring that the contract terms are adhered to.

The mandatory nature of these duties is reflected in the contract between the contract administrator and the employer and in contract between the employer and the contractor. As such, there is often considerable scope for disagreement between the contracting parties, both in contract and tort, on whether these duties have been satisfactorily performed.

It is with this background that those fulfilling the contract administrator's role should be clear on what is required of them.

As a contract administrator the following pre- and post-contract services should be considered important.

Pre-contract

- ❖ Agree detailed brief with client. Agree procedures for modifying the brief as commission proceeds, and for recording variations.
- ❖ Set budget and project time constraints and establish reporting procedures.
- ❖ Establish clear routes of responsibility for design, drawings and specification, and ensure client approval as scheme develops.
- ❖ Prepare tender documents and approve tendering processes with client, including the selection process.

Post-contract

- ❖ Administer the terms of the building contract during operations on site.
- ❖ Inspect the progress and quality of the work on a regular basis.
- ❖ Prepare interim financial reports to client, including the effects of any variations.
- ❖ Agree interim valuations with the contractor and issue interim certificates in accordance with the contract, allowing for the submission of interim applications for payment.
- ❖ Convene and chair site progress meetings on a regular basis to principally discuss progress, cost and quality issues. Record all principal matters in minutes distributed to all project team members.
- ❖ Prepare regular progress reports for client, including details of any applications for extensions of time or disputes.

❖ Agree practical completion of the works under the contract terms. This may include the preparation of 'snagging' lists detailing the non-completion of minor work items remaining outstanding at practical completion. However, the contract administrator may well need to unambiguously define practical completion for any given project in the pre-contract stage.

❖ Administer the contract conditions during the defects liability or rectification period ensuring that all items of disrepair are rectified before the issue of the making good defects certificate and release of retention monies.

For a precise understanding of the role of a contract administrator under various forms of contract, reference should be made to the various *Guides to Contract Administration* published by the Royal Institute of British Architects (RIBA).

Contributed by Steve Brewer, steve.brewer@watts.co.uk

Practical completion

Meaning of 'practical completion' in building contracts

Practical completion is clearly a significant, if not critical, part of a building contract and it is therefore surprising that an agreed definition of practical completion seems elusive. Indeed, *Keating on Construction, Construction Contracts* (8th edition, 2006) notes on page 774 that it 'is perhaps easier to recognise than to define'.

The issue of a Certificate of Practical Completion means that retention monies become due for release and liability for damage passes to the employer, insurances need to be in place, and the contractor's liability to pay liquidated and ascertained damages ceases.

Clearly then, arguments may frequently arise over whether practical completion has been achieved or not, but fortunately there is some help from the courts.

In *Skanska Corporation v Anglo-Amsterdam Corporation* (2002), a dispute arose between the parties as to the date by which the contractor had achieved practical completion.

The matter was referred to arbitration, which decided in favour of the employer and the contractor then successfully appealed. His Honour Judge Thornton QC interpreted the clause which deals with partial possession to mean that if the employer takes over a part of the building then, as far as that part of the works is concerned, the contractor is deemed to have achieved practical completion.

He explained his interpretation that responsibility for the part taken over rests squarely with the employer for such matters as damage and health and safety and that this would be the case even if the contract definition of practical completion had not been achieved.

Judge Thornton extended the principle to say that, while the contract did not deal with the situation where the employer takes possession of the whole of the works before practical completion, the same principle should be applied as if the employer had taken possession of part of the works. In other words practical completion is deemed to have taken place.

Other courts have decided that the term practical completion means completion for practical purposes and have defined this as being a situation where the employer can take possession of the works and use them as intended.

It has been stated that if practical completion meant doing everything down to the last detail then contract clauses containing provision for liquidated and ascertained damages would be penalty clauses and would be unenforceable.

Judge Newy, in *Emson Eastern v EME Developments* (1991), reinforced this in his summing up, saying; 'because a building can seldom, if ever, be built as precisely as required by drawings and specification, the contract realistically refers to "practical completion" and not "completion", but they mean the same. If contrary to my view, completion is something which occurs only after all defects, shrinkages and other faults have been remedied and a certificate to that effect has been given, it would make the liquidated damages provision unworkable.'

It seems from recent case law that the legal interpretation of practical completion in building contracts is taken to mean where the building has reached a state in which it is completed free from any patent defects, other than those which could be ignored as trivial.

This, of course, opens up a whole new argument about what is a patent defect and what is trivial, but it seems clear that the courts will decide that if a building can be used for its intended purpose, then practical completion has been achieved.

It also seems clear that if the employer takes possession of the works it will be deemed to have accepted practical completion, even if there are outstanding major works.

Need for an amendment

It would undoubtedly make the situation clearer if the Joint Contracts Tribunal (JCT) were to provide their definition of practical completion. However, this seems unlikely. Meanwhile, contract administrators who do not want the interpretation of the courts imposed upon them would be well advised to make sure that they include their own, unambiguous, definition of practical completion in the contract documentation.

Contributed by Steve Brewer, steve.brewer@watts.co.uk

Employer's agent

Employer's agent duties

Clients routinely wish to procure projects in the pursuit of certainty of cost. The JCT Design and Build contract, which is in frequent use, transfers most of the 'risk' in any development to the contractor, while allowing the contractor greater flexibility to deliver the product. As an employer's agent, it is essential that the following pre-contract and post-contract services are provided.

Pre-contract service

❖ Define the responsibilities of the employer, employer's agent and contractor.

❖ Appraise and quantify the risks.

❖ Formulate the employer's brief and identify specific requirements.

❖ Assess the contractor's proposals and ensure compliance with the employer's requirements.

❖ Undertake a design audit of the contractor's proposals for compliance with the employer's requirements.

❖ Evaluate the offer, the contract sum analysis and stage payments, and assess value for money.

Post-contract service

❖ Generally comply with the duties of the employer's agent under the building contract.

❖ Set up quality control procedure and report on works carried out on site. This may require the appointment of monitor design consultants on larger contracts.

❖ Provide site visits and chair meetings.

❖ Implement changes to the employer's requirements only on written approval of the client.

❖ Agree stage payments and recommendations for payments.

❖ Prepare monthly project control statements and cash flow forecasts to client.

❖ Advise on practical completion, preparation of snagging schedules and component literature.

❖ Make sure operation and maintenance manuals and/or purchaser packs are prepared and approved by appropriate consultation.

General exclusions

❖ Checking and verifying contractor's design in terms of adequacy and efficiency.

❖ Checking and verifying contractor's design in terms of fitness for purpose.

In undertaking duties as the employer's agent, it is important to recognise the contractor's freedom to design, while respecting the client's brief and auditing the quality of the end product. Make sure the employer's requirements are sufficiently tightly drawn up as to ensure the contractor delivers the project to meet the client's expectations.

Contributed by Tim French, tim.french@watts.co.uk

The quantity surveyor's role

The quantity surveyor (QS) is tasked with controlling construction cost by accurate measurement of the works and the application of expert knowledge of costs of labour, materials and plant. An understanding of the implications of design decisions at an early stage ensures that good value is achieved and clients receive accurate advice. A skilled QS needs:

❖ an ability to predict future costs from limited information at an early stage in a project;

❖ an ability to manage the procurement process to ensure that predictions of cost, time and quality are delivered;

❖ an ability to accurately value works carried out under a building contract;

❖ an awareness of risk with a capability to assess and manage risk;

❖ an ability to demonstrate value for money assisted by effective value engineering;

❖ the ability to communicate effectively with the client, design team and contractor throughout the life of a project;

❖ an understanding of how the client's business impacts the project; and

❖ an awareness of financial incentives and opportunities available to the client (such as VAT relief and capital allowances – for details, see the relevant sections in *Cost management*, page 101).

Current trends in the industry continue for cost reductions, with pressure coming from major purchasers; the importance of value for money remains the prime objective for most projects. Fixed out-turn costs are a necessity.

This is against a backdrop of continued upward cost pressure on construction materials and commodities and a general reduction in workload in all sectors. This scenario exerts additional pressure on the robustness of procurement information produced by the quantity surveyor.

Contributed by Tim French, tim.french@watts.co.uk

Managing construction risks during a recession

Offshore investors

Expect contractors and consultants to be wary of contracts with overseas investors using offshore accounts, making it difficult to enforce the payment provisions of UK building contracts. The risk of payment default can be reduced if a special purpose account is setup in the UK, either under the control of UK trustees or on an ESCROW account basis, whereby transfer balances can be automatic upon compliance with agreed preconditions.

Contractor failure

Contractor failure was always one of the highest *impact* risks on a project but the *probability* is now much higher in the current climate so it should be promoted as a risk and elevated to the top of a project risk register.

It is not possible to protect projects completely from contractor failure – but there are ways to considerably reduce the risk.

Consider the potential for contractor insolvency at the start of a project as part of the risk management strategy and put in place mechanisms to protect the project and the client.

The following protective measures may help:

❖ Adopt a pre-qualification procedure before finalising a tender list of contractors. Prepare a pre-qualification questionnaire (PQQ) which includes questions designed to assess a contractor's financial stability.

❖ Credit check the main contractors with a credit reference agency, for example, Dun and Bradstreet. This is the minimum level; more detailed checks are available (at a cost) from specialists.

❖ Check who owns the contractor and similarly check relevant parent companies, avoid offshore parents.

❖ Look out for significant restructuring; a name change can be subtle (e.g. from 'Southeast' to 'SE' LTD) and may have taken place to avoid dispute risk.

❖ Take credit references from the main contractors' supply chain – speak to at least three main suppliers and subcontractors. Ask whether they have changed their credit terms in the last 12 months and whether these have been honoured. Obtain references in writing signed by their financial directors.

❖ Contractors' cash rich reputations come from full order books – ask them how full their order books are and any changes (a reduction in turnover will create a cash demand). Look for any dips in turnover of more than 10%.

❖ Obtain warranties with step-in rights from key suppliers/subcontractors.

❖ Take out a performance bond – even a bargain basement bond will give up to 10% of the contract sum in cover should the contractor fail. The ease with which a contractor can provide a bond is a good third party financial health check.

❖ Ensure that contract payments are made (and processed) on time, don't create the situation you want to avoid.

❖ Check to see when their accounts were last lodged at Companies House – they should not be late. If they are, ask why.

❖ Check whether there are any outstanding court actions or arbitration proceedings.

❖ Be alert to slowdowns on site due to shortage of labour and late delivery of key materials. On the programme, establish key materials delivery dates and require the contractor to report labour levels – make sure you spot changes.

❖ Finally, make sure you understand the answers to these questions. If you don't, either recommend that the client takes further advice or that the contractor is not appointed. Better still, include as many of the above checks at pre-qualification – not after you find they are lowest bidder.

What to do if your contractor goes bust

Developments fail, or struggle, for a number of reasons, including developer, prospective tenant or contractor insolvency. Other reasons include a lack of funding (perhaps due to breached banking covenants), aggressive market conditions, or poor performance of contractors. This section focuses on contractor insolvency. The insolvency of the contractor will involve the preparation of a recovery plan that is specific to the particular circumstances of the case. However, a number of key actions are highlighted.

Stage 1 – immediate action

❖ Secure the site – including materials and plant.

❖ Ensure the site is safe.

❖ Terminate the employment of the contractor under the building contract.

❖ Verify the status of any performance bonds, parent company guarantee, and warranties with designers and design subcontractors.

❖ Verify the condition and quality of the works – e.g. highlight any defective or incomplete works.

❖ Notify the client, project team and any third party interest (e.g. lender) of the contractor's insolvency.

The next stage will be to decide whether to finish the building. Generally, the decision to proceed will be made, although market conditions may result in a later delivery date being preferred. Usually the existing consultant team, and possibly design subcontractors, will be available to complete the works.

Note: It is likely that an administrator will be appointed and will have adopted a presence on site before you get there. In this instance, most forms of building contract will still allow the contract to be terminated and possession of the site immediately regained. Recommend that your client seeks the services of a solicitor who specialises in insolvency.

Stage 2 – follow up action

❖ Prepare a recovery plan.

❖ Agree a preferred procurement route for completion of the remaining works.

❖ Establish the scope of works and programme.

❖ Assess the cost to complete the project. The costs to complete the works may be higher than the remaining amount due to the original contractor.

❖ Highlight any outstanding construction risks with the project. This will be partly dependent on the amount and quality of work completed by the original contractor and the status of the statutory consents.

❖ Tender the works and appoint a new contractor to complete the development.

❖ Keep records of all costs associated with the completion of the works.

❖ Complete the works on site.

Contributed by Tim French, tim.french@watts.co.uk

Cost management

Development and procurement

VAT in the construction industry – zero-rating

VAT and construction works

VAT in relation to buildings and construction is a complex area but below are some of the fundamental issues to consider when building new or carrying out works on an existing property.

Building new property

All goods and services supplied for use in the construction of a building are standard-rated (20% from 4 January 2011) except in the following circumstances, when they are zero-rated.

Where the new building is a dwelling and it:

- ❖ is self-contained;
- ❖ is able to be sold as a single dwelling;
- ❖ has been granted planning consent; and
- ❖ is entitled to be used as a dwelling throughout the year.

Note: Certain elements within a dwelling will always be standard-rated (see note on DIY projects later in this section). This zero-rating only applies to goods and services supplied in the course of construction of a new building and to the first grant of a major interest, by the developer.

Relevant residential building fulfilling the following criteria:

- ❖ facilities shared by residents, e.g. children's homes, old people's homes, hospices, living quarters for school pupils or armed forces; and
- ❖ an institution which is the sole or main residence for 90% of its residents.

Note: Flats and sheltered housing schemes made up of individual flats will be zero-rated as dwellings rather than relevant residential buildings.

Note: Prisons, hospitals and hotels are specifically excluded from zero-rating. This applies to goods and services and the first grant of a major interest.

Relevant charitable building is:

- ❖ a building used solely by a charity for the **non-business** use of the charity or as a village hall.

Note: The supply must be made to the person who intends to use the building for such purposes before the supply is made, then the person receiving it must give to the person making the supply a certificate that the intended use is for relevant residential or charitable purposes.

Works to an existing property

All goods and services supplied will be standard-rated except in the following circumstances.

Relevant Housing Association (HA) converting a building from non-residential to residential use, to allow zero-rating the HA must:

- ❖ be a Registered Social Landlord within the meaning of Part 1 of the *Housing Act* 1996; and
- ❖ be a registered HA within the meaning of the *Housing Associations Act* 1985 (or Part II of the *Housing (Northern Ireland) Order* 1992).

Note: This applies to goods and services only.

Approved alterations to existing protected buildings – basic principles to allow zero-rating are as follows:

- ❖ the work must be to a qualifying protected building as defined in VAT law and to the fabric of that building (e.g. a listed building or scheduled monument);

- ❖ the work must require and be granted listed building consent;

- ❖ the works must not be of a repair or maintenance nature; and

- ❖ the works must be apportioned if there is an element of both repair and maintenance, and approved alteration.

Note: Unlisted buildings in conservation areas do not qualify as protected buildings for VAT relief purposes. This applies to goods and services only.

Substantial reconstruction to existing protected buildings – basic principles to allow zero-rating are as follows:

- ❖ definition of protected buildings as above;

- ❖ the work must require and be granted listed building consent;

- ❖ at least 60% of the cost is attributable to 'approved alterations'; or

- ❖ only the wall(s) remain along with the other features of architectural or historic interest.

Note: This applies to the first grant of a major interest to the person carrying out the substantial reconstruction.

Conversion of buildings from non-residential use to dwellings or relevant residential use:

- ❖ if you are the person converting a building the first grant of a major interest can be zero-rated provided the building was neither designed nor adapted as a dwelling (or relevant residential purpose), or if it was designed as a dwelling and/or subsequently adapted, it has not been used as a dwelling for the whole of the previous ten years.

Residential conversions

A reduced rate of 5% applies to the following supplies of building services and related goods:

- ❖ a 'changed number of dwellings conversion', i.e. a conversion of a building (or part of a building) so that after conversion it has a different number of single-household dwellings (SHD) from the number before the conversion;

- ❖ a 'house in multiple occupation conversion', i.e. a conversion of a building (or part of a building) containing one or more single-household dwellings so that it contains only one or more multiple-occupancy dwellings; and

- ❖ a 'special residential conversion', i.e. a conversion of premises containing dwellings (single-household or multiple occupancy) for use solely for a relevant residential purpose or converting a care home into a single-household dwelling.

Renovation and alteration of dwellings

The lower rate of 5% also applies to supplies of:

- ❖ building services; and

- ❖ related goods;

in the course of the alteration (including extension) or renovation of a single-household dwelling that has been empty for three years. 'Empty' means unlived in, so use for another purpose, such as storage, is acceptable. The dwelling can remain a single household.

Specific conditions apply to both of these lower rate situations.

The reduced rate of VAT

The reduced rate of 5% VAT also applies to:

- ❖ converting a non-residential property into a care home or multiple occupancy dwellings, e.g. bedsits;

- ❖ converting a building used for 'relevant residential' purpose into a multiple occupancy dwelling;

- ❖ renovating or altering a care home or other qualifying building that has not been lived in for two years or more (amended from three years on 1 January 2008); and

- ❖ constructing, renovating or converting a building into a garage as part of the renovation of property that qualifies for the reduced rate.

Charity annexes

Since 1 June 2002, minor non-qualifying use (e.g. use where the annexe or part of an annexe is not used solely for a relevant charitable purpose) can be ignored with there being no requirement to apportion these between relevant charitable purpose and alternative usage.

Supplies to elderly and handicapped people

Certain goods and services supplied to a handicapped person, or to a charity for making them available to handicapped people for their domestic or personal use, may be zero-rated.

The supply and installation of certain mobility aids for elderly people also attracts the reduced rate of VAT.

Supplying and installing energy-saving materials and grant-funded installations

The supply and installation of certain energy-saving materials and equipment may attract the reduced rate of VAT. The reduced rate only applies to specified energy-saving materials and it only applies when installed in certain types of building.

In addition VAT at the reduced rate of 5% could be charged on certain items of heating and security equipment if installed in the homes of people who are either aged 60 or over or are on benefits.

DIY projects

HM Revenue and Customs (HMRC) will refund any VAT chargeable on the supply, acquisition or importation of any goods used in connection with construction or conversion work where the following criteria are met:

- ❖ the work is not part of a business project;

- ❖ the work comprises the construction of a dwelling, relevant residential or charitable building; or

- ❖ the work is the conversion of a non-residential building into a dwelling.

All works which fulfil the criteria set out above can be zero-rated. However, there are some items within these categories which will always be standard-rated:

- ❖ site investigations;

- ❖ temporary site fencing;

- ❖ concrete testing;
- ❖ site security;
- ❖ catering;
- ❖ cleaning to site offices;
- ❖ temporary lighting;
- ❖ transport and haulage to and from site;
- ❖ plant hire (without operator);
- ❖ professional services (architects, engineers, surveyors, solicitors, etc.);
- ❖ landscaping;
- ❖ furniture (other than fitted kitchens) – material only;
- ❖ some electrical or gas appliances – material only; and
- ❖ carpet/carpeting materials (including underlay and carpet tiles) – material only.

See the following notices issued by HM Revenue and Customs for further expanded information and definitions:

- ❖ Notice 708 *VAT Buildings and construction*;
- ❖ Notice 742 *Land and property*;
- ❖ Notice 719 *VAT refunds for 'do it yourself' builders and converters*;
- ❖ Notice 701/1 *Charities*;
- ❖ Notice 701/7 *VAT reliefs for people with disabilities*;
- ❖ Notice 701/19 *Fuel and power*; and
- ❖ Notice 708/5 *Registered social landlords (housing associations, etc.)*.

The primary legislation relating to this subject includes:

- ❖ Group 5 of Schedule 8 to the *VAT Act* 1994 as amended by SI 1995/280 and SI 1997/50 – buildings under construction;
- ❖ Group 6 of Schedule 8 to the *VAT Act* 1994 as amended by SI 1995/283 – approved alterations to protected buildings;
- ❖ Group 12 of Schedule 8 of the *VAT Act* 1994 – supplies to the handicapped;
- ❖ Section 35 of the *VAT Act* 1994 – DIY scheme;
- ❖ The *VAT (Input Tax) Order* 1992 as amended by SI 1995/281; and
- ❖ Schedule 10 to the *VAT Act* 1994.

Registered social landlords, VAT and 'Golden Bricks'

If a registered social landlord (RSL) commissions new build housing works via a building contract then works will be zero-rated with the RSL being liable for the payment of VAT on professional fees (and any other standard-rated elements).

If an RSL purchases land the RSL will be exempt from paying VAT on the condition that a specific form of certificate is issued to the seller at the time the price is agreed stating that it is the RSL's intention to construct residential dwellings. On the issue of the certificate the seller may choose to increase the price he or she is asking for the land as the seller will be unable to reclaim any VAT. This tightening of the rules was introduced on 1 June 2008.

If the seller of the land commences the RSL's development then the sale is potentially zero-rated. However, there are certain conditions which need to be achieved in order for this process to be accepted by HMRC. The building must be seen to be under construction on the land. It is generally accepted by the industry that the foundations require completion and the superstructure is commenced to one metre above the damp-proof course level ('Golden Brick'). This in itself poses some problems, as it will require cooperation between the seller and the RSL regarding design and specification and brings further complications when dealing with phased schemes. These Golden Brick agreements will require careful drafting to protect all parties.

Contributed by Stuart Russell, stuart.russell@watts.co.uk

Capital allowances

The following provides a brief summary of the capital allowances that are available to UK property owners, occupiers and investors. It is intended as an overview at the time of print and the authors would direct readers who require more detailed or specific advice to contact a capital allowances expert.

The UK taxation system has no general provision for tax relief for capital expenditure or for the depreciation in value of capital assets with the passage of time. Although there are numerous accounting standards detailing how the depreciation of capital assets must be dealt with for accounts purposes, there is no allowable deduction for tax purposes. Accounting depreciation is therefore added back to the accounting profits when computing the tax charge.

Capital allowances provide tax relief for at least some of this accounting and tax mismatch. Qualifying capital expenditure incurred on certain buildings, fixtures and chattels will attract specific rates or amounts of tax relief, which are available for offset against taxable profits.

This valuable form of tax relief is, in most cases, either under-claimed or not claimed at all due to a lack of understanding or application of the legislation and case law governing the availability of the relief.

General scheme of allowances

There are certain hurdles that must be cleared before capital allowances can be claimed. The entity incurring the expenditure must be within the charge to UK tax, therefore local authorities, government departments, charities, pension funds, etc. will not be in a position to use the relief (although they may be able to pass the benefit on for consideration).

The expenditure must be capital in nature, i.e. there must be an enduring benefit to the trade of the entity incurring it, e.g. the initial acquisition of an asset, or the subsequent improvement of it. Expenditure on the maintenance or general upkeep of an asset or on the development of an asset held as trading stock is likely to be revenue in nature.

Revenue expenditure will not qualify for capital allowances, but could still potentially be tax deductible in its entirety in the year it is incurred if it is written off through the profit and loss account. It should be noted that the revenue deduction is dependent on the accounting treatment of the expenditure. Revenue expenditure that is capitalised for accounts purposes, e.g. to improve the balance sheet, will not qualify for the 100% deduction in the year it is incurred.

The capital expenditure must be incurred for the purpose of a qualifying activity, e.g. a trade, profession, vocation, etc. In some situations, the asset that is acquired or created must also be 'in use' for the purpose of the qualifying activity.

Finally, the capital asset that is acquired or created must be qualifying for capital allowances purposes, and in this regard many tests have evolved through statute and case law.

Types and rates of allowances

Plant and Machinery Allowances (P&MAs)

These are currently given at a rate of 20% per annum on a reducing balance basis, i.e. 20% of the balance of the qualifying expenditure carried forward year on year. This rate will reduce to 18% per annum from 1 April 2012.

There is generally little help from the tax legislation on what constitutes qualifying plant and machinery (P&M) and therefore there has been much litigation in this area. Specialist advice should be taken, but typical examples will include IT equipment, fire-fighting equipment, catering installations and toilet facilities.

From 1 April 2008 (6 April 2008 for individuals) a new special rate pool of allowances was introduced to include integral features, such as:

- ❖ electrical systems (including lighting systems);
- ❖ cold water systems;
- ❖ lifts, escalators and moving walkways;
- ❖ space or water heating systems, powered systems of ventilation, air cooling or air purification, and any floor or ceiling comprised in such systems; and
- ❖ external solar shading.

Also within this special rate pool of allowances is the provision of thermal insulation to existing buildings, except dwellings. Expenditure incurred on P&M that is included within this special rate pool will attract relief at 10% per annum on a reducing balance basis, rather than the 20% for general P&M. From 1 April 2012, this rate will reduce to 8% per annum.

Qualifying P&M that has a useful economic life, when new, of exceeding 25 years is deemed to be a Long Life Asset (LLA) by the capital allowances legislation. The test applies from when the P&M is first used, therefore a second-hand asset with a useful economic life of less than 25 years at the date of purchase may still be a LLA in the new owner's business. LLAs attract allowances at a rate of 10% per annum on a reducing balance basis. Excluded from this is expenditure incurred on a dwelling house, hotel, office, retail shop and showroom.

All business entities are able to claim an Annual Investment Allowance (AIA) of £100,000 from 1 April 2010 (6 April 2010 for individuals). Up to the first £100,000 of annual qualifying capital expenditure incurred may therefore attract relief at 100% in the year that it is incurred. Any balance of qualifying expenditure will be relieved on the 20% or 10% reducing balance basis, depending on the nature of the expenditure. This AIA will reduce to £25,000 from April 2012.

Specific legislation exists to give a 100% first year allowance for expenditure incurred on new P&M that satisfies defined energy saving or environmentally friendly criteria.

Hotel Building Allowances (HBAs), Industrial Buildings Allowances (IBAs) and Agricultural Buildings Allowances (ABAs)

These categories of buildings have been grouped together as they all attract allowances at the rate of 4% per annum on a straight-line basis, i.e. the qualifying expenditure is written off over a period of 25 years from when the building is first used.

The properties must satisfy certain criteria specified in the capital allowances legislation in order to be 'qualifying':

- ❖ For HBAs, the property must be open for four months or more between April and October, have a minimum of ten letting bedrooms and provide guest services of at least breakfast, dinner and room cleaning.

❖ For IBAs and ABAs the test relates to the use to which the building is put, therefore there has to be qualifying industrial or agricultural use for the relief to be forthcoming.

This form of tax relief has been phased out from 1 April 2011.

Research and Development Allowances (R&DAs)

Expenditure incurred on facilities used for qualifying R&D attracts allowances at 100% in the first year. Again, the accounting treatment of the expenditure is key and this is supplemented by published guidelines providing more clarity. The underlying test is innovation.

Business Premises Renovation Allowances (BPRAs)

A new form of capital allowance was introduced from 11 April 2007 giving 100% tax relief for expenditure incurred on qualifying conversion, renovation or repairs to a building that is in a disadvantaged area (located using the postcode finder www.bis.gov.uk/analysis/statistics/sub-national-statistics/assisted-area-look-up) and which has remained unused for a period of at least a year up to the date that the work commenced.

The building must have previously been a business premises in use for a trade, for a profession or vocation, or as offices. It must not have last been used as a dwelling. The completed building must be used or available for use in a trade, profession or vocation, or as an office. The premises must not be available for use as a dwelling.

Expenditure is not qualifying if it is incurred on the acquisition of rights over land, the extension of the qualifying building, the development of land adjoining the qualifying building, or on the provision of plant and machinery (except where this is an integral fixture).

Where there is both qualifying and non-qualifying expenditure incurred, the relief must be apportioned on a just and reasonable basis. For example, if the premises are being extended, the extension work will not qualify for BPRA. There are also various anti-avoidance provisions to prevent any abuse of this form of tax relief.

Capital allowances issues for property transactions

Except where it has already been identified that qualifying expenditure must be on 'new' P&M, capital allowances are available on the purchase of second-hand assets. There are many tests and restrictions that apply to a property transaction to ensure that a subsequent owner is restricted in its claim to the original cost of the asset. Where no previous capital allowances claim has been made, there may be an opportunity to 'step up' the new owner's claim to reflect the price that it has paid for the asset, where this is greater than the original cost.

The vendor and the purchaser must apportion the purchase price, on a just and reasonable basis, between the components of the sale, i.e. the interest in the land, the building and the qualifying P&M. These figures are then compared to the original cost to establish what restriction may apply to the subsequent claim and conversely what disposal proceeds the vendor must account for on sale. In some situations, it is possible for the parties to the transaction to agree and formally elect for a specified value to be attributable to fixtures qualifying for P&MAs. The effect of the election is that all, part or none of the allowances can be passed between the transacting parties. Tax aware parties may be able to negotiate an adjustment to the purchase price to reflect the agreed capital allowances position.

It is important to establish the capital allowances history of a property during the pre-acquisition due diligence. The information that will be relevant to the claim is generally more readily made available at this time than post transaction and the opportunity to obtain any additional benefit through joint elections may not arise once the deal is concluded.

Following the introduction of the integral features capital allowances, there are significant opportunities to increase the value of a capital allowances claim on second-hand acquisitions even if a historic claim has been made.

The following table provides a guide to the expected levels of qualifying P&M (general P&M and Special Rate Pool P&M) that may be available on an unrestricted basis for differing property and transaction types.

Property type	Acquisition/disposal Qualifying %	New build Qualifying %
Office	15%–30%	15%–45%
Office refurb/fit-out	–	40%–100%
Retail	2%–25%	5%–40%
Retail refurb/fit-out	–	40%–90%
Industrial	2%–20%	5%–25%
Hotel	15%–45%	15%–50%
Hotel refurb/fit-out	–	40%–80%

Summary

The above is intended as an overview of the current availability of capital allowances. Specialist advice should be sought to maximise the availability and quantum of capital allowances.

Further information

- *Capital Allowances Act* 2001
- *Income and Corporation Taxes Act* 1988
- *Finance Act* 2004
- www.eca.gov.uk
- www.hmrc.gov.uk

Contributed by Chris Doyle, 020 8544 4810, chris.doyle@yewell.co.uk of Yewell Consulting LLP, 1 Hall Road, Wallington, Surrey SM6 0RT, www.yewell.co.uk

Land remediation tax relief

Various tax incentives have been introduced following the recommendations of the Urban Task Force set up by the government in 1998 to investigate causes of urban decline. Land remediation tax relief is one such generous incentive that provides up to 150% of tax relief for expenditure incurred in remediating contaminated land or, where a company is loss making, a tax credit (payment from the Exchequer) of 24% of the qualifying cost.

Availability of the tax relief

The qualifying expenditure must be incurred after 11 May 2001 on qualifying remediation works to land situated in the UK that was acquired for the purpose of a trade in a contaminated state. Land includes interests over land and buildings on the land.

The relief is available for companies but not for individuals or partnerships. A company in limited partnership can claim the relief in respect of its share in the partnership's expenditure on remediation. The relief is not available where the land is contaminated due to the actions of the acquiring company or someone connected with that company, or where the company has failed to prevent contamination.

Development and procurement

Land is in a contaminated state if there are substances in, on or under the land that are likely to cause harm to people, property or ecological systems or are likely to pollute controlled waters. Nuclear sites are specifically excluded from the definition of contaminated land.

From 1 April 2009 this tax relief is also extended to include the remediation of land that has been derelict since 1 April 1998, the removal of certain concrete foundations and post-tensioned concrete structures, and the removal of Japanese Knotweed.

This form of tax relief is likely to be withdrawn from 1 April 2012.

Qualifying expenditure

Expenditure must be incurred on the prevention, remediation or mitigation of the effects of the pollutant or on the restoration of the land to its former state. The expenditure must be directly linked to the remediation and as such, general site clearance will not qualify. Where in-house employees undertake the work, all of these costs are qualifying provided at least 80% of the time is spent on remediation tasks. Where employee time is less than 80%, some pro-rata adjustment will be necessary.

Preparatory works, such as site investigations and incidental professional fees, can be included in the claim for the relief. Where remediation work is subcontracted, then this cost will form the basis of the claim.

Claiming the relief

This relief is available to property owners, investors and developers. Any claim for the relief must be made within two years of the end of the accounting period in which the qualifying expenditure was incurred.

Summary

The above is intended as an overview of the principles and the current availability of land remediation tax relief. Specialist advice should be sought on the availability and to maximise the quantum of the tax relief.

Further information

- ❖ *Income and Corporation Taxes Act* 1988
- ❖ *Finance Act* 2001
- ❖ www.hmrc.gov.uk

Contributed by Chris Doyle, 020 8544 4810, chris.doyle@yewell.co.uk of Yewell Consulting LLP, 1 Hall Road, Wallington, Surrey SM6 0RT, www.yewell.co.uk

Tender prices and building cost indices

The Building Cost Information Service (BCIS) tender price indices (TPI) and general building cost indices (BCI) monitor the movement of tender prices and building costs. Both these indices include projections of usually at least two years. The Tender Price Index measures the trend of contractors' pricing levels in accepted tenders for new work (cost to client), whereas the General Building Cost Index measures changes in costs of labour, materials and plant (cost to contractor).

Over the last year the 'All-in TPI' has shown an increase of 2.3% from the third quarter of 2010 to the third quarter of 2011. The General Building Cost Index has also shown an increase of 3.5% in the same period. Over the year ahead to the end of the third quarter 2012, the 'All-in TPI' is forecast to increase by 3.1% and the BCI is forecast to increase by 2.8%.

It should be noted that, at the time of going to print, commentators are expecting tender prices to fall.

The following chart is based on the BCIS updated information as at December 2011 but should be adjusted to take into account price movement during the ensuing year.

Contributed by Tim French, tim.french@watts.co.uk

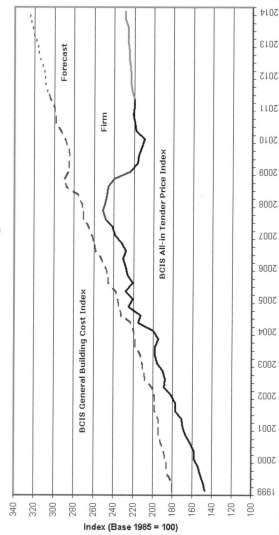

Tender prices and building cost indices

Indicative UK construction costs 2011

The scope of buildings covered in this section is limited but includes the majority of building types. The table is a quick guide to construction costs in the UK as a precursor to a detailed cost analysis.

Economic comment

Austerity measures introduced over the last year have impaired growth, but low interest rates still assist the economic recovery.

The construction sector is experiencing inflationary pressure on input costs, which is a reflection of a number of world events, such as the Euro-zone debt crisis (sovereign debt), Middle East uprisings (oil prices), the Japanese tsunami and emerging market demand (China and India consumption). Also events such as the flooding in Australia saw monthly increases in steel prices as mining halted.

The market is therefore challenged by how increased prices can be passed on in a low margin and low growth environment.

Location and site factors

Clearly, no two sites are the same. Factors such as geographic location, availability of utilities supplies, existing development, access, topography and planning all contribute towards the cost necessary to complete developments. Our indicative costs for new build only are factored to reflect the cost spread throughout the UK. A broad range of generic building types are covered, however, construction professionals and users of the guide are recommended to obtain detailed advice from Watts Group when assessing specific sites or developments.

Professional and statutory fees, and VAT

Professional fees (which are subject to negotiation and in some cases open tender), local authority fees, contributions and charges, and VAT (which are subject to legislation) have not been included in the guide costs. Indicative allowances for these and other additional costs have been outlined in the notes.

No guarantee is given by Watts Group, or any of its employees, as to this cost table's accuracy. More detailed advice must be obtained before relying on costs indicated.

Contributed by Neil Stevens, neil.stevens@watts.co.uk

Building type	Location factor	Benchmark 100		Greater London 111		North 93		Yorks & Hum 99		East Midlands 96		East Anglia 105		South East 107		South West 103		West Midlands 104		North West 94		Wales 92		Scotland 99		Northern Ireland 75	
		£/m²	£/sq ft	£/m²	£/sq ft	£/m²	£/sq ft	£/m²	£/sq ft	£/m²	£/sq ft	£/m²	£/sq ft	£/m²	£/sq ft	£/m²	£/sq ft	£/m²	£/sq ft	£/m²	£/sq ft	£/m²	£/sq ft	£/m²	£/sq ft	£/m²	£/sq ft
Houses* Local authority **		660–925	61–86	733–1027	68–95	614–860	57–80	653–916	61–85	634–916	59–85	693–971	64–90	706–990	66–92	680–953	63–89	686–962	64–89	620–870	58–81	607–851	56–79	653–916	61–85	495–694	46–64
Private estate, 2/3 bed **		720–950	67–88	799–1055	74–98	670–884	62–82	713–941	66–87	691–941	64–87	756–998	70–93	770–1017	72–94	742–979	69–91	749–988	70–92	677–893	63–83	662–874	62–81	713–941	66–87	540–713	50–66
Private detached, 4/5 bed **		730–980	68–91	810–1088	75–101	679–911	63–85	723–970	67–90	701–970	65–90	767–1029	71–96	781–1049	73–97	752–1009	70–94	759–1019	71–95	686–921	64–86	672–902	62–84	723–970	67–90	548–735	51–68
Luxury detached developments **		950–1580	88–147	1055–1754	98–163	884–1469	82–137	941–1564	87–145	912–1564	85–145	998–1659	93–154	1017–1691	94–157	979–1627	91–151	988–1643	92–153	893–1485	83–138	874–1454	81–135	941–1564	87–145	713–1185	66–110
Apartments Social and affordable ***		740–1260	69–117	821–1399	76–130	688–1172	64–109	733–1247	68–116	710–1247	66–116	777–1323	72–123	792–1348	74–125	762–1298	71–121	770–1310	71–122	696–1184	65–110	681–1159	63–108	733–1247	68–116	555–945	52–88
Private		845–1300	79–121	938–1443	87–134	786–1209	73–112	837–1287	78–120	811–1287	75–120	887–1365	82–127	904–1391	84–129	870–1339	81–124	879–1352	82–126	794–1222	74–114	777–1196	72–111	837–1287	78–120	634–975	59–91
Private luxury		1450–1875	135–174	1610–2081	150–193	1349–1744	125–162	1436–1856	133–172	1392–1856	129–172	1523–1969	141–183	1552–2006	144–186	1494–1931	139–179	1508–1950	140–181	1363–1763	127–164	1334–1725	124–160	1436–1856	133–172	1088–1406	101–131

Building type	Location factor	Benchmark 100	Greater London 111	North 93	Yorks & Hum 99	East Midlands 96	East Anglia 105	South East 107	South West 103	West Midlands 104	North West 94	Wales 92	Scotland 99	Northern Ireland 75
Investment	Student residence ***	1050–1625	1166–1804	977–1511	1040–1609	1008–1609	1103–1706	1124–1739	1082–1674	1092–1690	987–1528	966–1495	1040–1609	788–1219
		98–151	108–168	91–140	97–149	94–149	102–159	104–162	100–155	101–157	92–142	90–139	97–149	73–113
	Private apartments	1100–1300	1221–1443	1023–1209	1089–1287	1056–1287	1155–1365	1177–1391	1133–1339	1144–1352	1034–1222	1012–1196	1089–1287	825–975
		102–121	113–134	95–112	101–120	98–120	107–127	109–129	105–124	106–126	96–114	94–111	101–120	77–91
Offices	Medium rise, standard fit-out, no a/c	1090–1520	1210–1687	1014–1414	1079–1505	1046–1505	1145–1596	1166–1626	1123–1566	1134–1581	1025–1429	1003–1398	1079–1505	818–1140
		101–141	112–157	94–131	100–140	97–140	106–148	108–151	104–145	105–147	95–133	93–130	100–140	76–106
	Medium rise, standard fit-out, incl. a/c	1310–1820	1454–2020	1218–1693	1297–1802	1258–1802	1376–1911	1402–1947	1349–1875	1362–1893	1231–1711	1205–1674	1297–1802	983–1365
		122–169	135–188	113–157	120–167	117–167	128–178	130–181	125–174	127–176	114–159	112–156	120–167	91–127
	High rise, standard fit-out, incl. a/c	1690–2470	1876–2742	1572–2297	1673–2445	1622–2445	1775–2594	1808–2643	1741–2544	1758–2569	1589–2322	1555–2272	1673–2445	1268–1853
		157–229	174–255	146–213	155–227	151–227	165–241	168–246	162–236	163–239	148–216	144–211	155–227	118–172

* Residential developments may or may not be located within existing foul drainage schemes and may require construction of an individual treatment plant or connection to a local scheme. Costs for such installations will depend on site location and ground conditions, scheme layout etc. External works and drainage 12–15%. Professional fees 10–15%
** Rates based on large estates of multiple units utilising buying gains and economies of scale, not individual or one-off properties
*** Modular and prefabricated solutions are widely being explored to achieve low end of cost range products

Building type		Benchmark 100	Greater London 111	North 93	Yorks & Hum 99	East Midlands 96	East Anglia 105	South East 107	South West 103	West Midlands 104	North West 94	Wales 92	Scotland 99	Northern Ireland 75
Offices continued	Headquarters, high quality fit-out, incl. a/c	2100–3000	2331–3330	1953–2790	2079–2970	2016–2970	2205–3150	2247–3210	2163–3090	2184–3120	1974–2820	1932–2760	2079–2970	1575–2250
		195–279	217–309	181–259	193–276	187–276	205–293	209–298	201–287	203–290	183–262	179–256	193–276	146–209
	Business park, standard fit-out, no a/c	965–1415	1071–1571	897–1316	955–1401	926–1401	1013–1486	1033–1514	994–1457	1004–1472	907–1330	888–1302	955–1401	724–1061
		90–131	100–146	83–122	89–130	86–130	94–138	96–141	92–135	93–137	84–124	82–121	89–130	67–99
	Business park, standard fit-out, incl. a/c	1225–1710	1360–1898	1139–1590	1213–1693	1176–1693	1286–1796	1311–1830	1262–1761	1274–1778	1152–1607	1127–1573	1213–1693	919–1283
		114–159	126–176	106–148	113–157	109–157	119–167	122–170	117–164	118–165	107–149	105–146	113–157	85–119
	Call centre, standard fit-out, incl. a/c	1510–2315	1676–2570	1404–2153	1495–2292	1450–2292	1586–2431	1616–2477	1555–2384	1570–2408	1419–2176	1389–2130	1495–2292	1133–1736
		140–215	156–239	130–200	139–213	135–213	147–226	150–230	144–222	146–224	132–202	129–198	139–213	105–161
	Car parking, underground per space	17500–25000	19425–27750	16275–23250	17325–24750	16800–24750	18375–26250	18725–26750	18025–25750	18200–26000	16450–23500	16100–23000	17325–24750	13125–18750
	Car parking, multi-storey per space	8000–13000	8880–14430	7440–12090	7920–12870	7680–12870	8400–13650	8560–13910	8240–13390	8320–13520	7520–12220	7360–11960	7920–12870	6000–9750

Notes: Indicative costs for commercial buildings shown are for functional designs to current design norms. Specialised design features such as external feature detailing, security systems, building management systems (BMS), back-up power supplies (UPS), etc. will add substantially to indicative costs. External works and drainage 12–15%. Professional fees 10–14%

Building type	Location factor	Benchmark 100 £/m²	Benchmark 100 £/sq ft	Greater London 111 £/m²	Greater London 111 £/sq ft	North 93 £/m²	North 93 £/sq ft	Yorks & Hum 99 £/m²	Yorks & Hum 99 £/sq ft	East Midlands 96 £/m²	East Midlands 96 £/sq ft	East Anglia 105 £/m²	East Anglia 105 £/sq ft	South East 107 £/m²	South East 107 £/sq ft	South West 103 £/m²	South West 103 £/sq ft	West Midlands 94 £/m²	West Midlands 94 £/sq ft	North West 94 £/m²	North West 94 £/sq ft	Wales 92 £/m²	Wales 92 £/sq ft	Scotland 99 £/m²	Scotland 99 £/sq ft	Northern Ireland 75 £/m²	Northern Ireland 75 £/sq ft
Industrial	Units (shell only)	315–675	29–63	350–749	32–70	293–628	27–58	312–668	29–62	302–648	28–60	331–709	31–66	337–722	31–67	324–695	30–65	296–635	28–59	296–635	28–59	290–621	27–58	312–668	29–62	236–506	22–47
	Purpose built – base services	550–900	51–84	611–999	57–93	512–837	48–78	545–891	51–83	528–864	49–80	578–945	54–88	589–963	55–89	567–927	53–86	517–846	48–79	517–846	48–79	506–828	47–77	545–891	51–83	413–675	38–63
	Distribution warehouse	300–740	28–69	333–821	31–76	279–688	26–64	297–733	28–68	288–710	27–66	315–777	29–72	321–792	30–74	309–762	29–71	282–696	26–65	282–696	26–65	276–681	26–63	297–733	28–68	225–555	21–52
	Chilled distribution warehouse	780–1400	72–130	866–1554	80–144	725–1302	67–121	772–1386	72–129	749–1344	70–125	819–1470	76–137	835–1498	78–139	803–1442	75–134	733–1316	68–122	733–1316	68–122	718–1288	67–120	772–1386	72–129	585–1050	54–98
Retail (excl. fit-out)	Convenience store	575–950	53–88	638–1055	59–98	535–884	50–82	569–941	53–87	552–912	51–85	604–998	56–93	615–1017	57–94	592–979	55–91	541–893	50–83	541–893	50–83	529–874	49–81	569–941	53–87	431–713	40–66
	Supermarket	500–1050	46–98	555–1166	52–108	465–977	43–91	495–1040	46–97	480–1008	45–94	525–1103	49–102	535–1124	50–104	515–1082	48–100	470–987	44–92	470–987	44–92	460–966	43–90	495–1040	46–97	375–788	35–73

Building type	Benchmark 100	Greater London 111	North 93	Yorks & Hum 99	East Midlands 96	East Anglia 105	South East 107	South West 103	West Midlands 94	North West 94	Wales 92	Scotland 99	Northern Ireland 75
Retail (excl. fit-out) continued													
Stand-alone (out of town)	440-730	488-810	409-679	436-723	422-701	462-767	471-781	453-752	414-686	414-686	405-672	436-723	330-548
	41-68	45-75	38-63	40-67	39-65	43-71	44-73	42-70	38-64	38-64	38-62	40-67	31-51
Retail warehouse	440-675	488-749	409-628	436-668	422-648	462-709	471-722	453-695	414-635	414-635	405-621	436-668	330-506
	41-63	45-70	38-58	40-62	39-60	43-66	44-67	42-65	38-59	38-59	38-58	40-62	31-47
Shopping centres – retail units	625-830	694-921	581-772	619-822	600-797	656-872	669-888	644-855	588-780	588-780	575-764	619-822	469-623
	58-77	64-86	54-72	57-76	56-74	61-81	62-83	60-79	55-72	55-72	53-71	57-76	44-58
Shopping centres – service areas	930-1160	1032-1288	865-1079	921-1148	893-1114	977-1281	995-1241	958-1195	874-1090	874-1090	856-1067	921-1148	698-870
	86-108	96-120	80-100	86-107	83-103	91-113	92-115	89-111	81-101	81-101	79-99	86-107	65-81
Shopping centres – concourses	1050-1665	1166-1848	977-1548	1040-1648	1008-1598	1103-1748	1124-1782	1082-1715	987-1565	987-1565	966-1532	1040-1648	788-1249
	98-155	108-172	91-144	97-153	94-148	102-162	104-166	100-159	92-145	92-145	90-142	97-153	73-116
Retail fit-out — Superstore	830-1875	921-2081	772-1744	822-1856	797-1800	872-1969	888-2006	855-1931	780-1763	780-1763	764-1725	822-1856	623-1406
	77-174	86-193	72-162	76-172	74-167	81-183	83-186	79-179	72-164	72-164	71-160	76-172	58-131
Financial/high quality	1450-1820	1610-2020	1349-1693	1436-1802	1392-1747	1523-1911	1552-1947	1494-1875	1363-1711	1363-1711	1334-1674	1436-1802	1088-1365
	135-169	150-188	125-157	133-167	129-162	141-178	144-181	139-174	127-159	127-159	124-156	133-167	101-127
Hotels — Three star	1150-1550	1277-1721	1070-1442	1139-1535	1104-1488	1208-1628	1231-1659	1185-1597	1081-1457	1081-1457	1058-1426	1139-1535	863-1163
	107-144	119-160	99-134	106-143	103-138	112-151	114-154	110-148	100-135	100-135	98-132	106-143	80-108
Four star	1350-1650	1499-1832	1256-1535	1337-1634	1296-1584	1418-1733	1445-1766	1391-1700	1269-1551	1269-1551	1242-1518	1337-1634	1013-1238
	125-153	139-170	117-143	124-152	120-147	132-161	134-164	129-158	118-144	118-144	115-141	124-152	94-115
Five star	1650-2600	1832-2886	1535-2418	1634-2574	1584-2496	1733-2730	1766-2782	1700-2678	1551-2444	1551-2444	1518-2392	1634-2574	1238-1950
	153-242	170-268	143-225	152-239	147-232	161-254	164-258	158-249	144-227	144-227	141-222	152-239	115-181

Building type	Location factor	Benchmark 100	Greater London 111	North 93	Yorks & Hum 99	East Midlands 96	East Anglia 105	South East 107	South West 103	West Midlands 94	North West 94	Wales 92	Scotland 99	Northern Ireland 75
Education/ health	Primary school	990–1450	1099–1610	921–1349	980–1436	950–1392	1040–1523	1059–1552	1020–1494	931–1363	931–1363	911–1334	980–1436	743–1088
		92–135	102–150	86–125	91–133	88–129	97–141	98–144	95–139	86–127	86–127	85–124	91–133	69–101
	Secondary school	930–1350	1032–1499	865–1256	921–1337	893–1296	977–1418	995–1445	958–1391	874–1269	874–1269	856–1242	921–1337	698–1013
		86–125	96–139	80–117	86–124	83–120	91–132	92–134	89–129	81–118	81–118	79–115	86–124	65–94
	School gymnasium	830–1300	921–1443	772–1209	822–1287	797–1248	872–1365	888–1391	855–1339	780–1222	780–1222	764–1196	822–1287	623–975
		77–121	86–134	72–112	76–120	74–116	81–127	83–129	79–124	72–114	72–114	71–111	76–120	58–91
	Nursing home/ hospice	1250–1700	1388–1887	1163–1581	1238–1683	1200–1632	1313–1785	1338–1819	1288–1751	1175–1598	1175–1598	1150–1564	1238–1683	938–1275
		116–158	129–175	108–147	115–156	111–152	122–166	124–169	120–163	109–148	109–148	107–145	115–156	87–118
Leisure	Restaurants (shell only)	900–1300	999–1443	837–1209	891–1287	864–1248	945–1365	963–1391	927–1339	846–1222	846–1222	828–1196	891–1287	675–975
		84–121	93–134	78–112	83–120	80–116	88–127	89–129	86–124	79–114	79–114	77–111	83–120	63–91
	Public house (typical fit-out)	1200–1800	1332–1998	1116–1674	1188–1782	1152–1728	1260–1890	1284–1926	1236–1854	1128–1692	1128–1692	1104–1656	1188–1782	900–1350
		111–167	124–186	104–156	110–166	107–161	117–176	119–179	115–172	105–157	105–157	103–154	110–166	84–125
	Leisure centres	1050–2400	1166–2664	977–2232	1040–2376	1008–2304	1103–2520	1124–2568	1082–2472	987–2256	987–2256	966–2208	1040–2376	788–1800
		98–223	108–247	91–207	97–221	94–214	102–234	104–239	100–230	92–210	92–210	90–205	97–221	73–167

Notes: Indicative costs for industrial units are typical shell and basic services. Mezzanine flooring and storage racking not included. Hotels, shop units, restaurants and public houses may have expensive fitting-out costs in excess of those shown due to corporate image requirements or individual architectural or conservation requirements. Retail and industrial external works allowance 7–12%. Professional fees 10–15%.

No guarantee is given by Watts Group, or any of its employees, as to this cost table's accuracy. More detailed advice must be obtained before relying on costs indicated.

Value engineering

Value engineering (VE) is a means of evaluating the function, cost and objectives of all aspects of the design and construction of a project with a view to increasing the margin between cost and revenue. VE is not simply cost cutting, in fact it might lead to an increase in cost.

To succeed with value engineering, increases in value must be achieved with a lower cost impact and, similarly, decreases in value must be accompanied by a greater reduction in cost.

Value engineering is best undertaken in a workshop forum, ideally facilitated by a senior individual having some knowledge of the project but who is not part of the delivery team. Typically, a VE workshop will observe the following simple protocol:

❖ Representatives of the design team, the client and the construction team are present.

❖ The tone of the meeting should be constructive and the facilitator must encourage the notion of 'free enquiry'. No historic decisions should escape review.

❖ A member(s) of the team will present the project and will highlight key aspects of design, brief and cost.

❖ A process of functional analysis of the major components follows the general briefing. This process allows the team to fully appreciate the need for and role of each major component. An example of this would be a flat slab framing solution 'essential' to the avoidance of drop beams. Context is added by the consideration of cost, programme and sequence. The key is to concentrate upon the core components only.

❖ The definition of 'core components' will involve consideration of their cost, their effect upstream and/or downstream and their sensitivity, such as a client's personally-favoured solution.

❖ Analysis is followed by speculation and is the creative stage. Nothing (within reason) is off limits. The role of the facilitator is crucial here and he or she must keep the emerging alternatives to a manageable number.

❖ To arrive at a set of proposals, the alternatives must be evaluated against a set of criteria and the criteria must start with the basic test – what adds most value? This might be the alternative that also adds most cost.

❖ The end game is a list of alternatives, openly debated and validated by the team and worthy of more detailed consideration prior to presentation of recommendations to the client. This usually involves the assembly of a closure report.

Some golden rules for the facilitator:

❖ A group of eight is probably optimum – make sure all the design disciplines are represented.

❖ All must be encouraged to participate.

❖ All ground that is covered must be documented.

❖ The synthesis of ideas and concepts must be encouraged.

❖ Be flexible, but firm.

Contributed by Tim French, tim.french@watts.co.uk

Life cycle costing

The life cycle cost of an asset may be defined as the total cost of that asset over its operating life, including initial capital/acquisition cost, occupation costs, operating costs, and the cost or benefit of the eventual disposal of the asset at the end of its life.

Life cycle costing is essential to effective decision-making in four main ways:

* It identifies the total cost commitment undertaken in the acquisition of any asset.

* It facilitates an effective choice between alternative methods of achieving a stated objective, recognising different patterns of capital and running costs.

* It is a management tool that details the current operating costs of assets.

* It identifies those areas in which operating costs might be reduced.

The use of life cycle costing techniques has developed over recent years, driven predominantly by shifts in public sector procurement policy towards 'best value' rather than lowest cost. Publications such as *Construction Procurement Guidance, No 7 Whole Life Costs* (Office of Government Commerce) state that 'all procurement must be made solely on the basis of value for money in terms of the optimum combination of whole life costs and quality to meet the user's requirements'. The use of PFI/PPP for the procurement of major capital projects also contributed to the need to consider the whole life cost of an asset rather than simply the 'up front' capital outlay.

The benefits of life cycle costing should not be construed as being effective for the public sector alone – long-term investment returns on property can be influenced significantly by future maintenance/operational obligations which were not considered at the outset of a project. Energy efficiency of buildings, in particular, is considered to be a prime candidate for life cycle cost evaluation. In an era dominated by sustainability, European directives, the Climate Change Levy, etc., the higher capital cost of energy efficient installations can often be more than offset by longer term savings. Adding the benefit of potential tax advantages, the value of effective whole life cost techniques becomes apparent. See *Capital allowances*, page 106.

As a result, life cycle cost planning should, wherever possible, form an integral part of the design development process, being implemented from project outset to achieve maximum benefit.

Implementation of life cycle costing

Implementation of appropriate life cycle costing techniques must reflect not only the nature of the client's needs but also the client's property-specific objectives. The objectives of an owner-occupier client, retaining a long-term interest, will be significantly different from an investor seeking to transfer maintenance risk to a prospective tenant.

The following major elements should therefore be considered:

* the overall time period;

* all costs and revenues attributable to the project, including initial investment, recurring costs and revenues, proceeds from ultimate sale or other disposal and tax benefits;

* only those costs and revenues directly attributable to the project;

* the effects of time, including allowance for the impact of inflation; and

* the fact that pounds spent or received in the future are worth less than pounds spent or received today.

Stages of life cycle costing

Life cycle costing techniques can be split into the following stages.

Life cycle cost planning (LCCP)

Objectives are:

- ❖ to identify the total costs of the acquisition of a building or building element; and
- ❖ to facilitate the effective choice between various methods of achieving a given objective.

LCCP can be broken into seven basic steps:

- ❖ **Step 1**: Establish the objective.
- ❖ **Step 2**: Choose alternative options for achieving the objective (consider all realistic possibilities).
- ❖ **Step 3**: Formulate assumptions (e.g. discount rate, construction duration, asset replacement cycle, building life, basis of residual value).
- ❖ **Step 4**: Calculate all capital and recurrent costs over a defined period.
- ❖ **Step 5**: Compare costs and rank the alternatives.
- ❖ **Step 6**: Carry out a sensitivity analysis (i.e. when the results of step 5 are not demonstrably in favour of one choice).
- ❖ **Step 7**: Investigate capital cost constraints.

Applying the foregoing approach for each option under consideration will generate a life cycle cost plan, reflecting all costs and revenues over the selected time period. Recognising that monies spent in the future will be worth less than the same money spent today, the cash flows are discounted to a present day value. The total of all present day values over the life of the LCCP represent the net present value (NPV). Compared against alternative options, the NPV facilitates identification of the option which offers best value for money.

Life cycle cost management (LCCM)

Objectives are:

- ❖ to identify areas where running costs might be reduced;
- ❖ to establish where performance differs from the LCCP projection;
- ❖ to make recommendations on more efficient utilisation of the building;
- ❖ to provide information on asset lives and reliability factors for accounting purposes;
- ❖ to assist in the establishment of a maintenance policy for the building; and
- ❖ to give taxation advice on building-related items.

LCCM therefore applies throughout the operational phase of a building's life, focused upon maintaining and/or improving the asset's efficiency. LCCM should be read in conjunction with maintenance management.

Life cycle cost analysis (LCCA)

Objectives are:

- ❖ to provide a management tool which identifies actual operating costs incurred; and
- ❖ to relate cost and performance data to advisers about the running costs of occupied buildings.

LCCA is an ongoing operation, contributing to both LCCP and LCCM – in practice, one cannot take place without the other.

While each component can be viewed as a separate activity in its own right, there is a logical sequence that links them together. The sequence is demonstrated in the figure on the following pages, where a life cycle cost plan for a proposed project is based upon three similar buildings for which life cycle cost analyses are available.

Main components of life cycle costing

Components to consider when implementing life cycle cost techniques:

- ❖ Capital costs:
  - – land (including cost of acquisition)
  - – demolitions
  - – construction costs
  - – fit-out expenditure
  - – decanting charges (including rental of temporary accommodation)
  - – relocation expenses
  - – professional fees
  - – statutory fees
  - – VAT (and other taxes)
- ❖ Financing charges:
  - – cost of finance for land/site acquisition
  - – cost of finance during occupational period
- ❖ Operation costs:
  - – heating, electricity and other energy
  - – cleaning and caretaking
  - – rates
  - – insurance
  - – security and public health
  - – staff (building related)
  - – rent
  - – management charges
  - – land charges
- ❖ Maintenance costs:
  - – life cycle asset replacement (specific)
  - – annual maintenance (general)
  - – annual grounds maintenance (general)
- ❖ Residual values:
  - – disposal of existing buildings, land, etc.
  - – disposal of temporary decant accommodation
  - – retained value at end of evaluation period
- ❖ Revenue:
  - – other income derived from the accommodation
  - – benefit of capital allowances or other incentive.

Other considerations

The discount rate and inflation

When compiling life cycle cost plans, it is important to distinguish between the interest rate and the discount rate. Where project cash flows include an allowance for inflation, the discount rate should make an equivalent allowance. Alternatively, where estimates are in current prices, they should be discounted at the real discount rate.

The sequence linking LCCA, LCCP and LCCM

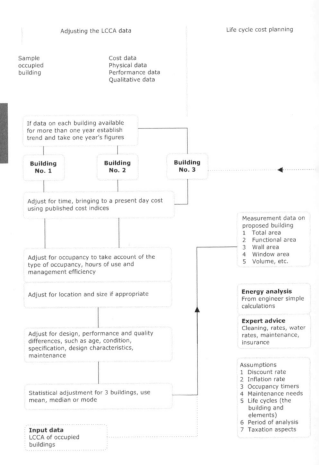

Adjusting the LCCA data

Life cycle cost planning

Sample occupied building

Cost data
Physical data
Performance data
Qualitative data

If data on each building available for more than one year establish trend and take one year's figures

Building No. 1 — **Building No. 2** — **Building No. 3**

Adjust for time, bringing to a present day cost using published cost indices

Measurement data on proposed building
1 Total area
2 Functional area
3 Wall area
4 Window area
5 Volume, etc.

Adjust for occupancy to take account of the type of occupancy, hours of use and management efficiency

Adjust for location and size if appropriate

Energy analysis
From engineer simple calculations

Expert advice
Cleaning, rates, water rates, maintenance, insurance

Adjust for design, performance and quality differences, such as age, condition, specification, design characteristics, maintenance

Statistical adjustment for 3 buildings, use mean, median or mode

Assumptions
1 Discount rate
2 Inflation rate
3 Occupancy timers
4 Maintenance needs
5 Life cycles (the building and elements)
6 Period of analysis
7 Taxation aspects

Input data
LCCA of occupied buildings

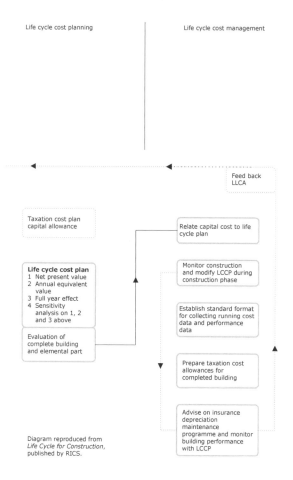

Life cycle cost planning

Life cycle cost management

Feed back
LLCA

Taxation cost plan
capital allowance

Relate capital cost to life
cycle plan

Life cycle cost plan
1 Net present value
2 Annual equivalent
   value
3 Full year effect
4 Sensitivity
   analysis on 1, 2
   and 3 above

Monitor construction
and modify LCCP during
construction phase

Establish standard format
for collecting running cost
data and performance
data

Evaluation of
complete building
and elemental part

Prepare taxation cost
allowances for
completed building

Advise on insurance
depreciation
maintenance
programme and monitor
building performance
with LCCP

Diagram reproduced from
Life Cycle for Construction,
published by RICS.

125

While there is no definitive approach, it is reasonable to state that if all cost estimates are expected to inflate at the same rate then it is not unreasonable to perform all calculations in current prices, applying a real discount rate. Alternatively, where cost estimates are likely to inflate at different rates (e.g. energy costs inflating significantly faster than construction prices) then it may be beneficial to account for the differing rates of inflation.

In the case of financing through borrowing, the discount rate will equal the long-term cost of borrowing money in the market place (net of inflation). While the discount rate will vary with the source of funding, it is worth noting that HM Treasury apply a discount rate of 3.5% in public sector option appraisal.

Project life

An estimate of the probable life of the project should be made. When ranking projects with identical lives, the option with the lowest present value should be chosen. However, where the options have different lives, the cost of each alternative should be expressed as an annual equivalent and the option with the lowest annual equivalent chosen.

Standardised Method of Life Cycle Costing for Construction Procurement

The UK *Standardised Method of Life Cycle Costing for Construction Procurement* was produced by BCIS in conjunction with the BSI and forms a Supplement to BS ISO 15686-5:2008 *Buildings and constructed assets – Service-life planning – Part 5: Life-cycle costing*.

It provides a standard cost data structure for life cycle costing along with standardised methods of applying life cycle costing. The intention is to provide an industry-wide accepted methodology to facilitate more accurate, consistent and robust application of life cycle costing.

Contributed by Simon Brereton, simon.brereton@watts.co.uk

Reinstatement valuations for insurance purposes

Generally it is considered prudent to insure a property for the value of complete reinstatement following total destruction (including partial destruction that necessitates demolition and rebuild). The calculation of construction costs can take different forms depending on the client brief and the information available. More complex or bespoke properties may benefit from detailed cost planning, while for simple structures a cost per m^2 is sufficient.

When preparing a reinstatement valuation the following points should be considered:

- ❖ Include demolition cost.
- ❖ Rebuilding costs to be valued (initially at 'day one' rates – using rates applicable at the time of preparation of the valuation).
- ❖ Include for any special features that are to be included to enable replacement of the property on a like-for-like basis. Examples include facade treatments (such as stonework embellishments) or internal features (such as specialist decorations).
- ❖ Ensure the scope of fixtures, fittings and installations is clearly defined, particularly in tenanted properties.
- ❖ Include professional fees at an appropriate level, depending on the complexity and location of the property.
- ❖ Account for geographical location factors either in rebuilding rates or separately by reference to recognised indices.

❖ Include local authority planning and building regulation fees as they are an unavoidable expense.

❖ The cost of rebuild should include for the impact of latest legislation, such as renewable energy installations.

If the valuation is being projected to cover the period of the policy (as opposed to 'day one' valuation) then account should be made for the:

❖ period of the policy;

❖ design period;

❖ planning period;

❖ construction period; and

❖ void (letting) period (if required by the owner).

This may result in projecting costs for anything up to and beyond a three-year period. A contingency should be included.

The 'declared value' is usually the 'day one cost' whereas an 'insured value' is usually the cost of construction plus allowances for inflation.

Reinstatement valuations for listed buildings

Listed buildings should be reinstated to the same design, quality, style and workmanship, and in the same material, but in accordance where necessary, with current legislation. Historic buildings therefore tend to be more expensive to reproduce than modern equivalents and hence more expensive to insure.

The building should be surveyed to establish the scope and specification of both the external and internal construction and finishes; this may also include archival research. A photographic report should be undertaken as a record of the survey and findings.

A design statement should be prepared detailing exactly how, in the event of loss, the building would be reconstructed. This should pick up the reconstruction of the shell, as well as all the historic features and points of historic interest and merit. A competent person, who can interpret the likely requirements of a conservation officer, should undertake the design statement.

A detailed estimate or cost plan should then be prepared to pick up the level of detail necessary to accurately price the scope contained within the design statement. The estimate should allow for appropriate skilled tradesmen and materials commensurate to the existing building.

It is unlikely that a reinsurance valuation based on unit rates multiplied by floor area will provide a reliable valuation.

Contributed by Tim French, tim.french@watts.co.uk

Office relocation and fit-out

Relocation of any business is a very significant undertaking and requires resolution of many disparate matters to achieve success. It embraces organisational change, legal agreements concerning the exit from existing premises and the acquisition or leasing of new premises, appointment of professional advisers, procurement and management of construction operations (to reorganise the office space from their landlord's basic specification, CAT A, to specific operational needs, CAT B), procurement of furniture, and the relocation of staff and equipment to the new premises. Above all, this project is vital as it will profoundly affect a business' day-to-day operations. In our experience, success requires strong project leadership on the client side and also in respect of the construction and technical project delivery.

Set out below are some of the key issues that should be considered in respect of office relocation and fit-out schemes:

- ❖ Plan ahead: Obtaining best value takes time; instigating organisational change takes longer. It is never too early to start the planning process.

- ❖ Appoint an internal project sponsor to provide a single point of liaison for all internal parties; this person will be responsible for briefing external consultants. This ensures clarity of communication.

- ❖ Appoint an independent project manager to guide you through this process to ensure that you achieve best value and that the project delivers.

- ❖ Agree a strategic programme with the project manager.

- ❖ Implement an internal consultation and communication strategy.

- ❖ Embrace the opportunity for change: consider new methods of working (such as hot desking, open plan offices, alternative IT strategies) and take the opportunity to reduce the amount of files and unwanted equipment. This is the ideal time to make changes and avoid replicating legacy solutions in a new location.

- ❖ Understand your exit cost and your liabilities; these will potentially include dilapidations in a leasehold situation. These exit costs and arrangements may inform your relocation decision.

- ❖ Determine an appropriate procurement route. Many options are available and each has different risk profiles and design team constituent requirements.

- ❖ Appoint a design team and/or design contractor (depending on the procurement route).

- ❖ Appoint a CDM coordinator (a mandatory, statutory appointment for most construction projects).

- ❖ Appoint a letting agent to commence a market search for suitable premises.

- ❖ Commence initial design and scoping activities to establish the actual space required (this may differ from the original expectations, especially if new methods of working are considered). The preliminary design and scoping will give an initial high-level requirement.

- ❖ Determine the best shortlist of available property assessed for compliance against the provisional design requirements.

- ❖ Begin legal and acquisition activity concerning the proposed premises including building surveying acquisition surveys. Allow for the necessary landlord approvals required in terms of the proposed fit-out works, if appropriate.

- ❖ Determine other approvals required; potentially these would include listed buildings consent, party wall consent, planning approval etc.

- ❖ Complete the tendering or a contractor selection process.

- ❖ Arrange for works to commence on site immediately after legal activities are completed.

- ❖ Consider all standing service contracts in existing premises which require termination or variation following the move.

- ❖ Procure telephone lines and data links for the new premises.

- ❖ Consider how IT can be migrated from existing to new premises while ensuring business continuity and minimising risk.

- ❖ Arrange for appropriate construction project review meetings together with methods of dealing with change and unforeseen circumstances.

- ❖ Establish what furniture will be relocated to the new premises, what requires disposal and what additional procurement requirements are generated. Ensure that furniture is procured carefully and that discounts which are available for bulk purchases are passed on to the end user.

- ❖ Implement a detailed move action plan, informing all staff of the intended relocation, the timing, impact and their duties.

- ❖ Arrange a relocation weekend or sequence of moves to minimise impact on the business and ensure business continuity as far as possible.

- ❖ Pay particular attention to handover and final commissioning activities. The last 5% of a project is crucial to its perception of success within your organisation. Ensure furniture installation occurs in good time.

- ❖ Coordinate IT installation to ensure it is in place, tested and commissioned in good time for occupation.

- ❖ Always plan contingencies where risk has been identified.

- ❖ Always make sure your insurance covers you through the proposed move.

Contributed by Daniel Webb, daniel.webb@watts.co.uk

Town and country planning in the UK

Primary legislation for town planning

Devolved government to Scotland, Wales and Northern Ireland means that each constituent has its own planning policies and guidance, separate to those of England. The basic structure of having one or more form of either national, regional or local plans remains, but the plans themselves are different for each constituent.

With the election of the coalition government in spring 2010, considerable changes are presently in train for England and Wales. However, the Scottish Parliament has put into place a planning regime that is now stable and certain, as is the status in Northern Ireland. The changes in England are dramatic and far reaching with both the proposed National Planning Policy Framework for England and the now enacted Localism Bill, which received Royal Assent on 15 November 2011.

The NPPF for England was the subject of a major consultation exercise which closed on 17 October 2011 and the results and subsequent legislative provisions are awaited. There are likely to be considerable deviations from the Draft NPPF of July 2011 which can be tracked on www.communities.gov.uk/documents/planningandbuilding/pdf/1951747.pdf

All that presently can be said is that the NPPF if enacted in full will result in the cancelling of 47 planning policy documents. The July Draft NPPF and the concurrent consultation document did indicate that the only policy documentation likely to remain (albeit incorporated elsewhere) was in respect of travellers, sustainable waste management, and eco-towns.

Separately but closely linked to the NPPF for England is the now enacted Localism Bill which seeks to:

❖ give new freedoms and flexibilities for local government;

❖ give new rights and powers for communities and individuals;

❖ reform the planning system to make it more democratic and more effective; and

❖ make reforms to ensure that decisions about housing are taken locally.

For a plain English guide to the Localism Act go to www.communities.gov.uk/publications/localgovernment/localismplainenglishguide. For the text of the Act see www.legislation.gov.uk/ukpga/2011/20/contents/enacted

England

Currently no national plan for England exists until such time as the NPPF for England comes into force.

It must also be noted that at the Conservative Party Conference in October 2010 the Secretary of State for the Department for Communities and Local Government, Eric Pickles, indicated 'there will be a presumption in favour of development in areas that do not put a new local plan in place'. This is in respect of the new Local Plans to replace Local Development Frameworks, which are to be followed by Neighbourhood Plans.

The *Planning Act* 2008 introduced an independent Infrastructure Planning Commission (IPC) to decide on planning permissions for 'nationally significant infrastructure projects'. On 29 June 2010, the coalition government announced the abolition of the IPC and the transfer of its responsibilities to a Major Infrastructure Planning Unit within the Planning Inspectorate.

In addition, the detailed provisions of the *Housing and Regeneration Act* 2008, the *Climate Change Act* 2008 and the *Local Transport Act* 2008 are now under review. The aim is to reconsider policies within the agenda for local political control – the 'Localism Agenda'.

Regional Planning Guidance, which was due to have been replaced by the Regional Spatial Strategy (RSS), presently remains in force following the announcement on 27 May 2010 of the abolition of Regional Strategies.

Two concurrent Parliamentary enquiries are now to develop the planning structure system following the abolition of Regional Strategies and to review the 'Localism Agenda'.

In Greater London, the present regional plan is provided by the London Plan. This is currently being reviewed and is subject to two separate Alterations.

Local Development Frameworks (LDFs), which may or may not survive the 'Localism Agenda' review, currently outline to local planning authorities how the local area may change over the next few years.

Supplementary to these documents are 25 Planning Policy Guidance Notes (PPGs) which were very gradually being replaced with equivalent Planning Policy Statements (PPSs).

To check on the current status of an individual PPG or PPS consult www.communities.gov.uk/planningandbuilding/planningsystem/planningpolicy/planningpolicystatements

The current PPSs (in bold) and PPGs, and projected replacements, as at the time of going to print, are listed in the following table (NR = no replacement planned/programmed). For England the implementation of the as yet Draft NPPF would result in wholesale abolition of PPGs and PPSs.

PPG/PPS number	Title	Date
PPS1	**Delivering Sustainable Development** – NR	2005
	Planning and Climate Change – Supplement to PPS1 (2007) and Ecotowns – A supplement to PPS1 (2009)	2007 and 2009
PPG2	Green Belts – NR	1995 (amended 2001)
PPS3	**Housing – make sure you have the amended version published 9 June 2010**	2010
PPS4	**Planning for Sustainable Economic Growth**	2009
PPS5	**Planning for the Historic Environment**	2010
PPS6	**Planning for Town Centres – cancelled**	cancelled
PPS7	**Sustainable Development in Rural Areas** – Note: now consulting on a new PPS, Planning for a Natural and Healthy Environment	2004
PPG8	Telecommunications – NR	2001
PPS9	**Biodiversity and Geological Conservation** – being reviewed and consolidated with open space, sport and reacreation PPG17 – consultation underway September 2010	2005
PPS10	**Planning for Sustainable Waste Management** – NR	2005
PPS11	**Regional Spatial Strategies** – is currently withdrawn from the DCLG website and may be expected to be replaced in the light of the Localism Bill	2004
PPS12	**Local Spatial Planning** – NR Note: PPG12 remains relevant for any Development Plans being prepared under the 1999 Development Plan Regulations.	2008

PPG/PPS number	Title	Date
PPG13	Transport – NR	2001
PPG14	Development on unstable land – NR	1990
PPG15	Planning and the historic environment – cancelled, see PPS5	cancelled
PPG16	Archaeology and planning – cancelled, see PPS5	cancelled
PPG17	Planning for Open Space, Sport and Recreation – see PPS9	2002
PPG18	Enforcing planning control – was to have been consolidated in new Development Management Policy Framework, now under Localism Agenda Review	1991
PPG19	Outdoor advertisement control – as PPG18	1992
PPG20	Coastal planning – now also with supplement to PPS25, published 9 March 2010	1992
PPG21	Cancelled and replaced in 2006 by *A Good Practice Guide on Planning for Tourism*	
PPS22	**Renewable energy** – see PPS1 *Planning and Climate Change* supplement	**2004**
PPS23	**Planning and Pollution Control** – NR	**2004**
PPG24	Planning and noise – NR	1994
PPS25	**Development and Flood Risk**, revised 29 March 2010 and accompanied by Supplement *Development and Coastal Change*, 9 March 2010	**2006**

There are supplementary annexes and Good Practice Guides for various PPGs/PPSs.

Policy on minerals and planning is contained within Minerals Planning Guidance Notes (MPGs) and their replacements, Minerals Policy Statements (MPSs).

Wales

A national plan for Wales is contained in *Planning Policy Wales* (Edition 2, 2010). This will be supplemented by Local Development Plans (LDPs) (the equivalent of the erstwhile English LDFs), currently being prepared by the local planning authorities.

Supplementary to these policy documents are 21 topic-based Technical Advice Notes (TANs). Procedural guidance is given separately in Welsh Office/National Assembly for Wales circulars. Use the website http://wales.gov.uk/topics/planning/policy/tans/?lang=en to find the relevant documentation.

Current TANs, which must be read with Planning Policy Wales 2002	
TAN1	Joint Housing Land Availability Studies – 2006
TAN2	Planning and Affordable Housing – 2006
TAN3	Simplified Planning Zones – 1996
TAN4	Retailing and Town Centres – 1996
TAN5	Nature Conservation and Planning – 2009
TAN6	Agricultural and Rural Development – 2000
TAN7	Outdoor Advertisement Control – 1996

Current TANs, which must be read with Planning Policy Wales 2002	
TAN8	Renewable Energy – 2005
TAN9	Enforcement of Planning Control – 1997
TAN10	Tree Preservation Orders – 1997
TAN11	Noise – 1997
TAN12	Design – 2009
TAN13	Tourism – 1997
TAN14	Coastal Planning – 1998
TAN15	Development and Flood Risk – 2004
TAN16	Sport and Recreation – undated in Welsh Government listings
TAN18	Transport – 2007
TAN19	Telecommunications – 2002
TAN20	The Welsh Language – Unitary Development Plans and Planning Control – 2000
TAN21	Waste – 2001
TAN22	Sustainable Buildings – 2010

Scotland

A national plan for Scotland is contained in the *National Planning Framework for Scotland 2*, which came into force in June 2009. Local Development Plans are also present at local planning authority level.

The Scottish Planning Policies (SPPs) and National Planning Policy Guidelines (NPPGs) only remained in force until they were replaced completely by the new consolidated Scottish Planning Policy Document of 2010 and the Scottish Historic Environment Policy of 2009. The previous 21 Scottish Planning Policies (now revoked) comprised 15 SPPs and 6 NPPGs.

Northern Ireland

In Northern Ireland, planning has long been devolved with Regional and Local Development Plans supplemented by (presently) a total of 16 Planning Policy Statements (PPSs) with a further 5 Clarification, Revision or Draft PPSs in the pipeline. The following website will enable an accurate check to be made: www.planningni.gov.uk/index/policy/policy_publications/ planning_statements.htm

Current PPSs are listed in the following table (revised editions currently out for consultation are noted as OFC).

Current PPSs	
PPS1	General Principles
PPS2	Planning and Nature Conservation
PPS3	Access, Movement and Parking – note with clarification/revision
PPS4	Industrial Development – OFC as Industry, Business and Distribution
PPS5	Retailing and Town Centres – OFC as Retailing, Town Centres and Commercial Leisure Developments

Current PPSs	
PPS6	Archaeology, The Built Heritage and Area of Townscape Character – note with an addendum as Areas of Townscape Character
PPS7	Quality Residential Environments – note with an addendum as Residential Extensions and Alterations
PPS8	Open Space, Sport and Outdoor Recreation
PPS9	The Enforcement of Planning Control
PPS10	Telecommunications
PPS11	Planning and Waste Management
PPS12	Housing in Settlements
PPS13	Transportation and Land Use
PPS14	Sustainable Development in the Countryside (cancelled) – the previous contentious draft is now published as PPS21
PPS15	Planning and Flood Risk
PPS17	Control of Outdoor Advertisements
PPS18	Renewable Energy
PPS21	Sustainable Development in the Countryside

The Channel Islands and the Isle of Man

In the Channel Islands, town planning controls and supplementary planning guidance varies between the islands. Jersey has a developed system of supplementary planning guidance, known as Planning Policy Notes and Planning Advice Notes. Guernsey is awaiting the adoption of the Shepley Report, published in April 2008, as regards such supplementary guidance, while Alderney and Sark are awaiting the results of the Shepley Report before adopting equivalent supplementary guidance.

The Isle of Man also has supplementary planning guidance.

Supplementary guidance

In all the constituent parts of the UK and the semi-autonomous islands, the various forms of planning policy and guidance are particularly relevant when the national, regional or local development plan or policy is outdated and does not reflect current government planning policies.

Thus far none of the constituent parts of the UK nor the semi-autonomous islands has defined rigid 'zoning' for different types of developments.

These 'plan-led' systems control the developments and alterations that can be undertaken on a given site or building.

For any proposal to undertake development the basic premise in the UK is that planning permission will be required.

Circulars

Departmental Circulars are also material considerations in the discharge of planning powers, but are more restricted and focus on advice on legislative matters and planning procedures. The current circulars may be consulted via English, Northern Irish, Scottish and Welsh Government planning websites.

❖ England and Wales: www.communities.gov.uk/ planningandbuilding/planningsystem/circulars

❖ Scotland: www.scotland.gov.uk/Topics/built-environment/planning

❖   Northern Ireland: www.planningni.gov.uk

A number of circulars have been subject to review and consultation and are likely to be superseded.

Contributed by Allen Gilham, allen.gilham@watts.co.uk

Heritage protection

Listed buildings, 'buildings of special architectural or historic interest', have long been recognised as a major asset in the built environment. The joint RICS, British Property Federation and English Heritage publication *Heritage Works* concluded, for example, that 'listed office buildings can be a sound financial investment'.

In a world increasingly concerned about reducing carbon emissions and protecting the environment, the 2002 study by the Investment Property Databank for English Heritage and the RICS Foundation concluded that 'the creative new use of historic buildings can bring a return on investment as good as any other type of building and is certainly the best form of "green" development'.

This very much connects with the emphasis in *Planning Policy Statement 5: Planning for the Historic Environment* (PPS5) on keeping historic buildings in active use and urging planning authorities to be flexible and imaginative in their approach to achieve the right balance between protecting the building's special architectural and historic interest and adapting it for different uses.

PPS5 and the accompanying *Historic Environment Planning Practice Guide* (which 'explains how to apply the principles in the PPS') were published in March 2010 and are available at: www.communities.gov.uk/publications/planningandbuilding/pps5

Paragraph HE1.2 in PPS5 contains a key policy statement:

> 'Where proposals that are promoted for their contribution to mitigating climate change have a potentially negative effect on heritage assets, **local planning authorities should**, prior to determination, and ideally during pre-application discussions, **help the applicant to identify feasible solutions that deliver similar climate change mitigation but with less or no harm to the significance of the heritage asset and its setting.'** [Author's emphasis]

> © *Crown copyright material is reproduced under the Open Government Licence v1.0 for public sector information: www.nationalarchives.gov.uk/doc/open-government-licence/*

A key principle is that the successful conservation of our national heritage needs to be based on sustainable development.

The 2004 White Paper included comprehensive changes to the heritage protection process in England and Wales but the abandonment of a draft *Heritage Protection Bill* in 2008/09 means that the only results so far are PPS5 and the Practice Guide. There are no indications at present of any replacement Bill, the nearest being the current proposals for England alone in the draft National Planning Policy Framework referred to below.

The key proposals for implementation post the White Paper and within the abandoned draft *Heritage Protection Bill* for England and Wales were to have been:

❖   The new unified register of historic sites and buildings: which aimed to offer a holistic approach to the statutory protection of the historic environment through a single designation regime and a new definition of 'historic assets'.

❖   A reformed heritage consent regime: to be implemented by local authorities with assistance from English Heritage and CADW (the Welsh equivalent). It was understood that this process would be likely to distinguish between the following three categories:
  –   below ground (and water) archaeology and monumental structures;

- historic buildings and structures suited to adaptive reuse; and
- historic landscapes and seascapes.

❖ Voluntary heritage partnership agreements: these are intended to provide an alternative management regime for:
- large assets;
- complex entities that comprise many similar or several different assets;
- assets of similar type and single ownership and management but in dispersed locations; and
- assets better managed alongside other regimes.

❖ New statutory requirements relating to Historic Environment Records (HER): local authorities would be required to maintain or ensure that they have access to an HER that meets nationally defined standards.

At the time of going to print no proposals exist for the reintroduction for consideration of the draft *Heritage Protection Bill*. However, for England alone the government's proposals for the simplification of English planning control laws under their Localism Agenda includes in the draft National Planning Policy Framework (NPPF) (in the Historic Environment Section, Clauses 176-191) a simplified all-embracing set of processes and procedures for the conservation of the historic environment and heritage assets in England. The consultation period for these proposals ended on 17 October 2011. Such was the level of considered objections and observations received that it had already been announced in the Daily Telegraph of 12 October 2011 that 'Department for Communities and Local Government officials will agree new wording with English Heritage'.

The prime considered concerns centred around the slavish reliance in the NPPF proposals of the practices and procedures already in place through *PPS5: Planning for the Historic Environment* of March 2010. These convoluted practices and requirements, in particular the requirements by the Heritage Authorities for applicants for Listed Building Consent to provide 'Statements of Significance' in respect of the Listed Building [or Heritage Asset] that are proportionate to the works proposed, have yet to be satisfactorily resolved in that the Heritage Authorities have been requiring Statements of Significance that are far greater in detail than could be considered as 'proportionate'.

Most interestingly, the consultation document for the projected NPPF indicated that one of the 47 Planning Policy Statements to be cancelled by the NPPF is PPS5.

A further and greater matter of concern has been the loss since 2006 of some 25% of trained and experienced conservation and historic building officers across England. The prompt processing of Scheduled Monuments, Listed Buildings and Conservation Area Consents is now at risk in England. In the current economic climate resolution of this will be difficult. Since PPS5 and the NPPF require 'Statements of Significance' for heritage assets to be provided by applicants using 'appropriate expertise where necessary' a possible radical answer could be for private sector heritage advisers approved by English Heritage to certify that the projected works are such as may be Granted Listed Building or Scheduled Monument or Conservation Area Consents as appropriate.

More positive action has been taken by the Scottish Government via the *Historic Environment (Amendment) (Scotland) Act* 2011. It is being implemented in two phases:

❖ the first came into effect on 1 June 2011;
❖ the second came into effect on 1 December 2011.

This Act amended and replaced the three previous pieces of Scottish primary legislation, the *Historic Buildings and Monuments Act* 1953, the *Ancient Monuments and Archaeological Areas Act* 1979 and the *Planning (Listed Buildings and Conservation Areas) (Scotland) Act* 1997.

A great advantage in Scotland is that there is a considered minimum staffing level of conservation and historic building officers at local and central government level.

In Scotland, as in England and Wales, a key purpose is to support sustainable economic growth. The Historic Environment Advisory Council for Scotland (HEACS) announced, in its 2007 annual report, four core topics for the then legislative review:

❖ the infrastructure of the historic environment sector;

❖ the economic impact of the historic environment;

❖ a strategy for conservation of ecclesiastical heritage; and

❖ strategies for engaging the interest of young adults in the historic environment.

As is the case for town planning, heritage protection is now subject to national variations across the UK.

These national differences in ethics, practices and procedures would be subject to further variations if a new *Heritage Protection Bill* for England and Wales ever sees the light of day and/or the historic environment provisions of the draft National Planning Policy Framework for England come to fruition.

However, a common primary aim of all the proposed/draft legislation is to create one or more forms of unified registers of historic assets warranting protection with a detailed explanation of what is important about them, why they merit protection and a detailed site map showing the exact extent of the designated site in the register. The resources available to all the controlling authorities in England (especially), Scotland and Wales are such that many years will pass before this aim will be achieved.

The Scottish and Northern Irish authorities have indicated that they are not following directly any of the previously proposed English and Welsh alterations to heritage protection laws and procedures.

The first step therefore in considering any proposals or works dealing with any UK heritage property is to establish in which jurisdiction the property is located.

To complicate matters further administrative and procedural variations exist if the property is situated in one of the semi-autonomous offshore islands of the UK – the Channel Islands of Jersey, Guernsey, Alderney and Sark, and the Isle of Man.

The present basis for heritage protection within the constituent parts of the UK is the product of a gradual recognition from the late 19th century that cultural heritage properties should be protected, preserved, conserved, restored and cared for, so as to benefit the population as a whole.

The present terms used in UK heritage protection legislation (although the term 'heritage assets' is also coming into vogue) are:

❖ Scheduled Ancient Monument;

❖ listed historic building;

❖ conservation area;

❖ parks and gardens on the Non-Statutory Register or Inventory (Scotland); and

❖ historic battlefields on the Non-Statutory Register.

All derive from the various heritage protection laws enacted from 1882–2007.

Scheduled Ancient Monuments

Scheduled Ancient Monuments derive from the *Ancient Monuments Protection Act* 1882, with an incorporated schedule of 69 unoccupied prehistoric Ancient Monuments, such as Stonehenge.

Present protection, which is UK wide, is under the *Ancient Monuments and Archaeological Areas Act* 1979. This requires Scheduled Monument Consent to be obtained from the relevant Secretary of State for any works proposed to the 27,000 plus scheduled monuments now contained on the National Schedules of Ancient Monuments.

Listed buildings

Listed buildings derive from the *Town and Country Planning Act* 1947, which came into force on 1 July 1948 and incorporated lists of historic buildings, the preservation of which was considered important for the cultural heritage of the UK. The original list incorporated previous lists, from circa 1939–1940, of buildings which were considered so important that they should be reconstructed in facsimile in the event of damage or destruction during the Second World War. Present protection for each constituent is under the following acts:

- ❖ **England and Wales**: the *Planning (Listed Buildings and Conservation Areas) Act* 1990.

- ❖ **Scotland**: the *Heritage Environment (Amendment) (Scotland) Act* 2011.

- ❖ **Northern Ireland**: the *Planning (Northern Ireland) Order* 1991.

- ❖ **Channel Islands**: the various Acts of the States, including the *Planning and Building (Jersey) Law* 2002, the *Ancient Monuments and Protected Buildings (Guernsey) Law* 1967 and the *Building and Development Control (Alderney) Law* 2002.

- ❖ **Isle of Man**: the *Manx Government Heritage Protection Laws*, in which the term 'Registered' building replaces 'Listed Historic' building.

The various Acts require that listed building or equivalent consent has to be obtained from the local planning authority (in England, Wales, Scotland, the Channel Islands and the Isle of Man) or the planning service of the Department of the Environment of Northern Ireland Environmental and Heritage Service (in Northern Ireland) for any works that, when considered, would 'affect the special architectural or historic interest of the listed or registered building'. This can include works and development proposals nearby which could affect the setting of the listed or registered building.

Categories of listed buildings in the UK

	England and Wales	Northern Ireland	Scotland
Buildings of exceptional interest (about 2% of listed buildings).	Grade I	Grade A	Grade A
Particularly important buildings of more than special interest (about 4% of listed buildings).	Grade II*	Grade B+	Grade B
Buildings of special interest which warrant every effort being made to preserve them. In Northern Ireland Grades B1 and B2 are buildings of local importance or good examples of some period or style.	Grade II	Grades B1 and B2	Grade C(S)

Government statistics are not totally accurate or comprehensive since an entry in the list or register can include more than one building but the total numbers of listed and registered buildings in the UK are estimated to be as follows:

- ❖ **England**: c500,000+ buildings on some 370,000 sites;
- ❖ **Wales**: c30,000+ buildings;
- ❖ **Scotland**: c47,000+ buildings;
- ❖ **Northern Ireland**: c1,500 buildings;

- ❖ **Channel Islands**: c450 buildings;
- ❖ **Isle of Man**: c200 buildings.

Listing

The basic criteria for listing were previously set out in PPG15 (modified for England by Circular 01/07) and 'spot listing' will still be considered for individual buildings overlooked or under threat, by reference of details by any member of the public to English Heritage, Historic Scotland, Welsh Heritage (CADW), and the Northern Ireland Environment and Heritage Service. The list reviews were to concentrate on finding the best examples of types and periods of buildings under-represented in the current lists. Since the cancellation of PPG15, the following references are the most applicable:

- ❖ The Department for Culture Media and Sport has a most useful brief *Principles of Selection for Listing Buildings* of March 2010 available at: www.culture.gov.uk/images/publications/ Principles_Selection_Listing.pdf
- ❖ English Heritage has a series of 20 themed selection criteria for scheduling heritage assets available at: www.english-heritage.org.uk/caring/listing/criteria-for-protection/ selection-guidelines
- ❖ Historic Scotland has a simple and helpful statement at: www.historic-scotland.gov.uk/index/heritage/ historicandlistedbuildings.htm
- ❖ CADW gives similar useful guidance for Wales at: http://cadw.wales.gov.uk/docs/cadw/publications/ What_Is_Listing_EN.pdf
- ❖ The Environment and Heritage Service of Northern Ireland has useful guidance at: www.ni-environment.gov.uk/built-home/protection.htm

What is a listed building?

A listed building is any structure or erection, and any part of a building including any object or structure within the curtilage, that forms part of the land and did so before 1 July 1948. There are of course 'Modern Movement' listed buildings that postdate 1948.

Material change of use

It is accepted that new uses for old buildings, the 'adaptive reuse of historic buildings', may often be the key to their conservation. In some instances, it may be appropriate that controls should be relaxed where this would enable historic buildings to be given a new lease of life.

The best use for a historic building is obviously the use for which it was designed and, wherever possible, the original use should continue.

Works for which listed building consent is necessary

Demolition of a listed building, or its alteration or extension in any manner that would affect its special architectural or historic interest, requires consent. Note that the setting of a historic building is considered of great importance and an essential feature of its interest and character. Consent is not normally required for works of repair that are on the basis of like-for-like materials and exact matching original details. However, this is a grey area.

Listed building consent for works already executed

Listed building consent may be sought even though the works have already been completed. If consent is granted this is not retrospective; the works are authorised only from the date of consent.

Conservation areas

Conservation areas derive from the *Civic Amenities Act* 1967 which introduced the concept of protecting areas as opposed to individual buildings or monuments. Present legislation covering these matters are the 1990–1997 Acts referred to under listed buildings above.

The relevant local planning authority designates 'an area of special architectural or historic interest the character or appearance of which it is desirable to preserve or enhance'.

The various Acts then require that an application be made to the local planning authority for conservation area consent for the complete demolition (note: **not** the partial demolition) of any unlisted or unregistered building in the conservation area.

When exercising its general planning functions, the local planning authority is under a duty to pay special attention to the desirability of the preservation and enhancement of the character or appearance of the conservation area.

In addition to permitted development rights removed by virtue of the designation of the conservation area, the planning authority may also remove further specific otherwise permitted development rights regarding buildings in the conservation area.

Such rights are removed by what is termed an 'Article 4 Direction' and can, for instance, then require owners of properties within the conservation area to repaint external woodwork to windows and doors of their properties in accordance with exact paint colours decreed by the planning authority.

Trees in conservation areas are also accorded limited protection against removal or works to them without prior notice to the planning authority.

No completely reliable statistics exist as to the total number of conservation areas across the whole of the UK. Best estimates appear to be in the order of between 10,600 and 11,000 conservation areas, with no records at all of the total number of buildings in these areas. Some buildings in conservation areas will be listed or registered buildings. There may also be Scheduled Ancient Monuments, which may be above-ground structures, underground structures or archaeological sites.

Non-statutory registers and inventories of historic parks and gardens, and battlefield sites

The inclusion of such a site on one of the registers or inventories does not accord any specific further protection under heritage protection legislation. The various national heritage protection authorities have indicated by advice to local planning authorities that should proposals for development or works be made as applications under the *Town and Country Planning Acts* then the entry of a site on such a register or inventory is a 'material consideration' when the authority considers the application for the site or where the application would affect the setting of the site.

Obtaining approvals, permissions and consents for works to heritage sites

Establishing the type of current heritage protection

Establishing the type of current heritage protection is a key first step. Consult the local planning authority (district, borough, burgh, city or county borough council) for information on the status of the site in question. The information that they hold can be variable, although in many cases it will be very helpful.

Where possible, speak with the local planning authority's conservation officer for initial verification and information. (Some authorities do not employ such a person or may just rely on advice from private firms contracted to provide advice when heritage protection applications are being considered.)

Online information is also available from national heritage agency websites:

- ❖ English Heritage: www.english-heritage.org.uk and www.imagesofengland.org.uk
- ❖ CADW (Welsh Heritage): www.cadw.wales.gov.uk
- ❖ Historic Scotland: www.historic-scotland.gov.uk
- ❖ Northern Ireland Heritage: www.ni-environment.gov.uk
- ❖ Channel Islands: www.jerseyheritagetrust.org; www.gov.je (Jersey); www.heritageguernsey.com; www.gov.gg (Guernsey); www.alderney.gov.gg
- ❖ Isle of Man: www.gov.im/dlge

If the property under consideration is a functioning Christian church of one of the established UK denominations, then the church authorities have degrees of exemption from the heritage protection legislation described above. The relevant church authorities will provide details of the procedures to be followed. Further useful guidance can also be found by consulting articles on www.buildingconservation.com

Applying for present forms of consent

Any application for Scheduled Monument, listed or registered building or conservation area consent requires the completion of the appropriate form:

- ❖ Application forms for Scheduled Monument consent are available from the relevant national heritage authorities listed above.
- ❖ Application forms for listed or registered building and conservation area consent are available from the relevant local planning authority.

The application packs give full details of the plans and documents that have to accompany the applications. The documentation should show the *present* condition, layout and use of the building and the *proposed* layout, changes and use. Clarity and depth of information will improve the prospect of success.

Formulating a proposal

The following are points to consider when preparing a proposal:

- ❖ The architectural and building construction history of the existing structure and building should guide you – not your ego or desire to impose your views on the property. You hold the building and structure in trust for future generations – do not seek to mutilate it; let the property guide you.
- ❖ Maximise the retention and repair of original historic fabric wherever possible rather than replacing with replicas, however good they might be.
- ❖ Any works must respect the style, design, detailing, materials, forms of construction, layout and, wherever possible, uses and plan forms of the original heritage properties and structures. Most heritage buildings and sites are of course an amalgam of many ages so there is real opportunity to mix and match into the various ages of the property.
- ❖ Changes of use should only be considered if the original use is now unsustainable or history has removed that possible use, e.g. monasteries are now schools; grand country houses are now hotels.

❖ The overriding aim is to secure the future life of the property while maintaining the architecture of the property for all to see.

❖ If necessity dictates doing something that crosses over a part of the architecture or plan form, for example, subdividing a room, you should seek to retain, for example, the original decorative room cornice and ensure the partition walls do not cut into it. One day someone may want to return the room to its original form. This is called 'reversibility'.

For example, long-abandoned, in-situ, folding, internal, timber, Georgian shutters that are 200 years old can be put back into use economically to help reduce heating energy loss and thereby reduce carbon emissions. 'Reversibility' = 'sustainability'.

❖ Use only materials that match the original materials of construction. Far too much damage has been caused to heritage properties and structures by imposing, for example, modern 'waterproofing' and 'water resistant' coatings to historic external fabric, forgetting that water will always be absorbed through micro-cracks but then cannot escape, thus condemning the structure to a slow death by decay and rot.

Processing the application

Scheduled Monument applications will be processed jointly by the national heritage authorities and the local planning authority, as will applications in respect of listed and registered buildings of Grades I and II* (Grades A and B respectively in Scotland).

Local planning authorities decide applications in respect of listed and registered buildings of Grade II (Grade C in Scotland) and conservation area consents.

In any event, it will take at least eight to ten weeks for applications to be processed. Complex and contentious applications may require longer.

At the time of going to print no fees are payable for Scheduled Monument, listed and registered building and conservation area consents.

Tree preservation and protection legislation

The importance of trees to the quality of life in towns and countryside was first recognised in the *Town and Country Planning Act* 1947 and the system and process of Tree Preservation Orders has followed through legislation across the constituent countries of the UK to this day.

A Tree Preservation Order (TPO) is an order made by the local planning authority in respect of trees or woodlands. The principal effect is to prohibit the cutting down, uprooting, topping, lopping, wilful damage or wilful destruction of trees without the authority's consent. Separately, in the case of trees in conservation areas, notice must be served on the planning authority before any such work can be undertaken. The authority then has six weeks to either give consent or serve a TPO on the tree(s) in question.

A detailed *Law and Good Practice Guide* (March 2000) can be found at: www.communities.gov.uk/publications/planningandbuilding/tposguide

While this guide is for England and Wales, the principles and practices are equally applicable elsewhere.

Contributed by Allen Gilham, allen.gilham@watts.co.uk

Planning appeals

One can appeal against:

❖ refusal of planning permission;

❖ conditions attached to a planning permission; and

❖ failure by the planning authority to determine an application within the statutory time period – generally 8 weeks, 13 weeks for major applications, and 16 weeks in the case of development proposals that are subject to Environmental Impact Assessment.

Appeals against a refusal or conditions must be made within six months of the decision date.

Appeal against the failure of the authority to determine an application within the statutory time period must be lodged within six months of the date when the decision was due.

Since April 2009, a new expedited appeals process has been introduced for appeals involving what are termed 'householder developments':

❖ developments involving the extension or alteration to an existing dwellinghouse or buildings or structures erected within the curtilage where they are to be used for purposes incidental to the enjoyment of the dwellinghouse.

The time period for lodging a householder appeal is 12 weeks. Appeals generally proceed on the basis that the local planning authority and appellant each have one opportunity to make their case with no opportunity to comment on the other party's case. Third parties have no further opportunity to comment on appeal.

Appeals are determined by independent inspectors employed by the Planning Inspectorate.

There are three appeals procedures:

❖ written representations by the exchange of written submissions;

❖ informal hearings which permit oral presentation of evidence; and

❖ public inquiries which require full written evidence to be submitted and presented in the hearing – this evidence is then subjected to cross examination.

With effect from April 2009, the Secretary of State has the right to determine how an appeal should proceed. This determination is made within seven days of receipt of a valid appeal.

The criteria adopted by the Secretary of State in determining the appeal method are available at www.planning-inspectorate.gov.uk

Guidance on the appeal process is provided in the Planning Inspectorate guidance note *Planning appeals and called-in planning applications* (PINS 01/2009).

❖ Each party to the appeal is expected to bear its own costs, but an opportunity to apply for an award of costs exists for all appeals.

❖ Costs awards are normally only considered where one party has behaved unreasonably.

❖ Circular 03/2009 contains guidance on the situations where an award of costs may be justified.

❖ Also see *Costs awards in planning appeals (England): A guide for appellants*, July 2009, available at www.communities.gov.uk

❖ An award of costs can be sought at all stages in the appeal.

The majority of appeals are decided by inspectors. Only specific types of cases are decided by the Secretary of State for Communities and Local Government. These relate to major or controversial development proposals, including:

❖ residential developments of over 150 units or sites of over 5 hectares which would significantly impact the government's housing objectives;

❖ town centre uses which exceed 9,000m² at edge-of-centre or out-of-centre locations;

❖ significant developments in the green belt.

Contributed by Allen Gilham, allen.gilham@watts.co.uk

Permitted development, use classes and the Development Management Procedure Order 2010

Town and country planning in the UK is generally dealt with through development control legislation. Development is defined as:

❖ the carrying out of building, engineering, mining or other operations in, on, over or under land; or

❖ the making of any material change in the use of any buildings or other land.

Section 55 of the *Town and Country Planning Act* 1990 details exceptions for which you do not require planning permission. These include:

❖ works carried out internally to a building to maintain, improve or alter a building;

❖ a change of use to agriculture (but note, a change of use from agriculture to another use will require planning permission);

❖ the use of buildings or other land within the curtilage of a dwellinghouse for a purpose that is incidental to its enjoyment.

Beyond these matters are works for which blanket planning permission is granted by virtue of the provisions of the *Town and Country Planning (General Permitted Development) Order* 1995 as modified by one or more of the currently 15 amending Orders from 1996 to 2010. The details of these can all be accessed at www.planningportal.gov.uk/permission/responsibilities/planningpermission/permitted and they do need to be carefully consulted.

On 1 October 2010 a consolidated version of the *Town and Country Planning (General Development Procedure) Order* 1995 (the GDPO), entitled the *Town and Country Planning (Development Management Procedure) (England) Order* 2010 (the DMPO) came into force.

The following list indicates where in the DMPO you will find the consolidated provisions. Two previous provisions were omitted, i.e. Article 4D *Access Statements: Wales* and Article 5A *Declaration to accompany application to a local planning authority in Wales for planning permission for certain telecommunications developments*.

❖ Article 1, Citation, commencement and application

❖ Article 2, Interpretation

❖ Article 3, Development to include certain internal operations

❖ Article 4, Applications for outline planning permission

❖ Article 5, Applications for approval of reserved matters

❖ Article 6, Applications for planning permission

❖ Article 7, Applications in respect of Crown land

❖ Article 8, Design and access statements

❖ Article 9, Applications for non-material changes to planning permission

❖ Article 10, General provisions relating to applications

❖ Article 11, Notice of applications for planning permission

❖ Article 12, Certificates in relation to notice of applications for planning permission

❖ Article 13, Publicity for applications for planning permission

❖ Article 14, Notice of reference of applications to the Secretary of State

- ❖ Article 15, Major infrastructure projects: economic impact report
- ❖ Article 16, Consultations before the grant of permission
- ❖ Article 17, Consultations before the grant of planning permission: urgent Crown development
- ❖ Article 18, Consultations before the grant of planning permission pursuant to section 73 or the grant of a replacement planning permission subject to a new time limit
- ❖ Article 19, Consultation with county planning authority
- ❖ Article 20, Duty to respond to consultation
- ❖ Article 21, Duty to respond to consultation: annual reports
- ❖ Article 22, Applications relating to county matters
- ❖ Article 23, Representations by parish council before determination of application
- ❖ Article 24, Notification of mineral applications
- ❖ Article 25, Directions by the Secretary of State
- ❖ Article 26, Development affecting certain existing and proposed highways
- ❖ Article 27, Development not in accordance with the development plan
- ❖ Article 28, Representations to be taken into account
- ❖ Article 29, Time periods for decision
- ❖ Article 30, Applications made under planning condition
- ❖ Article 31, Written notice of decision or determination relating to a planning application
- ❖ Article 32, Notice of appeal
- ❖ Article 33, Appeals
- ❖ Article 34, Local development orders
- ❖ Article 35, Certificate of lawful use or development
- ❖ Article 36, Register of applications
- ❖ Article 37, Register of local development orders
- ❖ Article 38, Register of enforcement and stop notices
- ❖ Article 39, Directions
- ❖ Article 40, Withdrawal of consent to use of electronic communications
- ❖ Article 41, Revocations, transitional provisions and savings
- ❖ Schedule 1, Letter to be sent to applicant on receipt of application
- ❖ Schedule 2, Notices under articles 11 and 32
- ❖ Schedule 3, Publicity for applications for planning permission
- ❖ Schedule 4, Major infrastructure projects: economic impact report
- ❖ Schedule 5, Consultations before the grant of permission
- ❖ Schedule 6, Notification where planning permission refused or granted subject to conditions
- ❖ Schedule 7 [new], Notices under article 34
- ❖ Schedule 8, Certificate of lawful use or development
- ❖ Schedule 9, Statutory instruments revoked in so far as they apply to England

Town and Country Planning (Development Management Procedure) (England) Order 2010

The key provisions of the *Town and Country Planning (Development Management Procedure) (England) Order* 2010 (the DMPO) brought in on 1 October 2010 are:

❖ a complete consolidation of all matters contained within the GPDO 1995 and all 15 amendments from 1995 to 2010;

❖ the new Article 18 procedure which relates to outline planning permissions that have been implemented in phases. This allows a local planning authority to grant a replacement outline planning permission subject to a new time limit where:

– the original development permitted was clearly intended, at the time of the initial decision, to be implemented in phases; and

– one or more of those phases has commenced.

Town and Country Planning (General Permitted Development) Order 1995 (as amended)

This Order (the GPDO) grants permission for certain defined classes of development or use of land:

❖ a wide range of small extensions or alterations to dwellings, the best guidance to these is contained in the DCLG publication *Permitted development for householders* available online at www.planningportal.gov.uk/uploads/100806_PDforhouseholders_TechnicalGuidance.pdf. These permitted rights were extended in 2008 to encompass domestic solar and microgeneration equipment and extensions to and development within the curtilage of a dwelling house that are incidental to the enjoyment of the dwelling; and

❖ there are numerous other minor permitted developments – always consult the Order.

Permitted developments granted under the GPDO can be withdrawn in a defined area under the terms of an article 4 direction made by the local planning authority or Secretary of State.

Town and Country Planning (Use Classes) Order 1987

Section 55 of the 1990 *Planning Act* provides that change of use of some buildings or land does not constitute development and is applicable where both the existing and proposed use fall within the same use class. Some changes of use between different use classes are also permitted development.

There are some uses which do not fall within any use class and these are referred to as *sui generis* uses.

The use classes have been subject to amendment and in the *Use Classes Amendment Order* 2005 the following changes were made:

❖ retail warehouse clubs and nightclubs are excluded from any use class;

❖ internet cafes are included within the A1 shops class;

❖ the former use class 'food and drink' is divided into three separate classes:
– restaurants and cafes;
– drinking establishments; and
– hot food takeaways.

One effect of these changes is that it is necessary to apply for planning permission to change from a restaurant or cafe to a drinking establishment such as a bar or pub or to a hot food takeaway.

The following list gives the use classes based on the *Town and Country Planning (Use Classes) Order* 1987 (SI 1987/764) and present subsequent amendments:

- ❖ **A1 Shops:** shops, retail warehouses, post offices, hairdressers, travel and ticket agencies, pet shops, showrooms, sandwich bars, domestic hire shops, undertakers, dry cleaners and funeral directors.

- ❖ **A2 Financial and professional services:** banks, building societies, professional and financial services, estate agencies, employment agencies and betting offices.

- ❖ **A3 Restaurants and cafes:** places where the primary purpose is the sale and consumption of food and light refreshments on the premises, e.g. restaurants, cafes, snack bars.

- ❖ **A4 Drinking establishments:** public houses, wine bars, etc. but not nightclubs.

- ❖ **A5 Hot food takeaways:** places where the primary purpose is the sale of hot food to take away.

- ❖ **B1 Business:** offices, research and development and light industry, appropriate in a residential area.

- ❖ **B2 General industrial:** covers a variety of industrial uses.

- ❖ **B3–B7 Special Industrial Groups:** see the Schedule to the *Use Classes Order* 1987.

- ❖ **B8 Storage or distribution:** includes open-air storage.

- ❖ **C1 Hotels:** hotels, boarding houses and guest houses where there is no care provided.

- ❖ **C2 Residential institutions:** residential care homes, nursing homes, hospitals, boarding schools, residential colleges and training centres.

- ❖ **C2A Secure residential institutions:** secure residential accommodation, e.g. prisons, detention centres, young offenders institutions, secure training centres, custody centres, short term holding centres, secure hospitals, secure local authority accommodation or military barracks.

- ❖ **C3 Dwellinghouses:** family houses or houses occupied by up to six people living as a single household including one where care is provided.

- ❖ **D1 Non-residential institutions:** clinics, health centres, crèches, day nurseries, day centres, schools, art galleries, libraries, museums, halls, places of worship, church halls, non-residential education and training centres, law courts.

- ❖ **D2 Assembly and leisure:** cinemas, music and concert halls, bingo and dance halls (but not nightclubs), skating rinks, swimming baths, gymnasiums and sports arenas (except motor sports or where firearms are in use).

- ❖ **Sui generis:** theatres, houses in multiple paying occupation, hostels providing no significant care, scrap yards, filling stations, shops selling and/or displaying motor vehicles, retail warehouse clubs, nightclubs, casinos, amusement centres, launderettes, taxi businesses.

Contributed by Allen Gilham, allen.gilham@watts.co.uk

Environmental impact assessments

Environmental impact assessment (EIA) is the process for identifying the environmental impact of proposed developments. The legal requirements derive from the *Town and Country Planning (Environmental Impact Assessment)*

Regulations 1999 as amended by the *Town and Country Planning (Environmental Impact Assessment) (England and Wales) (Amendment) Regulations* 2006 and 2007.

The requirement for an EIA to be undertaken is mandatory for certain development projects. These projects are referred to as 'Schedule 1' developments and are defined in the Regulations. For other developments, which are defined in the Regulations and referred to as 'Schedule 2' developments, the decision as to whether an Environmental Statement is required to support the planning application is contingent on:

❖ whether any part of the development is located within a defined sensitive area;

❖ whether the development exceeds an applicable development threshold or criterion; and

❖ whether the development is likely to have significant environmental effects.

A procedure is set out in the Regulations which allows the need for an EIA to be subject to a screening opinion (regulation 5(1)) obtainable on application to the local planning authority. The decision of the local planning authority in response to the request for a screening opinion must be made within three weeks of the receipt of the request, although there is provision for the local planning authority to request an extension. There is further provision within the Regulations for an applicant who disagrees with the local planning authority's screening decision to 'appeal' to the Secretary of State.

The Regulations also provide for a 'scoping opinion' to be obtained from the local planning authority. This provides guidance on the content and extent of matters that the authority considers should be covered by the EIA.

Further guidance on the EIA process can be found in the following:

❖ *Environmental Impact Assessment: A guide to procedures* produced by the Office of the Deputy Prime Minister (ODPM) (now Department for Communities and Local Government (DCLG)), 2000;

❖ *Preparation of Environmental Statements for Planning Projects that Require Environmental Assessment: A good practice guide* produced by the Department of the Environment, 1995; and

❖ *Evaluation of Environmental Information for Planning Projects: A good practice guide* produced by the Department of the Environment, 1994.

European Community Directives, UK case law and European Court of Justice judgments have also aided the interpretation of the EIA Regulations. To clarify the requirements, the then ODPM (now Department for Communities and Local Government (DCLG)) issued a *Note on Environmental Impact Assessment Directive for Local Planning Authorities* in April 2004 and this provides a further useful guidance note on the process. The DCLG also issued a letter to all local planning authorities in June 2006 providing further guidance in response to recent European Court of Justice (ECJ) judgments. The most recent development was the amendment to the *Town and Country Planning Regulations* in 2008, which now states that EIA can be required before approval of reserved matters where development consent comprises a multi-stage process (e.g. outline planning applications). The most important implication of the amendment is that it is now possible to allow for EIA to be undertaken at a later stage in a multi-stage development consent process if it has not been possible for it to have been carried out or completed at the initial stage.

A revised Circular and Practice Guide (*Amended Circular on Environmental Impact Assessment*) replacing Circular 02/99 was published in 2006 for consultation purposes and provides an updated policy and practice context for EIAs reflecting the changes brought about by UK and European case law.

Contributed by Janette Stevens, janette.stevens@watts.co.uk

Community planning gain

Section 106 agreements

Section 106 of the *Town and Country Planning Act* 1990 allows local planning authorities (LPAs) to enter into legally-binding agreements with property or land developers over issues related to planning applications. This type of agreement/obligation is usually known as a 'Section 106 agreement'.

Guidance on both the scope and the use of this form of agreement is given in Circular 05/2005: *Planning Obligations*.

Key to their use is that the matters to be the subject of a Section 106 agreement must be:

❖ relevant to planning;

❖ necessary to make the proposed development acceptable in planning terms;

❖ directly related to the proposed development;

❖ fairly and reasonably related in scale and kind to the proposed development; and

❖ reasonable in all other respects.

Section 106 agreements can cover almost any related issue and may include monies being paid to the LPA to carry out specific works. Examples of such agreements could include:

❖ a developer transferring ownership of woodland area to an LPA along with a sum to cover future maintenance;

❖ a local authority restricting future development of a portion of land (or permitting only specified operations to be carried out on it, such as amenity use);

❖ a developer planting an agreed number of trees and maintaining them for a certain period of time;

❖ a developer creating a nature reserve or similar amenity;

❖ a local authority executing a road improvement scheme associated with the development or property; and

❖ a local authority using the monies for repairs to historic buildings associated with the development.

Section 106 agreements can be used as a mechanism for placing restrictions on developers, often requiring them to minimise the impact on the local community and to carry out works which will provide community benefits.

The Section 106 agreement must specify exactly the works/land transfer/monies to be paid over **and** exactly the works to be funded by the monies.

An LPA cannot just ask for monies for unspecified works in exchange for a Section 106 agreement – this would be beyond its scope.

Contributed by Allen Gilham, allen.gilham@watts.co.uk

Occupier obligations

Legislation

Health and safety at work

In the following sections the term 'surveyors' has been used generically; the regulations apply to **all** persons at work, irrespective of their profession or trade.

Essential legal duties

The *Health and Safety at Work etc. Act* 1974 requires all surveyors to ensure, so far as is reasonably practicable, the health and safety of themselves and any other people who may be affected by their work.

In essence, the places where surveyors work must be safe and working practices must be clearly defined, organised, and followed to avoid danger. This requires safety training and the distribution of relevant information, followed up by diligent and regular supervision.

These duties extend to anyone who uses surveyors' professional services.

Those who lease part of their premises to other businesses also may be responsible for them with regard to safety matters.

In addition, all working people whether employees, managers, partners or directors (self-employed or not) must behave in a way that does not endanger themselves or others.

Health and safety policy statement

Firms that employ five or more people is obliged by the Act to draw up a health and safety policy statement, which should be kept up to date, with any significant revisions being notified to employees.

The Health and Safety Executive (HSE) in *Writing your health and safety policy statement: how to prepare a safety statement for smaller businesses* describes what the document should say and gives a useful pro forma.

It is suggested that employees, especially when taking a new job, should satisfy themselves that they have seen and understood the company's policy statement and have been made familiar with safe working practices. If they consider that the *Health and Safety at Work Act* is not being followed, they ought to say so, and if necessary ask advice from their local HSE office (listed in the telephone directory).

Practical procedures

Surveyors should identify the hazards they may encounter in practice, carry out a risk assessment and plan accordingly. The way they proceed will depend upon the working environment: when surveying old and derelict buildings, for example, there may be holes in floors, parts of the structure may be unstable or there may be health hazards. Particular care should be taken to protect against personal attack.

The Control of Substances Hazardous to Health Regulations 2002 (as amended)

The purpose of the *Control of Substances Hazardous to Health Regulations* 2002 (as amended in 2004) is to safeguard the health of people using or coming into contact with substances that are hazardous to health.

Substances are classified as being very toxic/toxic, harmful, corrosive or irritant. Under these Regulations employers are required to evaluate the risk of all products used that may be harmful to the health of their employees and take appropriate measures to prevent or control exposure.

The 'Six Pack' Regulations

The original six sets of Regulations were introduced in 1993. They were wide-ranging and, with some minor exceptions, apply to all places of work, replacing and consolidating various individual acts or regulations applicable to individual industries or sectors of industry, such as the *Factories Act*, the *Offices, Shops and Railway Premises Act*, and the *Construction Regulations*.

Provision and Use of Work Equipment Regulations 1998

These apply to all workplaces. Basically, all existing and new work equipment, which includes everything hired or purchased second hand, must comply with the Regulations.

Every employer must ensure that all work equipment is so constructed or adapted as to be suitable for the purpose for which it is used or provided. They identify specific hazards that the employer must prevent or adequately control.

Manual Handling Operations Regulations 1992

These require the employer to try to avoid the need for employees to undertake any manual handling operations at work that involve a risk of their being injured. Where this is not reasonably practicable the risk must be assessed and suitable provision made, including equipment, instruction and training for safe manual handling.

Management of Health and Safety at Work Regulations 1999

These Regulations are of a wide-ranging general nature and overlap with many others. They require the employer to carry out an assessment of the risks of the hazards to which his or her employees are exposed at work or to others arising from or in connection with this work. The employer must instigate appropriate protective or preventive measures, reviewing and amending these as necessary.

The employer must appoint a 'competent person' to provide assistance in respect of these duties. Emergency procedures must be put in force to deal with any serious and imminent danger. Employees must be informed of these measures and suitably trained where required. They are obliged to comply with these instructions and warn of any situation considered to be a serious and immediate danger to health and safety.

Personal Protective Equipment at Work Regulations 1992

Under these Regulations the employer has a duty to provide and maintain suitable personal protective equipment, including adequate instruction and training on its correct use when risks to health and safety cannot be avoided by other means. Employees have a duty to make full and proper use of such equipment provided, and to report any loss or obvious defects.

Display Screen Equipment Regulations 1992

The need for the Regulations is primarily the evidence of repetitive strain injury that is reported by keyboard users, the amount of time lost due to other causes of sickness among users and, of course, the European Directive.

These Regulations target full-time users of visual display units, mainly in the banking, insurance and data processing sectors but, given that most medium and larger companies will have in their offices a number of full-time or habitual users, then these Regulations will apply. They will also apply in the office facility of a construction site, if any persons are habitual users of visual display units.

Workplace (Health, Safety and Welfare) Regulations 1992

These apply to all workplaces. The Regulations set out the minimum requirements in respect of the provision and maintenance of the environmental and working conditions of employees. In addition, they impose particular safety requirements on forms of construction or circumstances which are considered to be high risk. The

Workplace Regulations do **not** apply to construction sites (see *The Construction (Design and Management) Regulations 2007* on page 188).

The following issues are addressed:

- ❖ ventilation;
- ❖ temperature;
- ❖ lighting (see below);
- ❖ cleanliness and waste materials;
- ❖ room dimensions and space;
- ❖ maintenance of the workplace;
- ❖ floors and traffic routes;
- ❖ ('glazing') transparent or translucent doors, gates, walls and windows – protection against breakage (see page 157);
- ❖ windows, doors and gates – cleaning and safety;
- ❖ escalators and moving walkways;
- ❖ sanitary conveniences and washing facilities (see page 158);
- ❖ drinking water;
- ❖ accommodation for work clothing and changing facilities;
- ❖ facilities for rest and eating facilities;
- ❖ working at height (see page 159).

Of the above list, four merit further detailed explanation:

- ❖ lighting;
- ❖ glazing;
- ❖ sanitary facilities; and
- ❖ working at height

Lighting

Regulations

The key provisions relating to lighting can be found in the following Regulations:

- ❖ *Workplace (Health, Safety and Welfare) Regulations* 1992:
  - – Lighting in workplaces should be suitable and sufficient to enable people to work and move about safely. If necessary, local lighting should be provided, and at places of particular risk, such as crossing points of traffic routes.
  - – Lighting shall, so far as is reasonably practicable, be by natural light.
  - – Lighting and light fittings should not create a hazard.
  - – Automatic emergency lighting, powered by an independent source, should be provided where sudden loss of light would create a risk.

- ❖ *Health and Safety (Display Screen Equipment) Regulations* 1992:
  - – Satisfactory lighting and appropriate contrast between screen and background to suit type of work and visual requirements of the operator.

- ❖ *Provision and Use of Work Equipment Regulations* 1992:
  - – Again, these Regulations require lighting to be both suitable and sufficient.

❖ **Building Regulations, Part L:**
  – Applies to all new non-domestic buildings over 100m² and certain buildings undergoing a change of use. Excludes exterior lighting.
  – Includes requirements for energy-efficient lighting, lamps and luminaires and controls. Aims to encourage maximum use of daylight and avoid unnecessary lighting when spaces are unoccupied.

Guidance

The Chartered Institution of Building Services Engineers (CIBSE) and the Society of Light and Lighting (SLL) (see www.cibse.org for both) have published a number of useful and authoritative guides:

❖ Guidance Note (GN2:1993) *Healthy Workplaces – on compliance with the Workplace Regulations*;

❖ *Code for Interior Lighting* generally, and other task-specific guides, e.g. LG1: *Industrial Environment*;

❖ LG3: *Areas for visual display terminals*; and

❖ TM12: *Emergency Lighting*.

ISO 9241 *Ergonomic requirements for office work with visual display terminals (VDTs)*.

BS 5266: covers minimum levels and for emergency lighting.

The absolute minimum lighting level for particular tasks is set out in HS(G)38 *Lighting at Work* published by the Health and Safety Executive (HSE).

Other considerations

Other considerations to take into account in relation to lighting would include:

❖ safe access for cleaning and maintenance;

❖ temperature of fitting(s);

❖ reflection and glare;

❖ ease of control;

❖ suitability for environment, including IP rating; and

❖ colour rendering properties of light source.

Glazing

Regulations

The *Workplace (Health, Safety and Welfare) Regulations* 1992, in regulation 14, require that glazed doors (and gates) be fitted with safety materials where any part of the glazing is below shoulder height. This requirement applies to glazing in the panels at the sides of the doors (and gates) because these areas are often struck or pushed when mistaken for part of the door.

The requirements also apply to windows, walls and partitions where there is glazing below waist height.

In situations where the width of the glass panel exceeds 250mm then safety materials must be used. Safety materials include:

❖ polycarbonates, glass blocks or other materials that are inherently robust; or

❖ glass that will break safely (i.e. shatters without a chance of sharp edges) or ordinary annealed glass that is of sufficient thickness relative to its area, as outlined in the following table.

Nominal thickness	Maximum size
8mm	1100 x 1100mm
10mm	2250 x 2250mm
12mm	3000 x 4500mm
15mm	Any size

Therefore, just because annealed glass exists, it does not follow that additional protection is required.

Glazing should always comply with British Standard 6262: Part 4: 2005 *Glazing for Building: Code of practice for safety related to human impact.*

In circumstances where glazing does not comply, it will be necessary to replace it with safety materials or to provide some physical protection that will ensure that it meets the impact performance levels required by BS 6262, Part 4: 2005.

A cheaper alternative would be to apply safety film to achieve the BS 6262 standard. Manufacturers of film should be consulted to ensure an appropriate grade of material for glass size.

All glass should be suitably marked as being of a safety standard. Where glass is protected by film, labelling should identify this.

Identification

Laminated and toughened glass can be detected using proprietary glass testing kits, for example, the Merlin glass laser and toughened glass detector: www.merlinlazer.com/Glass-Testing-Measurement

Note: ordinary Georgian wired glass does not comply with safety standards, but Georgian wired safety glass does.

Provision of sanitary facilities

Regulations

The *Workplace (Health, Safety and Welfare) Regulations* 1992 require that sanitary provision shall be suitable and sufficient for the numbers and types of workers employed.

British Standard 6465: Part 1: 1994

British Standard 6465: Part 1: 1994 sets out the minimum requirements.

It contains numerous tables illustrating the number and types of sanitary appliances required for a variety of different circumstances, depending on:

❖ the number of workers and, where relevant, customers;

❖ the ratio of males to females; and

❖ the different primary uses of the building in question.

The types of building include offices, shops, factories, restaurants, cafes, canteens and fast-food outlets, swimming pools, stadia, public houses, licensed bars, other places of public entertainment and non-domestic premises.

Comparison of requirements for 100 people evenly divided between the sexes (not including wheelchair users)								
Building type	Male			Female		Total		
	wc	urinal	whb	wc	whb	wc	urinal	whb
Workplaces	3	2	3	3	3	6	2	6
Workplaces (dirtier conditions)	3	2	3	3	5	6	2	8
Shops (customers) 1,000–2,000m²	1	1	1	2	2	3	1	3
Shops (customers) 2,000–4,000m²	1	2	2	4	4	5	2	6
Restaurants	1	1	2	2	2	3	1	4
Public houses, etc.	1	2	2	3	2	4	2	4

wc = water closet   whb = wash hand basin

The Equality Act 2010

The *Equality Act* 2010 received Royal Assent on 8 April 2010. The majority of its provisions came into force in October 2010. It may mean that other factors will also need to be considered, perhaps including the provision of unisex WCs to allow people not to disclose their physical gender.

Designing with transgender in mind may be relatively easily catered for in offices but in single sex accommodation in hospitals or educational establishments this could prove to be more difficult.

Working at height

Background

Falls from height are the most common cause of fatal injury and the second most common cause of major injury to employees in the workplace. Most falls are the result of poor management rather than equipment failure. Common examples include:

❖ failure to recognise a problem;

❖ failure to provide safe systems of work;

❖ failure to ensure that safe systems of work are followed;

❖ failure to provide adequate information, instruction, training or supervision;

❖ failure to provide safe plant or equipment; and

❖ failure to use appropriate equipment.

Regulations

The principles of good practice to prevent falls are contained within the *Work at Height Regulations* 2005. These Regulations came into operation on 6 April 2005 and apply to all work where there is a risk of a fall liable to cause personal injury, even if the fall is at or below ground level.

The Regulations place duties on employers, the self-employed and anyone who controls the work of others.

Employers must do all that is reasonably practicable to prevent falling by following a hierarchy for managing and selecting appropriate equipment:

❖ avoid work at height if possible;

❖ if unavoidable, use work equipment to prevent falls;

❖ where the risk of fall cannot be eliminated, use equipment or other measures to minimise the distance and consequences of any fall; and

❖ select collective measures to prevent falls (e.g. guardrails and working platforms) before measures which may only mitigate the distance and consequences of a fall (e.g. nets or airbags) or which may only provide personal protection from a fall (e.g. fall arrest lanyards).

Employees must report any safety hazards and properly use the equipment supplied to them.

Duty holders must ensure that:

❖ all work is properly planned and organised;

❖ work activities take account of weather conditions;

❖ persons involved are trained and competent;

❖ the place of work is safe;

❖ equipment is appropriately inspected; and

❖ risks arising from fragile surfaces and from falling objects are properly controlled.

Useful information

The Health and Safety Executive (HSE) has produced a number of free leaflets on falls from height that can be downloaded from their website at www.hse.gov.uk/falls. These include general advice, such as *Safe use of ladders and stepladders*, as well as the use of specific equipment such as *Safety in window cleaning using rope access techniques*.

Contributed by Paul Winstone, paul.winstone@watts.co.uk

The Regulatory Reform (Fire Safety) Order 2005

The *Regulatory Reform (Fire Safety) Order* 2005 (the RRFSO or the Fire Safety Order) came into force in England and Wales on 1 October 2006. Northern Ireland and Scotland have devolved responsibility for safety law (see subsections below).

The main effect of the Fire Safety Order was a move towards greater emphasis on fire prevention in all non-domestic premises, although it does also apply to the common parts of multi-tenanted residential accommodation, such as flats.

The RRFSO was brought in to simplify, rationalise and consolidate over 100 pieces of existing legislation in respect of fire safety. The aim was to reduce burdens on businesses caused by previous multiple overlapping fire safety regimes and responsibilities of enforcing authorities. Under the reform, fire certificates were abolished and ceased to have legal status. Instead, under the RRFSO, a 'responsible person' for each premises is required to carry out an assessment of fire risk and take reasonable steps to reduce or remove that risk. As with previous legislation, fire risk assessments need to be kept under review. While there is no separate formal validation process for higher risk premises, fire authorities will tend to base their inspection programmes on premises that they consider present the highest risk.

Multi-tenanted buildings

Where two or more responsible persons share or have duties in respect of premises, the RRFSO requires cooperation and coordination between the parties. For example, the landlord will generally be responsible for the common parts and the tenants responsible for their respective demised areas, with coordination between all of the parties concerned, ideally managed by the landlord.

Definition of 'responsible person'

Article 3 of the RRFSO defines 'responsible person' as:

'(a) in relation to a workplace, the employer, if the workplace is to any extent under his control;

(b) in relation to any premises not falling within paragraph (a)
   (i) the person who has control of the premises (as occupier or otherwise) in connection with the carrying on by him of a trade, business or other undertaking (for profit or not); or
   (ii) the owner, where the person in control of the premises does not have control in connection with the carrying on by that person of a trade, business or other undertaking.'

Fire safety duties

Under article 8 of the RRFSO, the 'responsible person' must:

'(a) take such general fire precautions as will ensure, so far as is reasonably practicable, the safety of any of his employees; and

(b) in relation to relevant persons who are not his employees, take such general fire precautions [as described below] as may reasonably be required in the circumstances of the case to ensure that the premises are safe.'

General fire precautions

The RRFSO cites, under article 4, the meaning of 'general fire precautions' as:

'(a) measures to reduce the risk of fire on the premises and the risk of the spread of fire on the premises;

(b) measures in relation to the means of escape from the premises;

(c) measures for securing that, at all material times, the means of escape can be safely and effectively used;

(d) measures in relation to the means for fighting fires on the premises;

(e) measures in relation to the means for detecting fire on the premises and giving warning in case of fire on the premises; and

(f) measures in relation to the arrangements for action to be taken in the event of fire on the premises, including –
   (i) measures relating to the instruction and training of employees; and
   (ii) measures to mitigate the effects of the fire.'

Risk assessment

The 'responsible person' is required to undertake a risk assessment, which will need to address, among other things, the following:

❖ assessed risks of young persons employed (i.e. under 18 years of age);

❖ elimination or reduction of risks from dangerous substances;

❖ fire fighting and fire detection provision;

❖ emergency routes and exits; and

❖ evacuation of disabled people.

Legislation

The government has produced a number of guidance documents which deal with fire safety in different types of premises and which reflect the legislation. There is also a supplementary guide dealing with means of escape for disabled people.

In addition to the above, the 'responsible person' will (in most cases) need to appoint a competent person to assist him or her in undertaking the risk assessment and fulfilling the obligations under the Order. 'Competent' is described in the Order as:

> 'where he has sufficient training and experience or knowledge and other qualities to enable him properly to implement the measures referred to' [in the Order].

On small simple buildings this might be the responsible person. However, on larger and more complex buildings, it is likely that the responsible person will need to appoint a qualified professional, trained and experienced in fire safety management.

Enforcement

The enforcing authority under the RRFSO depends upon the type of premises. The enforcing authorities include the fire and rescue authority for the area in which the premises falls, the Health and Safety Executive, the relevant local authority, fire inspector or any other person authorised by the Secretary of State. Enforcing authorities are empowered to serve a prohibition notice, an alterations notice, or an enforcement notice. Failure to comply with the RRFSO is an offence resulting in a fine up to the statutory maximum limit and/or imprisonment for a maximum of two years.

Northern Ireland

Sections 1 and 2 of the RRFSO were implemented in May 2006 and part 3 of the *Fire and Rescue Services (Northern Ireland) Order* 2006 and the *Fire Safety Regulations (Northern Ireland)* 2010 came into effect on 15 November 2010.

The *Fire Services (Northern Ireland) Order* 1984 was repealed on 15 November 2010 and the previous fire certification process has now ceased. It is now necessary for all premises, other than domestic dwellings, to have a current fire risk assessment.

To undertake a fire risk assessment under the RRFSO, the responsible person will need to address, among other things, the following:

- ❖ assessed risks of young persons employed (i.e. under 18 years of age);
- ❖ elimination or reduction of risks from dangerous substances;
- ❖ fire fighting and fire detection provision;
- ❖ emergency routes and exits; and
- ❖ evacuation of disabled people.

The government has produced 11 guidance documents which deal with fire safety in different types of premises and which reflect the latest legislation.

Northern Ireland Fire & Rescue Service is the enforcing authority. An inspector appointed by Northern Ireland Fire & Rescue Service (NIFRS) may do anything necessary for the purpose of enforcing fire safety duties under this Order and in particular shall have the power to:

- ❖ enter any premises and to inspect the whole or part of the premises and anything in them;
- ❖ require a person, who is subject to fire safety duties, to give such facilities, information, documents, records or assistance which the inspector may reasonably request;
- ❖ inspect and copy any documents or records on the relevant premises, or remove them from the relevant premises;

❖ carry out any inspections, measurements and tests, in relation to the relevant premises or an article or substance found on the premises, that are considered necessary;

❖ take samples of any articles or substances found on the premises for the purposes of ascertaining their fire resistance or flammability; and

❖ dismantle any article, deemed dangerous in the event of fire, for inspection or testing.

For more information see the website for the Northern Ireland Assembly www.niassembly.gov.uk or the Northern Ireland Fire & Rescue Service website www.nifrs.org

Scotland

The *Fire (Scotland) Act* 2005 came into force on 2 August 2005 with the exception of Part 3, which introduced a new fire safety regime in Scotland and which came into force on 1 October 2006.

The main purpose of the Act is to reform fire safety legislation in Scotland, modernising fire and rescue services. It also provides for the implementation of the provisions of a number of EU Directives on health and safety at work.

The Act does not include private dwellings but common areas of private dwellings are dealt with.

The Act consolidates existing legislation relating to duties of employers to their staff and in respect of premises. Provision is made regarding fire safety measures, risk assessment and enforcement.

The introduction of the Act has allowed enabling orders and regulations to be made. In conjunction with Part 3 of the Act, the *Fire Safety (Scotland) Regulations* 2006 came into force on 1 October 2006. The Regulations, among other things, cover fire safety, means of fighting fire, means of escape, procedures in dangerous areas, maintenance of premises and equipment, and information to and training of employees.

The Scottish Government, in September 2011, deliberated to reform the Fire Service in Scotland by forming a single fire authority covering the whole country. The public consultation period ended on 2 November 2011. The Scottish Government website (www.scotland.gov.uk) should be consulted for an update on current developments.

Fire, residential property and houses in multiple occupation (HMOs)

Purely domestic properties are excluded under the RRFSO, however, it still applies to the common areas of houses in multiple occupation and the common parts of flats. Residential landlords also have a general common law duty to keep tenants' homes fit for them to live in and to ensure that they do not endanger tenants' health, including ensuring that there are no fire hazards. Where a house is in multiple occupation and meets the 'HMO' classification, there are additional fire safety responsibilities. (For details see: www.direct.gov.uk/en/ HomeAndCommunity/Privaterenting/Repairsandstandards/DG_189200). This will include the provision of adequate fire precautions, such as fire alarms and extinguishers, and of suitable and sufficient means of escape, usually providing at least 30 minutes protection. The local council or Fire and Rescue Service can inspect the property to see whether the landlord or managing agent is complying with the law. If the property is not an HMO, there are no specific fire safety laws to comply with, although there is a general duty to keep the property habitable. There is also an obligation to ensure that the property is properly maintained, so for example, a fire hazard does not occur as a result of a faulty electrical installation. There is also a requirement to ensure that upholstered furnishings provided in the property are fire resistant.

Further information

❖ www.communities.gov.uk/housing

Contributed by Harry Dowey, harry.dowey@watts.co.uk, Ian Laurie, ian.laurie@watts.co.uk and Andrew Murray, andrew.murray@watts.co.uk

Social inclusion

The DDA (the Disability Discrimination Act 1995 as amended by the Special Educational Needs and Disability Act 2001 and the Disability Discrimination Act 2005)

The *Disability Discrimination Act* 1995 (DDA) came into force on 2 December 1996. It brought in measures to prevent discrimination against disabled people. The *Disability Discrimination Act* 2005 further amended the DDA 1995 by increasing and creating new rights for disabled people. However, from 1 October 2010, much of the DDA was superseded by the *Equality Act* 2010.

The DDA 1995 is split into different sections:

❖ **Part 1**: defines the term 'disability'.

❖ **Part 2**: deals with discrimination in employment, trade organisations and qualifications bodies.

❖ **Part 3**: deals with discrimination in the provision of goods, facilities and services to members of the public and the disposal and management of property.

❖ **Part 4**: deals with provisions for education.

❖ **Part 5**: deals with provisions for public transport.

❖ **Part 6**: deals with the setting up of the National Disability Council.

❖ **Part 7**: supplemental provisions (details duties and responsibilities covering Codes of Practice, victimisation, liability of employers, help for people suffering discrimination, aiding unlawful acts and exclusion for acts done with statutory authority or done for the purpose of safeguarding national security).

❖ **Part 8**: miscellaneous provisions (including government appointments, regulations and interpretation).

Part 2 – Employment, trade organisations and qualifications bodies

Employment

This section of the Act applies when a disabled person is employed, or an employee becomes disabled. The Act places a duty on all employers to make reasonable adjustments to enable disabled employees to carry out their work. (The armed forces are excluded under the employment provisions.)

An employer is expected to take reasonable measures to allow a person to do his or her job. This may involve:

❖ making adjustments to premises;

❖ moving a disabled person's place of work;

❖ altering hours of work;

❖ reallocating a disabled person's duties;

❖ acquiring or modifying equipment; and

❖   providing a reader or interpreter.

In addition to the above, employers should ensure that their equal opportunities policy addresses disability, in addition to preparing a disability statement and policy. Employers are not required to make changes in anticipation of employing a disabled person, however the Code of Practice suggests that employers should take opportunities to make improvements as they arise, e.g. as part of planned maintenance or refurbishment works. In addition, employers must not unjustifiably discriminate against current employees or job applicants on the grounds of disability, and may have to make reasonable adjustments to their employment arrangements or premises if these substantially disadvantage a disabled person.

Part 3 – The provision of goods, facilities and services including discrimination in relation to premises

The Act covers:

❖   any place where the public may enter;

❖   accommodation in hotels, boarding houses, etc.;

❖   all retailers or tradesman's premises;

❖   any building owned by a public authority; and

❖   facilities for entertainment or recreation.

Discrimination is deemed to have arisen if a provider of services treats a disabled person less favourably than he or she would treat others and:

❖   cannot show the treatment in question was justified; and

❖   failed to undertake his or her duty to make adjustments to physical features or practices and policies.

The Act does not require a service provider to take any steps which would fundamentally alter the nature of its service, trade, profession or business.

Public authority functions

The DDA 2005 introduced new duties (which amend Part 3 of the DDA 1995) in respect of public authority functions. The Act now prohibits discrimination in relation to every function of a public authority. The new duties came into force on 4 December 2006. The Act does not define a public authority but states that a public authority 'includes any person certain of whose functions are functions of a public nature'. For example, this includes NHS Trusts and Boards, the Prison Service, courts and tribunals, police authorities, governing bodies of higher education institutions, colleges and universities, and local authorities among others.

Public authorities have duties to make reasonable adjustments, which fall into three distinct areas:

❖   practices, policies and procedures;

❖   auxiliary aids and services; and

❖   physical features.

Disability Equality Duty

The DDA 2005 introduced a duty on public authorities to promote disability equality to cover disabled people in every area of their work. The duty is not necessarily about alterations to buildings or adjustments for individuals.

There are both general duties and specific duties under the Disability Equality Duty. The general duty sets out what the public authorities need to consider in order to promote equality of opportunity. Those covered by the specific duties (which applies to most public authorities) must also have produced a Disability Equality Scheme.

Private clubs

Private clubs with more than 25 members have a duty to make reasonable adjustments to policies, practices and procedures, with the provision of auxiliary aids and to undertake reasonable adjustments to physical features.

Discrimination in relation to selling, letting and management of premises

Under the DDA 2005 (in relation to letting of premises), there is a duty to make reasonable adjustments to policies, practices and procedures and to provide auxiliary aids and services, where reasonable to do so. Landlords therefore have a duty to take reasonable steps to facilitate access for disabled tenants and leaseholders.

However, landlords will not be under any duty to carry out adjustments to physical features of the premises. Furthermore, the cost of any reasonable adjustments that a landlord may have to make (in respect of policies, practices, procedures, auxiliary aids and services) cannot be recovered by way of increased rent or service charges.

Landlords have an obligation under the DDA to change letting terms, where reasonable to do so, to enable a tenant to undertake alterations which ordinarily might not be permitted under the lease.

Disability Discrimination (Providers of Services) (Adjustment of Premises) Regulations 2001

These Regulations apply to service providers and landlords of premises occupied by service holders. They prescribe particular circumstances in which it is reasonable or unreasonable for service providers to make physical alterations to the premises they rent or own or for lessors to withhold their approval to same.

Since the introduction of the Disability Equality Duty (DED) from December 2006, public authorities such as councils need to consider how the DED could affect them as landlords. This is likely, among other things, to include the need to consider access improvements to the common and demised parts of rented premises. The provisions of the original DDA 1995 have been extensively amended and extreme caution should be taken when referring to material that may now be out of date. There is no substitute for professional legal advice in an environment where incorrect interpretation of the provisions is widespread.

Part 4 – Education (as amended by the Special Educational Needs and Disability Act 2001 and the Disability Discrimination Act 2005)

Construction professionals should note that there are differing requirements between schools and post-16 education. Duties under post-16 education apply to higher education, further education, adult and community education, schools providing further education for adults (but excluding sixth form) and youth and community services.

The Disability Rights Commission (DRC) (now superseded by the Equality and Human Rights Commission – EHRC) published two Codes of Practice that set out, separately, in detail, the duties and responsibilities for both schools and post-16 education. The codes warrant detailed examination for those who are involved in educational establishments as they provide clarification and examples of potential scenarios covering the various duties and responsibilities under the Act.

Part 5 – Public transport

Part 5 of the Act allows the government to set access standards for buses, coaches, trains, trams and taxis. Regulations have been introduced by the government to apply minimum access standards.

Codes of practice and advice notes

The government has drawn up various codes of practice to help implement the Act and interpret its requirements.

The codes are available on the EHRC website: www.equalityhumanrights.com/advice-and-guidance/information-for-advisers/codes-of-practice/

The DDA and the Building Regulations

Where a physical feature of a building is covered by Approved Document M of the Building Regulations, if that feature conforms or is deemed to conform to the requirements of the edition current at the time of approval or installation, a ten-year exemption applies to that specific feature from the date of installation or construction. This exemption applies to service providers only.

BS 8300:2009

British Standard 8300:2009 *Design of buildings and their approaches to meet the needs of disabled people – Code of Practice* came into effect on 28 February 2009 and superseded BS 8300:2001. This is an important document in the field of access for disabled people and provides extensive and detailed guidance on good practice in the design of and access to buildings and their approaches. It forms the basis for much of the amendment to the Part M Approved Document under the Building Regulations. This document is much more comprehensive than the Approved Document and, therefore, it may not be sufficient to rely simply on Part M.

Part M Approved Document

This revised guidance is based on and is complementary to BS 8300:2009, although the BS contains much additional material that is not included in the Part M Approved Document. In some cases, the guidance in the Part M Approved Document differs from the recommendations in BS 8300. Compliance with the recommendations in the BS, therefore, while ensuring good practice, is not necessarily equivalent to compliance with the guidance in the Part M Approved Document and appropriate care should be taken when dealing with both documents.

The National Register of Access Consultants

The National Register of Access Consultants (NRAC) was established in 1999 to accredit access auditors and access consultants. Its website can be accessed at www.nrac.org.uk. There are two levels of membership: auditor or consultant. The fundamental difference between an auditor and a consultant is that consultants are required to have construction-related qualifications. Therefore, there are some limitations to the extent and detail of the advice that auditors can provide. Construction professionals such as surveyors and architects are therefore well placed to advise in this field.

The Royal Institution of Chartered Surveyors (RICS) 'Certificate in Inclusive Environments'

The RICS scheme was introduced in spring 2006 to 'promote excellence in the field of inclusive environments'. The scheme is similar to that of the NRAC with the setting up of a register of individuals with appropriate knowledge, experience and skills in inclusive environments. However, it is focused on RICS members, in particular, chartered building surveyors. See www.rics.org for more information.

Access Statements

Essentially, an Access Statement is a document which shows how an applicant is addressing accessibility issues within the design of a building or space.

An Access Statement is required to be submitted with all planning applications with the exception of householders and changes of use. Access Statements are recommended to be submitted with all Building Regulations applications and should certainly be provided where the applicant deviates from Approved Document M.

The DDA, listed buildings and conservation areas

Contrary to popular belief, listed buildings are not excluded from the DDA. There is nothing in the Act stating that if a building is listed or located within a conservation area there is any exemption from the DDA. Buildings that fall into this category will invariably be more difficult to work with in improving physical access. However, access improvements have been made to numerous historic buildings where alterations have remained sympathetic to the original character and features. Any proposed alterations will need to meet the approval of the relevant conservation authority.

Equality Act 2010

Over the last four decades discrimination legislation has been important in helping to make Britain a more equal society. However, the legislation was complex and, despite the progress that has been made, inequality and discrimination persist.

The *Equality Bill* was published on 27 April 2009, setting new laws to strengthen anti-discrimination legislation, extending the use of positive action and helping to narrow the gap between gender pay.

On 8 April 2010 the *Equality Bill* received Royal Assent and became the *Equality Act* 2010. The purpose of the Act is to advance equality of opportunity for all; to update and strengthen the previous legislation; and to deliver a simple and accessible framework of discrimination law that protects individuals from unfair treatment and promotes a more equal society.

Everyone in Britain is protected by the Act in respect of their:

- ❖ age;
- ❖ disability;
- ❖ gender reassignment;
- ❖ marriage and civil partnership;
- ❖ pregnancy and maternity;
- ❖ race;
- ❖ religion and belief;
- ❖ sex; and
- ❖ sexual orientation.

The provisions in the *Equality Act* 2010 came into force at different times to allow time for people and organisations affected by the new laws to prepare for them. Most of the Act came into force on 1 October 2010, however, the new public sector equality duties did not come into force until 5 April 2011.

The key points of the Act include:

- ❖ **Socio-economic duty**: this requires certain public bodies to consider reducing socio-economic inequalities when making strategic decisions about spending and service delivery, giving a more effective way to address issues surrounding youth crime, housing, health care, etc.

- ❖ **A new equality duty** on public bodies: public bodies need to think about the needs of everyone who uses their services or works for them.

- ❖ **Extended positive discrimination**: public bodies are able to take positive action measures in service delivery to meet the particular needs of disadvantaged groups, and, in certain circumstances, are allowed to recruit and promote in favour of an under-represented group.

❖ **Equality through public procurement**: public bodies are expected to use their purchasing power to drive equality outcomes in contract practice, suppliers' employment practices and service delivery.

❖ **Equal pay**: public bodies with more than 150 employees and private employers with 250 or more employees will be required to provide a gender pay report with effect from 2013.

❖ **Banning age discrimination** outside the workplace: it is already unlawful to discriminate against older people at work and the Act makes this apply outside work.

❖ **Strengthening protection from discrimination for disabled people**: the Act makes it easier for disabled people who live in homes with common areas to be able to use these areas. It also makes 'poor treatment' unlawful.

❖ **Protecting carers from discrimination**: It is unlawful to discriminate against or harass someone because they are 'linked to' or 'associated with' someone who is elderly, has a disability or has had gender reassignment. Thus, for example, an employer cannot refuse to promote a member of staff just because he or she cares for an older relative.

❖ **Stronger protection for breastfeeding mothers**: the Act makes it clear that it is unlawful to stop a mother breastfeeding in a public place, or to ask her to leave.

❖ **Banning discrimination in private clubs**: it is unlawful for associations to discriminate against members or guests of members invited to a club. This does not mean that clubs for people with a shared characteristic will be banned, e.g. single-sex, gay, single faith, simply that members must be treated equally.

❖ **Strengthening the powers of Employment Tribunals**: Tribunals are able to make recommendations in discrimination cases that benefit the whole workforce, not just the individual who won the claim.

Disabled people's rights in everyday life

The *Equality Act* 2010 aims to protect disabled people and prevent disability discrimination. The Act provides legal rights for disabled people in the following five areas:

1 Employment

❖ The Act makes it unlawful for an employer to discriminate against a disabled person and requires that they make reasonable adjustments for disabled people. There are duties involved with:
  – recruitment;
  – working hours;
  – pay and benefits;
  – career development;
  – managing workers;
  – dismissal and redundancy;
  – equality training;
  – making reasonable adjustments to accommodate disabled people.

2 Education

❖ The Act makes it unlawful for education providers to discriminate against disabled students.

3 Access to goods, services, facilities and premises

❖ The Act provide rights not to be discriminated against:
  – in accessing everyday good and services such as shops;
  – in buying or renting property;
  – in accessing or becoming a member of a private club with more than 25 members; and
  – in accessing the functions of public bodies.

4 Health

❖ The Act gives disabled people rights not to be discriminated against or harassed in access to health services, including social services, doctors' surgeries and hospitals. Adjustments must be made to assist in accessing these services if it is reasonable to do so.

5 Functions of public bodies

❖ The Act requires public bodies to consider disabled people in their daily operations of policy making and the delivery of services.

The Act also provides rights for people not to be directly discriminated against or harassed because they have an association with a disabled person. This can apply to a carer or parent of a disabled person. In addition, people must not be directly discriminated against or harassed because they are wrongly perceived to be disabled.

Further information may be found on www.equalities.gov.uk

Contributed by Alex Odell, alex.odell@watts.co.uk

Rating

Since the introduction of the *Local Government Finance Act* 1988, rating assessments on business premises have been subject to five-yearly revaluations. The latest rating lists came into force on 1 April 2010.

Business or non-domestic premises include most commercial properties. The following are exceptions:

❖ places of public religious worship;
❖ fish farms;
❖ most farmland and farm buildings;
❖ moveable moorings;
❖ public parks;
❖ sewers; and
❖ some types of property used by the disabled.

If part of a building is used for business and part for residential purposes, then the part used for business counts as non-domestic premises.

The national valuation organisations responsible for undertaking independent valuations of local business and domestic property are:

❖ **England and Wales**: the Valuation Office Agency (VOA): www.voa.gov.uk
❖ **Scotland**: the Scottish Assessors Association: www.saa.gov.uk
❖ **Northern Ireland**: the Land & Property Services Agency: www.lpsni.gov.uk/index.htm

Basis of valuation

The new rateable values are based on rental values and are designed to reflect the changes in the property market across the country. This is intended as a means of maintaining fairness in the system rather than to raise revenue overall. The new multiplier will be set to ensure that the overall national rates bill will remain the same and will only change with inflation.

The new rateable values that came into effect on 1 April 2011 were based on market rental values at 1 April 2008 in England, Scotland and Wales (April 2003 in Northern Ireland) and remain effective for five years. To ensure consistency, the same fixed valuation date is used for all properties.

Transitional relief

Transitional relief is a government scheme which ensures that large increases or decreases in rates bills that are due to the revaluation are phased in gradually over the next five years. This sets limits on the percentage by which your rates liability can change each year, prior to inflation but before any other relief such as small business rate relief. Small properties are defined as those with rateable valuies below £25,500 in Greater London or £18,000 elsewhere.

Any transitional relief you are entitled to will be calculated by your local authority and included in your rates bill.

Transitional relief only applies in England.

Small Business Rate Relief

Businesses may be eligible for Small Business Rate Relief if their rateable value is below a certain level. Thresholds were increased after the April 2010 revaluation.

There was also a temporary increase in Small Business Rate Relief announced in the June 2010 budget and extended in the March 2011 budget and the Autumn Statement. Between 1 October 2010 and 31 March 2013, eligible ratepayers will receive Small Business Rate Relief at 100% on properties up to £6,000, rather than 50%, and a tapering relief from 100% to 0% for properties up to £12,000 in rateable value for that period.

This is administered by local councils and the system varies between England and Wales. Full details on how rate relief works for each are given on the VOA website under the heading 'Rate Relief Schemes'.

A Small Business Rate Relief Scheme has been introduced in Northern Ireland. In Scotland, the Small Business Bonus Scheme has replaced the Small Business Rates Relief.

Empty properties

Since 1 April 2008, all empty business properties in England and Wales have been exempted from business rates for the first three months that they are empty. Industrial and warehouse properties qualify for a further three months' exemption from business rates. After that full business rates are payable. They are not payable on listed buildings, vacant storage land, properties of companies in administration, buildings used for charity and community sports club buildings. Buildings with a rateable value below £2,600 are exempt as long as they remain empty.

Empty properties with a rateable value below £18,000 were exempted from business rates until 1 April 2011, when the threshold dropped to £2,600.

In Scotland empty properties are exempt for the first three months and are then charged at 50% of the occupied rate. Properties such as factories and listed buildings and properties with a rateable value of less than £1,700 pay no rates.

Scottish ministers announced last September in their spending plans that, from April 2013, long-term empty property rate relief would be scrapped in Scotland.

In Northern Ireland rating of empty commercial properties remains at 50% afer three months.

Certain other reliefs may apply and advice is available from local authorities.

Business Rates Deferral Scheme

The deferral scheme allowed ratepayers to defer some of their 2009–10 liability until 2010–11 and 2011–12.

It was announced in the Autumn Statement that all businesses will be allowed to defer 60% of the increase in next year's business rates to the two following years.

Business Rate Supplements Act

The Business Rate Supplements Act (BRS) was given Royal Assent on 2 July 2009. It gives county councils, unitary district councils and, in London, the Greater London Authority a new discretionary power to raise a supplement on the business rate and to use those funds on projects aimed at economic development. In England, properties with a rateable value of £50,000 or less will be exempt from the BRS.

Uniform Business Rates

The Uniform Business Rate (UBR), sometimes known as the multiplier, is an amount set by the government each year. It is set to ensure that the overall amount collected in rates only ever increases by the rate of inflation.

Different multipliers are used for England, Wales, Scotland and Northern Ireland.

Country	UBR 2011/12	Notes
England	43.3p	City of London Uniform Business Rate = 43.7p
	42.6p for small businesses	City of London Small Business Rate = 43.0p Small Business = One whose rateable value (RV) is up to £18,000, or in Greater London £25,500 The Small Business Rate Relief Scheme provides further discounts, calculated by the relevant local authority. Greater London business rate supplement – 0.2p on RVs greater than £55,000 (proceeds to Crossrail).
Wales	42.8p	Small businesses with an RV of £6,000 or less are entitled to 100% reduction.
Scotland	42.6p	UBR in Scotland is known as the 'poundage rate'. Businesses with a total ratable value of £18,000 or less are eligible for a discount of between 25% and 100%.. All businesses with an RV of £35,000+ pay a supplement of 0.7p on the poundage rate to fund the Small Business Bonus Scheme.
Northern Ireland	55.7p on average	The rate varies according to location. Manufacturing industries receive substantial reductions (70% for 2011–12).

Further information

- ❖ www.voa.gov.uk
- ❖ www.scotland.gov.uk
- ❖ www.lpsni.gov.uk
- ❖ www.wales.gov.uk

❖ www.businesslink.co.uk

Contributed by Angela Dawson, angela.dawson@watts.co.uk

The Building Act 1984 and the Building Regulations 2010

The technical requirements of the Building Regulations are generally expressed as functional requirements; by themselves they may be difficult to interpret or understand. For this reason, the Department for Communities and Local Government (DCLG) publishes guidance on meeting the requirements in what are known as 'Approved Documents'. The Approved Documents cover all of the parts A–P of the Regulations, although building work will also have to comply with the requirements of any other relevant paragraphs in Schedule 1 to the Regulations. The Approved Documents also refer to additional texts – Associated Guidance.

The Approved Documents are intended to provide guidance for some of the more common building situations. In themselves they are not mandatory and there is no obligation to adopt any particular solution contained in an Approved Document if it is desired to meet the relevant requirement in some other way. They are given legal status by the *Building Act* 1984.

The most recent versions of the Approved Documents for the 14 technical 'Parts' of the Building Regulations' requirements can be downloaded free of charge from www.planningportal.gov.uk/buildingregulations/approveddocuments/downloads

For links to guidance to the Approved Documents see each Approved Document. See in particular, with effect from 1 October 2010, the new Approved Documents for Parts F, J and L, and see Part G which came into force on 6 April 2010. A government consultation exercise started in July 2010 as to the future of the Building Regulations; it has yet to bear fruit.

The legislative framework of the Building Regulations comprises:

❖ the *Building Regulations* 2010 (SI 2010/2214); and

❖ the *Building (Approved Inspectors etc.) Regulations* 2010 (SI 2010/2215).

For Scotland the most useful website is www.scotland.gov.uk/Topics/Built-Environment/Building/Building-Standards. Note particularly the availability online of the Building Standards Technical Handbooks and the annual amendments.

Note: the two Scottish Handbooks are very comprehensive – Domestic Buildings being 600+ pages and Non-Domestic Buildings 700+ pages.

In the following table the Domestic Handbook is abbreviated to DH and the Non-Domestic Handbook to NDH.

For Northern Ireland the most useful website is www.buildingcontrol-ni.com

Contributed by Allen Gilham, allen.gilham@watts.co.uk

Current Approved Documents

England and Wales – Approved Documents	Guidance to the England and Wales Approved Documents	Scotland – Technical Handbooks	Northern Ireland – Technical Booklets
Part A: Structure	**Disproportionate collapse:** ❖ *DTLR Framework Report: Proposed Revised Guidance on meeting Compliance with the Requirements of Building Regulation A3: Revision of Allot and Lomax Proposal*, Project report number: 205966 ❖ *DTLR, Guidance On Robustness And Provision Against Accidental Actions* ❖ NHBC, *Guidance on Disproportionate Collapse* **Multi-storey car parks:** ❖ *Department for the Environment Transport and the Regions Partners in Innovation Scheme Contract Ref: 39/3/570 CC1806 EDGE PROTECTION IN MULTISTOREY CAR PARKS – Assessment Method For Installed Restraint Systems*, Final Report, October 2001 ❖ *Enhancing the Whole Life Structural Performance of Multi-Storey Car Parks*, September 2002, OPDM and Mott Macdonald **Thaumasite:** ❖ *Thaumasite Expert Group One-Year Review* ❖ *Thaumasite Expert Group Report: Review after three years' experience.* **Garden walls:** ❖ *Your garden walls: better to be safe*	DH0 General DH1 Structure NDH0 General NDH1 Structure	Part C: Preparation of site and resistance to moisture Part D: Structure
Part B: Fire safety	❖ *Building Regulations and Fire Safety: Procedural Guidance*, July 2007 ❖ *Fire Safety in Adult Placements: A Code of Practice*, September 2005	DH2 Fire DH4 Safety NDH2 Fire NDH4 Safety	Part E: Fire safety (1994) Part E: Fire safety (2005)

177

England and Wales – Approved Documents	Guidance to the England and Wales Approved Documents	Scotland – Technical Handbooks	Northern Ireland – Technical Booklets
Part C: Site preparation and resistance to contaminates and moisture	None	DH3 Environment NDH3 Environment	Part C: Preparation of site and resistance to moisture
Part D: Toxic substances	None	DH3 Environment DH4 Safety NDH3 Environment NDH4 Safety	Part C: Preparation of site and resistance to moisture
Part E: Resistance to the passage of sound	None but see Robust Details part E: www.robustdetails.com	DH5 Noise NDH5 Noise	Part G: Sound insulation in dwellings
Part F: Ventilation	None Note: amendments to Part F came into force on 1 October 2010.	DH3 Environment DH6 Energy NDH3 Environment NDH6 Energy	Part F: Conservation of fuel and power Part K: Ventilation Part F1: Conservation of fuel and power in dwellings
Part G: Sanitation, hot water safety and water efficiency	None Note: sanitation, hot water safety and water efficiency revisions came into force on 6 April 2010.	DH3 Environment NDH3 Environment	Part N: Drainage Part P: Sanitary appliances and unvented hot water storage

England and Wales – Approved Documents	Guidance to the England and Wales Approved Documents	Scotland – Technical Handbooks	Northern Ireland – Technical Booklets
Part H: Drainage and waste disposal	None	DH3 Environment NDH3 Environment	Part J: Solid waste in buildings (Note: modified to Parts J1 and J2 as at March 2010) Part N: Drainage Part P: Sanitary appliances and unvented hot water storage
Part J: Combustion appliances and fuel storage systems	❖ *Solid fuel, wood and oil burning appliances* – safety leaflet ❖ *Risk assessment of concrete flue liners* ❖ *Danger – carbon monoxide poisoning* ❖ Approved Document J: 2002 edition: *Guidance and Supplementary Information on the UK Implementation of European Standards for Chimneys and Flues* Note: amended regulations came into force on 1 October 2010.	DH1 Structure DH3 Environment NDH1 Structure NDH3 Environment	Part L: Heat-producing appliances and liquefied petroleum gas
Part K: Protection from falling, collision and impact	None	DH2 Fire DH4 Safety NDH2 Fire NDH4 Safety	Part H: Stairs, ramps, guarding and protection from impact (2000) Part R: Access and facilities for disabled people

179

England and Wales – Approved Documents	Guidance to the England and Wales Approved Documents	Scotland – Technical Handbooks	Northern Ireland – Technical Booklets
Part L: Conservation of fuel and power	See www.planningportal.gov.uk/buildingregulations/approveddocuments/partl/bcassociateddocuments9/ for: ❖ *National Calculation Methodologies* (includes SAP 2005, SBEM and the criteria for assessing software interfaces for SBEM) ❖ *Accredited Construction Details* (for steel, timber and masonry construction) ❖ Other reference documents on multi-foiled insulation, low or zero carbon energy sources, domestic and non-domestic heating systems, gas and oil central-heating boilers and condensing boiler installations ❖ *Monitoring the Sustainability of Buildings* ❖ *Sustainable and Secure Buildings Act 2004, A Biennial report and supporting documents (Baseline key performance indicators and Impact of policy measures)* ❖ *Climate Change and Sustainable Energy Act 2006* – section 14: A report regarding compliance with Part L Note: amendments to Part L came into force on 1 October 2010.	DH3 Environment DH6 Energy NDH3 Environment NDH6 Energy	Part F: Conservation of fuel and power
Part M: Access to and use of buildings	None	DH4 Safety NDH4 Safety	Part H: Stairs, ramps, guarding and protection from impact Part R: Access and facilities for disabled people
Part N: Glazing – safety in relation to impact. opening and cleaning	None	DH4 Safety DH5 Noise NDH4 Safety NDH5 Noise	Part V: Glazing

England and Wales – Approved Documents	Guidance to the England and Wales Approved Documents	Scotland – Technical Handbooks	Northern Ireland – Technical Booklets
Part P: Electrical safety	❖ *New Rules for Electrical Safety in The Home*, DCLG 2004	DH4 Safety DH6 Energy NDH4 Safety NDH6 Energy	No current electrical safety technical booklets under the Building Regulations
Approved Document to support Regulation 7 – Material and workmanship	None		

Building Regulations approval

The Building Regulations are made under powers, provided within the *Building Act* 1984, that apply throughout England and Wales. The current regulations, the *Building Regulations* 2010 came into force on 1 October 2010, replacing the *Building Regulations* 2000 (as amended). The purpose of the Building Regulations is to protect the health and safety of people and users in and around all types of buildings.

The Building Regulations are supported by the Approved Documents. These are divided into 14 separate parts, ranging from A (Structure) through to P (Electrical). The Approved Documents provide functional requirements, and are expressed in terms of what is seen as reasonable, adequate or appropriate.

Where developers or clients are considering undertaking building works, by law, they are required to ensure that the works are fully compliant with the Building Regulations where they apply. The developer or client has one of two building control services available:

- ❖ Local Authority Building Control Service; or
- ❖ Approved Inspector Building Control Service.

Local Authority Building Control Service

Where the developer or client opts for the Local Authority Building Control Service option, dependent on the size and type of the building works, an application can be considered by one of two options:

- ❖ a Building Notice application; or
- ❖ a Full Plans application.

Note: Both applications are valid for a period of three years from the date the submission is issued to the local authority.

Key points of the Building Notice procedure are:

- ❖ it enables smaller works to proceed onto site quickly; and
- ❖ it does not require a 'full plans' application (detailed design drawings).

Once a Building Notice has been issued to the local authority stating the developer's or client's intention to commence work, the local authority will advise whether the proposed work complies with or contravenes the Building Regulations. Where required, the local authority may request further information and details to aid the application. Once on site, the local authority will make periodic inspections and provide advice on compliance.

Key points of the Full Plans procedure are:

- ❖ detailed design drawings, plans, structural calculations and construction details are required to be submitted in advance of work commencing;
- ❖ the designated local authority verifies the submission to check for compliance;
- ❖ the local authority decision may be to reject, to approve unconditionally or to approve together with set conditions within a five-week period;
- ❖ further information or amendments will need to be submitted where conditional approval has been made; and
- ❖ work can commence once the Full Plans application has been submitted, provided that the local authority is given 48 hours' notice via a 'Commencement Notice'.

Approved Inspector Building Control Service

In comparison to the previous building control service, an Approved Inspector (AI) is essentially a private sector company or practitioner who is registered under the Construction Industry Council (CIC). The AI will take responsibility for approving the plan submissions and undertaking periodic inspection of the work throughout the duration.

Key points of the AI procedure are:

❖ together, the developer/client and AI provides an 'initial notice' to the local authority notifying them that responsibility for the works to comply with the Building Regulations rests with the AI;

❖ the AI checks plans and construction details;

❖ the AI issues a 'plans certificate';

❖ the AI carries out periodic inspections; and

❖ the AI issues a 'final certificate' to the local authority formally stating that the works have been constructed in compliance with the Building Regulations.

If the AI is not satisfied with the works, in that they contravene the Building Regulations, the inspector will not consequently issue the 'final certificate' and may potentially cancel the 'initial notice', thereby terminating the inspector's involvement in the project.

Unlike the local authority, the AI has no direct power to enforce the Building Regulations if the proposals or work in progress does not comply. Cancelling the 'initial notice' results in the building control service being taken on by the local authority, who do have certain enforcement powers to ensure the works comply with the Building Regulations.

Further information

❖ Construction Industry Council: www.cic.org.uk

❖ Association of Consultant Approved Inspectors (ACAI): www.approvedinspectors.org.uk

Contributed by Allen Gilham, allen.gilham@watts.co.uk

Part L 2010 compliance

As part of the drive towards a carbon-zero standard for all new buildings from 2019, several of the Approved Documents to the Building Regulations have been updated. The changes to Part L took effect from 1 October 2010 and are aimed at achieving a further 25% reduction of CO_2 emissions (in dwellings and non-domestic buildings) in comparison with the savings required within the 2006 documents.

Looking specifically at the changes to Part L relating to existing buildings only, the key points are summarised as follows:

❖ Existing dwellings (Part L1B):
 – The standards are tightened in the 2010 version, with a reduction in Limiting Fabric Parameters for roofs, walls, floors, party walls, windows and pedestrian doors.
 – Consequential improvements now apply to buildings over 1,000m².
 – Conservatories and porches that are provided with heating or cannot be sealed off from the dwelling are no longer exempt in terms of thermal compliance.
 – A 'Commissioning Notice' is also now required.

- ❖ Existing non-domestic (Part L2B):
  - – 'Commissioning Notices' are required for alterations to building services.
  - – Consequential improvements are the same as the 2006 Regulations.
- ❖ The worst acceptable airtightness target remains at 10m³/h.m² at 50 pascals.
- ❖ For existing buildings undergoing refurbishment or extension that fall under L2B, there is a requirement to reduce unwanted air leakage. Submission of a report signed by a suitably qualified person is required to demonstrate that appropriate measures have been taken to minimise air leakage.
- ❖ The Target Emission Rate (TER) changed significantly. It is now determined by a 2010 Notional Building – Improvement Factors and LZC Factors have been removed.
- ❖ A mandatory requirement for CO_2 emissions calculations (BER and TER as designed) must be submitted to the local authority prior to start on site.
- ❖ A revised definition of dwelling type provides greater clarity.
- ❖ There are additional measures for dwellings within a 'type' that have not been subjected to testing.
- ❖ Temporary sealing for all natural ventilation devices, i.e. trickle vents, is now acceptable when carrying out air leakage testing – refer to Part F.
- ❖ ATTMA TSL1 and TSL2 documents are referenced for testing airtightness for dwellings and non-dwellings respectively.
- ❖ BINDT (British Institute of Non-destructive Testing) registered airtightness testing is the only recognised certification within the Approved Documents.

Contributed by Ian Laurie, ian.laurie@watts.co.uk

Airtightness

Airtightness (air permeability) is the degree of air leakage that takes place through the fabric of a building and is expressed in m³ per sq. metre of external surface area when subjected to a pressure difference of 50 Pascals (Pa).

Air leakage is the leakage of air that takes place through gaps, cracks and fissures in the fabric of the building. The 2010 Approved Document L requires a minimum level of air permeability of 10m³/(h.m²)@50Pa, however, this represents a fairly leaky building. A better target would be 7m³/(h.m²)@50Pa, and best performance would be 3m³/(h.m²)@50Pa.

Achieving an airtight building means following three essential steps:

- ❖ design for airtightness;
- ❖ build for airtightness; and
- ❖ test for airtightness.

It is not practicable to construct a building and then try to make it airtight. Remedial sealing can be difficult and costly. By designing in airtightness at the drawing stage you can deal with air barrier continuity and sealing details at critical elements – and ensure long-term performance by specifying the correct seal or sealant.

The main air leakage problems in buildings occur typically:

- ❖ around doors, windows, panels and cladding details;
- ❖ in gaps where the structure penetrates the construction envelope;
- ❖ in service entries: such as pipes, ducts flues, ventilators;

❖ in porous construction: such as bricks, blocks, mortar joints; and

❖ in joist connections within intermediate floors.

Designers should identify all the problem areas (e.g. sealing around pipe entries), and spell out responsibility for finishing off in the contract documents. Detailed guidance and typical details for different forms of construction can be found in *Accredited Construction Details* available at: www.planningportal.gov.uk/ buildingregulations/approveddocuments/partl/bcassociateddocuments9/acd

Constructing the building to the airtightness specification is down to the main contractor and subcontractors. For this to be successful, all of the workforce should be aware of airtightness issues in the same way as safety issues and codes of conduct are dealt with.

Inspection during construction is essential. Talking to and working with contractors is the best way of ensuring that the team understands the importance of airtightness and how to incorporate it.

The only real way to be confident that the building meets an airtightness specification is to carry out a fan pressurisation test prior to handover. Large buildings (e.g. hypermarkets or industrial buildings) need specialist larger capacity equipment.

If the three essential steps listed earlier are followed, the building should pass the test. In the event they are not and the building fails, the proposals in Part L state: 'If on first testing the building fails to comply, the major sources of air leakage should be identified using the techniques described in TM23 [CIBSE Technical Memorandum].' (Fan pressurisation – see description in *Airtightness testing* below.) This usually requires specialist help.

Despite improved understanding of construction techniques, few buildings are sufficiently airtight – this is true of new buildings as well as old. In a recent survey, only one out of 39 buildings tested met a good practice benchmark for airtightness. While the degree of leakage varies considerably from building to building, it has been claimed that the problem is equivalent to having a $9m^2$ hole in the building envelope.

Both the government and the Chartered Institution of Building Services Engineers (CIBSE) regard airtightness as a serious issue and encourage protective measures.

Airtightness testing

Within the UK, air pressurisation/depressurisation testing must be undertaken in accordance with relevant national standards (CIBSE TM23 *Testing Buildings for Air Leakage* and BS EN 13829: 2001 *Thermal performance of buildings – Determination of air permeability of buildings – Fan pressurization method*). Testing organisations should have United Kingdom Accreditation Service (UKAS) accreditation in accordance with BS EN 17025 *General requirements for the competence of testing and calibration laboratories* and be members of the Air Tightness Testing and Measurement Association (ATTMA).

ATTMA standard TS1: 2006 (applicable to planning applications submitted post 6 April 2006) and TM23 describe the testing methodology for the fan pressurisation testing of buildings to show compliance with Part L of the Building Regulations. In addition to the testing methodology, these documents lay down recommended air leakage specifications for different building types.

Single or multiple fan units can be used to identify whole-building leakage rates by producing artificial positive or negative pressures within a building. Air is supplied to the building through the fan(s) for a range of measured airflow rates, with a maximum difference of typically 50–60 Pa. The fan speed is increased in steps up to the maximum and then decreased in steps. The air leakage through the envelope is represented by the air volume flow rate through the fans and the pressure difference across the building envelope is recorded.

The external barometric pressure and temperature are measured and compared with the internal temperature so that corrections can be applied to the measured airflow rates if necessary.

Wind speeds above 6m/sec. can also influence the measured envelope leakage rates and so tests are usually conducted when weather conditions are favourable.

Smoke tests

Air leakage paths can be determined using smoke and the normal forces acting on the building envelope, or smoke used in conjunction with artificially-induced internal pressurisation or depressurisation. Hand-held generators can be used to pinpoint leakage that may need remedial sealing either before a pressure test, or after a test that has revealed inadequacies.

By comparison, large-scale smoke generators are generally used to smoke log buildings. The buildings are then typically pressurised to blow the smoke out through any discontinuities in the envelope. Smoke leaking from the building can then be identified and recorded photographically.

Smoke logging tests are a less accurate means of detection than hand-held generators, as smoke can travel for significant distances before it escapes. For example, while smoke may appear to be leaking from the ridge of the building, it may in fact be travelling up through a cavity wall from a discontinuity, rather than leaking out from the roof void.

Infrared thermography

Infrared thermography produces a visual representation of the surface temperatures of a subject. Large areas can be surveyed in a relatively short time and a visual record of the results produced as the survey proceeds. Instead of using smoke, the infrared camera detects the amount of heat radiated from the surface and by depressurising the building, colder external air can be drawn in through discontinuities in the fabric, cooling the adjacent areas and enabling identification. In the alternative, creating a positive internal pressure will enable the external identification of leakage points as warm air escapes.

Contributed by Trevor Rushton, trevor.rushton@watts.co.uk

Building Regulations and historic building conservation

Striking the balance between energy conservation requirements of the Building Regulations and historic building conservation

A key statement now contained in *Planning Policy Statement 5: Planning for the Historic Environment* (PPS5), in paragraph HE1.2 is:

> 'Where proposals that are promoted for their contribution to mitigating climate change have a potentially negative effect on heritage assets, local planning authorities should, prior to determination, and ideally during pre-application discussions, help the applicant to identify feasible solutions that deliver similar climate change mitigation but with less or no harm to the significance of the heritage asset and its setting.'

> © *Crown copyright material is reproduced under the Open Government Licence v1.0 for public sector information: www.nationalarchives.gov.uk/doc/open-government-licence/*

This in effect should mean that sensible and pragmatic compromises are to be reached between Building Control Officers and Conservation Officers when Part L is applied to historic buildings.

The Approved Documents L1 A and B and L2 A and B impose energy conservation requirements on properties when undergoing certain types of refurbishment or alteration works, details of which can be found at www.planningportal.gov.uk. Historic buildings protected under planning law will not necessarily have to comply with the full extent of these documents, however, that is not to say that their protection under planning law will necessarily exempt them from all or part of the requirements.

Note that the 2002 and 2006 revisions to Part L of the Building Regulations have been subject to further revisions which came into effect from 1 October 2010.

The fields of energy conservation and building conservation are two very large overlapping subject areas and a pragmatic approach needs to be adopted in order to reach a satisfactory compromise. Due consideration of this is given within the Approved Documents, however, further useful guidance is contained in the English Heritage publication *Building Regulations and Historic Buildings – Balancing the needs for energy conservation with those of building conservation: an Interim Guidance Note on the application of Part L.*

For the latest guidance consult the English Heritage website: www.english-heritage.org.uk/professional/advice/advice-by-topic/climate-change

Separate guidance is available from www.historic-Scotland.gov.uk (for Scotland), www.ni-environment.gov.uk (for Northern Ireland), and www.cadw.wales.gov.uk (for Wales).

The present Approved Documents provide guidance on buildings that currently do not have to comply with the full requirements, i.e:

❖ listed buildings, as listed in accordance with section 1 of the *Planning (Listed Buildings and Conservation Areas) Act* 1990;

❖ buildings in a conservation area; and

❖ Scheduled Ancient Monuments.

Special considerations apply to buildings in the three categories above where meeting the energy conservation requirements would alter the character or appearance unacceptably.

Planning Policy Statement 5 and Approved Documents L1B and L2B point out that improved energy efficiency should not be at the risk of the character or long-term viability of the building. They suggest that taking advice and enlisting the services of local authority conservation officers would be beneficial (for example, in cases involving restoration, rebuilding and work undertaken to enable fabric to 'breathe').

Although ultimately the extent and type of any energy conservation works to a historic building will be agreed through discussion with conservation and building control officers, the professional contemplating works to such a building should be mindful of the issues discussed.

The Planning Minister Greg Clarke announced in October 2011 that he aims to have a final version of the National Planning Policy Framework (NPPF) for England by 31 March 2011. In the event that the NPPF abolishes PPS5 then the above references to PPS5 will become null and void. There are presently no indications as to what might replace it.

Further information

❖ Approved Documents L1 A and B and L2 A and B, see www.planningportal.gov.uk/buildingregulations/approveddocuments/partl/approved

❖ *Building Regulations and Historic Buildings – Balancing the needs for energy conservation with those of building conservation: an Interim Guidance Note on the application of Part L,* English Heritage, 2004 (www.english-heritage.org.uk/publications/building-regulations-and-historic-buildings-balancing-the-needs/ignpartlbuildingregs.pdf).

Contributed by Allen Gilham, allen.gilham@watts.co.uk

The Construction (Design and Management) Regulations 2007

The *Construction (Design and Management) Regulations* 2007 (CDM 2007) (SI 2007/320) came into force on 6 April 2007, replacing the previous CDM Regulations 1994 and the *Construction (Health, Safety and Welfare) Regulations* 1996 (CHSW).

CDM 2007 provides a statutory framework for managing health and safety during the construction, repair, maintenance and demolition of civil engineering and construction work, with legal duties for everyone involved in the project from design through construction and beyond, including the maintenance, use and demolition of the building or structure.

The Health and Safety Commission has published an accompanying Approved Code of Practice *Managing health and safety in construction* (L144).

The key aim of the Regulations is to integrate health and safety into the management of the project and encourage everyone involved with the project to work together to:

- ❖ improve the planning and management of projects from the very start;
- ❖ identify hazards early on, so they can be eliminated or reduced at the design stage and the remaining risks can be properly managed;
- ❖ target effort where it can do the most good in terms of health and safety; and
- ❖ discourage unnecessary bureaucracy.

The Regulations apply to all 'construction work', with additional requirements if the project is notifiable. In the following text the latter are highlighted with an asterisk *.

The key matters are as follows:

* Project notification: a project must be notified to the Health and Safety Executive (HSE) if it is expected to last more than 30 working days or involve more than 500 person days of construction work. The client is required to confirm his or her agreement of the details.

* CDM co-ordinator (CDMC): replaces the previous role of the 'planning supervisor' and is the adviser and 'friend' of the client. The CDMC:

- ❖ advises the client on measures necessary for compliance;
- ❖ ensures adequate arrangements are in place for cooperation and coordination generally;
- ❖ takes all reasonable steps to ensure designers comply with their duties;
- ❖ liaises with the principal contractor regarding the contents of the health and safety file, and information needed to prepare the construction phase plan and for subsequent design development;
- ❖ prepares, or if existing, otherwise reviews and updates, the health and safety file and passes it to the client at the end of the construction phase.

Competence: anyone who is appointing another party, or is being appointed, must ensure that they are competent for the specific project.

Cooperation and coordination: everyone involved in the project is required to cooperate and coordinate their activities with each other and also to cooperate with those involved in concurrent projects on neighbouring sites to ensure the safety of those carrying out the construction work, and others who may be affected by it.

The client:

- ❖ cannot abrogate responsibility to an agent;
- ❖ must appoint the CDMC as early in the project as possible and before the scheme design progresses beyond the concept stage;
- ❖ must ensure that suitable project management arrangements are in place;
- ❖ must provide the CDMC with all available relevant information, including the minimum time to be allowed for the principal contractor for planning and preparation prior to start on site;
- ❖ must ensure that there are reasonable management arrangements in place throughout the project to ensure that the construction work can be carried out, so far as is reasonably practicable, safely and without risk to health;
- ❖ must ensure that relevant information, likely to be needed by designers, contractors or others to plan and manage their work, is passed to them;
- ❖ if the project is a fixed workplace, must ensure that the design and materials used comply with the *Workplace (Health, Safety and Welfare) Regulations* 1992;
- ❖ must appoint a principal contractor to manage health and safety during the construction phase;
- ❖ must ensure that contractors have made arrangements for suitable welfare facilities to be in place from the start and throughout the construction phase;
- ❖ must ensure that the construction phase does not commence until satisfied that the principal contractor has prepared a suitable construction phase plan; and
- ❖ must ensure that the CDMC is provided with all relevant information needed for inclusion in the health and safety file, with the information clearly separated for each discrete project, site or structure and keep the file available for inspection thereafter.

Pre-construction information (the equivalent of the previous tender stage of the health and safety plan): this is a collection of information, contributed to by all relevant parties, to be provided to all designers and to every contractor (who has been, or may be, appointed by the client). It includes information:

- ❖ about or affecting the site or construction work;
- ❖ concerning the proposed use of the structure as a workplace;
- ❖ about the 'mobilisation time' for contractors; and
- ❖ that contained in any existing health and safety file.

Health and safety on construction sites: every contractor and every person who controls the way in which construction work is carried out by a person at work must comply with the requirements of regulations 26 to 44 inclusive. These are the general health and safety requirements that were previously described in the CHSW Regulations 1996 and include general matters such as good housekeeping, emergency procedures, fire fighting and detection, and safe working environments, as well as specific high risk activities and forms of construction. In addition, construction workers are obliged to report to their supervisors any defects which they are aware may endanger themselves or others.

Health and safety file: the health and safety file is a record of significant information relevant to health and safety to be retained by the client, made available and used throughout the life of the building or structure to assist its safe maintenance, alteration or demolition. The file is prepared by the CDMC using information supplied by other duty holders.

Where a file relates to more than one project or structure, the client must ensure that the information relating to each part can be easily identified.

Contributed by Paul Winstone, paul.winstone@watts.co.uk

Dispute resolution

Disputants and their advisers have a variety of dispute resolution mechanisms that they can select to resolve their disputes.

The principal dispute resolution procedures are as follows.

Adjudication

This process is enshrined in the *Housing Grants, Construction and Regeneration Act* 1996 (as amended by Part 8 of the *Local Democracy, Economic Development and Construction Act* 2009). A wide variety of the disputes arising under construction contracts can be referred to adjudication. From 1 October 2011 in England and Wales, disputes regarding *oral* contracts can also be referred to adjudication. The Act does not deal with disputes with residential occupiers unless the parties agree that adjudication will apply. Adjudication is popular not least because an adjudication award has to be made within 28 days of the case being referred to an adjudicator unless the parties agree otherwise. The decision of an adjudicator is binding pending agreement of the parties or the decision of a court or arbitrator.

Arbitration

Arbitration is based on the contractual provisions agreed by the parties. Procedures under the *Arbitration Act* 1996 have given the arbitrator wide powers to resolve disputes without unnecessary cost or delay, and in a fair manner without undue interference from the courts. The right of appeal is limited.

Early Neutral Evaluation (ENE)

Technology and Construction Court judges are prepared to arrange a short hearing of a case, on specific issues, on a without prejudice basis and give preliminary views on the merits, as an aid to settlement discussions between the parties. If a judge determines a particular issue by ENE, the parties are free to agree whether or not they will be bound by it. If the ENE does not result in settlement, the case can proceed to trial but will be heard by another judge with no knowledge of the outcome of the ENE.

Independent expert

This forms a valuable means for the speedy resolution of technical disputes. The procedure is generally straightforward and flexible. Issues in dispute are referred to an expert to decide using his or her own professional expertise or judgment. It has been successfully used for many years in rent review matters, but has much wider application to technical disputes. If the parties agree to be bound by the expert's decision the right of appeal exists in limited circumstances only.

Litigation

The *Civil Procedure Rules* 1998 have led to more efficient running of cases both in terms of costs and time. The Technology and Construction Court (TCC) in the High Court deals with construction disputes and has considerable experience of doing so. Before court proceedings are commenced, the parties should comply with the *Pre-Action Protocol for Construction and Engineering Disputes* (the Protocol). This requires the parties to set out their respective cases in correspondence and to meet on a without prejudice basis to seek to settle the dispute or narrow the issues involved, prior to the issue of court proceedings. A TCC working party is currently reviewing the Protocol following the recommendations set out in Lord Jackson's report: *Review of Civil Litigation Costs*. The working party is considering the future role of the Protocol, in particular whether it should be retained, abolished or amended to be voluntary rather than compulsory.

Mediation

Mediation is a voluntary and non-binding procedure. It is a private process in which an independent neutral person helps the parties reach a negotiated settlement. The mediator usually does not make a determination on the dispute but may do so if the parties agree and he or she considers that it will assist in reaching a settlement.

Dispute Review Boards

Dispute Review Boards (DRBs) are used on larger projects. A panel is appointed at the start of the project and visits site a number of times per year to deal with disputes by providing interim binding decisions (similar to an adjudicator). The decisions can be challenged via litigation or arbitration.

Contributed by Suzanne Reeves, 020 7395 3168, sreeves@wedlakebell.com of Wedlake Bell, 52 Bedford Row, London WC1R 4LR, www.wedlakebell.com

Latent Damage Act 1986

The *Latent Damage Act* 1986 enhances case law relating to certain cases of negligence, by imposing statutory limits in relation to the time in which cases may be brought to court if a defect is found.

The Act applies specifically to those cases of negligence that relate to latent damage and not to personal injury. In addition, recent case law suggests that in the meaning of the Act, negligence covers only a breach of a tortious duty of care and not a contractual duty of care.

Previous statute exists indicating time limits in which legal action must commence; section 14 of the *Limitation Act* 1980. The 1986 Act enhances section 14 by limiting any claims to six years after the damage occurred. This, however, can be extended under section 14A by a further three years from the date when the defect is discovered. In all cases however, a 15-year time limit is placed under section 14B of the Act. When considering claims for latent defects, the most important points to establish are the dates from which the negligence occurred and the cause of the negligence. For example, the negligence may have been caused by defective construction, design, or a combination of both. The date on which the defect technically arises may be confused by the ongoing contractual state of the project, i.e. whether a final certificate has been issued or a defect liability period is still active. In certain cases proceedings may be delayed on the basis that the damage has not yet occurred, but is in fact imminent.

Contributed by Paul Lovelock, paul.lovelock@watts.co.uk

Discovery of building defects – statutory time limits

The *Limitation Act* 1980 ('the 1980 Act') as modified by the *Latent Damage Act* 1986 (see above) lays down the periods within which proceedings to enforce a right must be brought. Upon the discovery of a defect in a building or structure, possible claims against the designers and constructors of that building or structure could arise in contract, in tort or under statute.

Contract

To bring an action for breach of a simple contract, court proceedings must be commenced within six years of the date on which the breach of contract occurred. If the contract has been completed under seal, rather than under hand, then the time limit prescribed by the 1980 Act is 12 years. Under the *Companies Act* 1985 (as amended), the 12-year limitation period also applies to companies when a contract is signed as a deed by two directors or a director and a company secretary.

Tort

The general time limit for actions in tort is six years from the date when the damage was suffered, with the exception that a time limit of three years applies to personal injury actions involving negligence. This period runs from the date of the accident concerned, although special rules apply for illnesses, which may not manifest themselves for many years after exposure to their cause, for example, asbestos.

Also, for negligence claims involving latent damage, the time limit laid down by the *Latent Damage Act* 1986 for commencing proceedings is six years from the date the damage was suffered. However this period can be extended for a further three years from the 'starting date'. The starting date is defined by the *Latent Damage Act* 1986 as the date on which the plaintiff first had both the required knowledge and the right to bring an action. The *Latent Damage Act* also includes a 'long-stop' provision preventing the instigation of any proceedings after the expiry of 15 years from the date of the negligence concerned.

Statute

Where a right derives from a breach of statutory duty, reference should, in the first instance, be made to the particular statute concerned, which may specify a time limit for the commencement of proceedings. The *Defective Premises Act* 1972 provides a particularly germane example. If the statute concerned is silent as to the time limit, then a period of six years will generally apply. If an action is brought in respect of a defective product, under the *Consumer Protection Act* 1987 there is a cut-off point of ten years from the 'relevant time' (usually the date of a supply).

It should be noted that the time limits for both tortious and contractual claims might be postponed where there is concealment, mistake or fraud.

Contributed by Paul Lovelock, paul.lovelock@watts.co.uk

Expert witness

Expert evidence in court proceedings is dealt with by Part 35 of the *Civil Procedure Rules* (CPR) and accompanying practice direction which came into force on 26 April 1999. This has been supplemented by the Civil Justice Council's *Protocol for the Instruction of Experts to give evidence in civil claims* ('the Protocol') which took effect from 5 September 2005. The Protocol is intended to assist in the interpretation of the provisions of CPR Part 35. Reference should also be made to the relevant Court Guides:

- ❖ Section H2 and Appendix 11 of the Admiralty and Commercial Courts Guide;
- ❖ Section 13 of the TCC Guide;
- ❖ Chapter 4 of the Chancery Guide;
- ❖ Section 7.9 of the Queen's Bench Guide; and
- ❖ to any specific pre-action protocol relevant to your case.

The CPR states that it is the duty of experts to help the courts on matters within their expertise. This duty overrides any obligation to the person from whom experts have received instructions or by whom they are paid. The expert should therefore:

- ❖ be independent/impartial – the Protocol sets out a useful test of 'independence' namely, whether the expert will 'express the same opinion if given the same instructions by the opposing party';
- ❖ state any reservations about the case he or she is instructed upon;
- ❖ identify areas outside his or her expertise;

- ❖ consider all material facts in his or her report and state all facts and assumptions upon which his or her opinion is based;

- ❖ state where necessary that it is only a provisional report, because only limited information/data was available when it was compiled;

- ❖ advise instructing solicitors if further information, i.e. the other expert's report, changes his or her opinion;

- ❖ make available all documents referred to in the report (i.e. survey reports, plans, calculations, photographs, etc.); and

- ❖ keep the report as brief as possible, but without losing the reasoning and conclusions upon which his or her opinion is based.

The written report

There needs to be a statement setting out the brief and instructions given.

The report is to be written in the first person and it must be an individual who prepares the report and not the company or firm.

The report should be addressed to the court.

Although the report should be as brief as possible, accuracy should not be sacrificed to brevity.

The expert witness must be able to substantiate each and every sentence of the report and highlight any areas where his or her opinions are based on inadequate factual information. It is not the expert's role to make or advance legal arguments.

The details of experts' qualifications to be given in reports should be commensurate with the nature and complexity of the case. It may be sufficient merely to state academic and professional qualifications. However, where highly specialised expertise is called for, experts should include the detail of particular training and/or experience that qualifies them to provide that highly specialised evidence.

The report must contain statements that the expert: (i) understands his or her duty to the court and has complied and will continue to comply with it; and (ii) is aware of the requirements of Part 35 and practice direction 35, the Protocol and the practice direction on pre-action conduct. The report must also be verified by a statement of truth.

The form of the statement of truth is as follows:

'I confirm that I have made clear which facts and matters referred to in this report are within my own knowledge and which are not. Those that are within my own knowledge I confirm to be true. The opinions I have expressed represent my true and complete professional opinions on the matters to which they refer.'

The Protocol emphasises that this wording is mandatory and must not be modified.

Under the CPR, each party has 28 days after receipt of the opposing expert's report to put written questions. Unless the court gives permission for or the other party agrees to (CPR 35.6(2)(c)(ii))) more general questions, these can only be for the purpose of clarifying the report.

Without prejudice meetings

Unless a single joint expert is appointed (as is more common in lower value cases), without prejudice meetings between experts are necessary and important. The court, under the CPR, may, and normally does, require the experts to produce a joint statement from 'without prejudice' meetings setting out what has and has not been agreed. Reflecting the provisions of CPR Part 35, the Protocol states that agreements between experts during discussions 'shall not bind the parties unless the parties expressly agree to be bound by the agreement'. However, the Protocol adds a strong caveat that in view of the overriding objective of the CPR, which encourages that cases are dealt with expeditiously and fairly, 'parties should give careful consideration before refusing to be bound by such an agreement, and be able to explain their refusal should it become relevant to the issue of costs'.

Giving evidence in court

Oral expert evidence can only be given at trial with the court's permission. If the case is large or complex, permission is usually given at an early stage in the proceedings (at the case management conference). In most other cases, permission is not given until much later, if at all. A single joint expert does not normally attend trial, his/her evidence and the answers to any questions being contained in his/her report.

If the case gets to a hearing, and expert witnesses are required to give evidence, the court will consider the best way to do so. The TCC Guide suggests various ways including:

- ❖ an expert giving evidence followed by other experts of the same discipline;
- ❖ an expert giving evidence on a particular issue, followed by other experts doing the same;
- ❖ concurrent evidence or 'hot-tubbing', usually after the experts have been cross-examined on general matters and key issues. The experts sit in the witness box together and the court chairs a discussion between them.

A few helpful hints in giving evidence are listed below:

- ❖ Take time, don't rush.
- ❖ Succinctly answer only the questions that are asked. Use plain language.
- ❖ Do not digress from the question asked.
- ❖ Do not act as advocate.
- ❖ If the question is not understood nor heard – say so.
- ❖ Know the report 'inside out'.

Cross-examination will challenge credibility, so consider the following:

- ❖ Do not feel obliged to fill a silence.
- ❖ Do not be afraid to answer repeated or different questions with the same answer again and again.
- ❖ If asked a closed question, if appropriate state that there may not be a yes or no answer.
- ❖ Do not be rattled by a number of quick fire questions.
- ❖ Do not argue with counsel.
- ❖ If he or she becomes aggressive, stay cool.
- ❖ Beware of the important question slipped in among a number of trivial questions.

The above notes only deal briefly with the CPR and Protocol. These notes should not be considered as comprehensive text. The role of the expert is evolving through the interpretation of the CPR in case law and any expert should ensure that he or she fully understands that role in the light of the current law.

Lord Jackson's recommendations

In January 2010, Lord Jackson published his final report following his extensive review of civil litigation costs. In relation to the use of expert witnesses he made two key recommendations:

- ❖ The CPR should be amended to require a party seeking permission to adduce expert evidence to provide an estimate of the costs of that evidence to the court.

Lord Jackson noted that effective case management could lead to huge cost savings provided that all parties were committed to preparing for case management conferences properly and the judge has had time to read the case. He further commented that although the court has power under the CPR to make an order to limit the fees and expenses of expert witnesses recoverable from the other party this power is seldom exercised. He recommended that judges be more willing to exercise this power.

❖ Concurrent evidence or 'hot tubbing' (see *Giving evidence in court* on the previous page) should be piloted in cases where all parties give consent. This method of hearing evidence is already popular in the Australian courts and commonplace in international arbitration. It has been trialled in Manchester since June 2010 and the TCC Guide (updated in October 2010) now includes hot-tubbing as a recognised way for expert evidence to be given.

A bill was laid before Parliament on 21 June 2011 which would implement the majority of Lord Jackson's recommendations.

Liability of expert witnesses

In the recent case of *Jones v Kaney* [2011] UKSC 13, the Supreme Court held that the immunity from suit for breach of duty that expert witnesses have previously enjoyed in legal proceedings (relating to both performance in the witness box and the contents of expert reports) should be abolished. This means that expert witnesses are now potentially liable to their clients for a breach of duty (whether in contract or negligence), even where the work carried out by the expert relates to preparation for or involvement in legal proceedings. So expert witnesses will need to tread carefully in the future.

Further information

❖ The *Civil Procedure Rules* can be found at www.justice.gov.uk/civil/procrules_fin/

Contributed by Suzanne Reeves, 020 7395 3168, sreeves@wedlakebell.com of Wedlake Bell, 52 Bedford Row, London WC1R 4LR, www.wedlakebell.com

Part II of the Housing Grants, Construction and Regeneration Act 1996

The following aims to set out a brief outline of the issues which need to be considered when determining whether contractual terms are compliant with Part II of *the Housing Grants, Construction and Regeneration Act* 1996 (the Act) as amended by the *Local Democracy, Economic Development and Construction Act* 2009 (LDEDCA) or whether certain provisions will be incorporated into the contract by the Scheme for Construction Contracts.

Parties to a construction contract are free to negotiate and agree the terms and conditions under which the works and services are to be carried out. However, there are times where a contract fails to comply with the minimum requirements relating to adjudication and payment laid down by the Act. Consequently, certain provisions will automatically be incorporated into the contract by the Scheme for Construction Contracts.

The original Act provisions will apply to construction contracts entered into before 1 October 2011. Contracts entered into on or after 1 October 2011 will be subject to the Act as updated by the provisions of LDEDCA. The principal amendments made by LDEDCA include:

- ❖ Parties who have an oral or partly oral contract will be able to rely on the provisions of the Act.

- ❖ The payment and withholding notices provisions are overhauled. For example, either party (rather than only the payer) can issue a payment notice stating how much is due, and payment notices must be given even if the amount due is zero. If no notice to pay less is given then the notified sum becomes due.

- ❖ There is a provision in the Act, as amended by LDEDCA, dealing with pre-agreeing the allocation of costs of future adjudications in the contract (known in the industry as 'Tolent' clauses). The intention is that clauses that provide that the party bringing an adjudication claim will be liable to pay all costs of the adjudication will be outlawed unless agreed by both parties at the time of the adjudication. Arguably, however, the relevant legislation wording is ambiguous and the courts may need to interpret the legislation before it can be said with certainty that such clauses are illegal.

- ❖ 'Pay when certified' clauses will be prohibited in most contracts. The main contractor cannot make payment to its subcontractors conditional on its own payment by the employer being certified.

- ❖ The suspending party can claim the costs from the exercise of the right to suspend and can claim an extension of time to complete its work for the delays resulting from the exercise of the right.

- ❖ Contracts will need to include a right for the adjudicator to correct typographical or clerical errors (such as miscalculations) in his or her decision (the courts had previously confirmed this right, the 'slip rule').

When does the Act apply? (S104–107)

The Act applies to:

- ❖ contracts entered into on or after **1 May 1998**;

- ❖ and contracts entered into on or after **1 October 2011** are subject to the Act **but** as amended by LDEDCA;

- ❖ **contracts in writing** – it is sufficient if the contract is evidenced in writing, and for contracts entered into on or after 1 October 2011 the Act (as amended by LDEDCA) will apply to **oral** contracts;

- ❖ contracts for **construction operations** which include the construction, alteration, repair, maintenance, decoration, demolition and installation in buildings forming or to form part of the land, and also architectural, design, surveying or engineering advice; and

- ❖ the carrying out of construction operations in England, Wales or Scotland, whatever the applicable law of the contract.

The Act does not apply to:

- ❖ contracts with **residential occupiers** for work on their property where they intend to occupy the property as their residence;

- ❖ certain mining, drilling and extraction operations;

- ❖ installation or demolition of plant or machinery or steelwork to support or provide access to plant or machinery on a site where the primary activity is nuclear processing, power generation, water or effluent treatment, or the production processing of chemicals, pharmaceuticals, oil, gas, steel, food or drink;

- ❖ manufacture and delivery of materials not involving installation; and

- ❖ artistic works.

Letters of intent may be subject to the Act where they are sufficient to amount to a legally binding contract in their own right.

Adjudication (S108)

The contract must:

- ❖ allow either party to refer a dispute to adjudication at any time;
- ❖ provide for the appointment of an adjudicator within 7 days;
- ❖ require the adjudicator to reach a decision within 28 days **after** the dispute has been referred to the adjudicator (or a longer period if agreed by the parties);
- ❖ allow the adjudicator and the party who referred the dispute to the adjudicator to extend the period for the decision by up to 14 days;
- ❖ impose a duty on the adjudicator to act impartially;
- ❖ enable the adjudicator to take the initiative in ascertaining the facts and the law surrounding the dispute;
- ❖ provide for the decision of the adjudicator to be binding on the parties until the dispute is taken to arbitration or the courts;
- ❖ provide that the adjudicator is not liable for anything he or she does unless he or she acts in bad faith; and
- ❖ for contracts entered into on or after 1 October 2011 (where the Act as amended by LDEDCA applies), include a provision permitting the adjudicator to correct his or her decision to remove a clerical or typographical error arising by accident or omission.

If the contract does not comply with the adjudication provisions of the Act in full, all the adjudication provisions of the contract will be set aside and the adjudication procedures under the Scheme for Construction Contracts will apply. The procedures under the Scheme cover the points listed above and introduce time limits.

These provisions must be in writing; therefore if the contract is entirely oral (and after 1 October 2011 the Act, as amended by LDEDCA, applies to oral contracts) the adjudication procedures under the Scheme for Construction Contracts automatically apply.

See also *Adjudication under the Scheme for Construction Contracts – how to get started*, page 200.

Adjudication costs (S108A)

LDEDCA has introduced a new section 108A to the Act. The intention of this provision was to ensure that parties could only agree the allocation of the costs of an adjudication after the date of the relevant adjudication notice. This was intended to preclude what is known in the industry as a 'Tolent clause' (a clause which requires the party bringing the adjudication to pay the costs). There is concern, however, that the wording of the legislation is ambiguous and that parties could still use Tolent clauses in their contracts. The courts may have to interpret this provision to determine whether or not Tolent clauses are illegal.

Payment

The Act and the Scheme for Construction Contracts provide a 'menu' of payment provisions covering:

- ❖ payment by instalments;
- ❖ final payment;
- ❖ withholding payment; and
- ❖ conditional payment.

If a contract fails to comply with any one of the provisions from the 'menu' the relevant provisions from the Scheme will apply. The remainder of the contractual provisions that do comply with the Act will remain intact. It is therefore possible to end up with a contract where the payment provisions are a mixture of express terms agreed between the parties and implied terms from the Scheme.

Payment by instalments (S109–110/110B)

A party to a construction contract is entitled to payment by instalments, stage payments or other periodic payments unless:

❖ the contract specifies that the duration of the work is less than 45 days; or

❖ the parties agree that the work is estimated to take less than 45 days.

Where the work falls within the 45-day limit, the right to instalment payments is excluded but all other payment provisions (notice of withholding payment, set-off, etc.) will apply, as will the adjudication provisions outlined above.

Where a contract falls below the 45-day limit, payment of the contract price falls due 30 days after completion of the work (or 30 days after the contractor's claim if later) and payment must be made within 17 days.

In all other cases, the parties can agree between themselves:

❖ the amounts of each payment;

❖ the intervals between each payment;

❖ the date each payment becomes due; and

❖ the final date by which each payment must be made.

If the contract does not contain a clear mechanism for determining each of these four elements they will be determined by the Scheme for Construction Contracts, namely:

❖ The amount of each payment will be based on the value of the work and other costs to which the contractor is entitled during the payment interval.

❖ There will be 28-day payment cycles.

❖ Payment is due 7 days after each 28-day period (or 7 days after the contractor's claim for payment if later).

❖ The final date for each payment is 24 days after each 28-day period (or 24 days after the contractor's claim for payment if later).

The contract must provide for the paying party to give notice within 5 days of the date on which each instalment becomes due, specifying the amount proposed to be paid and the basis on which it is calculated (for contracts to which the Act as amended by LDEDCA applies it is immaterial whether the amount due is zero). Any attempt in the contract to vary or exclude this requirement will be ineffective and this provision will be implied by the Scheme for Construction Contracts.

In contracts entered into on or after 1 October 2011, if the paying party (or another party specified in the contract as being responsible for giving the payment notice) fails to give such notice then the payee may give the notice specifying how much the payee considers to be due and the basis on which that amount is calculated.

Final payment

The contract must contain a clear mechanism for determining when the final payment due under the contract becomes payable and the final date by which that payment must be made.

The parties are free to agree the dates or periods within which the final payment is due and is payable but if there is no such mechanism, in accordance with the Scheme, the final payment:

- ❖ is due 30 days after completion of the work (or 30 days after the contractor's claim for payment if later); and

- ❖ the final date for making the final payment is 47 days after completion of the work (or 47 days after the contractor's claim for payment if later).

Withholding payment (S111)

- ❖ No payment can be withheld unless a 'notice of intention to withhold payment' has been given for contracts entered into before 1 October 2011 where the original Act applies, specifying the amount to be withheld and the grounds for withholding payment. For contracts entered into on or after 1 October 2011 which are subject to the Act as amended by LDEDCA, the payer (or other specified person) must serve a notice to 'pay less' specifying the amount the payer considers due and the basis on which that sum is calculated.

- ❖ The notice must be given before the final date for payment.

- ❖ The contract can specify how long before the final date of payment the notice must be given (even if it is just one day) but if this notice period is not specified, the Scheme applies and at least seven days notice must be given.

Conditional payment (S113)

Any provision in a contract which makes payment conditional upon the paying party receiving payment from someone else (and also for contracts entered into on or after 1 October 2011, payment being certified as due under a superior contract) is ineffective and the payment provisions of the Scheme outlined above will apply.

The only exception is where the contract provides that payment may be withheld if the reason for non-payment is the insolvency of someone else in the payment chain.

Suspending performance (S112)

If any payment is not received by the final date for payment and a notice of withholding payment or a 'pay less' notice has not been served, the contractor may suspend work after giving seven days notice of its intention. The right to suspend performance ceases when the relevant payment is received. The period in which to complete the works is automatically extended by the number of days of the suspension.

This brief summary of Part II of the *Housing Grants, Construction and Regeneration Act* 1996 is not intended to be a detailed explanation of the provisions and we recommend that legal advice is sought on any specific issues.

Contributed by Suzanne Reeves, 020 7395 3168, sreeves@wedlakebell.com of Wedlake Bell, 52 Bedford Row, London WC1R 4LR, www.wedlakebell.com

Adjudication under the Scheme for Construction Contracts – how to get started

Adjudication under the *Housing Grants, Construction and Regeneration Act* 1996 (as amended by the *Local Democracy, Economic Development and Construction Act* 2009) (the Act) allows for a quick fix method of dispute resolution. The right to refer a dispute to adjudication is available to a party to a construction contract within the meaning of the Act at any time.

Below is a brief explanation of the steps required to commence an adjudication under the Scheme for Construction Contracts, i.e. **where there are no contractual adjudication provisions**.

Where adjudication is your chosen method of dispute resolution, it is essential that you comply with the strict time limits laid down by the Scheme and any timetable imposed by the adjudicator. The adjudicator is under an obligation to reach a decision within 28 days of receipt of the Referral Notice unless the parties agree otherwise.

It is not possible to contract out of the time constraints laid down for adjudication by the Act.

Procedure

To commence adjudication you must take three steps:

- ❖ give notice of adjudication;
- ❖ request an adjudicator to act; and
- ❖ serve a Referral Notice.

Notice of Adjudication

This must be in writing, be given to every other party to the contract and contain:

- ❖ details of the parties involved;
- ❖ a brief description of the dispute;
- ❖ details of when and where the dispute arose;
- ❖ what you are seeking from the adjudicator, for example, an award for a specific sum; and
- ❖ names and addresses of the parties to the contract (including the addresses which the parties have specified for the giving of notices, if any).

Note: In view of the very tight timescale for adjudication you should ensure that your claim is fully prepared before issuing the Notice of Adjudication.

Appointing an adjudicator

After giving notice of adjudication you must make a request for an adjudicator to act. The timescale for the appointment of an adjudicator is extremely tight and a request for the appointment of an adjudicator should be made at the same time as giving the Notice of Adjudication. In order to determine who to appoint you should consider the following:

- ❖ If your contract names an adjudicator, contact that person to ensure that he or she is ready and willing to act.
- ❖ If an Adjudicator Nominating Body (ANB) is named in your contract, contact that body and ask for an appointment to be made.

❖ If no adjudicator or ANB has been named in your contract you can contact any ANB such as:

– the Association of Independent Construction Adjudicators, 0870 429 6353;
– the Royal Institution of Chartered Surveyors, Dispute Resolution Service, 020 7334 3806;
– the Chartered Institute of Arbitrators, 020 7421 7444;
– the Royal Institute of British Architects, 020 7580 5533;
– the Technology and Construction Solicitors Association, 020 7367 2000; or
– the Construction Industry Council, 020 7637 8692.

❖ Contact the most appropriate ANB depending upon the nature of the dispute and the issues involved. Some ANBs will be able to offer a greater diversity and breadth of experience.

❖ If an ANB is used: the ANB has five days to inform you of the nominated adjudicator. The nominated adjudicator then has up to two days to confirm his or her appointment.

Caution: If a named or nominated adjudicator refuses to act, another adjudicator can be agreed or nominated by any ANB, but beware the time limit for issuing the Referral Notice. If an alternative adjudicator cannot be appointed within seven days of the Notice of Adjudication the safest course is to issue a fresh Notice of Adjudication.

Referral Notice

Within seven days of the Notice of Adjudication you must send the Referral Notice to the adjudicator formally referring the dispute to him or her. The Referral Notice must be in writing, and must be given to the adjudicator and every other party to the dispute and:

❖ contain the basis of your claim, including an explanation of how the dispute arose and identifying the issues in dispute;

❖ be accompanied by copies of (or relevant extracts from) your contract (whether this is a standard printed form or evidenced in correspondence);

❖ include any documents upon which you wish to rely in support of your case;

❖ contain the remedies and award you are seeking; and

❖ give the adjudicator wide jurisdiction by giving him or her an alternative, for example, 'such other sum as the adjudicator may determine'.

It is important that the Referral Notice clearly sets out the issues in dispute which the adjudicator is being asked to determine, including the history of the case and any arguments raised by the other party, as well as identifying the remedies sought. Claims not identified in the Notice of Adjudication cannot be introduced later in the same adjudication.

Following service of the Referral Notice the adjudicator must inform every party to the dispute of the date it was received and should set a timetable for dealing with the adjudication, including a response from the opposing party, and request any further information or evidence in order to reach his or her decision.

Contributed by Suzanne Reeves, 020 7395 3168, sreeves@wedlakebell.com of Wedlake Bell, 52 Bedford Row, London WC1R 4LR, www.wedlakebell.com

Landlord and tenant

Legislation

Dilapidations

The term 'dilapidations' refers to breaches of lease obligations, either express or implied, and usually relates to: reinstatement; repair; decoration; breaches of statute or other specific requirements; and associated costs.

The legal remedy for a breach of dilapidations obligations is typically a claim for damages, and the fundamental purpose of a 'Schedule of Dilapidations' is to identify the breaches of covenant. The surveyor should be mindful that the matter may end up in court, though is not necessarily acting as an expert in the early stages of the instruction.

The Schedule of Dilapidations is usually prepared as part of a claim which itself should represent the damage actually suffered by the landlord, and which is capped under section 18(1) of the *Landlord and Tenant Act* 1927, as well as by common law principles. (See *Section 18(1) of the Landlord and Tenant Act 1927* on page 215.)

While schedules may be prepared on behalf of a tenant where there are alleged breaches by the landlord of its obligations, the more common approach is for the document to be prepared on behalf of a landlord in relation to tenants' alleged breaches.

Preparation of schedules on behalf of tenants is more usually restricted to interim schedules. Schedules commonly fall into the following categories:

- ❖ **Interim**: served during the term.
- ❖ **Terminal**: served around the end of the term.
- ❖ **Final**: served after the term.

Broadly speaking, landlords' schedules of dilapidations are prepared either in respect of claims arising during the term or at the end of the term.

The Property Litigation Association (PLA) Protocol and RICS guidance note

The fifth edition of the RICS *Dilapidations* guidance note (the guidance note) was published at the beginning of June 2008 and represents a 'guide to best practice'.

The guidance note was drafted having regard to the *Civil Procedure Rules* Binding Practice Direction and the third edition of the Property Litigation Association (PLA) *Pre-action protocol for claims for damages in relation to the physical state of commercial property at the termination of a tenancy* (the Dilapidations Protocol).

The PLA Dilapidations Protocol was formally adopted by the Civil Justice Council (CJC) on 14 October 2011 and came into force on 1 January 2012. The Protocol should be read in conjunction with the Practice Direction under the *Civil Procedure Rules* (CPR).

Key issues to note from the RICS guidance are:

- ❖ recommended reasonable response times;
- ❖ standardisation of various procedures;
- ❖ emphasis on the requirement for the initial claim to be reasonable;
- ❖ requirement for the surveyor to endorse the schedule of dilapidations, rather than the landlord's claim;
- ❖ requirement for a formal Diminution Valuation only prior to issue of proceedings;
- ❖ consideration of Alternative Dispute Resolution;
- ❖ consideration of the role of the surveyor as either 'adviser' or 'expert';
- ❖ consideration of the assessment of loss;

❖ clarification of the surveyor's endorsement; and

❖ endorsements are required by both landlord and tenant surveyors.

The modern approach to commercial leases is to encourage a more equitable balance of power between landlord and tenant. Various initiatives in the industry encourage both parties to be reasonable in their dealings, including the *Code for Leasing Business Premises in England and Wales 2007* (often referred to as the Lease Code) and the Commercial Landlord's Accreditation Scheme. Guidance aims to discourage landlords' spurious or inflated claims, given the underlying principle that the purpose of dilapidations is not to enrich the landlord or punish the tenant.

The provisions of the *Fraud Act* 2006 further emphasise the need for all parties to adhere to this position.

Stages in the dilapidations process

Stage 1 – preparation

Obtain and appraise all relevant documentation including:

❖ leases;

❖ licences to alter;

❖ schedules of condition;

❖ side letters;

❖ photographs;

❖ fit-out specifications;

❖ agents' letting brochures;

❖ any statutory notices served;

❖ deeds of variation;

❖ schedules of landlord's and tenant's fixtures and fittings;

❖ details of outstanding service charges; and

❖ any rent deposit agreements.

This list is by no means exhaustive.

Stage 2 – the inspection

This must be comprehensive and thorough. With increasingly complex buildings specialist input, such as that provided by a structural engineer or mechanical or electrical consultant, may be required.

The surveyor should establish the original condition at the beginning of the term (if possible) and the standard of repair that the tenant has covenanted to achieve, taking into account the age, character and locality of the premises when let (*Proudfoot v Hart* 1890).

❖ Identify items of disrepair.

❖ Check if the item falls within the demise.

❖ Check if the item is subject to the covenant or covenants.

❖ Consider if the item is out of repair, i.e. has there been a change from a previously better condition.

❖ Consider the nature of remedial work reasonably necessary.

❖ Take measurements to aid calculation of the cost of the remedial works and use as proof as required at a later date.

❖ Consider the impact of 'green' lease clauses (see *Green leases*, page 400).

Stage 3 – preparation of the Schedule of Dilapidations and claim

The example below shows a typical format for a Schedule. The initial document should contain information in the first five columns, with the additional columns relating to the tenant's and landlord's subsequent negotiations. The combined document is commonly referred to as a Scott Schedule.

The Schedule of Dilapidations should be accompanied by a claim letter, which must include:

- ❖ the landlord's and tenant's names and addresses;
- ❖ a clear summary of the facts on which the claim is based;
- ❖ the Schedule of Dilapidations (a separate document);
- ❖ any documents relied upon, such as invoices and evidence of costs and losses;
- ❖ confirmation that the landlord and advisers will attend meetings;
- ❖ a date by which the tenant should respond;
- ❖ a summary of the claim including: cost of works, preliminaries, overheads and loss of profit, surveyors' fees for preparing the Schedule (quantified and substantiated), loss of rent, loss of service charge, surveyors' fees for negotiating a settlement (projected), and any sums paid to a superior landlord; and
- ❖ depending on the landlord's intent, obtain a diminution valuation.

The Schedule of Dilapidations should be served within a reasonable time before the termination of the tenancy and typically not more than 56 days afterwards, though the landlord may have up to six years before it may commence proceedings.

If a notice from the landlord has to be given to the tenant for reinstatement of alterations then this must be served within a reasonable period before the end of the tenancy so that the tenant is still able to start these works in time.

Item	Clause No.	Breach	Remedial work required	Landlord cost (£)	Tenant's comments on		Landlord's comments on	
					Breach and remedy	Cost (£)	Breach and remedy	Cost (£)

Electronic copies of the Schedule of Dilapidations should be provided to facilitate easier negotiation, preferably in a Scott Schedule format as shown above.

Stage 4 – the response and negotiations

Following submission of the claim, the tenant should respond within a reasonable period, usually 56 days. However, in interim dilapidations the period for response required by statute, or under the lease, may be considerably shorter if the tenant's position is to be protected.

Ideally the surveyors should meet on site to review the facts, usually on a without prejudice basis, before the tenant is required to respond to the claim. If further meetings are necessary a strict timetable should be adopted. In any case it is expected that experts of the respective parties in their like disciplines should also meet within 28 days of the tenant's response.

Final dilapidations claims

The approach to a Final Schedule of Dilapidations will be similar to that adopted for a Terminal Schedule. However, the Final Schedule is served after the end of the term, so care should be taken to ensure that a suitable notice requiring the tenant to reinstate alterations is served separately before the term date, if so required.

Interim dilapidations claims

These claims are made during the lease term and are typically as a consequence of one of the lease parties becoming concerned with breaches of the lease obligations by the other. This is a complicated area of law so legal advice should always be taken on the appropriate drafting, and the service and timing of notices and counter-notices.

Interim dilapidations claims by the landlord are typically subject to one of three remedies: determination of the lease; damages; or specific performance. A tenant may also seek: specific performance; damages; the right to undertake works; offset against rent; or repudiation and quitting of the premises. The tenant's options will, however, differ in each case and should be considered carefully.

Concentrating on the more usual service by a landlord, to be successful, a landlord would need to satisfy one or more of five grounds (summarised below):

- ❖ that immediate remedying is necessary to protect the value of the landlord's interest in the property, or that the value has already been affected;

- ❖ that the work is necessary to comply with legislation;

- ❖ that where the tenant does not occupy the whole building, the work is necessary in the interests of other occupiers;

- ❖ that immediate remedying of the defect will be substantially cheaper than would be the case if the work was delayed; or

- ❖ special circumstances exist.

Jervis v Harris Notices (Repairs Notices)

Where the lease specifically allows, landlords may have the option of entering the tenant's demise and completing the works themselves, often at the cost of the tenant. Depending on the terms of the lease, the cost to the tenant is calculated as a debt, rather than as damages, so avoiding the complications of section 18(1) of the *Landlord and Tenant Act* 1927 and common law. However, the lease will set out a series of events that the landlord must comply with before this opportunity is available to enter and carry out the works. Typically these are:

- ❖ that a notice must be served on the tenant setting out exactly the alleged breaches; and

- ❖ that the tenant is given a reasonable time to comply with the notice.

Carrying out work within a tenant's demise is complicated. Significant problems could be encountered such as: trespass by the contractor, access to power and water, disruption of the tenant's quiet enjoyment, and the effect on the relationships between the parties. The right of entry is, as a result, used sparingly.

Break clauses

Increasingly leases include an option for the landlord or the tenant to bring the lease to an end before the contractual expiry date. It is important to establish whether the break clause is 'condition precedent' or not.

Where the clause is conditional, the party exercising the break may be required to comply with a variety of conditions before the break can be deemed effective. Compliance may range from absolute compliance with all obligations within the lease, to simply requiring that vacant possession be provided at the break date.

The risk of non-compliance with a conditional break clause is often substantially greater than the cost of the works necessary to comply. It is therefore essential to fully understand and adhere to the lease requirements.

Two leading cases shed some light as to how break clauses might be interpreted by the courts.

The first case, *Fitzroy House Epworth Street (No 1) Ltd v The Financial Times Ltd*, has assisted practitioners in understanding the extent of work that may be necessary for the tenant to 'materially' comply with its obligations. The tenant undertook approximately £900,000 worth of works, but approximately £20,000 worth of works remained incomplete at the relevant date. The court held that, because there had been no consequential delay to the landlord in reletting or selling the property, the tenant had indeed complied materially with the lease obligations. Conversely other cases have accepted that the lack of a single coat of paint may be sufficient to invalidate a break clause.

Importantly in the Fitzroy case, the Appeal Court went on to rule that there was no disadvantage to the tenant as a consequence of the landlord and its advisers declining to assist the tenant in determining the extent of works that would be required to comply with the obligations.

Legal and General Assurance Society Ltd v Expeditors International (UK) Ltd highlighted the importance of careful drafting of any settlement agreement associated with the operation of a break clause. The break clause was conditional on the tenant observing the lease covenants and giving vacant possession on the break date. Prior to this date the landlord and tenant agreed a cash payment in settlement of dilapidations to ensure the lease would end on the break date. On the break date the tenant had moved out but had not removed all possessions or handed over keys. Vacant possession had not been given but on appeal it was held that the tenant was able to rely on the settlement agreement. The lesson for landlords is to ensure that they do not inadvertently waive the right to rely on other preconditions and for tenants that they are at risk if they do not give full vacant possession.

Dilapidations and the Equality Act 2010

In October 2010 the *Equality Act* 2010 replaced large parts of the *Disability Discrimination Act* as well as the *Disability Discrimination (Providers of Services) (Adjustments of Premises) Regulations* 2001. Further guidance in this respect is given in the *Social inclusion* section starting at page 164.

It is now the property controller who has the obligation to take reasonable steps to ensure that they are complying with their duties under the *Equality Act* 2010, in relation to the facilities provided at the premises. While this shift in definition is remains untried in court, it appears that there remains a link with the service provision and therefore the vacant demise at the end of the lease cannot be in breach of any duty imposed by the Act. It is noted, however, that there are separate requirements in respect of 'disposing' of property which may separately require changes to be made. Initial published guidance indicates that the Act does not extend to altering physical features of the property but rather it requires auxiliary aids to be introduced as necessary.

Based on guidance available at the time of going to print, it appears therefore that a landlord remains unable to require a tenant to undertake works to comply with the duties imposed by the Act during the term of a lease. Neither can it impose this as a part of a dilapidations claim at the end of, or during, a lease.

Where a tenant has undertaken works to comply with the DDA, there are implications. If a landlord wishes to remove the alteration, there is nothing to prevent the landlord doing this after the outgoing tenant has vacated, but all reinstatement of these elements might be at the landlord's own cost and, further, they must consider their own obligations with regard to disposing of the property. Any requirement on the outgoing tenant to remove these alterations may be considered unreasonable and could be challenged in the courts. As with the original DDA, this is as yet untested, and it remains to be seen whether a tenant will be able to use this in defence against a reinstatement claim.

Asbestos

The presence of asbestos products in a property is often a contentious point in dilapidations. Current law does not require removal of asbestos products if they can be made safe. However, there is a requirement for the presence of asbestos materials to be formally recorded in appropriate detail. This does not apply to buildings built since the use of asbestos in construction was outlawed.

In the context of dilapidations, the asbestos register should be passed on by the tenant to the landlord. If relevant information is not available there will be additional costs associated with obtaining sufficient documentation or in treating unidentified materials as asbestos. Depending on the exact lease terms an allowance should be included within the dilapidations schedule.

VAT and dilapidations

VAT in respect of dilapidations is a complex subject with its own set of rules, regulations and case law. The Dilapidations Protocol, Clause 4.5, requires that the VAT status of the landlord should be stated. Where a tenant is making a payment to a landlord in full and final settlement of its dilapidation liabilities, under Customs and Excise rules, the payment is not a 'taxable supply' for the purposes of VAT as the payment is deemed to be one of damages and not a supply. VAT may be payable if the landlord passes the payment on to an incoming VAT registered tenant.

The *Finance Act* 1989 introduced major changes that included giving UK payers of VAT the option to pay VAT on supplies relating to an interest in commercial land.

Where a person or company is registered for VAT there is a special statutory exemption to the charging of VAT on such supplies. Taxpayers can waive this exemption if they desire by notifying HM Revenue and Customs. If a landlord has elected to waive its exemption on a building, it must charge VAT on such items as rent received and it will not be appropriate to include VAT as part of a dilapidations claim. If the VAT exemption has not been waived then VAT may form part of a dilapidations claim.

Once the landlord's VAT position has been established, a simplified VAT analysis might follow the steps shown in the diagram below.

Dilapidations VAT analysis

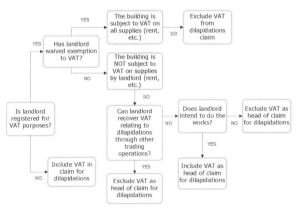

Valuation – diminution in value

See *Section 18(1) of the Landlord and Tenant Act 1927* on page 215.

Summary of important statutes

- ❖ **Landlord and Tenant Act 1927, section 18(1)**
  - – Limits the cost of a claim for breach of covenant.

- ❖ **Law of Property Act 1925, section 146**
  - – Prescribes the form of notice for re-entry for forfeiture.

- ❖ **Law of Property Act 1925, section 147**
  - – Provides relief for tenants on long leases in respect of internal redecorations.

- ❖ **Leasehold Property (Repairs) Act 1938**
  - – Gives protection to certain tenants in respect of section 146 notice above.

- ❖ **Landlord and Tenant Act 1954, Part IV**
  - – Extension of *Leasehold Property (Repairs) Act* 1938.

- ❖ **Defective Premises Act 1972**
  - – Provides that a landlord shall be liable for lack of repair in cases where the landlord knew or ought to have known of the defect.

- ❖ **The Civil Procedure Rules 1998**
  - – Introduced by Lord Woolf, they provide rules and practice directions for dispute procedures.

- ❖ **The Fraud Act 2006**
  - – The injured party need not suffer loss, implications for practitioners in preparing and defending claims.

Summary of important case law

There have been a number of leading decisions relating to dilapidations law in the last few years. The following cases give an indication of developing areas of law.

- ❖ *Scottish and Mutual Assurance Society Ltd v British Telecommunications plc* (1994) (unreported)
  - – Section 18(1) of the *Landlord and Tenant Act* 1927 Part II.
  - – Loss of rent.
  - – Notice for reinstatement of alterations.

- ❖ *Shortlands Investments Ltd v Cargill plc* (1995) EGLR 51
  - – Section 18(1) of the *Landlord and Tenant Act* 1927 Part II.

- ❖ *Trane (UK) Ltd v Provident Mutual Life Assurance Co Ltd* (1995) WGLR 78
  - – Compliance with conditions of break clauses.

- ❖ *Jervis v Harris* (1996) EGLR 78
  - – Use of provision for landlord's re-entry.
  - – Extent of recovery of expenditure.

- ❖ *Mannai Investments Co Ltd v Eagle Star Life Assurance Co Ltd* (1997) EGLR 69
  - – Accuracy of notice showing intent to break tenancy.

- ❖ *Credit Suisse v Beegas Nominees Ltd* (1994) 4 All ER 803
  - – Establishing the interpretation of the repairing covenants and the different types of obligation placed on the tenant.

- ❖ *Fitzroy House Epworth Street (No 1) Ltd and Fitzroy House Epworth Street (No 2) Ltd v The Financial Times Ltd* (2006) CA1 2207
  - – Test of 'material compliance' of a conditional break clause.
  - – Requirements of landlords and their advisers to assist tenants under conditional break clause circumstances.

- ❖ *Legal and General Assurance Society Ltd v Expeditors International (UK) Ltd* (2006) EWHC 1008
  - – Financial settlements in respect of dilapidations associated with break clause preconditions and vacant possession.

- ❖ *Latimer v Carney* (2006) EWCA Civ 1417
    – Measure of damages, section 18(1) of the *Landlord and Tenant Act* 1927.

- ❖ *Janet Reger International v Tiree Holdings* (2006) EWHC 1743 (Ch D)
    – Liability for disrepair, deterioration from a previous better condition.

- ❖ *Riverside Property Investments Ltd v Blackhawk Automotive* (2005) 01 EG 94
    – Standard of repair and recovery of costs.

- ❖ *Carmel Southend Ltd v Strachan & Henshaw Ltd* (2007) EHWC 1289 (TCC); (2007) 35 EG 136
    – Standard of repair, patch repair sufficient, tenant not required to put premises into perfect repair or pristine condition.

- ❖ *Lyndendown Ltd v Vitamol Ltd* [2007] EWCA Civ 826; (2007) 47 EG 170
    – Damages not recoverable if subtenant remains in occupation under the same terms.

- ❖ *Business Environment Bow Lane Ltd v Deanwater Estates Ltd* (2008) EWHC 2003 (TCC)
    – Exaggerated claims, conduct of parties and costs awards.

- ❖ *PGF II SA v Royal & Sun Alliance* [2010] EWHC 1459 (TCC)
    – The award of costs as damages and clarification of supersession and the landlord's intentions.

Dilapidations in Scotland

At a practical surveying level, dilapidations work in Scotland differs very little from that in other parts of the UK. There are, however, a few significant differences in the legal principles and the statutory background to dilapidations work in Scotland, all of which are potential pitfalls for the unwary.

In Scotland, unlike England and Wales, there is little statute or case law regulating commercial leases and their effect. As a result, the liability for repair of a commercial property, under a contract of lease, is principally determined by Scots common law, and the extent to which this has been displaced by the wording of the conditions set out in the lease.

It is therefore essential to understand the legal relationship between the landlord and tenant under Scots common law, any relevant statute law and, in particular, that imposed by the contract of lease.

At Scots common law, a landlord provides the tenant with an implied warranty that the leased premises are wind and watertight and are reasonably fit for their purpose at the outset of the lease. The landlord also has a continuing duty to keep the premises in a tenantable condition and wind and watertight during the currency of the lease. The tenant, therefore, has very little liability for repairs at common law. The tenant is expected to use reasonable care in the management of the premises and is only liable for any damage attributable to his or her negligence.

Most modern leases of commercial property will transfer some or all of the landlord's common law repairing liability onto the tenant. Where doubt or ambiguity exists over the meaning of the wording of the lease, as to where the repairing obligations may lie, then the courts will apply these common law principles. This may have the effect of leaving the obligation with the landlord unless it can be otherwise clearly shown to be that of the tenant.

Scots common law is also derived from the limited number of decisions in cases heard in the Scottish courts. Decisions from courts in other parts of the UK, although persuasive, are certainly not treated as binding precedents in Scotland.

There are few statutory provisions that affect the Scots common law position outlined above or, more importantly, the obligations set out in the contract of lease. This is significantly different to the situation in England and Wales.

Scotland has no equivalents to the *Landlord and Tenant Acts* of 1927, 1954 and 1988, the *Leasehold Property (Repairs) Act* 1938, the *Law of Property Act* 1925, or the *Defective Premises Act* 1972. Equally importantly, the *Civil Procedure Rules* do not apply in Scotland. The third edition of the Property Litigation Association so-called 'Dilapidations Protocol' published in May 2008, has no legal significance in Scotland. The RICS *Dilapidations* guidance note (5th edition, published June 2008) states in its introduction that it applies only to England and Wales. However, Scotland now has its own RICS guidance note. *Dilapidations in Scotland*, the RICS guidance note (1st edition), was published in January 2011.

There are, however, many other statutes and statutory instruments which may have an influence upon commercial property leases in Scotland, including:

❖ the *Occupiers Liability (Scotland) Act* 1960;

❖ the *Factories Act* 1961;

❖ the *Offices, Shops and Railway Premises Act* 1968;

❖ the *Environmental Protection Act* 1990;

❖ the *Clean Air Act* 1993:

❖ the *Disability Discrimination Act* 1995;

❖ the *Fire (Scotland) Act* 2005; and

❖ the *Control of Asbestos Regulations* 2006.

These and many others have, however, only an indirect bearing on the relationship of the landlord and the tenant in Scotland, and there are therefore very few statutory implications that have to be taken into account when interpreting Scottish commercial leases. Accordingly, in almost all cases relating to commercial property in Scotland, the text of the lease can largely be taken to mean what it says, subject to the overriding requirements of the common law.

The terms 'interim' and 'terminal' schedules of dilapidation have now become widely used in Scotland. They are borrowed from England and Wales. These terms have no legal relevance under Scots law and as a general rule their use is not essential.

As with the practice in other parts of the UK, there are differences between what might be found in a schedule served during the currency of a lease (an *interim* schedule) and one served at or near termination of the lease (a *terminal* schedule).

A schedule served during the currency of the lease and some time before expiry is normally limited to requiring the tenant to remedy what is alleged as a breach of a repairing obligation or some other specific obligation of the lease. Unlike in England and Wales, there is no limit imposed on the nature, extent or significance of the defects raised in an *interim* schedule, or their cost in relation to the value of the property. The only test is whether the tenant is in breach of its repairing obligation. In preparing an *interim* schedule, however, the landlord would not do its cause much good in being over zealous by including insignificant items that are of limited relevance to the landlord's interest in the property at that time.

A schedule served at or near expiry of the lease tends to be a much more comprehensive document and would include not only current breaches of a repairing obligation but might forewarn the tenant of other breaches for which the tenant will be held liable at expiry. In addition, redecoration, minor repairs, and the reinstatement of the premises by removal of tenants' fixtures and fittings or alterations would all normally be included, where these are relevant.

In default of the tenant, the main remedies open to the landlord under Scots law are as follows:

❖ The landlord can apply to the courts for a *decree of specific implement*. In this case the courts issue an order requiring the tenant to comply or alternatively give the landlord authority to enter the premises and carry out the work at the cost of the tenant. This remedy is mainly used in circumstances where the lease still exists rather than where it has already terminated.

❖ If the lease makes available such a provision, the landlord can lawfully **enter the premises**, usually after a stipulated period of time, and carry out the works itself and recover any costs from the tenant as a debt.

❖ The landlord can **terminate or 'irritate' the lease** through the irritancy clause in the lease (assuming there is one), usually on the grounds of breach of contract. The landlord may then sue the tenant for damages. This remedy is, by its nature, only of relevance during the period of the lease and is subject to the provisions of the *Law Reform (Miscellaneous Provisions) (Scotland) Act 1985*.

❖ At termination of the lease, if the tenant has failed to honour its repairing obligation then the landlord might claim a sum in lieu or, if all else fails, **sue the tenant for damages** for breach of contract.

❖ There may of course be **alternative dispute resolution** (ADR) provisions within the lease which can be used in lieu of pursuing a claim for damages through the courts.

So what is the measure of damages to the landlord in the event of tenant default? There is no definitive answer to this question in Scotland. In England and Wales, statute and the 'diminution in value' approach limit the amount of damages recoverable. There is no such limit on the damages recoverable in Scotland. A more pragmatic approach is needed and there may indeed be more than one method of quantifying the measure of damages.

It is often said that the 'diminution in value' is the English approach, and the 'cost of repairs' the Scottish approach. This is an oversimplification. The courts in Scotland have confirmed that a landlord is 'entitled' to quantify the claim in the first instance by reference to the cost of repairs, but that it is open to the tenant to prove the 'actual loss' to the landlord is less than that, perhaps measured by some other means. The burden of proof in the first instance to prove loss is that of the landlord.

Tacit relocation

In Scotland, with the absence of a statutory right of lease renewal (there are a few exceptions), the common law doctrine of **tacit relocation** applies. In simple terms, in a situation where a landlord or tenant fails to give notice to quit within the appropriate timescale then the lease will continue for a period of one year or the period of the lease if it was for less than one year. All of the lease terms remain in force, including the repairing obligations.

Case law

There a number of cases which clarify key elements of dilapidations and repair in Scotland. These can be summarised as follows:

❖ *Turner's Trustees v Steel* (1900) 2F 363
   – The implied warranty of fitness for purpose.

❖ *Blackwell v Farmfoods (Aberdeen) Ltd* (1991) GWD 4-219
   – The landlord's implied warranty at common law of fitness for purpose in relation to common parts.

❖ *Hastie v City of Edinburgh District Council* (1981) SLT 61 & 92
   – Inadequate description of the premises.

❖ *Marfield Properties v Secretary of State for the Environment* (1996) SCLR 749
   – The common Law of the Tenement does not apply in leases to assist in determining what would or would not be common parts.

❖ *Taylor Woodrow Property Co. Ltd v Strathclyde Regional Council* (1996) GWD 7-397
   – A comprehensive examination of the language of a repairing clause.

❖ *Thorn EMI Ltd v Taylor Woodrow Industrial Estates Ltd* (1982), unreported
  – Wording sufficient to extend liability of tenant to include extraordinary repairs.

❖ *Cantor's Properties (Scotland) Ltd v Swears & Wells Ltd* (1980) SLT 165
  – The importance which the courts place on the interpretation of words in the context in which they appear in the lease.

❖ *West Castle Properties Ltd v Scottish Ministers* (2004) SCLR 899
  – Replacement of plant and equipment.

❖ *Scottish Discount Co. Ltd v Blin* (1985) SC 216
  – Identified the proper tests to determine whether an item is or is not a heritable fixture.

❖ *Cliffplant Ltd v Kinnaird; Mabey Bridge Co. Ltd v Kinnaird* (1982) SLT 2
  – Tenant's fixtures and fittings.

❖ *House of Fraser Plc v Prudential Assurance Co. Ltd* (1994) SLT 416
  – Landlord's obligation to repair, and service charges.

❖ *Kidneat Ltd v N.C.R. Ltd* unreported
  – Common repairs.

❖ *Lowe v Quayle Munro Ltd* (1997) GWD 10-438
  – Landlords to carry out work in a 'fair and reasonable' manner.

❖ *Mars Pension Trustees Ltd v County Properties & Developments Ltd* (1999) SC 267
  – Exclusion of landlord's implied warranty at common law on both the leased premises and any common parts to be made in the clearest terms.

❖ *Prudential Assurance Co. Ltd v James Grant & Co. (West) Ltd* (1982) SLT 423
  – This case established that the absolute rule for the measure of damages in the English case *Joyner v Weeks* was not parts of Scots Law. It also confirmed that the ceiling on damages (i.e. the diminution in value of the landlord's reversionary interest) was inapplicable in Scotland.

❖ *Admiralty v Aberdeen Steam Trawling & Fishing Co.* (1910) SC 553
  – Landlord must take (even if in fact he has not) all reasonable steps to minimise his loss.

❖ *Euro Properties Scotland Ltd v Alam* (2000) GWD 23-896
  – Irritancy and the principles of the 'fair and reasonable landlord'.

Dilapidations in Northern Ireland

The foundation of dilapidations law in Northern Ireland is the *Conveyancing Act 1881*. In addition, the *Business Tenancies (Northern Ireland) Order 1996* may be held as applicable in certain circumstances. The *Law of Property Act 1925, Landlord and Tenant Act 1927* and the *Leasehold Property Repairs Act 1938* do not extend to Northern Ireland.

In practice the current RICS *Dilapidations* guidance largely sets the protocol for the execution of dilapidations work in Northern Ireland. One important difference between Northern Ireland, and England and Wales is that diminution valuation is not an alternative remedy because the absence of specific legislation in Northern Ireland means that a working representation is applied that is self evident that the cost of repairs that are due to be done equals the diminution in the value of the reversion.

Significantly, unlike England and Wales, Northern Ireland has to date no recorded case law on the subject of dilapidations.

Green leases

With increasing requirements upon businesses to reduce their carbon footprint, a new breed of 'green lease' has come into being which addresses both energy usage and sustainable construction methods. Cardiff University has produced a Good Practice Guide on the subject and undoubtedly the profession will see more extensive use in coming years.

Green leases are largely untested with regard to dilapidations but are likely to impact on the way both terminal and interim dilapidations schedules are compiled in the future. Examples of the additional dilapidations considerations of green leases include:

❖ works required to restore, or indeed improve, an EPC rating to its former level – this may be particularly contentious in coming years as EPC ratings gain additional legal standing with regard to the ability to sell or let a property;

❖ does the condition of the property affect energy usage – this may be particularly relevant for interim schedules;

❖ the cost of repairs using environmentally sourced materials may be considerably higher than standard products;

❖ the extent of reinstatement required at the end of the term. For example, should a tenant be required to remove wind turbines that represent a high maintenance liability, but which may significantly improve the property's environmental rating;

❖ the extent of renewal (as opposed to repair) required at the end of the term; and

❖ the cost, or benefit, of recycling materials removed from the building.

No doubt further clarification and guidance, both from professional and legal sources, will be required.

Contributed by Harry Dowey, harry.dowey@watts.co.uk, Ian Laurie, ian.laurie@watts.co.uk, Allan Robertson, allan.robertson@watts.co.uk

Section 18(1) of the Landlord and Tenant Act 1927

Section 18(1) of the *Landlord and Tenant Act* 1927 in effect caps the landlord's claim for damages for breach of covenant at the end of the term. The section is divided into two limbs.

Limb 1 provides that:

> 'damages for a breach of a covenant … to keep or put premises in repair … shall in no case exceed the amount … by which the value of … the premises is diminished owing to the breach …'.

> © *Crown copyright material is reproduced under the Open Government Licence v1.0 for public sector information: www.nationalarchives.gov.uk/doc/open-government-licence/*

Limb 1 of section 18(1) applies in all dilapidations cases. The common law claim in dilapidations usually comprises the following components:

❖ cost of works;

❖ fees for preparation and service of the Schedule;

❖ fees for carrying out of the works;

- ❖ fees for negotiating the claim;
- ❖ loss of rent, loss of empty rates and service charge;
- ❖ loss of insurance; and
- ❖ VAT.

Limb 1 of section 18(1) provides that whatever the amount of the common law claim, the landlord's entitlement in damages is limited to the amount by which the value of its interest has been diminished owing to the breach of the covenant to repair. This is not the same as the covenant to redecorate or to reinstate.

Section 18(1) relates to repair only and traditionally it has been considered that the redecoration and reinstatement covenants of the lease were not subject to the S18(1) cap. However, in the case of *Latimer v Carney* (2006), Lady Justice Arden questioned this approach and concluded that decorations may, in certain circumstances, fall with the scope of S18(1).

Reinstatement and decoration are also governed by common law principles under which the landlord's entitlement is to be reimbursed for its financial loss. For this reason, assessment of the landlord's loss is commonly described as a 'diminution valuation'. It will be relevant, however, in assessing the loss, whether the landlord truly intends to reinstate tenant's alterations, for example, a mezzanine floor in a warehouse.

The operation of S18(1) of the Act requires comparison to be made between two valuations:

- ❖ **Valuation A**: assuming compliance;
- ❖ **Valuation B**: assuming actual condition.

The difference between Valuation A and Valuation B assesses the statutory cap on the amount of damages payable.

It has been held that even where Valuation A is a negative figure and Valuation B is a greater negative figure the difference, amounting to the landlord's loss, is payable (*Shortlands Investments Ltd v Cargill plc*).

Limb 2 of section 18(1) deals with what is often referred to as supersession, and provides:

> 'no damage shall be recovered … if it is shown that the premises, in whatever state of repair they might be, would at or shortly after the termination of the tenancy have been or be pulled down, or such structural alterations made therein as would render valueless the repairs …'.

> © *Crown copyright material is reproduced under the Open Government Licence v1.0 for public sector information: www.nationalarchives.gov.uk/doc/open-government-licence/*

The second limb of section 18(1) would operate, for example, where it could be demonstrated that the landlord of an unmodernised 1960s office building intended, as at the expiry of the lease, to carry out refurbishment works to install a suspended ceiling, a raised floor and air conditioning.

In such a case, the landlord's proposals would significantly impact upon the repairs required to the interior of the building, rendering the benefit of the required repair valueless. As a consequence, to the extent that this work is rendered valueless, it would fall out of the claim.

However, the claim for those repairs unaffected by the landlord's alterations would remain valid.

The critical date upon which to establish the landlord's intention is at the expiry of the lease (see *Salisbury v Gilmore* (1948), *Cunliffe v Goodman* (1950) and, more recently, *PGF II SA v Royal & Sun Alliance* (2010)).

The fact that the landlord is contemplating a number of options, including a potential refurbishment, as at the expiry of the lease is not a sufficient basis itself to render the value of the repairs nugatory. A clear and fixed intention must be demonstrated.

The PLA Dilapidations Protocol and RICS *Dilapidations* guidance note require the surveyor to have regard to the common law principles of loss and section 18(1) and, as a consequence, both landlords and tenants should obtain advice as to the likely impact of section 18(1) on their claim at an early stage. The value itself may not, however, require preparation until later in the process, depending on the intended course of action.

Contributed by Ian Laurie, ian.laurie@watts.co.uk

Tenant fit-out and licences to alter

Specific professional advice should be sought to ensure any application for landlord approval is administered correctly.

What are they and how are they used?

A licence is a legally enforceable document granted by a landlord to a tenant enabling the latter to exercise a right within a formal lease agreement. The *Code for Leasing Business Premises* encourages that landlord's control over alterations should be limited to that necessary to protect the value of the property belonging to the landlord.

This section refers specifically to licences for alteration, for example, where a tenant seeks to carry out significant alterations such as subdivision works, provision of mezzanine floors, changing shop fronts, etc.

It is important to review the lease with regard to proposed alterations, as while minor changes may be permitted, the lease may prevent any changes or activities being undertaken at all. Such prohibitions may take the form of two types:

❖ **absolute**: where the landlord is not obliged to grant any consent or approval to an application; and

❖ **qualified**: where the landlord's approval is required but such approval should not be unreasonably withheld.

A licence affords the landlord a degree of control as to how more substantial work is carried out. For example, the licence may require that noisy work is done out of hours to reduce the likelihood of other tenants alleging a breach of their right to quiet enjoyment.

Licences for alteration are also used in some dilapidations claims. Depending on the time elapsed since works were undertaken, if there is no licence in place for works undertaken, the landlord may have the right to insist on removal and reinstatement to the former condition and layout. However, if the licence is worded to avoid any form of reinstatement the changes made may be left in situ at the expiration of the tenure period. Valuation matters relating to reinstatement are discussed elsewhere, see page 126.

Where an application may be required to satisfy certain legal and statutory requirements, for example, to comply with the *Disability Discrimination Act*, the landlord's consent must not be unreasonably withheld.

The application and appraisal process

In certain situations an application by the tenant for formal approval may not necessarily be required, but the lease terms should clarify this. Nevertheless, the tenant should offer the professional courtesy of notifying the landlord when the work is to be carried out.

There is no benchmark or minimum requirement governing the information to be submitted as part of the application. The tenant should ensure that full details of the proposals are forwarded to the landlord and it is advisable that parties discuss the extent of works and establish what information is expected as early as possible in the process, to avoid any delays in the application.

Legislation

The landlord should behave reasonably as to turnaround time, the level of information and detail needed, and whether any amendments or conditions would be necessary. It can be prudent to make use of a standard template checklist to ensure the basic and critical information is provided, thus allowing for further communication if more detail is needed. Often tenants seek approval in order to improve their premises to enhance business performance, and this should be considered in a pragmatic manner by the landlord.

It is not unreasonable for an application to include the following technical information:

> ❖ a complete set of architectural, structural and building services plans, specifications and scope of work;
>
> ❖ a typical programme with commencement and completion dates;
>
> ❖ details of the tenant project team for ease of communication; and
>
> ❖ copy of applications for statutory consents, and subsequent consent/discharge confirmation.

Consideration should also be given to inspection and sign-off of the works by the parties.

Where a chain of leases is present, then superior landlord approval may be required. The superior landlord's interests, however, may not necessarily be the same as the tenant-landlord's and all respective interests and requirements should be contained in the licence for alteration.

Factors to consider

There are a number of factors that may need to be determined when a landlord assesses an application. These may be reported on by external advisers from various professional disciplines depending on the scope, magnitude and complexity of the proposals.

While not a comprehensive list, examples of factors to be considered include the following:

> ❖ Will other tenants be disturbed or inconvenienced by the works?
>
> ❖ Are the proposals sensible for the property and the tenant's business objectives?
>
> ❖ If the proposals increase the rental value, the landlord should consider financing the works pursuant to the *Landlord and Tenant Act* 1927, in exchange for additional rent.
>
> ❖ Will the proposals have any bearing on changes to floor areas, service charge agreements, rateable values and similar?
>
> ❖ Will the work be carried out in a single contract, or phased over time?
>
> ❖ Will building services installations be affected temporarily or permanently?
>
> ❖ Will the structural integrity of the property be compromised temporarily or permanently?
>
> ❖ Will the building work or the completed alterations affect the building insurance cover?
>
> ❖ Will any fire precautions be affected during or after the work?
>
> ❖ Who will be responsible for settling the landlord's costs and professional fees?
>
> ❖ The need for any additional enabling or remedial work after the proposals are complete.
>
> ❖ Responsibility and liability for all design, construction work and the securing of all appropriate consents.
>
> ❖ The requirement for temporary additional parking areas, refuse collection point and similar.

❖ The need and frequency for landlord work inspections, to ensure compliance with the agreed documents.

Form of consent

Whether the licence is initially drafted by the landlord's or tenant's solicitor, it is usually the case that each party will have technical consultants and their agreed version of the plans and proposals would be appended to the main licence. Similarly, if the landlord wishes to insert specific conditions, such as sequencing of work, then these can be agreed and incorporated into the licence.

A signed and certified copy of the agreed licence should be held with the lease bundle for cross-reference purposes.

It is normal practice that, to complete the licence conditions, once the work has been completed, the tenant submits final copies of all statutory consents secured for the works, and permits the landlord to inspect the completed activity to ensure these are fully signed-off and agreed, promptly in writing.

Where tenants carry out alterations without formal approval, the landlord could insist on reinstatement (depending on the lease terms). The landlord's position, however, may be reduced if the alterations are left unchallenged for a period of time. In particular, if an unlicensed alteration has been undertaken but not discovered within 12 years, or 6 years if the lease is not executed as a deed (England and Wales), then it is possible the *Limitation Act* 1980 may apply.

Further information

❖ See also the RICS guidance note *Handling Tenant's Applications for Approval to Alterations*.

Contributed by Ian Laurie, ian.laurie@watts.co.uk

Recovery of service charges for major works

Service charges are a wide and complex subject. This section deals with:

❖ the basic principles of service charges payable for any major works in the maintenance of a property, in conjunction with the express repairing obligations of the lease; and

❖ the general implications for any tenants/leaseholders.

This section is intended as a general guide and is not a substitute for legal advice.

The administration and notification for recovery of service charges will vary subject to the type of property tenure, length of lease, and legislation. In simple terms, a landlord will undertake repair and maintenance works and may contribute to the cost, however, it is often the leaseholder who will be liable to pay for the works under the lease terms.

Surveyors and/or other professional advisers acting for property owners should be aware of the basic principles, current practice and legislation relevant to service charge recovery.

Commercial property

There is no specific legislation regulating the administration and/or recovery of service charges in commercial properties. The administration and recovery of service charges is a system largely self-administered and regulated by the industry. The Royal Institution of Chartered Surveyors (RICS) has published an RICS Code of practice, which is based upon the second edition of *Service Charges in Commercial*

Legislation

Property: A Guide to Good Practice. Separate editions are available for England and Wales, for Scotland and for Northern Ireland, as practices differ slightly in these jurisdictions.

While it is not a legal requirement to follow these guidelines, by doing so a practitioner will be deemed to be embodying best practice and endorsing the notion of value for money, and hopefully good landlord and tenant relationships are likely to be fostered.

The mechanisms for charging and recovering service charges should be laid out within the lease covenants; these have legal force in contract law. Case law has also clarified some points over the years, though this is subject to change.

The apportionment of service charge liability is usually stipulated in the lease and commonly based upon (but not restricted to) the following:

❖ percentage of the value of the total cost of the works;

❖ floor area;

❖ rateable value;

❖ a fixed amount.

Service charges may include for payment into a sinking fund, or other account intended to cover the cost of major works, and often leases include a separate clause allowing the landlord to recover sums in addition to the standard service charge.

Residential property

Service charges are not normally recoverable under Assured Shorthold Tenancies (ASTs), which are usually for a minimum period of 6 or 12 months.

Residential properties sold on long leaseholds are protected by various Acts of Parliament, but the two principal legislative instruments governing service charges recovery for major works for leaseholders are:

❖ The *Landlord and Tenant Act* 1985, which sets out the basic ground rules for service charges, and defines what a service charge is, reasonableness of service charges and consultation.

❖ The *Commonhold and Leasehold Reform Act* 2002, which introduced new requirements for statutory consultation.

Section 153 of the 2002 Act requires that: 'A demand for the payment of a service charge must be accompanied by a summary of the rights and obligations of tenants of dwellings in relation to service charges'. Section 151 of the 2002 Act replaced section 20 of the *Landlord and Tenant Act* 1985, and introduced a new section 20ZA on consultation procedures for major works and long-term contracts; comprising two separate 30-day periods for leaseholders to put forward their observations, and also nominate their own contractors, where any lessee has to pay more than £250 for works, or in excess of £100 in any accounting period, towards costs incurred under a long-term agreement.

Note: Section 20 procedures for local authorities and other public sector landlords differ and further guidance should be sought in this regard.

The above Acts provide limitations on the amounts a landlord can recover unless the landlord has complied with the requirements as to estimates, consultation and nomination of contractors, and/or has received dispensation from either the Leasehold Valuation Tribunal or the Land Tribunal.

Landlords and leaseholders have rights to ask the Residential Property Valuation Tribunal (Tel: 0845 600 3178) whether a service charge demand is reasonable, in respect of costs already incurred or an estimate or budget.

Overview

If either a landlord or tenant is in any doubt about their leasehold rights and duties, they should seek specific advice, from either a property lawyer or a chartered surveyor specialising in this field, or from one of the professional bodies listed below:

- ❖ the Lease (an Executive Non Departmental Public Body (ENDPB) funded by government): www.lease-advice.org
- ❖ the Lands Tribunal: www.landstribunal.gov.uk
- ❖ the Law Society: www.lawsociety.org.uk/home.law
- ❖ the Royal Institution of Chartered Surveyors: www.rics.org

The Leasehold Valuation Tribunal

The Leasehold Valuation Tribunal was originally created by the *Housing Act* 1980 and is a statutory body for determining landlord and tenant disputes in relation to residential leases. The tribunal is an alternative to court proceedings. Tribunals usually comprise three members and are empowered to:

- ❖ decide the sum the leaseholder would be required to pay to buy (enfranchise), extend or renew the lease of their home, where a value cannot otherwise be agreed with the leaseholder;
- ❖ modify estate management schemes under the *Leasehold Reform, Housing and Urban Development Act* 1993;
- ❖ adjudicate disputes about the right of first refusal;
- ❖ determine the liability for payment of service charges; and
- ❖ determine applications on the dispensation of service charge consultation requirements, administration charges, the right to manage, the appointment of managers, the variation of leases and estate charges.

Further information can be found on the website: www.direct.gov.uk/en/HomeAndCommunity/BuyingAndSellingYourHome/Leaseholdproperties/DG_191691

Contributed by Ian Laurie, ian.laurie@watts.co.uk

Neighbourly matters

Rights to light

The subject of rights to light usually concerns the assessment of whether proposed obstructions (for example, new developments) are likely to interfere materially with neighbours' easements of light. Interpretation of whether a material right to light issue is likely to arise requires knowledge of the law, particularly easements and nuisance, and an understanding of the technical measurements of skylight entering a room. It is then possible to assess the risk of injunction and, where appropriate, the likely level of damages that could be awarded. It is also possible to determine how to modify a proposed scheme in order to reduce or overcome potential problems.

Legal background

Rights to light problems bring together two distinct but different areas of English law, namely private nuisance (a subdivision of the law of torts) and easements (a subdivision of land law).

Private nuisance

The tort of private nuisance, like the tort of public nuisance, regulates activities affecting individual rights in or rights over real property (land).

A private nuisance may be defined as an unreasonable interference with a person's use or enjoyment of land itself, or some right over or in connection with land (i.e. a right to light).

The law of nuisance tries to balance the legitimate activities of neighbours – a give and take approach. Interference with a right to light must be objectively unreasonable in its extent and severity if it is to be sufficient to constitute a nuisance in the eyes of the courts. Only when the courts are satisfied that the interference is unreasonable will they remedy the situation by awarding an injunction and/or damages. It should be appreciated that levels of natural light can often be interfered with to a marginal extent and this will not necessarily constitute an infringement of a proprietary right that will be recognised as a nuisance.

Easements

An easement may be defined as a right annexed to land to use or to restrict use of neighbouring land in some way. For an easement to be valid, four essential characteristics must be satisfied:

- ❖ There must be a dominant tenement and a servient tenement.
- ❖ The right must accommodate (benefit) the dominant tenement.
- ❖ The dominant tenement and the servient tenement must be owned or occupied by different persons.
- ❖ The right concerned must be capable of forming the subject matter of a grant.

Rights to light have been recognised as a valid easement for centuries. The general rights to light principles set out below have been distilled from the large body of case law that exists.

A right to light can be defined generally as a negative easement providing a right for a building to receive sufficient natural light through a defined aperture (usually a window), over the land of another, in perpetuity or for a term of years.

Nature of a right to light

A right to light is not personal – it runs with property/buildings. It benefits the dominant tenement and burdens the servient tenement.

A right to light is for 'sufficient' natural light only and this is taken to mean enough light, 'according to the ordinary notions of mankind' for:

❖ comfortable use and enjoyment of a dwelling house; or

❖ beneficial use of and occupation of a warehouse, shop or other place (office, etc.).

The test for 'sufficiency' is whether or not the dominant tenement will be left with enough light according to the ordinary requirements of mankind. Sufficiency is not based on the measure of light lost. See *Colls v Home & Colonial Stores* [1904] AC 179.

Actionable injury and measurement of light

No specific rule has been developed by the courts to define exactly when a reduction in natural light becomes actionable. The test for injury is uncertain but flexible. The court will have regard, in all cases, to the specific facts and circumstances and it will usually hear objective technical evidence from a rights to light expert, as well as more subjective evidence from the injured party.

A form of technical evidence has evolved that entails analysis of the amount of the notional sky dome that can be seen from a series of points in an affected room at table level. At any given point on the working plane there is a minimum amount of sky area below which the level of daylight at that point will be inadequate. Adequacy is considered to be just enough for undertaking work that requires visual discrimination, such as reading, drawing or sewing. In technical terms this is one lumen or 1/500th of a standard uniform dome of overcast sky in December (i.e. 0.2% sky factor).

It is possible to plot the 0.2% sky factor contour in the subject room and measure the area of the room that will receive more than adequate light both before and after development. Today, leading rights to light experts tend to do this with the aid of 3D computer modelling and specialist software, which is more accurate and efficient than the laborious manual Waldram method.

Having measured the area that will be adequately illuminated, it is possible to assess whether an actionable injury will arise. Very generally, for day-to-day practical purposes, light specialists have adopted the general conventions that:

❖ A commercial property may be considered actionably damaged when less than 50% of an office floor area is lit to the critical one lumen (0.2% sky factor) level, i.e. the so-called 50/50 rule.

❖ A residential/domestic property should be considered actionably damaged when less than 55% of a room area is lit to the critical one lumen (0.2% sky factor) level.

It must be understood that the percentages mentioned above are not strongly founded in specific legal authority, although courts will make reference to previously decided cases where the facts are similar. The courts regard the so-called 50/50 rule as a 'convenient rule of thumb'.

Acquisition of a right to light

A right to light may be created by:

❖ express grant or reservation (sometimes encountered);

❖ implied grant or reservation (rarely encountered); or

❖ prescription (very common and often called 'ancient lights').

Prescription means the procuring of a right on the basis of a long-established custom and three methods of prescription exist, namely:

❖ time immemorial (right enjoyed since before 1189);

❖ doctrine of lost modern grant (right enjoyed continuously for minimum 20 years); and

❖ *Prescription Act* 1832: sections 3 and 4 (right enjoyed continuously for 20 years).

(Note: In the City of London, because of the 'Custom of London', the acquisition of a right by the doctrine of lost modern grant is not available – see *Bowring Services Ltd v Scottish Widows* [1995] 16 EG 206.)

Defeating a right to light

Prescription through the doctrines of lost modern grant or time immemorial can be defeated if it can be shown that the easement has not been enjoyed, 'as of right', i.e. through force, secrecy or with permission.

Statutory prescription, under the *Prescription Act* 1832, may be defeated if the servient party can show that:

❖ at some time within the last 19 years, it has prevented the entry of natural daylight through the subject apertures by erecting an opaque physical obstruction for a continuous period of at least one year;

❖ at some time in the last 19 years, it registered a light obstruction notice under the *Rights of Light Act* 1959 for a whole year (see below); or

❖ the right has been enjoyed under some consent or agreement expressly given for that purpose by deed or in writing.

Defending a right to light

A prescriptive right to light may be lost if it is not defended in the face of development. A neighbour who acquiesces in or submits to an interruption of light for one year or more will lose a claim to a prescriptive right under section 4 of the *Prescription Act* 1832. (See *Dance v Triplow and Another* [1992] 17 EG 103.)

Successful defence of a prescriptive right to light relies much on eternal vigilance and prompt protestation in writing to the obstructor. The protestations should also be repeated at regular intervals. Ultimately legal proceedings will need to be brought against a developer who ignores the objections and the timing of this may considerably affect the chances of obtaining an injunction.

Remedies

The current legal system permits the awarding of:

❖ prohibitory or mandatory injunctions; and/or

❖ common law damages.

Injunctions

The courts are reluctant to sanction a wrongdoing by a servient party in allowing that party to purchase its neighbour's rights. Generally, an injunction is regarded as the normal remedy, with damages the exception. The Court of Appeal has recently reminded all of this principle in their decision in *Regan v Paul Properties Ltd and Others* [2006] EWCA Civ 1319.

The court may award damages in lieu of an injunction if all the four requirements below can be answered in the affirmative:

❖ Is the injury small?

❖ Would a small money payment be an adequate remedy?

❖ Would it be oppressive to the defendant to grant an injunction?

❖ Is the injury one that can be estimated in money terms?

These requirements are derived from *Shelfer v City of London Electric Lighting Co* [1895] 1 Ch 287 31, however, the courts have departed from a strict application of the test and it is not necessarily applicable to every rights to light situation.

The conduct of parties will also have a significant bearing on the matter. If a developer ignores the communicated protestations from its neighbour and continues developing regardless then once a nuisance is proved an injunction should be the default remedy.

Damages (compensation)

Compensation for injury to a right to light may be assessed using one of two methods:

❖ the traditional valuation approach; or

❖ the share of developer's profit approach.

Compensation/damages based on a share of the developer's profit is the method more likely to be used since the case of *Tamares (Vincent Square) Ltd v Fairpoint Properties (Vincent Square) Ltd* [2007] All ER(D) 1034 (assessment of damages). This method will often derive a significantly larger sum in compensation than will the traditional valuation approach. In *Tamares*, the court set out eight principles, derived from previous cases, to give guidance on how damages should be assessed.

Whichever method is adopted, the valuation approach is based on a freeholder in possession. With a traditional valuation approach, a 'base book value' is calculated for the light loss, which may then be enhanced by a multiplier of up to three or four times, having regard to the case of *Carr Saunders v Dick McNeil Associates Ltd and Others* [1986] 1 WLR 992. Any compensation will be appropriately apportioned between the various interests in the dominant tenement. For leases, this is generally dependent upon the number of years remaining until the next rent review. For residential property, however, the assessment of compensation is more subjective.

Compensation based on a share of the developer's profit requires an (often complicated) assessment to be made of the amount of profit that a developer will be expected to realise if construction of the infringing part of a proposed development actually occurs. The owner(s) of the injured building will then expect a share of that element of profit, which share could be anything between 5% and 50% depending on the circumstances. This approach essentially considers the possibility of sharing the profit that a developer will make from floor space that could not be built if the adjoining owner obtained an injunction. There is no consistent guidance from the courts indicating when profit-based compensation is to be preferred over the traditional valuation approach.

Dos and don'ts

❖ Do establish whether surrounding properties enjoy rights to light, including other tenanted parts of the client's property, and identify all parties with an interest.

❖ Do establish whether development proposals are likely to leave the surrounding buildings with inadequate light.

❖ Do take specialist advice from a rights to light consultant at an early stage.

❖ Do obtain copies of all leases, deeds, transfers, restrictive covenants, and so on, that could have a bearing on the legal position.

❖ Don't be fooled by buildings that look less than 20 years old or have blocked-up windows: case law is complex and there could still be a right to light.

❖ Do consider whether the Crown has ever had an interest in the development site: the surrounding buildings may not be entitled to rights to light.

❖ Do consider whether the development site has ever been acquired or appropriated by the local authority for planning purposes under section 237 of the *Town and Country Planning Act* 1990, as this affects the potential for injunctions. Local authorities are able to override rights to light that would otherwise hinder a development by using powers conferred on them by section 237. The development land concerned has to have been 'appropriated for planning purposes' and the development must be executed in accordance with a planning permission. An injury caused by the proposed development must be addressed by paying the injured party compensation but the sums concerned are calculated on compulsory purchase principles and not the common law principles described above. (Other legislation relating to development by government-funded agencies, for example, the *Housing and Regeneration Act* 2008, also exists and contains provisions that are similar to section 237.) Use of section 237 powers has become more prominent for major landmark developments since the case of *HKRUK II (CHC) Ltd v Heaney* [2010] 44 EG 126.

❖ Do obtain copies (if available) showing the massing and profile of the existing building on the development site, and the proposed building or extension, and also up to date floor layout plans for the surrounding buildings.

❖ Do establish the extent of a right (i.e. the number, size and location of apertures).

❖ Do consider whether transferred or 'incorporated' rights to light exist.

❖ Do seek the advice of lawyers if the legal position is complicated beyond your experience by any controlling deeds or similar documents.

❖ Do ensure that your client understands that the law relating to rights to light, and the valuation techniques, are not an exact science.

❖ Do remember that recent case law has reminded all that the primary remedy of interference with a right to light is an injunction – not damages.

❖ Do remember that you cannot rely on a neighbour, particularly a residential owner, settling for compensation.

❖ Do explain to your client that there are no general statutory procedures for dealing with rights to light issues and that there are no prescribed periods and deadlines during or by which parties are obliged to settle issues.

❖ Don't allow a 'dominant' party to be pressured into early agreement of compensation.

Light obstruction notices

Light obstruction notices can be used to either defeat an existing right to light that has been acquired by statutory prescription or prevent such a right from being acquired. They are a useful tool for preserving the development potential of a site and can also be used to 'flush out' potential claims.

Under section 2(1) of the *Rights of Light Act* 1959, a light obstruction notice can be registered with the local authority as a local land charge for a period of one year.

References

❖ *Rights of light: Practical guidance for chartered surveyors in England and Wales* (1st edition), RICS guidance note, 2010.

❖ *Rights of Light: The Modern Law* (2nd edition), S. Bickford-Smith and A. Francis, Jordan Publishing Ltd, 2007.

❖ *Anstey's Rights of Light* (4th edition), J. Anstey and L. Harris, RICS Books, 2006.

Further information

The two main statutes that are relevant to rights to light are:

❖ the *Prescription Act* 1832; and

❖ the *Rights of Light Act* 1959.

There exists a large body of rights to light case law. The selection of case reports listed below includes the more recent and more important decisions.

❖ *Allen and Another v Greenwood and Another* [1975] 1 All ER 819 6, 35-6.

❖ *Bowring Services Ltd v Scottish Widows Fund & Life Assurance Society* [1995] 16 EG 206.

❖ *Carr Saunders v Dick McNeil Associates Ltd and Others* [1986] 1 WLR 992 37, 43.

❖ *Charles Semon & Co v Bradford Corporation* [1922] 2 Ch 737.

❖ *Colls v Home & Colonial Stores* [1904] AC 179 4, 9, 10, 29, 31-2, 34.

❖ *Colls v Laugher* [1894] 3 Ch 659.

❖ *Dance v Triplow and Another* [1992] 17 EG 103.

❖ *Deakins v Hookings* [1994] 14 EG 133.

❖ *Ecclesiastical Commissioners for England v Kino* [1880] 14 ChD 213 40.

❖ *Fishenden v Higgs and Hill Ltd* [1935] 153 LT 128 33.

❖ *Forsyth-Grant v Allen and Another* [2008] EWCA Civ 505.

❖ *HKRUK II (CHC) Ltd v Heaney* [2010] 44 EG 126.

❖ *Lyme Valley Squash Club Ltd v Newcastle under Lyme Borough Council and Another* [1985] 2 All ER 28–9.

❖ *Marine and General Mutual Life Assurance Society v St. James Real Estate Co Ltd* [1991] 2 EGLR 178.

❖ *Midtown Ltd v City of London Real Property Co Ltd* [2005] 14 EG 130.

❖ *Ough v King* [1967] 3 All ER 859 34.

❖ *Price v Hilditch* [1930] I Ch 500 5, 37, 43.

❖ *Pugh and Another v Howels and Another* [1984] 48 PCR 298 36–7.

❖ *Regan v Paul Properties Ltd and Others* [2006] EWCA Civ 1319.

❖ *RHJ Ltd v (1) FT Patten (Holdings) Ltd and (2) FT Patten Properties (Liverpool) Ltd* [2007] EWHC 1655 (Ch).

❖ *Salvage Wharf Ltd and another v GS Brough Ltd* [2009] EWCA Civ 21.

❖ *Scott v Pape* [1886] 31 ChD 554 6, 80.

❖ *Sheffield Masonic Hall Co v Sheffield Corporation* [1932] 2 Ch 17 43.

❖ *Shelfer v City of London Electric Lighting Co* [1895] 1 Ch 287 31.

❖ *Tamares (Vincent Square) Ltd v Fairpoint Properties (Vincent Square) Ltd* [2006] EG41 226 (injunction v damages ruling).

❖ *Tamares (Vincent Square) Ltd v Fairpoint Properties (Vincent Square) Ltd* [2007] ALL ER(D) 1034 (assessment of damages).

❖ *Wheeldon v Burrows* [1879] 12 ChD 31 78.

❖ *Wrotham Park Estate Co v Parkside Homes Ltd* [1973] ChD 321.

Contributed by Paul Lovelock, paul.lovelock@watts.co.uk

Daylight and sunlight amenity

As greater emphasis is placed on environmental issues, local planning authorities are increasingly concerning themselves with the effect of developments on the daylight and sunlight enjoyed by neighbouring properties. A local authority's Unitary Development Plan or Local Plan should always be consulted, as it will give an indication of what they expect in this regard. Also bear in mind supplementary planning guidance issued by the local authority.

The Building Research Establishment (BRE) published the second edition of Report 209 in October 2011 titled *Site layout planning for daylight and sunlight: A guide to good practice*. It is intended to give guidance on how to ensure good daylight and sunlight to proposed new development through good design, while avoiding detrimentally affecting neighbours' daylight and sunlight amenity. It sets out various tests that can be undertaken to establish if a noticable reduction in amenity is likely to result from a scheme.

The BRE report is not intended to be mandatory. However, it is not uncommon for planning authorities to require a developer to submit a daylighting and sunlighting study in support of a planning application and some may expect compliance with the recommendations given in the guidelines.

It is important to note that even if a scheme is granted planning consent this will not override the private rights of individuals, and therefore, rights to light may still be an issue. (See *Brewer and another v Secretary of State for the Environment and others* [1988] 2 PLR 13.)

The BRE report treats the assessment of daylight and sunlight differently.

Daylight

The BRE report states that if any part of a new building or extension, measured in a vertical section perpendicular to a main window wall of an existing building, from the centre of the lowest window, subtends an angle of more than 25° to the horizontal, then the diffuse daylighting of the existing building may be adversely affected. This will be the case if either:

❖ the vertical sky component measured at the centre of an existing main window is less than 27%, and less than 0.8 times its former value; or

❖ the area of the working plane in a room which can receive direct skylight is reduced to less than 0.8 times its former value.

In such circumstances the occupants of the existing building will notice the reduction in the amount of skylight and more of the room will appear poorly lit.

The BRE report also presents another method of assessing the interior daylight levels within a room, called the average daylight factor (ADF), which it takes from British Standard 8206-Part 2: 2008. There are recommended minimum ADF values for dwellings, namely 1% for bedrooms, 1.5% for living rooms and 2% for kitchens.

Sunlight

The BRE report advises that new development should take care to safeguard access to sunlight for existing dwellings and any non-domestic buildings where there is a particular requirement for sunlight. If a living room of an existing dwelling has a main window facing within 90° of due south, and any part of a new development subtends an angle of more than 25° to the horizontal, measured from a point two metres above ground in a vertical section, perpendicular to the window, then the sunlighting of the existing dwelling may be adversely affected.

The sunlight amenity of the existing dwelling will be considered to be adversely affected if the window reference point receives less than one quarter of annual probable sunlight hours, and/or less than 5% of annual probable sunlight hours during the winter months between 21 September and 21 March, and the available sunlight hours in either period is reduced to less than 0.8 times its former value.

Overshadowing

BRE Report 209 also provides guidance concerning overshadowing created by a proposed scheme. It notes that sunlight to open spaces is 'valuable for a number of reasons', namely to:

❖ provide attractive sunlit views (all year);

❖ make outdoor activities like sitting out and children's play more pleasant (mainly during the warmer months);

❖ encourage plant growth (mainly in spring and summer);

❖ dry out the ground, reducing moss and slime (mainly in the colder months);

❖ melt frost, ice and snow (in winter); and

❖ dry clothes (all year).

The BRE report suggests that the availability of sunlight should be checked for all open spaces where it will be required. It goes on to state that this would normally include gardens, allotments, parks and playing fields, children's playgrounds, outdoor swimming pools, paddling pools, public sitting-out areas, and focal points for views (such as a group of monuments or fountains).

BRE Report 209 gives guidance concerning the degree of change in overshadowing to open areas, resulting from an adjoining development, which is thought to be permissible before the change becomes noticeable to users of the space. The BRE report advises that:

'for it to appear adequately sunlit throughout the year, no more than two-fifths and preferably no more than a quarter of any garden or amenity area should be prevented by buildings from receiving any sun at all on 21 March. If, as a result of new development, an existing garden or amenity area does not meet these guidelines, and the area which can receive some sun on 21 March is less than 0.8 times its former value, then the loss of sunlight is likely to be noticeable.'

BRE material is reproduced with permission from Building Research Establishment Ltd. BRE publications are available from www.brebookshop.com

Analysis

The BRE report sets out the methods by which the effect of a development on existing neighbouring buildings and open spaces may be assessed. If the local planning authority requires an assessment to be undertaken and submitted in support of a planning application, it is usual for the analysis to follow the methodologies in BRE Report 209.

The target values recommended in BRE Report 209 are quite demanding and can be difficult to achieve, particularly in dense urban environments. Care should be taken when applying the guidance and interpreting the results of analyses.

Further information

❖ BRE Report 209, *Site layout planning for daylight and sunlight: A guide to good practice* (second edition, 2011), by P. J. Littlefair.

❖ BS 8206-2: 2008, *Lighting for buildings: Code of practice for daylighting*.

❖ *Brewer and another v Secretary of State for the Environment and others* [1988] 2 PLR 13.

❖ Planning appeal by St George Central London, decided 20 April 2004.

❖ *Malster v Ipswich Borough Council* [2001] EWHC ADMIN 711.

❖ Planning appeal by West End Green (Properties) Ltd, decided 10 October 2005.

❖ Planning appeal by Inner Circle Ltd, decided 16 March 2007.

Contributed by Paul Lovelock, paul.lovelock@watts.co.uk

High hedges

The *Anti-social Behaviour Act* 2003 came into operation in England on 1 June 2005. Part 8 of the Act provides local authorities with powers to deal with complaints about high hedges.

The legislation means that neighbours who are in dispute over a high hedge can now go to their local authority for resolution. Note that 'in dispute' does not mean one neighbour can simply bypass the other and expect a favourable response from the local authority. The legislation provides a vehicle for neighbours who have discussed the matter and have tried, but exhausted, all other possibilities for resolving their dispute.

Note also that the local authority is not expected, nor empowered, to mediate between the neighbours or to assist or progress negotiations. Its role is simply to adjudicate on whether 'the hedge is adversely affecting the complainant's reasonable enjoyment of their property'.

In its deliberations the local authority must consider all the relevant factors and must try to strike the right balance between the interests of the two neighbours. It may also consider the interests of the wider community if it considers this may be adversely affected.

Once it has considered all the relevant issues (not the neighbours' arguments), the local authority will either dismiss the matter and write to the neighbours telling them its reasons, or it will write to the hedge owner in a formal notice setting out what the owner must do to the hedge (and by what date he or she must do it) in order to remedy the problem.

A hedge owner who fails to comply with the notice or in any way fails to carry out the works which are required by the local authority will be guilty of an offence. Upon summary prosecution the failing hedge owner could receive a fine of up to £1,000 and continuing fines which will accumulate on a daily basis while the owner remains in breach of the order.

Common misconceptions

High hedges are all those which are over two metres tall

Not true: The legislation does not apply to all hedges, only to those which are evergreen or 'semi-evergreen'. It does not cover single or deciduous trees. For clarification this means a hedge which has two or more consecutive trees or shrubs which are evergreen, or one which is predominantly evergreen. Furthermore, some hedges over two metres do not block light, do not cause a nuisance and do not prevent anyone from enjoying their own land. Therefore, they are not going to be the subject of a dispute and can safely be allowed to grow as high as they will.

You need permission to grow a garden hedge over two metres tall

Not true: A hedge owner can grow a hedge as high as he or she likes in the first instance. Permission is not required and the local authority will take no automatic action unless a dispute is referred to it. If both neighbours want a tall hedge and are not in dispute over it then it is very unlikely that a local authority will become involved.

If the local authority receives a complaint it will order the hedge to be cut down to two metres

Not true: If a local authority receives a complaint it will weigh up all the relevant matters and consider the merits of each case in isolation. It may order a reduction in height, either in one cut or in stages if a single cut could be drastic enough to kill the hedge. The local authority may stipulate a greater height than two metres if it considers that this height will abate the nuisance sufficiently. The confusion seems to stem from the fact that the local authority may not order a reduction to less than two metres. Additionally, the local authority cannot require the hedge to be removed completely.

The hedge will be a nuisance if it blocks light to a neighbouring property

Not true: While a hedge which is blocking a neighbouring owner's light may be interpreted as a nuisance, this is not unequivocal. Each case will be considered individually and an appropriate order will be made, but the legislation does not guarantee an adjoining property access to uninterrupted light.

Anyone served with an order under Part 8 of the Anti-social Behaviour Act 2003 will be the subject of an ASBO

Not true: There is no provision in the Act to serve an Anti-social Behaviour Order in respect of high hedge complaints.

Further information

There is, of course, a lot more to high hedges and their problems than has been outlined above. Much of the information is somewhat confusing and needs to be interpreted carefully.

Be aware, also, that a number of organisations exist purely to complain about high hedges. Some of these organisations can be really helpful, however they do not all consider the interests of fair play and some may offer confusing, if not misleading, information.

It is better then, to get information from an official source.

The Department for Communities and Local Government (DCLG) has more information, including guidance from the Building Research Establishment on calculating light loss and appropriate hedge height. *Hedge height and light loss* can be found at: www.communities.gov.uk/publications/planningandbuilding/hedgeheight

Although the Act applies in Wales, the situation is slightly different. Further information can be found on its application in Wales at: www.wales.gov.uk/legislation/?lang=en

Contributed by Paul Lovelock, paul.lovelock@watts.co.uk

Party wall procedure

The *Party Wall etc. Act* 1996 came into force throughout England and Wales on 1 July 1997. All previous local enactments, including the *London Building Acts (Amendment) Act* 1939 Part VI and the *Bristol Improvement Act* 1847, have now been repealed.

The general principle of the Act is to enable an owner to undertake certain specific works on, or adjacent to, adjoining properties while giving protection to potentially affected neighbours. As suggested by the word 'etc.' in its title, the Act relates not just to party walls. Its purpose is to facilitate the execution of work not to prevent it. Today's legislation is the latest incarnation of legislation that was originally born out of the Great Fire of London in 1666.

The parties

The owner of the property where the work is to be undertaken is the 'building owner'. The owner of the adjoining property is the 'adjoining owner'. There can be many adjoining owners including freeholder, leaseholder and anyone with an interest greater than from year to year.

Under the Act, the word 'owner' can also include people with a contract to purchase or an agreement for lease; this arrangement allows a prospective owner to serve notice, and even commence work, before completion of the contract.

Party structures

A party wall is one that stands on the land of two owners, by more than its footings, or one which separates buildings of different owners. In the first case, the whole wall is a party wall whereas in the second, it is only a party wall for the extent to which the two buildings are using it and the whole of the rest of the wall belongs to the person on whose land it stands. Other types of party structure are party fence walls (i.e. shared garden walls) and party floors (e.g. separating different flats).

In the case of a party wall, each owner owns the part of the wall that stands on their own land, but also has rights over the remainder of the wall. The Act allows owners to treat the whole of the party wall as if it were their own, and debars them from dealing with their half on its own without informing their neighbours.

Before exercising any of the rights bestowed upon them, owners must follow the procedures set down in *the Party Wall etc. Act* 1996. If an owner wishes to underpin, raise, cut into, thicken or demolish and rebuild a party wall, that owner must give notice of his or her intention to do so. In the event that the adjoining owner disagrees, each party must appoint a surveyor and a formal agreement known as a party wall award must be entered into.

An adjoining owner may respond to a party structure notice by serving a counter notice requiring certain specified works to be undertaken to the party wall for his or her future purposes. However the notice must be served within one month of the original notice and the adjoining owner will be responsible for the cost of the additional work.

Excavations adjacent to structures

The *Party Wall etc. Act* 1996 requires notice to be served on adjoining owners of certain intended excavations within three metres or six metres of adjacent buildings or structures. The excavations could be for any purpose, not just for a building or its foundations.

Refer to the following diagrams for details of these notifiable excavations.

Three metre notice

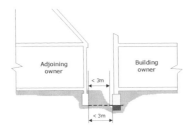

Six metre notice

New walls at boundaries

Where it is proposed to build at the 'line of junction' (i.e. the boundary), notice may need to be given to the adjoining owners. This will be the case where the boundary is not already built upon, or is built upon only to the extent of a boundary wall (not being a party fence wall or external wall of a building). In return, a right to construct projecting mass concrete footings work may be claimed.

General rights and obligations

The *Party Wall etc. Act* 1996 grants various general rights and obligations in relation to work undertaken in pursuance of the Act. The key ones are:

- ❖ obligation to serve notice on adjoining owners before undertaking the work;
- ❖ obligation to execute the work in compliance with other statutory requirements and in accordance with details agreed either by the parties or by appointed party wall surveyors in an award;
- ❖ ability to enter and remain on adjoining owners' land so far as is reasonably necessary to facilitate the work;
- ❖ duty not to cause unnecessary inconvenience;
- ❖ duty to compensate adjoining owners for loss or damage arising as a consequence of the work; and
- ❖ obligation to make good damage caused by work to party structures.

Agreeing the works

The building owner and adjoining owner may agree the details of the works between them. Where disagreements occur, either deemed or actual, the Act provides a mechanism for resolving them through the appointment of party wall surveyors. The appointed surveyors have a duty to settle the matter by making an award and they must act expediently and impartially, having regard to the interests and rights of both parties.

Entry to adjoining land

There are differing views on whether a building owner may enter adjoining land for all work covered by the Act or only where the Act expressly grants a right to do work, such as raising a party wall. The Act is ambiguous, which may potentially create difficulties for building owners who wish to build a new wall wholly on the line of junction and who need to erect scaffolding on adjoining land. For such work it is important to establish the views of the surveyors and adjoining owners concerned at an early stage.

Dos and don'ts

- ❖ Do consider whether proposed excavations and building works require the serving of notices under the Act.

- ❖ Do allow adequate time in the project programme for identifying and resolving all party wall issues. Time periods stated in the Act are statutory minimums, and often longer periods should be allowed.

- ❖ Do establish which party will act as the 'building owner' and verify his or her legal interest in the property.

- ❖ Do remember that if the building owner parts with his or her interest in the property part-way through proceedings, matters will have to start afresh.

- ❖ Do remember that the interests of all relevant adjoining owners will have to be identified with certainty and each owner notified separately.

- ❖ Do remember that each adjoining owner has a right to disagree with the proposals and to appoint a surveyor.

- ❖ Don't let unreasonable or unresponsive adjoining owners or surveyors hinder progress: use the mechanisms in the Act to force matters along.

- ❖ Do make allowance within the cost plan for the reasonable fees of the adjoining owners' surveyors and any necessary subconsultants (typically structural engineers).

- ❖ Do ensure that the design team and contractors cooperate and produce all necessary drawings, method statements, calculations, etc. in good time.

- ❖ Do ensure that the proposed time and manner of carrying out the work is reasonable and that no unnecessary inconvenience will be caused.

- ❖ Do consider making provision within tender documents for restrictions on working hours and/or methods of working for noisy elements of work falling within the scope of the Act.

- ❖ Do consider whether access will be required onto adjoining land to build a wall at the line of junction and bear in mind that differing views exist as to whether a right of entry exists for such work.

- ❖ Do ensure that the procedures required by the Act are followed meticulously; otherwise, notices and awards could be invalidated.

❖ Do remember that the party wall surveyors are administering the Act impartially and not representing clients.

❖ Do ensure that awards are agreed prior to starting the relevant work.

❖ Don't confuse common law and rights to light matters as being part of party wall procedures.

❖ Do establish a line of communication between adjoining owners and contractors for dealing with day-to-day issues of noise, dust, and so on.

❖ Do ensure that any variations in the agreed works are agreed between the parties, or by their appointed surveyors.

❖ Finally, do ensure that all parties fulfil their obligations.

Further information

❖ *Party Wall Legislation and Procedure* (5th edition), RICS guidance note, 2002.

❖ *The Party Wall Act Explained – A Commentary on The Party Wall etc. Act 1996* (The Green Book), Pyramus and Thisbe Club, 2nd edition, 1997.

❖ *Party Walls – The New Law*, S. Bickford-Smith and C. Sydenham, 2nd edition, Jordans, 2003.

❖ *A Practical Manual for Party Wall Surveyors*, J. Anstey, RICS Books, 2000.

❖ *Anstey's Party Walls and What to Do with Them*, G. North, 6th edition, RICS Books, 2005.

❖ *An Introduction to the Party Wall etc. Act 1996*, J. Anstey and V. Vegoda, Lark Productions, 1997.

❖ *The Party Wall Casebook*, P. Chynoweth, Blackwell Science, 2003.

❖ *Party Wall etc. Act 1996*, audio cassette, Owlion.

❖ *Party Walls – Best Practice Roadshow*, audio CD, Owlion, 2002.

❖ *Party Wall etc. Act, 1996: explanatory booklet*, Department for Communities and Local Government.

❖ *Practical Neighbour Law Handbook*, A. Redler, RICS Books, 2006.

❖ *Boundaries: procedures for boundary identification, demarcation and dispute resolution in England and Wales* (2nd edition), RICS guidance note, 2009.

Useful websites

❖ *Party Wall etc. Act* 1996 – Office of Public Section Information: www.legislation.gov.uk/ukpga/1996/40/contents

❖ Royal Institution of Chartered Surveyors: www.rics.org/partywallsguide

❖ Pyramus and Thisbe Club: www.partywalls.org.uk

❖ Department for Communities and Local Government (DCLG): www.communities.gov.uk

❖ Party Wall and Rights to Light Discussion Forum: www.partywallforum.co.uk

Contributed by Paul Lovelock, paul.lovelock@watts.co.uk

Access to adjoining property

The safe and economic execution of construction work on, or close to, site boundaries frequently requires access to adjoining land for plant and/or materals and/or operatives.

Rights to access land belonging to adjoining owners for specific construction works exist in the form of:

- ❖ the *Access to Neighbouring Land Act* 1992;
- ❖ the *Party Wall etc. Act* 1996; and
- ❖ compulsory purchase legislation.

This legislation does not provide access rights for every conceivable construction activity and, when this is the case, express consent from adjoining owners has to be sought for access. Express consent is often given in the form of a licence.

Access to Neighbouring Land Act 1992

Under the *Access to Neighbouring Land Act* 1992, a court may grant an order for access to land where such access is required to enable the execution of basic preservation works and where access has been refused by the neighbour. Such works include:

- ❖ maintenance, repair or renewal of any part of a building or structure;
- ❖ clearance, repair or renewal of drains, sewers, pipes and cables;
- ❖ cutting back or felling trees and hedges in certain circumstances; and
- ❖ filling in or clearing any ditch.

The Act contains provisions for the preparation of schedules of condition and for overseeing of the work by surveyors. Surveyors can also be called upon to provide evidence where claims for damage under the Act are made.

The access order made by the court may require the payment of consideration, having regard to the likely financial advantage to the applicant and the degree of inconvenience, except where the works are to residential land.

Often the knowledge that rights exist under the Act will prompt neighbours to be accommodating, but, even then, it is still sensible to enter into an informal access agreement in the form of a licence with accompanying schedule of condition.

This Act is available online at: www.legislation.gov.uk/ukpga/1992/23/contents

Party Wall etc. Act 1996

Party wall legislation (section 8 of the Act) enables plant (including scaffolding), materials and operatives to enter and stay on the land of an adjoining owner, but only to the extent and for the duration of time that such plant, materials and operatives are required to execute the specific items of work contemplated by the Act.

This Act is available online at: www.legislation.gov.uk/ukpga/1996/40/contents

Compulsory purchase legislation

Compulsory Purchase Orders, obtained by local authorities, if properly prepared, can include the acquisition of temporary rights of access over adjoining land for scaffolding, cranes, hoarding, etc. over land and buildings that are outside of the land in respect of which legal title is being acquired. Such Orders normally result from comprehensive redevelopment of only the largest of urban sites, with complex title arrangements and boundary conditions. The right of access must obviously be exercised sensibly so as to avoid disruption to occupants of the adjoining land or buildings and might require temporary works designs and method statements to be approved, and insurances and a schedule of condition to be prepared.

Rights of way and fire escape agreements

More intense use of an existing right of way often requires renegotiation of the right altogether. One type of right commonly encountered relates to fire escape routes benefiting properties that adjoin a development. The rights are often disrupted by large-scale redevelopment and negotiations for both temporary escape rights during the redevelopment and for revised escape rights over the new permanent development will be required.

Oversailing cranes and encroaching scaffolds

Most large developments necessitate the use of at least one crane. There are benefits to the developer or contractor of using fixed-jib tower cranes, as opposed to luffing-jib or folding-jib cranes, such as reduced cost and increased speed and load capacity. However, where the jib of a crane will oversail adjoining land, the agreement of the adjoining land owner, and any other party with an interest in the air space above it, will be needed.

Without such agreement the developer will be committing a trespass on every oversailing occasion.

The law on this matter comes from the tort of trespass. The position was clarified in the case of *Anchor Brewhouse Developments Ltd and others v Berkeley House (Docklands Developments) Ltd* [1987], in which the plaintiffs sought, and were granted, injunctive relief in relation to an unauthorised oversailing crane.

While some developers manage to place oversailing risks on their contractors, when work is abundant contractors will often not accept such risks or, if they do, their tender prices are significantly enhanced.

Similar trespass issues often arise in relation to temporary independent scaffolding, although, wherever possible, rights granted by the *Party Wall etc. Act* 1996 and emanating from the *Access to Neighbouring Land Act* 1992 should be exercised.

Developers and/or their contractors should give consideration at an early stage to the issue of access onto or over adjoining land or the airspace above it. Neighbours should be approached in advance for consent and the terms of such consent will be the subject of negotiation by the parties. It is sensible to enter into an access agreement or licence and the developer may be expected to pay a sum of money in consideration or grant reciprocal oversailing rights. Typically such agreements will provide for indemnities, insurance arrangements, schedules of condition, payment of fees and costs and so on.

Contributed by Paul Lovelock, paul.lovelock@watts.co.uk

Construction noise and vibration

The level of permissible construction noise and vibration is controlled by the common law of nuisance and a number of statutes, in particular the *Control of Pollution Act* 1974. A range of guidance is available, including BS 5228-Part 1: 2009 (Noise), Part 2: 2009 (Vibration) and BRE papers entitled *Controlling particles, vapour and noise pollution from construction sites*, Parts 1 to 5.

Nuisance

A private nuisance is 'an unreasonable interference with a person's use or enjoyment of the land'. If a neighbour can demonstrate that a nuisance exists and that he or she has suffered substantial damage as a result, then he or she may be successful in bringing an action against the parties creating the nuisance.

The remedies available are injunctions and/or damages. The courts have, however, traditionally regarded demolition and construction sites as a special case as far as noise is concerned. It would appear that as long as the works are carried out with proper skill and care, and all reasonable precautions are taken to minimise disturbance to neighbouring occupiers, no action in nuisance will arise.

Developers and contractors have to ensure that they take 'reasonable precautions'. They must be aware of the definition of 'best practicable means' in the *Environmental Protection Act* 1990. This includes considering local conditions and circumstances, the current state of technical knowledge and financial implications.

A leading case on construction noise and nuisance is *Andreae v Selfridge* [1938] 3 All ER 264, where the judge held that provided demolition and building operations are 'reasonably carried on, and all proper and reasonable steps are taken to ensure that no undue inconvenience is caused to neighbours, whether from noise, dust or other reasons, the neighbours must put up with it'.

More recently, vibration arising from demolition works was considered in the case of *Hiscox Syndicates Ltd and another v The Pinnacle Ltd and others* [2008] PLSCS 21 in which the court decided, on the balance of convenience, that the claimant was entitled to injunctive relief against, among other things, nuisance caused by vibration and water spray used in the demolition process.

Control of Pollution Act 1974

The *Control of Pollution Act* 1974 deals, in part, with the control of noise on construction sites. Section 60 empowers a local authority to serve notice imposing certain limitations. These limitations include specifying the hours of work, permitted noise levels and the particular plant and machinery that may be used. The recipient may appeal against the notice within 21 days. Contravention of the notice is an offence under the Act. Section 61 provides an opportunity for a developer or contractor to apply to the local authority in advance of the works and seek agreement to such matters as the method of carrying out the work and the steps that will be taken to minimise noise. The local authority is not obliged to give its consent and, even if it does, it may attach conditions to it. It may also change the conditions if it sees fit.

The local authority will often specify that 'best practicable means' are used. The developer/contractor will be expected to adopt the quietest viable method of working within reasonable cost limits. The local authority may also require continuous noise and vibration monitoring and regular liaison meetings with neighbours.

Planning legislation

Planning law and procedures do not avail adjoining owners of the ability to influence how developers and contractors undertake building works. That is not the purpose of the legislation; it is not there to determine the balance of convenience between an adjoining owner and an applicant (developer).

Occasionally, planning permissions are granted subject to the condition that the applicant must, before commencing any work, submit a construction management plan identifying how, in a general sense, the applicant will proceed with the development so as to minimise the nuisance and disruption that it causes to the public and the occupants of immediately-surrounding property.

Contributed by Paul Lovelock, paul.lovelock@watts.co.uk

Architectural and design criteria

Design

Project stages

For the ease of understanding, it is very helpful to adopt a common vocabulary to describe the different stages of a project life cycle. Many such descriptions exist, the most popular being the *RIBA Outline Plan of Work* (the most recent version is the 2007 edition, amended in January 2009 with the publication of a Corrigenda). A simplified table setting out the key stages and associated descriptions is set out below.

RIBA Work Stages		Colloquial terms	Description of key tasks
Preparation	A Appraisal		Identification of client's needs and objectives, business case and possible constraints on development. Preparation of feasibility studies and assessment of options to enable the client to decide whether to proceed.
	B Design Brief	Feasibility	Development of initial statement of requirements into the Design Brief by or on behalf of the client confirming key requirements and constraints. Identification of procurement method, procedures, organisational structure and range of consultants and others to be engaged for the project.
Design	C Concept	Outline design	Implementation of the Design Brief and preparation of additional data. Preparation of Concept Design including outline proposals for structural and building services systems, outline specifications and preliminary cost plan. Review of procurement route.
	D Design Development	Scheme design	Development of concept design to include structural and building services systems, updated outline specifications and cost plan. Completion of Project Brief. Application for detailed planning permission.
	E Technical Design	Detailed design	Preparation of technical design(s) and specifications, sufficient to co-ordinate components and elements of the project and information for statutory standards and construction safety.

RIBA Work Stages		Colloquial terms	Description of key tasks
Pre-Construction	F Production Information		F1 Preparation of production information in sufficient detail to enable a tender or tenders to be obtained. Application for statutory approvals. F2 Preparation of further information for construction required under the building contract.
	G Tender Documentation	Tendering	Preparation and/or collation of tender documentation in sufficient detail to enable a tender or tenders to be obtained for the project.
	H Tender Action		Identification and evaluation of potential contractors and/or specialists for the project. Obtaining and appraising tenders; submission of recommendations to the client.
Construction	J Mobilisation		Letting the building contract, appointing the contractor. Issuing of information to the contractor. Arranging site handover to the contractor.
	K Construction to Practical Completion	Construction	Administration of the building contract to Practical Completion. Provision to the contractor of further information as and when reasonably required. Review of information provided by contractors and specialists.
Use	L Post Practical Completion	Defects period and beyond	L1 Administration of the building contract after Practical Completion and making final inspections. L2 Assisting building user during initial occupation period. L3 Review of project performance in use.

The project stages and descriptions from the RIBA Outline Plan of Work 2007 (as amended in January 2009), copyright Royal Institute of British Architects, are reproduced here with the permission of the RIBA.

Significant advantages can be obtained through alignment to one method of project description including:

❖ Gateway reporting at the end of each work stage, seeking approval to proceed to the next stage. This allows the client to review deliverables (including design development, associated costs and implications) on a staged basis as the project progresses.

❖ The ability to link consultant terms of appointment to each work stage ensuring alignment of deliverables at each stage, together with associated payment terms – providing the client with a staged release of information and phased cost exposure as the project progresses.

Contributed by Daniel Webb, daniel.webb@watts.co.uk

Design data

Building types

Design data for different building types exists from a number of sources and examples are listed below.

Housing

Typical housing equivalent densities:

> (Note: hr/ha = habitable rooms per hectare)

- ❖ c. 125 hr/ha: low-density layout (e.g. 4+-bedroom detached houses with gardens);
- ❖ c. 200hr/ha: high-density 2-storey housing with traditional street pattern;
- ❖ c. 250 hr/ha: 3-storey flats, street pattern still possible;
- ❖ c. 250+ hr/ha: block of flats, no street pattern.

English Partnership (EP), the national regeneration agency, launched minimum space standards that apply to all EP schemes from 1 November 2007.

The agency's requirement for minimum internal floor areas (MIFA), calculated in line with the RICS Gross Internal Floor Area, are:

Unit type	Space standard (m²)
1 bed / 2 person dwellings	51
2 bed / 3 person dwellings	66
2 bed / 4 person dwellings	77
3 bed / 5 person dwellings	93
4 bed / 6 person dwellings	106

English Partnership has additional standards relating to space and usage, including the demand that all dwellings provide access to private outdoor space 'of sufficient size to enhance the use of the dwelling' (winter gardens/conservatories, used in addition to MIFA, can count as outdoor space).

Other sources of housing design data exist.

Hotels

Typical space allocation by star rating

Star rating	m²/room gross
2*	20–22m²
3*	25–27m²

Star rating	m²/room gross
4*	30–34m²
5*/exclusive	36m² minimum

Car parking

❖ Resident guests: 1.2–1.3 spaces per room.
❖ Conference facilities: 1 car space per delegate.

The required provision must be agreed with the local authority.

Industrial

Typical design data for industrial property

Site coverage		Plot ratio normally maximum of 1:1, including office content. Site coverage should not normally exceed 75% (normally approx. 50–60%)
Car parking (factories)	Staff	1 car/50m² of gross floor area
	Visitors	Typically 10% of parking
Car parking (warehouses)	Staff	1 car/200m² of gross floor area
Factory building types	'Light duty' industrial	Spans 9m–12m Ht. to eaves 4.5m Floor loading 16kN/m²
	'Medium duty' industrial	Spans 12m–18m Ht. to eaves 6.5m Floor loading 25kN/m²
	'Heavy duty' industrial	Spans 12m–20m Ht. to eaves 7m–12m Floor loading 15–30kN/m²
Warehouses	General purpose	Spans 12m–18m Ht. to eaves 8m Floor loading 25kN/m²
	Intermediate high bay	Spans 11.1m–20.5m Ht. to eaves 14m Floor loading 50kN/m²
	High bay	Ht. to eaves 30m Floor loading 60kN/m²

Offices

Methods of calculating areas

❖ For planning purposes, gross total area measured over external walls (GEA).
❖ For cost purposes, gross total area measured inside external walls (GIA).

The RICS guidance note, *Code of Measuring Practice*, gives further detail.

Definition of space

Deep plan (triple zone)	20m+
Medium depth (double zone)	15–20m
Shallow plan (double zone)	12–15m
Shallow plan (single zone)	8–12m

Sanitary provision

Regulation 20 of the *Workplace (Health, Safety and Welfare) Regulations* 1992 requires employers to provide sanitary conveniences in sufficient numbers. For further information see page 158.

Car parking

❖ Staff: 1 car/25m² of gross floor area

❖ Visitors: 10% of parking provision.

The required provision must be agreed with the local authority.

Basic design data

Basic design data is available from a number of sources: examples are listed below.

Typical design values – internal environmental

Lighting (maintained illuminance) requirements

Activity	Illuminance
Circulation	100 Lux
Offices	500 Lux
Drawing office	750 Lux
Very fine work	1,500 Lux

Acoustics requirements

Use	Noise rating
Auditoria	15–30 NR
Bedroom	25 NR
Open plan office	35 NR
Light industrial	45–55 NR

Temperature requirements

Dwellings	Living rooms	22–23°C
	Bedrooms	17–19°C
Offices	General	21–23°C
	Circulation	19–21°C

Retail	Small	19–21°C
	Supermarket	19–23°C
	Restaurants	21–23°C
Factories	Sedentary work	19–21°C
	Light work	16–19°C
	Heavy work	11–14°C
Hotels	Bedrooms	19–21°C
	Bathrooms	20–22°C

Vehicle car parking/circulation

Car parking	Standard European bay 2.4 x 4.8m	Total area per car 24m²
Ramps	Car parking garages	Max. gradient 10%
Carriageway widths	One-way two lanes	7.3m
Vehicle movement turning circles	Standard car	4.5m long: 3.5m inner radius, 5m outer radius
	Standard articulated truck	18m long: 12m radius

Sources of information

- ❖ CIBSE, *Environmental Design: CIBSE Guide A* (7th edition), CIBSE Publications, 2006
- ❖ English Partnerships, *Quality Standards Policy Guidance*, English Partnerships, 2007
- ❖ Littlefield, D., *Metric Handbook: Planning and Design Data* (3rd edition), Architectural Press, 2008
- ❖ Neufert, E. and Neufert, P., *Architects' Data* (3rd edition), Blackwell Science, 2000
- ❖ Pickard, Q. (editor), *The Architects' Handbook*, Blackwell Science, 2005

Contributed by Michael Lee, michael.lee@watts.co.uk

BCO best practice for new offices and fitting out works

It has long been recognised that good design can help improve the workplace environment and contribute to business performance. The British Council for Offices (BCO) researches and develops best practice in the specification of commercial offices.

The BCO launched its first guide to the specification of offices in 1994. Its latest guide, *2009 Guide to Specification: British Council for Offices Best Practice in the Specification for Offices* (the BCO Guide), sets out guidance on current best practice for shell and core developments.

The BCO Guide considers:

- ❖ Drivers for change.

- ❖ **Site issues**: The location of the development and proximity to local amenities, the plot ratio, the orientation of the development to surrounding buildings and developing a strategic brief.
- ❖ **Building form**: Plan shape and floor plate efficiency, the coordination of building elements and services (the planning grid), requirements for circulation space and the design of the building core, lifts and toilet accommodation.
- ❖ **Engineering design**: Design criteria and objectives for the structure and envelope, building services and security considerations.
- ❖ **Sustainability**: Cost effectiveness of sustainability measures.
- ❖ **Envelope**: Design consideration and integration with other building elements.
- ❖ **Fit-out/completion**: Early consideration of fit-out issues, completion checklist.

Throughout the BCO Guide reference is made to good practice published by recognised organisations such as the Centre for Window and Cladding Technology (CWCT), the Building Research Establishment (BRE) and the Chartered Institution of Building Services Engineers (CIBSE).

Legislative changes in recent years have focused designers' attention on environmental and sustainability issues and this is reflected in the latest edition of the BCO Guide.

In the BCO Guide various design criteria are given (see their *Quick guide to key criteria*) which cover typical items such as:

- ❖ workplace density;
- ❖ floor plan efficiency (NIA/GIA);
- ❖ finished floor to underside of ceiling;
- ❖ plan depth (window to window or atrium, not core);
- ❖ column grid;
- ❖ raised floor depth;
- ❖ live load (general) for bulk of the lettable floor area and (high) for a percentage of the lettable floor area for special requirements such as filing and paper storage;
- ❖ office lighting;
- ❖ comfortable temperature ranges for summer and winter;
- ❖ fresh air standard;
- ❖ noise criteria for open plan offices, cellular offices, meeting rooms.

While every development will have its own set of requirements and objectives, the BCO guides provide a useful source of benchmark information and guidance on processes for successful execution.

The BCO also produces guidance on fit-out design. The *2011 Guide to fit-out* (the Fit-Out Guide) provides guidance on good practice and is intended to complement the 2009 BCO Guide.

The Fit-Out Guide examines how occupiers' requirements for optimising productivity, providing value for money and meeting the needs and aspirations of staff can be realised.

Guidance is provided on architectural, engineering and services design, procurement and sustainability. Consideration is given to facilities management issues and the employment of post-occupancy evaluation techniques to measure the success of a project. The Fit-Out Guide also includes a number of helpful management 'checklists'.

Contributed by Michael Lee, michael.lee@watts.co.uk

Project extranets as a method of coordinating project information

Some of the specific characteristics of the construction industry make the quality, quantity and timing of information flows difficult to administer. These include:

- ❖ large numbers of participating companies collaborating on projects of relatively short duration;
- ❖ diverse locations and working conditions related to the building site;
- ❖ comparatively low levels of management support; and
- ❖ diverse sources of information – CAD, Power Project, Microsoft Project, etc.

Despite this, the use of electronic systems for information management, 'project extranets', can have significant benefits including:

- ❖ direct 24-hour access to project-related material;
- ❖ enhanced communications, faster drawing/document approvals;
- ❖ reduced paper trails on labour intensive tasks;
- ❖ reduced distribution/production costs and associated time savings;
- ❖ improved management of information providing accountability and an audit trail;
- ❖ competitive differentiation;
- ❖ less chance of losing information;
- ❖ a platform to stimulate innovation; and
- ❖ the support of a green agenda.

As with any application there are also drawbacks which need to be considered:

- ❖ systems, no matter how secure, are threatened by malicious intrusion from a remote, often untraceable, source; and
- ❖ the sharing of information assumes all parties have access to the relevant software to view the files posted.

Relevant legislation/best practice information

The British Standards Institution's section for delivering information solutions to customers (BSI-DISC) sets out five principles which should be the starting point for coordinating information in DISC PD 0010:1997. BSI considers that the key principles of good practice for information management are to:

- ❖ be aware of all information types and sources;
- ❖ recognise your responsibilities in the use of the information;
- ❖ find a procedural solution;
- ❖ resolve a support network/resource for the solution; and
- ❖ review the results and apply lessons learnt.

Other relevant legislation/best practice information includes:

- ❖ The Construction Project Information Committee (CPIC), *Production Information: A Code of Procedure for the Construction Industry*, May 2009;
- ❖ BS 7799 (ISO 27001), *Information Security Management*; and
- ❖ the *Data Protection Act* 1998.

Examples of project document management systems

The following list summarises a small sample of project document management systems currently available:

- ❖ Asite: www.asite.com
- ❖ BIW Technology: www.biwtech.com
- ❖ Business Collaborator: www.unit4collaboration.com
- ❖ Cadweb: www.cadweb.co.uk
- ❖ Meridian: www.meridiansystems.com
- ❖ Sarcophagus: www.sarcophagus.co.uk
- ❖ 4 Projects: www.4projects.com

Key issues

In order to ensure the successful adoption of a project extranet, a number of key issues need to be carefully considered and resolved. These include the following:

- ❖ Adopt document handling procedures within the project team that prevent double handling, e.g. the benefits of a project extranet system will only be realised if information is distributed electronically and not with simultaneous hard copy.

- ❖ A principal barrier to entry is the selection of an appropriate system with appropriate pricing arrangements, reflecting the project particulars. The availability of project extranet systems appropriately scaled to project needs has greatly enhanced over recent years. Accordingly, it should be possible to identify a suitable system. System selection should include consideration of:
  - – ownership of data;
  - – post project archive access;
  - – procedures for recovery of information should a hosting company cease trading;
  - – system redundancy; and
  - – numbers of users.

- ❖ A suitable policy or system feature is required to ensure that all required users are aware of and review new information when posted to the website. This can either be resolved through separate communication or an extranet site design that ensures all personnel are notified of new postings and are required to review them within a certain period, allowing the project manager to audit compliance.

- ❖ Policies are required concerning the information exchange format, e.g. are Autocad drawings to be posted in DWG format for design team use or in a finalised common exchange format such as Adobe PDFs. Perhaps both editable and fixed information is required.

- ❖ The system should provide different levels of ownership allowing data to be available to the whole project team, to other stakeholders, such as letting agents or tenants, and to the contractor. However, full availability of data to all parties is unlikely to be appropriate.

- ❖ The system administration arrangements should be simple and clear, as unlimited opportunity to amend the procedures and systems will inevitably generate a large barrier to the effective use of the system.

- ❖ Systems requiring a specialist appointed information coordinator may be less appropriate on all but the largest schemes, as this provides an additional workload to one particular team member and may delay information distribution. Of additional benefit can be a system allowing direct posting by all enrolled stakeholders, however, the notification points discussed above remain key.

❖ Team members experienced in utilising project extranets should be a factor in the selection protocol for the team.

❖ Adopting a suitable framework to resolve the above matters throughout the team might most usefully be documented within the Project Execution Plan and matching provisions should be reflected in all appointments.

Web tendering

Web tendering is now commonplace on the web and is offered by many of the organisations previously mentioned in this section including RICS: www.ricsetendering.com. Through the use of tendering websites construction project tender documents are posted by the client (otherwise known as the 'buyer') onto a website. 'Suppliers' are then able to access the tender documentation and submit a price online. The service is able to satisfy most types of procurement method including open (open to any supplier) and closed (restricted to a preferred tender list) tenders, as well as negotiation.

See also the *Contracts and procurement* chapter (page 67 onwards) for information on web-based public procurement processes and procedures.

Contributed by Robert Staton, robert.staton@watts.co.uk

Building into the basement

In 2005, the then government called on the UK house-building industry to increase the provision of domestic basements. This was a complete reversal of previous policies, based on the perception that a basement area as living, working or storage space represented a poor relation to housing the same functions above ground. It also represents considerable challenges for both new and adaptive construction in providing dry, warm and decent environments below ground level.

Basements for Dwellings Approved Document 2005

Basements for Dwellings Approved Document 2005 was subsequently approved by the Secretary of State, under section 6 of the *Building Act* 1984, as practical guidance on meeting the requirements of the Building Regulations in force at the time as they applied to the incorporation of basements into dwellings. It has the same standing as Approved Documents.

The Approved Document brings into one text all of the relevant Building Regulations for dwellings that are affected by the inclusion of a basement. The sections covered are:

❖ **Part A**: Structure

❖ **Part B**: Fire safety

❖ **Part C**: Site preparation and resistance to contaminants and moisture

❖ **Part E**: Resistance to the passage of sound

❖ **Part F**: Ventilation

❖ **Part J**: Heat producing appliances

❖ **Part K**: Stairs, ramps and guards

❖ **Part L1**: Conservation of fuel and power

❖ **Part M**: Access and facilities for disabled people

❖ **Part N**: Drainage and waste disposal

The sections are laid out in order of construction, rather than in the strict alphabetic order of the Building Regulations.

An **Addendum** covering **Plain Basement Retaining Walls**, published in December 2007, covers both plain concrete and plain masonry retaining walls of height up to 2.7m. The complete set of Approved Documents are presently being revised by the Basement Information Centre and will incorporate references to Euro Codes EC2 and EC6.

Keeping water out

Where basements are concerned, whether for new build or alterations and adaptations, the key issue is that of water resistance. The Approved Document details four grades of construction to achieve various levels of water resistance:

❖ **Grade 1**: which allows water seepage and is almost certainly going to be inappropriate for any dwelling use;

❖ **Grade 2**: which is the reasonable minimum for garages;

❖ **Grade 3**: which is the reasonable minimum for accommodation; and

❖ **Grade 4**: which is for totally dry conditions or for premises which require a very controlled environment. This is unlikely to be appropriate for housing except in very exceptional circumstances.

The Approved Document also details different types of wall construction. Typically, there are three:

❖ **Type A**: which is geared around total reliance on waterproofing;

❖ **Type B**: where the structure provides the main resistance; and

❖ **Type C**: where the structure provides some resistance but the principal reliance is on an internal system which intercepts moisture ingress, controls it and carries it away so the internal environment is not affected. In simple terms, the moisture is intercepted by a drainage layer on the internal face of the wall directing the moisture downwards to gutters which, in turn, direct the water into a sump from which the water is pumped away into the drainage system to the outside.

Environmental exposure

The Approved Document contains the phrase 'acceptability of construction types'. Commencing with the three forms of construction (A, B and C above) you introduce different levels of severity, or environmental exposure, to the construction types. A key factor is where the water table lies in relation to the proposed, or existing, basement. This is referred to as 'low', 'variable' and 'high'. However, water tables are almost invariably 'variable' on a seasonal basis – higher in winter and lower in summer – unless you have water tables that are high all year round, particularly as a result of proximity to a river or a sea coast. Design therefore must take into account the highest water table levels.

Adapting existing basements

The most complex cases are where existing basements are being considered for refurbishment. Almost without exception, Georgian, Victorian and Edwardian houses had basements, varying from limited storage and coal cellars to complete basements. These were either fully below ground level or semi-basements originally designed to provide storage, kitchens and servants' accommodation. They worked quite happily on the basis that any moisture that did ingress was removed by natural air flow movements.

Houses built pre-1914 and some constructed pre-1939 should be dealt with cautiously. The brickwork of such properties will have been constructed using lime-based mortars rather than Portland or similar cements. Lime mortars are hygroscopic and take up water readily, with the result that the mortars can decay and, in the worst conditions, can crumble away completely. Their ongoing stability and the retention of the strength of the mortars relies on their being able to release the moisture into the internal environment through plaster facings into the rooms. In other words, such construction has to be able to release moisture inwards. The last thing one would want to do in dwellings constructed in this way is to lock moisture into the brickwork by means of waterproof renders on the internal face of the walls.

Moisture ingress into basements of buildings such as these should primarily be dealt with by the Type C wall construction described above. Any use of Type A internal waterproofing to the building should be thought through very carefully to ensure the lime-based brickwork is not compromised.

Further information

❖ BS 8102:2009 *Code of practice for protection of below ground structures against water from the ground*, effective from 30 November 2009.

Contributed by Allen Gilham, allen.gilham@watts.co.uk

Structural and civil engineering design

A basic introduction to structures

While in many respects parallels can be drawn between the work of a structural engineer and the work of the building surveyor, the approach of each discipline to the appraisal of a building will be fundamentally different. While a surveyor will inevitably concentrate upon the condition of the fabric (the areas where he or she is most comfortable), an appreciation of the way in which the building resists the forces applied to it will often be of secondary importance. Conversely, the engineer will be reviewing the load paths within the building and considering its stability first before worrying about the condition of the fabric. There is nothing wrong with either approach, but surveyors are often called upon to make judgments of the building that will be expected to include some assessment of its structural stability. If the stability has not been analysed, how accurately can that judgment be made? This section sets out some basic information on structures and structural mechanics: some generalisations must be permitted for the sake of brevity.

Essential terminology

❖ **Force or action**: an influence upon something measured in newtons (N) or kilonewtons (kN).

❖ **Mass**: the amount of matter in an object, measured in grams or kilograms.

❖ **Weight**: in engineering commonly expressed as the force exerted by an object, i.e. mass x acceleration due to gravity ($9.8m/s^2$).

❖ **Density**: mass/volume, measured in kilogrammes per cubic metre (kg/m^3).

❖ **Limit state**: a condition which makes the structure unfit for use.

❖ **Stress**: the internal pressure that exists within the body of a structural member as a result of an external influence. Direct stress is expressed as force/area and measured in N/mm^2.

❖ **Shear stress**: the internal pressures resulting from shear (slicing) forces and expressed as shear force/area in N/mm^2.

❖ **Strain**: the physical extension or shortening of a member as a result of stress. Strain is not expressed in units; it is the ratio of change in length to original length. This may be a very small number hence the use of the term 'microstrain'. Strain can be expressed as a percentage.

❖ **Young's Modulus (E)**: a constant that expresses the ratio of stress to strain in any given material.

A mass of 1kg will have a weight of 10N, i.e. (1kg x 10).

❖ A 1kg bag of sugar will impose a force of 10N upon a table.

❖ Four 25kg bags of cement (100kg) will impose a force of 1kN on a floor.

❖ An 80kg man will impose a force of 800N or 0.8kN on a bar stool.

❖ A 1,000kg car will impose a force of 10kN on a car park.

❖ 1 litre of water = 1kg = 10N.

Types of load

❖ **Dead load**: a permanent load – the self weight of a structural element and the parts of the building that are supported by it.

❖ **Live load**: imposed load – variable loads that result from the use of the building – people and furniture, snow, stock, etc.

❖ **Lateral load**: a load (which may or may not be variable) acting horizontally or at an angle to the horizontal, e.g. a wind load or the load resulting from soil or water against a retaining wall.

❖ **Point load or concentrated load**: a load acting on a single point, e.g. the base of a storage racking system.

❖ **Uniformly distributed load (UDL)**: a load that is distributed equally over the length of a beam or over the area of a floor.

❖ **Uniformly varying load**: a load that is distributed continuously but not equally and in a linear manner, e.g. over the height of a retaining wall the force is greatest at the bottom and least at the top.

One of the fundamental engineering principles is Newton's third law:

'For every action there is an equal and opposite reaction'.

Effectively, for a structure to remain stable it must be capable of resisting the forces applied to it. Stability means that all of the forces are held in equilibrium. Structural members will be subjected to forces acting in different ways:

❖ **In bending**: a simply supported beam spanning between two points will, depending upon its span and the loads it carries, gradually bend. If the loads are increased, the bending will increase until failure occurs. Failure will not occur if the beam is able to provide equal resistance to the load imposed upon it. Floor slabs are effectively wide, shallow beams and, although they are often designed to span between two supports, they may also span in two directions between four supports.

❖ **In compression**: a column in a building may be supporting a floor slab or other structural elements. These loads act axially in a downward direction and must be resisted by an equal and opposite reaction – hence the column is in compression.

❖ **In shear**: a short beam with a heavy load close to one of the supports would be subjected to a slicing type force; rather than bending, the beam may fail as a result of this slicing action.

❖ **In tension**: the opposite of compression forces, occurring, for example, in the bottom tie member of a roof truss. The ends of the tie are resisted from moving outwards by an equal and opposite reaction within the tie.

❖ **In torsion**: a twisting or rotational force possibly caused by a load that does not pass through the centroid of a structural element.

A structural component will fail when the stress created by bending or shear exceeds the maximum permissible stress of a particular material.

The analysis of structures that are subjected to different forces is complex and for this reason engineers will often seek to simplify the design concept by making individual elements do specific tasks. Different structural elements can be designed to resist different forces. For example:

❖ An arch is held in compression throughout its span; thus materials that are weak in tension (brick, stone, etc.) can be made to span considerable distances.

❖ A truss is an assembly of components that are either held in compression or tension and so do not require an analysis for bending or shear.

The analysis of these elements and indeed the whole structure will depend upon an understanding of the routes that the loads must take. The sum of the live and dead loads will eventually be transferred via a load path down to foundation level. Here, the combined load must be resisted by an equal and opposite reaction otherwise the building would not stand up. However, the transmission of loads will depend to a large extent on how the individual members are jointed. Engineers use different types of joint to permit different load transfers:

❖ **Pin joints** (in reality these joints are rarely pins but the structure is analysed as if they were): pin joints can be considered as pivot points: they can provide a reaction to horizontal or vertical loads but cannot resist rotation. Components in a pin-jointed frame can thus be treated as if they have axial loads – either compression or tension.

❖ **Roller joints**: roller joints will provide a reaction to vertical loads but not to horizontal loads. So, for example, a bridge deck that is likely to expand and contract may have provision for movement in the form of a roller joint.

❖ **Moment joints or connections**: these joints are fixed in all axes, thus preventing vertical, horizontal or rotational movement at the joint.

Frames and bracing

If one were to consider a simple frame constructed of two inclined members with a pivot joint at the apex, it would be clear that the bottom ends of the frame would be free to move apart. However, if the two ends were to be joined by a third member, the frame would be rigid. Similarly, a square frame could easily be distorted into a parallelogram if a horizontal load were applied to one corner. If a diagonal member were to be inserted, the square would be rigid – in effect the insertion of a single diagonal 'brace' has created two triangular structures.

A framed building behaves in exactly the same way; unless it can be suitably braced it would be free to move under lateral load. Hence the provision of diagonal bracing to stiffen the structure and prevent lateral buckling. Steel framed structures, particularly large sheds, must be braced in this way. However, the provision of diagonal members may not be desirable for architectural reasons and so alternative forms of bracing are often employed. In buildings constructed during the 1960s and 1970s a very common form of bracing was the provision of a rigid core (e.g. a staircase or lift enclosure), or alternatively the provision of a reinforced concrete shear wall at the ends of a building as a means of providing resistance to lateral loads.

Today, the following ways of resisting lateral loads are most common:

❖ cross or diagonal bracing to one bay of a series of steel frames;

❖ stiff cores or shear walls; and

❖ sway (or unbraced) frames. In a sway frame, resistance to lateral loads is provided by very stiff joints (moment connections) as described above. Such a system would be found in a large steel-framed building with unobstructed internal spaces and 'lightweight' enclosures to staircases and lifts.

High-rise buildings may utilise a variety of structural techniques which are beyond the scope of this handbook.

Contributed by Graeme Lees, graeme.lees@watts.co.uk

Soils and foundation design

For very light residential buildings, a visual assessment of the soils with a minimum of physical testing may be sufficient if local knowledge of the area is good. For larger buildings, a proper geotechnical investigation is usually recommended. This allows the measurement of relevant soils (geotechnical) data on which the foundation design will be based. Accurate testing of samples of soil obtained from boreholes usually leads to economies in foundation design. Samples are usually tested for consolidation, compressibility (both of these affect settlement) and shear strengths. In certain circumstances, testing for chemicals which could affect the structure may be included.

Where soil conditions are good, and building loads are relatively light, a simple spread foundation is usually sufficient. This will be in the form of either simple strips or pad bases of non-reinforced concrete. As loads increase and soil conditions become more complex, foundations may need to be reinforced to allow loads to be spread sufficiently. Heavy building loads and poor ground often require piled foundations to take the foundation loads into suitable (deeper) soils.

Other features, such as trees (in shrinkable soils), groundwater and basements, all require special consideration in foundation design.

Further information

For a long time, the relevant British Standard for site investigations was BS 5930:1990 *Code of Practice for Site Investigations*. This document is now partly superseded, although it remains current and is cited in the Building Regulations. Further detailed guidance is listed below.

BSI Standard	Title
BS EN ISO 22476-2:2005	*Geotechnical investigation and testing. Field testing. Dynamic probing* (AMD Corrigendum 16932)
BS EN ISO 22476-3:2005	*Geotechnical investigation and testing. Field testing. Standard penetration test* (AMD Corrigendum 16931)
BS EN ISO 14688-2:2004	*Geotechnical investigation and testing – Identification and classification of soil. Principles for a classification* (AMD Corrigendum 16928)
BS EN ISO 14689-1:2003	*Geotechnical investigation and testing. Identification and classification of rock. Identification and description* (AMD Corrigendum 16929)
BS EN ISO 14688-1:2002	*Geotechnical investigation and testing – Identification and classification of soil. Identification and description* (AMD Corrigendum 14181) (AMD Corrigendum 16930)
BS EN 1997-2:2007	*Eurocode 7: Geotechnical design. Ground investigation and testing*
BS EN ISO 22475-1:2006	*Geotechnical investigation and testing – Sampling methods and groundwater measurements. Technical principles for execution*

For preliminary design purposes only, the following table gives typical allowable bearing values under static loading for various types of soils and may be used to size certain strip or pad foundations.

Category	Soil type	Presumed allowable bearing pressure (kN/m²)
Unweathered rocks	Strong igneous rocks	10,000
	Strong sandstones and limestones	4,000
	Strong shales	2,000
Non-cohesive soils	Dense gravel	600
	Medium dense gravel or sand and gravel	200–500
	Loose gravel or loose sand and gravel	up to 200
	Loose sand	up to 100

Category	Soil type	Presumed allowable bearing pressure (kN/m²)
Cohesive soils	Very stiff clay	300–600
	Stiff clay	150–300
	Firm clay	75–150
	Soft clay	up to 75

Note: some types of ground, including very soft clays, made ground and fills, etc. are not normally suitable to support foundations.

Contributed by Graeme Lees, graeme.lees@watts.co.uk

Soil surveys

Soil surveys may be required to determine either, or both, of the following:

❖ geotechnical properties; and
❖ environmental contamination.

Geotechnical

The purpose of a geotechnical site investigation is to provide sufficient geotechnical information to enable design of foundations, floors and hardstandings. Investigations will be designed specifically to suit the anticipated geology and development proposals. A geotechnical site investigation is intrusive and may include in-situ and laboratory tests. A geotechnical site investigation is often procured with an environmental site investigation given the significant overlap with the fieldwork requirements.

Environmental

An intrusive investigation may be required to establish the nature of any subsurface contaminated soil and/or groundwater. Site investigations are based upon site-specific factors such as the presence of likely contaminants, the anticipated subsurface geology and the location of the site. They are often referred to as Phase II investigations where they follow a non-intrusive Phase I audit. Samples of soil and groundwater are taken for laboratory analysis. The results are interpreted and a risk assessment undertaken for any contamination identified.

Fieldwork

The following methods of soil and groundwater sampling are common to both environmental and geotechnical investigations.

Trial pits

Trial pits are extremely valuable if the depth of investigation required is less than about three metres. They allow a detailed examination of the ground conditions in situ with some indication of stability and groundwater conditions. Trial pitting is a relatively fast and efficient means of exploring subsurface conditions.

Auger holes

Auger holes are normally made by hand-turning a very light auger into the ground, or by using light power-auger equipment. However, while auger holes are effective in preliminary investigations, they do not provide the depth or range of sampling and in-situ testing provided by conventional site investigation boreholes.

Window samplers

A window sampler is a steel tube, usually about one metre long, with a series of windows along the tube through which disturbed soil conditions or extract samples can be viewed. A lightweight percussion hammer drives the sampler into the ground. It is then extracted with jacks. A depth of approximately ten metres can be achieved, depending on soil conditions, using a sequence of progressively smaller diameter samplers.

Boreholes

Light percussion drilling (shell and auger) is the most commonly used method in the UK. Samples are often unsuitable for soil description on the basis that the drilling process will have changed the strength of the soil by remoulding it and increased the moisture content of the soil through lubrication. For this reason U100 tube samples are often taken from boreholes at regular depths by driving a small diameter tube into the soil at the base of the borehole, thus extracting an undisturbed sample for laboratory analysis. Lubrication may be required if the subsurface is not cohesive, making it unsuitable for some types of environmental site investigations.

Geotechnical in-situ testing

In-situ testing is typically undertaken on cohesionless soils (i.e. sands and gravels) where the strength characteristics may only be established on undisturbed in-situ samples.

Cone Penetration Test (CPT)

This technique involves hydraulically pushing a 10 or 15cm^2 cone into the ground at a standard rate of penetration and measuring the penetration resistance. The equipment necessary for this type of investigation is housed in a large truck. The results from a CPT can be very valuable providing a soil profile, estimates of the soil types encountered, including consistency and density, and evidence of the presence of voids beneath the site.

Dynamic probing

Much less sophisticated than CPT, dynamic probing involves driving a steel rod into the ground by using repeated blows of a hammer of a specified mass falling through a fixed distance. The number of blows required for each 100mm is recorded and plotted as a depth versus blow-count log. However, the information given by dynamic probing is very restricted and is difficult to interpret. Further investigations are usually necessary to supplement this test.

The Standard Penetration Test (SPT)

This test involves driving an open-drive sampler into the bottom of a borehole with repeated blows of a hammer falling a predetermined distance. The number of blows necessary to drive the sampler six increments of 75mm are counted and recorded, giving the penetration resistance value. The test is undertaken on cohesionless soils such as gravels.

Other methods of testing and sampling are used depending on the soil type and conditions on site.

Geotechnical laboratory testing

Laboratory testing is typically undertaken on cohesive soils, i.e. clays, where an undisturbed sample may be retrieved from the field. Such testing is not appropriate to cohesionless soils such as gravels. Tests include:

- ❖ **Soil Classification**: Particle Size Distribution, Plasticity Index, Moisture Content.
- ❖ **Consolidation**: to assess the settlement characteristics.

❖   **Triaxial**: to assess the compressive strength characteristics.

Geotechnical reporting

The results of the fieldwork and laboratory tests are assessed. For development purposes, preliminary designs for foundations may be prepared. Sufficient information would be provided to enable design of building foundations. For diagnostic purposes, the investigation would assist with identifying the cause of defects in a building superstructure, allowing remedial solutions to be specified with confidence.

Environmental sampling and analysis

Information on soil, water and gas sampling for environmental information can be found in the *Contaminated land* section (see pages 369 and 370).

Contributed by Graeme Lees, graeme.lees@watts.co.uk

Floor loadings in buildings

Guidance on the selection of appropriate imposed loads in new and existing buildings is set out in BS EN 1991-1-1: 2002 *Actions on structures* and its UK National Annex. This is one of the suite of new Eurocodes which have superseded earlier British Standards used in structural design (the Standard). Reliance upon Standards does not confer immunity from legal obligations, and strict adherence to the guidance may not necessarily provide a design that is suitable for a particular use.

Some useful definitions (see also *A basic introduction to structures*, page 256) include:

❖   **Permanent or dead load**: the self weight of all permanent partitions, walls, floors, roofs, finishes, etc. (in crude terms anything that would not fall out if you turned the building upside down). Dead loads may be calculated by reference to BS EN 1991-1-1: 2002 or ascertained from other published data.

❖   **Imposed load**: the load that is produced by the occupants and use of the building, moveable equipment, impact loads, demountable partitions, furniture, etc. Imposed loads will in all probability vary from day to day or even moment to moment.

❖   **Storage height**: the height that is available for the storage of goods, extending from floor level to another physical obstruction such as a soffit, roof or element of structure. Usually measured to the underside of the haunch in a portal framed industrial building.

❖   **Uniformly distributed load (UDL)**: the load per square metre of plan area measured in kN/m^2.

❖   **Concentrated load**: a load applied over a relatively small area of the structure.

❖   **Reduction in load**: given that the imposed design load values in some types of buildings are unlikely to be in place on all floors simultaneously, a design that is based simply upon the selection of a stated imposed load could result in an unnecessarily high calculation of total load – a factor that would be relevant say in the design of foundations or columns in multi-storey buildings. In certain cases therefore, a reduction in total loads can be factored into the calculations and permissible reductions are set out in the Standard.

❖ $1kN/m^2$ = approx. 20lbs per sq ft.

Typical minimum imposed loadings

❖ For offices in general use, a UDL of 2.5kN/m² has been commonly used as a minimum but the new Standard requires the use of 3.5kN/m² for floors at or below ground. A few years ago 'institutional standards' regularly dictated an imposed load of 5kN/m² but this is generally considered to be over-design. The British Council of Offices recommends as a minimum 2.5kN/m² plus a further 1kN/m² to allow for partitions and 0.85kN/m² for raised access floors. They further recommend an allowance of 7.5kN/m² for 5% of the floor area for heavy filing, safes, etc. Specialised storage equipment such as proprietary, rolling filing systems can impose loads greater than 7.5kN/m² and need special consideration.

See also *Imposed floor loading for offices: a re-appraisal* (Stuart, J., archives of the *Structural Engineer*).

❖ Plant rooms are often designed to 7.5kN/m².

❖ Loads in industrial buildings should be assessed considering the intended use and equipment to be used. The Standard refers to PD 6688, the background paper to the UK National Annex to BS EN 1991-1 for information. For general storage, the Standard recommends 2.4kN/m² for each metre of storage height or a concentrated load of 7kN. However, many engineers will argue that floor design calculations based upon these criteria are too simplistic as they do not take into account the effects, for example, of rolling loads. Point loads, i.e. concentrated loads, from storage racking systems can be very high, while the practice of block stacking will be punishing.

Over the years a number of different studies into methods of specifying floor loads in industrial and warehouse premises have been published. See the BRE Report *Floor loading in warehouses: a review*, 1984, BRE IP 19/87; *Classes of imposed loads for warehouses*, Concrete Society TR34; and C&CA Technical Report 550:1982.

❖ Areas in general retail shops and department stores are recommended under the Standard to have a minimum capacity of 4kN/m², although again this may not be truly reflective of actual conditions. The British Council of Shopping Centres' *Survey of Tenants Requirements 1998* sets out more detailed guidance according to use. Under this guide, bookshops and food shops would be designed to 5kN/m², while some household stores and sports shops may be as high as 7kN/m².

❖ Residential uses are usually designed to 1.5kN/m² (for living rooms and bedrooms in private dwellings), while hotel bedrooms are normally to 2kN/m².

❖ Car parks for vehicles not exceeding 30kN gross weight are to be designed to 2.5kN/m².

Historic buildings

The adaptive reuse of historic buildings often demands an analysis of floor loading capacity. The application of floor loadings in strict compliance with the Standard will often be very difficult to achieve in practice – at least without substantial and intrusive work – itself contrary to the principles of minimum intervention set out in BS 7913. In its June 2001 paper *Floor loadings in historic buildings* (Hume, I.), the IHBC Technical Subcommittee argues for a more realistic approach to design, based upon a careful analysis of the actual proposed use rather than a generalised 'one size fits all' approach.

Specific dynamic loadings

Certain types of building use can generate enhanced vertical or horizontal loads on a structure or alternatively an amplification of the dynamic response to loadings. Dance floors, lightweight, long span structures, or buildings containing certain types of machinery are examples of building types where this type of loading must be taken into account. Floors or balconies have been known to collapse under conditions of crowding accompanied by, for example, dancing to music with a heavy beat. Under such conditions, the building must be designed to avoid resonance by limiting the natural frequency of the building or by designing for dynamic loads. Such design will involve specialist techniques.

In existing buildings, testing can be carried out to assess the natural frequency of the floors, and from this a comparison with other buildings can be made so that the probability of discernable vibration under footfall can be made.

Contributed by Graeme Lees, graeme.lees@watts.co.uk

Floors in industrial and retail buildings

In the UK, industrial buildings are being increasingly constructed for use as storage and distribution facilities, or for retail use such as DIY stores, rather than for production. In these buildings the floor forms a vital part of the operation of the facility, and the specification of the floor must suit the tolerances of the storage and materials handling equipment which is to be installed.

Specification

The main factors which need to be considered in the specification of a floor are:

❖ durability and suitability of floor finish for intended use;

❖ tolerance on finished levels across the floor;

❖ accommodation of movement due to constructional and in-service movements; and

❖ type and intensity of loading.

In bespoke facilities, where the use of the floor and the location of plant or storage racking and aisles are known, the specification of all of the above can be quite precise. Where the final use of the building and the layout of the facility is not known, as is the case for speculative development, assumptions must be made, but it may still be beneficial in terms of costs and usability to define as much as possible before design of the floor commences.

Support

Structurally, floors in industrial buildings may be either ground supported or suspended. Suspended construction is where the floor is supported on piles and not designed to bear directly onto the ground immediately below the building. The design of such slabs is not dissimilar to the design of concrete upper floors in multi-storey buildings, with the concrete section being reinforced to span between supports.

The more common arrangement, ground conditions allowing, is the use of a ground-bearing slab. With this type of construction, the load capacity of the floor is derived largely from the strength of the underlying ground and the imported capping (sub-base). Reinforcement is included in the slab but does not contribute to strength, being essentially there to control cracking which, in an unreinforced concrete section, would result from shrinkage as water in the freshly placed concrete dries out. The rate of drying and resulting shrinkage depends on many things, including the method of curing, the thickness of the slab, the concrete mix design and the presence of a membrane under the slab.

Loadings

Floor slabs are subject to distributed loads, for example, from materials stored on the floor, and to concentrated loads from materials handling plant, storage racking, mezzanine floors and internal division walls. Of these, it is generally the concentrated loads which are more critical to the design of the slab and hence there are moves to specify floor capacities in these terms rather than in terms of distributed loadings. See also *Floor loadings in buildings*, page 262.

In general, the weakest parts of a floor slab are the edges and the sections immediately adjacent to joints, particularly where joints intersect.

Construction methods

The proposed construction method will influence the design of the slab. Increasingly, large floor slabs are constructed using specialised plant which only trade contractors specialising in floor construction, rather than general contractors, are likely to have. With this type of procurement and construction much of the design and specification of materials is done by the contractor. In particular, the use of fibre reinforcement instead of conventional reinforcement is common for large bay construction.

Components

❖ **Concrete**: the concrete mix will be specified by the structural engineer or specialist trade contractor to meet the requirements of the floor in terms of constructability, durability and finish. The concrete will include reinforcement in the form of either reinforcing bars or mesh, or fibres. Such fibres may be of steel or polypropylene.

❖ **Joints**: joints are provided in a concrete floor slab to split it into easily constructed sections, and to cater for inevitable movement within the construction. This movement arises from shrinkage of the concrete soon after casting and from expansion and contraction due to changes in temperature over the life of the slab. Joints are expensive to provide and introduce weaknesses into the floor and therefore much design and specifying expertise has been expended into trying to reduce their number, or even to omit them entirely.

❖ **Membranes**: the provision of a membrane immediately below the concrete slab can assist in reducing the friction which develops between the shrinking concrete as it dries out and the material below (sub-base). Good preparation of the sub-base and the inclusion of a membrane can reduce the amount of reinforcement required to control cracking. A membrane may also be used to minimise loss of fine particles from the concrete mix during placing and, if specified and laid appropriately, as a damp-proof membrane to protect against rising damp.

❖ **Sub-base**: this is the imported material which forms the foundation of the floor slab and is necessary on all but the best natural ground (sub-grade).

❖ **Sub-grade**: this is the upper level of the existing ground below the floor. An investigation, undertaken on site with laboratory testing, to determine the nature of the ground on the site, is required to allow design of the floor slab. This investigation is normally undertaken by geotechnical firms to a specification that is usually drawn up by the structural engineer.

Flatness

Sophisticated materials-handling equipment in warehouse and distribution facilities requires tight control of variation in level between different parts of the slab. In general terms, it is not economic to construct all concrete floor slabs to meet these requirements. Where tolerances are inappropriately specified, the slab may be unnecessarily expensive or unsuitable for certain uses.

Specialist surveying equipment is necessary to confirm compliance with the higher categories of level specification. Such surveys are usually undertaken soon after construction and records of survey results should be sought where flatness is important. Visual survey will not pick up failure of a floor slab to meet level tolerances unless the variation in level is extremely large.

Finish

In contrast to the majority of upper floors in buildings, the concrete often forms the finished surface of the floor in warehouse and retail buildings. Durability of the concrete surface against impact damage and wear, including tendency to form dust, is important.

Defects

Most defects in floor slabs affect the serviceability of the floor, but occasionally more fundamental structural defects occur. The most common defects are:

- ❖ dusting or breakdown of surface or finishes;
- ❖ lack of flatness;
- ❖ cracking;
- ❖ breakdown of joints; and
- ❖ structural defects due to slab or sub-base defects, or poorer than anticipated ground.

Increasingly, floor slabs will be considered as important components of buildings in the way that cladding and services are, and recorded information on aspects of their construction and performance will be required during the life of the building, particularly at times of change in use or ownership.

Further information

- ❖ Technical Report No 34 *Concrete industrial ground floors – A guide to design and construction* (ISBN 1 904482 01 5), The Concrete Society.

Contributed by Graeme Lees, graeme.lees@watts.co.uk

Office floors

Suspended upper floors for modern office buildings are generally of some form of concrete construction, usually precast or cast in situ, but in some cases pre- or post-stressed concrete. Earlier buildings have a greater variety of floors, including some unusual or proprietary forms. Timber floors will be found in some older buildings. Modern concrete floors may take many forms, including solid, waffle or voided slabs. The concrete may have been cast on timber shuttering, subsequently removed, or on proprietary profiled metal decking, in which case the metal decking is incorporated into the final construction, providing part of the strength of the floor by acting as all or part of the tensile reinforcement to the combined steel and concrete floor construction.

Floor slabs are usually supported on a grid of beams which may be of steel or concrete construction, and which are normally visible below the soffit of the slab. The term 'flat slab construction' is used to describe concrete floor slabs supported directly off columns without the use of downstand beams. In these floors, bands of reinforcement within the slab perform a similar function to that of conventional beams.

Choice of floor construction normally includes consideration of issues such as cost, construction programme, proposed spans, column layout, and distribution of building services between and through floors, etc. Increasingly, environmental aspects of the building construction will also influence the type of construction chosen.

Service distribution through floor structures

Various structural systems are available which allow horizontal service distribution within the overall depth of the structure. Generally, with these systems, the overall depth of the floor structure is increased, but savings in overall floor depths are made because there is no need for a service distribution zone between the ceiling and the underside of the structure.

Small openings can often be formed through floors to allow distribution of building services between floors, but larger openings will normally require some form of trimming to avoid compromising the strength of the floor. The acceptability of forming openings in floors varies depending on the type of structure and on the location of the hole relative to spans and columns.

Environmental aspects

Environmental issues may influence the choice of floor structure used in a new building. In particular, concrete floor slabs can be utilised as a heat sink to reduce fluctuations of temperature within a building.

Loading

See *Floor loadings in buildings*, page 262, for a discussion on loading.

Finishes

Office floors may be directly finished concrete, or finished with some form of sand-cement screed or concrete topping, or be finished by the addition of a raised floor system, usually a proprietary product, often supported on pedestals.

Whereas screeds are generally used solely to provide a level wearing surface to a floor, concrete toppings usually have a structural function as well, providing strength and lateral stiffness to the floor.

Defects

Some forms of floor construction have a higher incidence of defects in certain circumstances than others. Some defects may be common to all types of floors, whereas others are specific to certain types of construction. Defects may relate to structural or to serviceability aspects of the construction. Although not exhaustive, the following list comprises some of the more common defects:

  ❖ Requirement for strengthening, where particularly heavy equipment or storage is required, or where additional finishes are required, such as when kitchen facilities or shower rooms are to be installed, or where heavy acoustic or sliding partitions are added.

  ❖ Occupants being disturbed by vibration of the floor, as a result of people walking in open areas or corridors.

  ❖ Weakening of floor structures as a result of inappropriate alterations, overloading, removal of structural toppings, etc. or as a result of fire, or reduction in fire resistance following inappropriate work.

  ❖ Cracking of finishes, which sometimes occurs where brittle finishes are laid onto floors not designed specifically for them.

❖ Floor constructions containing high alumina cement (HAC). High alumina cement concrete has been found to lose strength over time, associated with a chemical process referred to as conversion. Site inspection may reveal the possibility of concrete containing HAC, but laboratory testing is needed to confirm its existence. Where HAC is found, further investigation and appraisal of the structure is necessary to assess its capacity. See also HAC on page 291.

❖ Defects in the original construction, such as inadequate concrete cover to reinforcement, poor compaction of concrete between pots or in narrow ribs, or in concrete cast on certain types of formwork, which may affect strength, reduce durability and/or fire resistance.

❖ Filler-joist floor constructions with clinker-aggregate concrete that may contain inclusions, which in damp conditions can create an acidic and therefore corrosive environment to the embedded steel sections.

❖ Floor construction that contains concrete with high levels of calcium chloride, which can lead to severe pitting corrosion of embedded steel sections or reinforcement.

❖ Floor constructions containing reinforced autoclaved aerated concrete planks which, in early designs before 1980, may have insufficient strength leading to excessive deflection.

Contributed by Graeme Lees, graeme.lees@watts.co.uk

Building services design

Design

Air-conditioning systems

Air conditioning (AC) refers to a system or process for controlling within predetermined limits the temperature, humidity and sometimes the purity of the air in a building. The air, as well as being filtered, is heated or cooled as necessary and moisture is added or extracted to give a controlled humidity. A comfort cooling system is essentially an air-conditioning system but without full control of the humidity.

The effectiveness, cooling capacity and plant/riser size implications of system arise from the mechanism to remove heat from the building and the way cooling is delivered within the conditioned spaces. Older systems used air to carry 'coolth' from the conditioned spaces to outside but, as air is a poor carrier of coolth, large risers were required. Developments from the 1970s led to the use of chilled water and now refrigerant gas to deliver coolth. Water and refrigerant-based systems provide no ventilation and are usually matched with air-handling plant to provide full conditioning.

The range of systems used in modern buildings is too extensive to be considered in detail here. The reader should consult the Building Services and Research Information Association (BSRIA) publication *Illustrated Guide to Mechanical Building Services* for system details and a full comparison of characteristics. Typical systems used in modern buildings are:

❖ **Fan coil units**: High to very high capacity system suitable for a range of building types. Very flexible and can provide both cooling and heating.

❖ **Active chilled beam**: Medium capacity system suitable for large open plan buildings. Limited flexibility and typically provides cooling only, OFTEN matched with trench heaters.

❖ **Passive chilled beam/ceiling**: Low capacity system suitable for larger open plan buildings. Very limited flexibility and provides cooling only.

❖ **Split system**: Flexible, high capacity system suitable for small- to medium-sized single rooms.

❖ **VRF/VRV**: As fan coil units but utilises refrigerant gas based external condensers rather than boilers/chillers to provide both heating and cooling. Ideal where independent systems are required for each tenant demise.

❖ **VAV**: Large scale, medium capacity, legacy system. Economically suited to very large speculative buildings.

See also *Air-conditioning inspections*, page 385.

Contributed by Mark Rabbett, mark.rabbett@watts.co.uk

Plant and equipment

Boilers (purpose is to heat water for distribution to central or local plant)

❖ Fuel can be gas, oil, coal, electric, dual fuel (oil/gas) or biomass;

❖ air is required for combustion and cooling (not for electric);

❖ some form of flue is required (not for electric); and

❖ usually quiet in operation with insignificant vibration.

Water chillers (purpose is to cool water for distribution to central or local emitters)

- ❖ Normally electrically driven, but can be gas driven;
- ❖ conventionally air cooled to avoid the need for cooling towers that can be susceptible to bacteriological contamination – cooling towers provide significantly better cooling/energy efficiency and are enjoying a resurgence;
- ❖ best located externally but can be internal and ducted to the atmosphere;
- ❖ refrigeration machines are complex and expert maintenance is required;
- ❖ high noise and vibration levels can be generated; and
- ❖ old machines incorporated CFCs and HCFCs but new ones must not. (The use of the refrigerant HCFC R22 will be banned from 1 January 2015. R22 has been widely used throughout commercial and industrial plant.) See *Refrigerant phase out*, page 387.

Air-handling units (purpose is to deliver heated/cooled and filtered air to spaces)

- ❖ Units incorporate fans, heaters, coolers, humidifiers and filters in various combinations;
- ❖ may be located externally or internally with fresh air ducts to outside;
- ❖ low tech equipment and easily maintained; and
- ❖ noise and vibration levels can be contained (but additional space required in plant room for silencers).

Diesel generators (purpose is to provide a standby electrical supply to compensate for a breakdown in the main utility supply)

- ❖ Normally diesel oil fed for commercial developments;
- ❖ high fresh air and exhaust requirements demanding large louvred areas (for cooling);
- ❖ noise and vibration levels require special attention;
- ❖ oil storage facility – daily use and possibly long-term storage; and
- ❖ flue is required.

Contributed by Trevor Rushton, trevor.rushton@watts.co.uk

Lift terminology

Power systems

Traction systems

- ❖ Ideally requires motor room above (possible planning problem);
- ❖ can be positioned at other levels, usually below or adjacent to lift pit – more expensive (doubles load on structure);
- ❖ machine room-less (MRL) models now available and commonly used;
- ❖ incorporates counterbalance weight;

- ❖ high efficiency; and
- ❖ high speed available.

Types of traction system:

- ❖ Single speed AC motor: up to 0.5m/sec jolt stop;
- ❖ dual speed AC motor: up to 1.0m/sec, more accurate levelling;
- ❖ geared variable voltage/frequency: smoother ride and greater speed; and
- ❖ gearless variable voltage/frequency above 2.0m/sec, very quiet, long travel.

Hydraulic systems

- ❖ Higher starting current, in older lifts can cause electrical spikes;
- ❖ maximum travel 20m, lower speed, up to 1.0m/sec;
- ❖ less efficient, higher energy consumption due to lack of counterbalance; and
- ❖ motor and pump house can be remote from shaft (up to 10m from lift pit), ventilation important for cooling.

Types of hydraulic system:

- ❖ Direct acting: ram and bore hole below car;
- ❖ side acting: usually 'fork lift' action ram and cylinder within shaft; and
- ❖ indirect: combined ram and ropes, ram raises and lowers pulley.

Control systems

Push button control systems

- ❖ Lifts respond to car or landing calls in sequence (fully/up/down collective control);
- ❖ collective, which can lead to several lifts stopping at every floor unnecessarily.

Destination despatch systems

- ❖ Requires passengers to enter their destination at the landing – can improve overall journey time and is commonly retrofitted to existing installations to improve lift capacity.

Packaged lifts

While it is still possible to buy bespoke lifts, it is much more common to select standard lift products from a catalogue. The evolution of 'motor-roomless' packaged lifts manufactured to European standards has revolutionised the lift market and significantly reduced lift costs at the expense of design flexibility. Compliance with accessibility requirements can be an issue with packaged lifts. Such lifts rarely comply with BS 7255, which requires improved controls on top of the car for the safety of maintenance staff. There can also be issues with a lack of waterproofing to the car top controls when these lifts are used for fire fighting purposes.

Contributed by Mark Rabbett, mark.rabbett@watts.co.uk

Lighting design

Categories of lighting, their respective lux levels, and the areas for which they are typically suitable are identified in the following table.

Category	Lux	Typical areas
Casual	100–150	Storage areas, plant rooms, lifts, circulation areas, bathrooms
Casual rough work	200–300	Dining areas, lounging rooms, bars, sports halls, libraries, rough machining
Routine work	300–500	General office, retail areas, lecture rooms, laboratories, kitchens, medium machining, supermarkets
Demanding work	750	Drawing offices, inspection of medium machining
Detailed work	1,000	Colour discrimination, fine machining and assembly, inspection rooms
Very fine work	1,500–3,000	Hard engraving, precision works, inspection of fine works

Lighting design should generally comply with the recommendations as laid down in the CIBSE/SLL *Code for Lighting*.

Lighting in offices should comply with the requirements of CIBSE/SLL *Lighting Guide* LG7. The purpose of LG7 is to promote the overall visual environment (i.e. surface reflections, direct daylight, etc.) and its effect on display screens and their users. Emphasis is also placed on designing schemes that avoid very high luminance patches in a space and abrupt changes in luminance across a surface or between adjacent surfaces.

Fluorescent lamps

The most common form of fluorescent lamp in commercial buildings is a straight tube. The letter T denotes that the shape of the lamp bulb is tubular. The number after the T is the diameter of the lamp in eighths of an inch (sometimes in millimetres, rounded to the nearest millimetre). Fluorescent lamps come in several sizes, ranging from T1 to T17, but the more commonly used diameters are T12 or T38 (1½" or 38.1mm), T8 or T26 (1" or 25.4mm) and T5 or T16 (⅝" or 15.8mm).

At the ends of the tube are bases with pins that connect the lamp to the sockets in the luminaire. Most bases have two pins and are called bi-pin bases; most common are the medium bi-pin, (found on T12 and T8 tubular lamps) and a smaller version, the minature bi-pin (found of T5 lamps).

The table overleaf summarises the most commonly found sizes.

Contributed by Tony Churchill, tony.churchill@watts.co.uk

Fluorescent lamps explanation of designations

Lamp designations		Tube diameter measurements		Socket	Notes
Imperial	Metric 100–150	inches	mm		
T5	T16	⅝	15.8	G5 bi-pin	The fluorescent lamp of choice for new commercial installations.
T8	T26	⅞ (1″)	25.4	G13 bi-pin	The T8 fluorescent lamp is probably the most widely found lamp in commercial premises today, although it is being rapidly replaced with T5 lamps to achieve energy savings and improve EPC ratings.
T12	T38	1²⁄₈ (1½″)	38.1	G13 bi-pin	These lamps are still found in schools and some older office installations even though they have not been widely specified since the early 1980s. Good energy savings can be achieved without loss of light levels by replacing these lamps with T5 lamps. One other consideration is there are no high frequency versions of this fitting.

Data installations

Data installations and information technology require extensive cabling which, in turn, demands adequate access through the building. Therefore, it is important to consider access via risers, suspended floors or floor trunking in order to present the user with these services.

A raised floor is normally a basic prerequisite to enable full flexibility of outlet positions. The minimum clear void would typically be 100–150mm depending upon floor plate size and riser arrangement.

Modern buildings are now usually block wired for voice and data using common telephone/data jack outlets.

Definitions

❖ **MER**: Main equipment room – typically houses: main servers, switches, patching frames, UPS equipment.

❖ **SER**: Satellite or secondary equipment room – typically houses: switching, patching frames.

Field wiring types:

❖ **Backbone**: typically fibre cabling – used to interconnect MERs to SERs.

❖ **UTP**: unshielded twisted pair – commonly used where low risk of electromagnetic interference.

❖ **STP**: shielded twisted pair – used where medium risk of electromagnetic interference.

❖ **FSTP**: fully shielded twisted pair – used where high risk of electromagnetic interference.

Cabling categories (to EIA/TIA 568 Standards):

❖ **Cat-5e**: up to 100 MHz bandwidth.

❖ **Cat-6**: up to 250 MHz bandwidth.

❖ **Cat-7**: up to 600 MHz bandwidth.

Field cable lengths are generally limited to 90m + 10m patch cords. Fibre cables are used for greater transmission distances.

Wireless LAN (to IEEE 802.11) utilising Wi-Fi technology:

❖ **802.11a**: up to 20 Mbit/s raw data rate (line of sight only).

❖ **802.11b**: up to 11 Mbit/s raw data rate.

❖ **802.11g**: up to 54 Mbit/s raw data rate.

❖ **802.11n**: up to 300Mbit/s raw data (more likely up to 200 Mbit/s), approved by the IEEE in October 2009.

Range typically restricted to tens of metres. Repeaters or access points are required to extend coverage. Can have data security issues.

Contributed by Trevor Rushton, trevor.rushton@watts.co.uk

Materials

Materials and defects

277

Deleterious materials

The definition of so-called deleterious materials is difficult. Many materials, if used incorrectly, can perform badly but other materials, when used in accordance with their known working parameters, can perform perfectly well. In many respects it is better to be more specific and identify materials according to their propensity to cause harm – either to people or to buildings. The property market has grown accustomed to a range of materials that it considers to be deleterious. In some cases the description is fair and reasonable (for example, asbestos); in other cases it is unjustified.

The presence of deleterious materials in a building may affect its market value and could, in severe cases, result in element failure or could affect the health of persons working or living there.

The reaction of investing institutions to these materials depends on a number of factors and often the presence of a deleterious substance will not prevent a purchase. However, great care must be taken to assess the actual risks or consequences involved, so that a proper judgment can be made.

Materials hazardous to health

The more common hazardous materials, and associated risks, are identified in the following table.

Materials	Common use	Use risk
Lead	When used in water pipes and lead paint (lead roofing materials pose little or no risk).	Risk of contamination of drinking water in lead pipes, or from lead solder used in plumbing joints. Risk of inhalation of lead dust during maintenance of lead-based paint. Risk to children of chewing lead painted surfaces (Pica). Concentration of lead in paint now generally much reduced. Beware of lead content in brass fittings.
Urea Formaldehyde foam	Cavity wall insulation. Some insulation boards but rare in UK.	There is some evidence that UF foam may be a carcinogenic material although this is not proven. Vapour can cause irritation. Poorly installed insulation can lead to passage of water from outer leaf of brick to inner leaf in cavity wall situation. There are some worries over formaldehyde used as an adhesive in medium density fibreboard and chipboard but this is likely to be a problem only in unventilated areas with large amounts of boarding.
Asbestos (see also page 281)	Commercial and residential buildings as boarding, sheet cladding, insulation and other uses, particularly in the 1950s, 1960s and 1970s.	Airborne asbestos fibres may be inhaled and eventually lead to either asbestosis, lung cancer or mesothemelioma.

Materials	Common use	Use risk
Machine made mineral fibres (MMMF)	Common in contemporary construction	MMMF are classed as carcinogenic, but there are certain derogations and in practice the materials that are most commonly used in buildings are considered (currently) not to cause harm to human health (other than in terms of local irritations and similar transitory reactions). However, certain types of fibre, such as special ceramic fibres, are considered harmful – these are rare in buildings and are more likely to be found in specialised industries. Despite the above, precautions need to be taken when fibres are of respirable size. Generally health trials are based on investigations of laboratory animals; the fact that health risks to humans have not been fully established does not mean that they are 'safe' – it simply means that at present a relationship has not been established.

Materials damaging to buildings

Those materials which may affect building performance or structure are identified in the following table.

Materials	Common use	Use risk
Calcium silicate brickwork	Used in lieu of concrete or clay bricks, often as an inner leaf in cavity work. Often cited as deleterious but if used correctly will perform well.	Calcium silicate brickwork shrinks after construction with further movement due to wetting. Construction must provide measures of control to distribute cracking. Concrete bricks may display a similar propensity to shrinkage and again care must be taken in the design of movement joints, etc. Note that concrete bricks perform in ways that are very similar to calcium silicate bricks and yet it is rare to consider them as deleterious.
Calcium chloride concrete additive	Commonly used in in-situ concrete as an accelerator and often added in flake form. Often found in buildings constructed before 1977. May also be present from atmospheric or traffic exposure.	Reduces passivity of concrete in damp conditions. Subsequent risk of corrosion of steel reinforcement. See also *Calcium chloride* page 293, *Corrosion of metals* page 298 and *Steel frame corrosion* page 323.

Materials	Common use	Use risk
High Alumina Cement (HAC) (see also HAC on page 291)	Mainly used in manufacture of precast X or I roof or floor beams together with some lintels, sill members, etc. 1954–1974. HAC was first produced commercially in the UK in 1925.	Strength of concrete can decrease significantly, often when high temperatures and/or high humidity is involved. Defects may be due to faulty manufacture.
Sea dredged aggregate not in compliance with BS EN 1260 (previously BS 882)	In-situ concrete or precast concrete.	May contain salts such as sodium chloride. If salts not properly washed out, risk of corrosion reinforcement. Provided the aggregates are properly washed and controlled in accordance with British Standard requirements, the indications are that there are no greater risks involved than with the use of aggregates from inland sources. Risk of inclusion of reactive aggregates that could contribute to ASR, although this is unlikely with most UK-sourced aggregates.
Mundic blocks and Mundic concrete	Concrete blocks and concrete manufactured from quarry shale, commonly found in the West Country.	Loss of integrity in damp conditions. Further research required to identify level of risk across the country.
Woodwool slabs (also woodcrete and chipcrete)	Often used as (a) decking to flat roofs, or (b) permanent shuttering.	Use in (a) may be considered acceptable providing material is kept dry. Use in (b) as a permanent shutter may result in grout loss (honeycombing) or voidage of concrete near to or surrounding reinforcement, particularly with ribbed floors. May result in reduced fire resistance, reinforcement corrosion or in extreme cases loss of structural strength. May be repaired by application of sprayed concrete. Condition investigated by cut-out removal of woodwool in many locations.

Materials	Common use	Use risk
Brick slips	Typically 1970s and 1980s to conceal flow nibs in cavity walls.	Risk of poor adhesion, lack of soft joints can transfer load to slips and cause delamination.

Materials that can have harmful effects on buildings

Materials that have not been classed as hazardous or deleterious but which can have harmful effects on a building are identified in the following table.

Materials	Common use	Use risk
Clinker concrete	Typically late 19th and early 20th century construction for fire resisting floors reinforced with steel joists.	In damp conditions, produces sulphuric acid from combustion products and unburnt coal in the clinker concrete has corrosive effect on steel joists leading to loss of section.
Masonry encased steel	Typically late 19th and early 20th century construction.	Corrosion of steel frame due to poor protection against moisture and corrosion. Results in cracking and possible dislodgement of building stone.
Marble cladding	Late 20th century construction using thin stone panels as cladding (does not affect ashlar).	Natural characteristics of calcitic and dolomitic marbles lead to anisotropic movement and thermal hysterisis. Bowing and sugaring of marble panels is prevalent leading to eventual failure. Process is irreversible.

For a fuller description refer to *Investigating Hazardous and Deleterious Building Materials*, Rushton, T., RICS Books, 2006 (see page 440).

Contributed by Trevor Rushton, trevor.rushton@watts.co.uk

Asbestos

Asbestos is the generic term for several mineral silicates occurring naturally in fibrous form. Because of its various useful properties (resistance to heat, acids and alkalis, and good thermal, electrical or acoustic insulator) it has been extensively used in the construction industry.

Three main types used in the UK were Chrysotile (white), Amosite (brown) and Crocidolite (blue). It was used in a variety of forms varying from boards or corrugated sheets to loose coatings or laggings and, generally, the more friable the material, the greater the asbestos content.

Health risk

Inhalation of its microscopic fibres can constitute a serious health risk and is associated with several terminal diseases.

Not all asbestos, irrespective of its circumstances, constitutes an immediate risk, although the effects of possible future disturbance or deterioration must be considered. Factors to be taken into account are the type, form, friability, condition and location of the source material.

The (1987) Joint Central and Local Government Working Party on Asbestos concluded that 'Asbestos materials which are in good condition and not releasing dust should not be disturbed … Materials that are damaged, deteriorating, releasing dust or which are likely to do so should be sealed, enclosed or removed as appropriate. Materials which are left in place should be managed and their condition periodically reassessed. The risk to the health of the public from asbestos materials which are in sound condition and which are undisturbed is very low indeed. Substitute materials should be used where possible, provided they perform adequately'.

The Health and Safety Executive (HSE) actively discourages the unnecessary removal of sound asbestos materials and each case should be decided on its own merits following an assessment of the risks arising.

In the past the people most at risk have been workers in the asbestos industry involved in the importation, storage, manufacture and installation of materials or components containing this material.

These activities are now banned in the UK and the removal, treatment or intentional working with asbestos is strictly controlled and generally limited to specialists. The risk however continues for anyone who inadvertently disturbs the asbestos in the course of their routine business, including builders, maintenance workers, electricians, etc., and the most recent legislation is intended for their protection.

Legislation

The enabling act for asbestos legislation is the *Health and Safety at Work etc. Act* 1974 and failure to comply with its requirements is a criminal offence.

The principal Regulations that apply to works that could expose persons to the risk of respirable asbestos fibres are the *Control of Asbestos Regulations* 2006 (CAR 2006) which came into operation on 13 November 2006 and implement the 2003/18/EC amendment to the *European Asbestos Worker Protective Directive* 83/477/EEC.

In addition the HSE has produced various Approved Codes of Practice and Guidance:

- ❖ L143, *Work with materials containing asbestos, Control of Asbestos Regulations* 2006 (ISBN 0 7176 6206 3); and

- ❖ L127, *The management of asbestos in non-domestic premises: Regulation 4 of the Control of Asbestos Regulations 2006* (ISBN 0 7176 6209 8).

In addition to legislation specifically focused on asbestos, more general health and safety legislation that may also need to be taken into account includes:

- ❖ the *Management of Health and Safety at Work Regulations* 1999; and

- ❖ the *Construction (Design and Management) Regulations* 2007.

CAR 2006 introduced fundamental changes to the previous legislation and these are set out below:

- ❖ The concept of 'action levels' was abandoned and a **single** 'control limit' is applicable to **all** types of asbestos.

- ❖ The applicability of specific regulations and methods of control are based on risk assessment, using the hierarchy of risk assessment of Control of Substances Hazardous to Health (COSHH).

- ❖ In principle, CAR 2006 changed the concept of previous legislation by applying all of its many and varied regulatory requirements to **any** work involving **any** form of asbestos, subject to only a few limited and specific exceptions on a risk-based assessment basis.

These exceptions are known as the regulation 3(2) exceptions and in such cases the regulatory requirements relating to licensing, notification, arrangements to deal with accidents, incidents and emergencies, designation of asbestos areas and of health records and medical surveillance do **not** apply.

At the time of going to print the EU has determined that such concessions are in breach of the European Asbestos Worker Protectice Directive and has instructed the UK to amend the regulation. The HSE is currently considering a suitable revision.

Control limit

This is a specific level of concentration of asbestos in the atmosphere, measured in accordance with the World Heath Organisation (WHO) recommended method, or approved equivalent. It is the trigger point for the application of specific regulations and/or controls. If the risk assessment for the works indicates it is liable to be exceeded, then regulation 18(1)(2) 'Designated areas' requires the establishment of 'respirator zones', where access is restricted to 'competent' persons and suitable respirators must be worn at all times. In addition, if it is **not** liable to be exceeded, then this is one of a number of circumstances set out in regulation 3(2) for which specific regulatory requirements **may** not necessarily apply.

The current control limit is 0.1 fibres per cubic centimetre of air averaged over a continuous period of four hours.

What are the regulation 3(2) exceptions?

The regulations in the table below do **not** apply to the circumstances set out in regulation 3(2), i.e. where:

'(a) the exposure of employees to asbestos is *sporadic and low intensity*;

(b) it is clear from the risk assessment that the exposure of any employee to asbestos will not exceed the control limit; and

(c) the work involves:
   (i) *short, non-continuous maintenance activities*,
   (ii) removal of *materials in which the asbestos fibres are firmly linked in a matrix*,
   (iii) encapsulation or sealing of asbestos-containing materials which are in good condition, or
   (iv) air monitoring and control, and the collection and analysis of samples to ascertain whether a specific material contains asbestos.'

© *Crown copyright material is reproduced under the Open Government Licence v1.0 for public sector information:* www.nationalarchives.gov.uk/doc/open-government-licence/

The phrases in italics are explained in the Approved Code of Practice (ACOP) and guidance accompanying the Regulations and should be referred to for detail.

Regulation	Title	Details
8	Licensing of work with asbestos	Licensed asbestos contractor
9	Notification of work with asbestos	Informing enforcement authority
15(1)	Accidents, incidents and emergencies	Arrangements in anticipation

Regulation	Title	Details
18(1)(a)	Asbestos areas	Designated area where employee(s) liable to be exposed to asbestos
22	Health records and medical surveillance	Health monitoring requirements for employees exposed to levels of asbestos fibres in excess of control limit

Generally this means that, subject always to the results of the risk assessment in the specific circumstances, work to asbestos-containing decorative coatings will fall into this exclusion category. Also, subject to the control limit not being likely to be exceeded, the definition of 'sporadic and low intensity' will also apply to:

- ❖ asbestos cement;
- ❖ bituminous, plastic, resin or rubber articles where thermal and acoustic properties are only incidental; and
- ❖ sundry products with no insulation purposes, including paper linings, cardboard, felt, textile, gaskets, washers and ropes;

effectively thus taking these low risk materials outside of the previous licensing requirements and allowing the works to be carried out by competent contractors, but who need not necessarily be licensed by the HSE.

Training

The accompanying ACOP sets out the detailed requirements.

In addition to the general training requirements for any employee, set out in the *Management at Work Regulations*, regulation 10 of CAR 2006 requires every employer to ensure that adequate information, instruction and training is given to employees who:

- ❖ are, or are liable to be, exposed to asbestos, and to their supervisors; and
- ❖ carry out work in connection with the employer's duties under these Regulations so that they can carry out that work effectively.

The ACOP, which accompanies CAR 2006, provides a full and detailed list of these training requirements.

There are three main types of information, instruction and training, namely:

Type	For
Awareness training	Those who are liable to be exposed to asbestos while carrying out their normal everyday work, e.g. maintenance staff; electricians; demolition and construction workers; installers of computers, fire or burglar alarms; and '**construction professionals**'.
For non-licensable asbestos work	For example, a roofer removing whole asbestos cement sheet in good condition.
For licensable asbestos work	For example, a contractor removing asbestos lagging or asbestos insulating board.

The topics which the training should cover are listed and should be given in appropriate detail by both written and oral presentation and by demonstration (as necessary). In particular, training is to be in a manner appropriate to the nature and degree of exposure identified by the employer's risk assessment, giving the significant findings of the assessment and the results of any air monitoring carried out, together with an explanation of the findings.

A competent person should give the training and the procedures for providing the information, instruction and training should be clearly defined and documented, and reviewed regularly, particularly when work methods change.

Records should be kept of the training undertaken by each individual. For licensable work, copies should be given to each individual.

Refresher training should be given at least **every year** and more frequently if the work methods, equipment used or type of work changes.

Where **non-employees** are on the employer's premises, they should also be given adequate information, instruction and training as far as is reasonably practicable.

Management of asbestos

Regulation 4 requires the dutyholder(s) to 'manage' asbestos in 'non-domestic premises' and also, for 'every person' to cooperate with the dutyholder so far as is necessary to enable him or her to comply with his or her duties.

Accredited personnel

Regulations 20 and 21 require, respectively, that only persons accredited as complying with ISO 17025 must be employed to measure the concentration of airborne asbestos fibres and analyse a bulk sample of material to determine whether it contains asbestos.

In addition, since 1 April 2007, anyone issuing a clearance certificate for reoccupation following asbestos removal work has been required to meet the relevant accreditation requirements of ISO 17025 and ISO 17020 extended to include all **four stages** of the clearance and not just the air testing part.

Distinguishing between asbestos insulating board and asbestos cement

Because of the relatively higher potential risks to health arising, working with asbestos insulating board (AIB) is subject to different and more stringent controls than working with asbestos cement.

As the two materials are very similar in physical appearance, depending upon the circumstances, it is necessary to distinguish between them.

The distinction is one of density, the general rule being that the greater the proportion of cementitious matrix to asbestos, the greater the density. Conversely, the more friable the material, the greater the asbestos content.

The ACOP that accompanies CAR 2006 defines asbestos cement as 'a material which is predominantly a mixture of cement and asbestos and which in a dry state absorbs less than 30% water by weight'. The guidance in the document includes a comprehensive description of the testing procedure.

Asbestos insulating board (AIB) is defined as a flat sheet, tile or building board consisting of a mixture of asbestos and other material except asbestos cement or any article of bitumen, plastic, resin or rubber which contains asbestos, and the thermal or acoustic properties of which are incidental to its main purpose.

It is relatively easy to identify asbestos cement when it is used in preformed components such as corrugated sheeting, tanks or toilet cisterns, but when it is used in flat board form the only sure way of distinguishing the material from AIB is by laboratory analysis.

Where there is doubt, the Regulations require that caution be taken, and the material is presumed to be AIB until proven otherwise.

Summary of CAR 2006

Regulation(s)	Title (in italics) plus explanatory notes
1	*Citation and commencement*
2	*Interpretation*
3	*Application of the Regulations*: see 'regulation 3(2) exceptions' on page 283
4	*Duty to manage asbestos in non-domestic premises*: see separate detailed explanation following this table
5	*Identification of the presence of asbestos*
6	*Assessment of work which exposes employee to asbestos*: prior to the works, assess the likely level of risk, determine the nature and degree of exposure and set out steps to control it
7	*Plans of work*: produce a suitable written plan of the proposed works
8*	*Licensing of work with asbestos*: All work except 'regulation 3(2) exceptions' must only be undertaken by licence holders
9*	*Notification of work with asbestos*: notify the enforcing authority of licensable work (min. 14 days notice)
10	*Information, instruction and training*: see 'Training' on page 284
11	*Prevention or reduction of exposure to asbestos*: prevent exposure to employees as far as is reasonably practicable, and where not reasonably practicable, reduce to lowest level reasonably practicable, both the exposure (without relying on use of respirators) and the number of employees exposed
12	*Use of control measures*: ensure that any control measures are properly used or applied
13	*Maintenance of control measures*: maintain control measures and equipment (keeping records of the latter)
14	*Provision and cleaning of protective clothing*: provide suitable personal protective equipment (PPE) and ensure it is properly used and maintained
15*	*Arrangements to deal with accidents, incidents and emergencies*
16	*Duty to prevent or reduce the spread of asbestos*: where not reasonably practicable, reduce to lowest level reasonably practicable
17	*Cleanliness of premises and plant*: keep asbestos working areas and plant clean and thoroughly clean on completion; four-stage clearance procedure and certification for reoccupation
18*	*Designated areas for asbestos work*: 'asbestos areas' where any employee would be liable to be exposed to asbestos and 'respirator zones' where control limit liable to be exceeded
19	*Air monitoring*: monitor exposure of employees to asbestos

Regulation(s)	Title (in italics) plus explanatory notes
20	*Standards for air testing and site clearance certification*: see 'Accredited personnel' on page 285
21	*Standards for analysis*: of bulk samples, see 'Accredited personnel' on page 285
22*	*Health records and medical surveillance*: of employees liable to be exposed to asbestos
23	*Washing and changing facilities*
24	*Storage, distribution and labelling of raw asbestos and asbestos waste*: if received, dispatched from, transported or distributed, waste must be in sealed, labelled, appropriate bags or containers
25–31	*Prohibitions and related provisions*
32–37	*Miscellaneous*: exemptions, etc. and defence 'must have taken all reasonable precautions and exercised all due diligence'

Regulations marked with an asterisk do **not** apply in whole or part where the work falls within any of the circumstances set out in 'regulation 3(2) exceptions'.

Duty to manage asbestos in non-domestic premises (regulation 4)

The dutyholder responsible for the management of asbestos in non-domestic premises as set out in regulation 4(1) is every person who has, by virtue of a contract or tenancy, an obligation for its repair or maintenance, or, in the absence of such, control of those premises or of access to or egress from the premises.

This includes those persons with any responsibility for the maintenance, or control, of the whole or part of the premises.

When there is more than one dutyholder, the relative contribution required from each party in order to comply with the statutory duty will be shared according to the nature and extent of the repair obligation owed by each.

This regulation does not apply to 'domestic premises', namely a private dwelling in which a person lives, but legal precedents have established that common parts of flats (in housing developments, blocks of flats and some conversions) are not part of a private dwelling.

The common parts are thus classified as 'non-domestic' and therefore regulation 4 applies to them, but not to the individual flats or houses in which they are provided.

Typical examples of common parts are entrance foyers, corridors, lifts, their enclosures and lobbies, staircases, common toilets, boiler rooms, roof spaces, plant rooms, communal services, risers, ducts, and external outhouses, canopies, gardens and yards.

The regulation does not however apply to kitchens, bathrooms or other rooms within a private residence that are shared by more than one household, or communal rooms within sheltered accommodation.

The duties are identified in the following table.

Materials and defects

Subject	Requirement
Cooperate (see also 'Duty to cooperate', page 289)	Cooperate with other dutyholders so far as is necessary to enable them to comply with their regulation 4 duties.
Find and assess condition of asbestos containing materials (ACMs)	Ensure that a suitable and sufficient assessment is made as to whether asbestos is or is liable to be present in the premises and its condition, taking full account of building plans or other relevant information, the age of the building and inspecting those parts of the premises which are reasonably accessible. (Must presume that materials contain asbestos unless strong evidence to the contrary.) (See HSG264 *Asbestos: The survey guide* for guidance on asbestos surveys.)
Review	Review assessment if significant change to premises or suspect that it is no longer valid and record conclusions of each review.
Records	Keep an up to date written record of the location, type (where known), form and condition of ACMs.
Risk assessment	Where asbestos is or is liable to be present assess the risk of exposure from known and presumed ACMs.
Management plan (see also below)	Prepare and implement a written plan, identifying those parts of the premises concerned, specifying measures for managing the risk, including adequate measures for properly maintaining asbestos or, where necessary, its safe removal.
Provide information to others	Ensure the plan includes adequate measures to ensure that information about the location and condition of any asbestos is provided to every person likely to disturb it and is made available to the emergency services.
Review and monitor	Regularly review and monitor the plan to ensure it is valid and that the measures specified are implemented and that these are recorded.

Management plan

The management plan is an important legal document that, in addition to its health and safety significance, will be required to be made available to, and inspected by, a variety of interested parties.

The absence of such a document may therefore have significant financial implications or affect the liquidity of the premises as an asset.

A plan is not required when the assessment whether asbestos is present or is liable to be present in the premises confirms that it is not. For example, the building is post-2000 and there is confirmation from the project team that asbestos has not been used in its construction.

Nevertheless a record must be kept of the assessment carried out and its conclusion to show to an inspector or prospective purchaser or occupant.

The dutyholder owns and is responsible for the safekeeping of the plan, however, he or she is is obliged to make the information available 'at a justifiable and reasonable cost' to anyone who is likely to disturb asbestos, and this includes new owners or occupants.

(See the HSE publication *A comprehensive guide to managing asbestos in premises* HSG227.)

Duty to cooperate

Every person has a duty to cooperate with the dutyholder so far as is necessary to enable the dutyholder to comply with his or her duties under regulation 4. This includes the landlord, tenants, occupants, managing agent, contractors, designers and planning supervisor.

The possible scenarios envisaged by the ACOP include:

❖ anyone with relevant information on the presence (or absence) of asbestos; and

❖ anyone who controls parts of the premises to which access will be necessary to facilitate the survey and management of asbestos (i.e. its removal, treatment or periodic inspection).

Cooperation does not extend to paying the whole or even part of the costs associated with the management of the risks of asbestos by the dutyholder(s), who must meet these personally.

Where there is more than one dutyholder for premises, the costs of compliance will be apportioned according to the terms of any lease or contract determining the obligation to any extent for repair and maintenance of the premises. If there is no such documentation then the apportionment of costs will be based on the extent to which parties exercise physical control over the premises.

In the final analysis, the courts will decide financial responsibility using the principles outlined above.

Guidance in the ACOP states that architects, surveyors or building contractors who were involved in the construction or maintenance of the building and who may have information that is relevant 'would be expected to make this available at a justifiable and reasonable cost'.

The duty to cooperate is not subject to any limitation or exclusion, thus there is an obligation to do whatever is necessary to cooperate with the dutyholder.

Short lease tenants, licensees or other occupants who control access but do not have any contractual maintenance liabilities would be required to permit the landlord access to fulfil his or her duties.

In October 2011, RICS published the third edition of its guidance note *Asbestos and its implications for members and their clients* (GN 38/2011) to take account of HSG264.

HSG264 Asbestos: The survey guide (guidance on asbestos surveys)

Issued by HSE in January 2010, this replaces and expands on MDHS 100 *Methods for the determination of hazardous substances – surveying, sampling and assessment of asbestos-containing materials* (July 2001). The key changes are:

Categories of survey: previously there were three types of asbestos survey – this has been reduced to two, 'Management survey' and 'Refurbishment and demolition survey'. The former is that necessary to meet the CAR regulation 4 duty during normal occupancy, including foreseeable maintenance and installation. The latter is required **before** any refurbishment or demolition and for all work which disturbs the building fabric in areas where the management survey has not been intrusive.

Competence and quality assurance procedures: clarification on the technical competence of asbestos surveyors 'strongly recommend[ing] the use of accredited or certified asbestos surveyors', requiring the use of 'adequate quality management systems' and that the survey is carried out in accordance with the survey guide.

Survey planning: emphasis on the importance of pre-inspection planning with a survey strategy for both non-domestic and domestic properties, with the aim of reducing caveats and ensuring the completeness of the survey.

Contributed by Paul Winstone, paul.winstone@watts.co.uk

Polychlorinated biphenyls and buildings

Polychlorinated biphenyls (PCBs) are mixtures of up to 209 individual chlorinated organic compounds. Their commercial use began in 1929 and they have since been used as a component in insulation, as cooling fluids in transformers, as dielectric fluid in capacitors, in hydraulic fluids, in grouting and sealants, and as plasticisers in paints. Since their introduction, over 1m tonnes of PCBs have been produced worldwide (OSPAR Commission, 2001).

Health implications

Concerns have been raised since the 1970s regarding PCBs' toxicity, persistence and tendency to bio-accumulate – once they are in the environment or have been ingested by humans, it is very difficult to dispose of them. They can adversely affect reproduction, immune and nerve systems and children's ability to learn. Extensive exposure has been proven to result in skin problems, lung and liver damage, and disruption to hormone and enzyme systems.

One of the effects that has received most media attention is the damage to an animal's ability to reproduce. These effects have been observed among seals, minks, guillemots and sea eagles. When the PCB content in the environment was at peak levels, these species were adversely affected and population levels dropped. Studies have also shown that pregnant women who ate fish from lakes (implying a moderate exposure to PCBs) have given birth to children with reduced learning abilities.

PCB audits and what to look for

PCBs were widely used as a dielectric fluid in electrical transformers and capacitors up to 1977 when manufacture of these materials ceased. Buildings constructed prior to this may therefore harbour materials or components containing PCBs.

Joints containing PCBs can be found, for example, in facades (dilatation joints), around facade elements, around doors and windows, hidden underneath thresholds, in connections between facades and balconies, and also hidden from sight, for example, behind steel sheet claddings. PCBs in plastic-based floor coverings, especially with non-slip qualities, were used in industrial premises and institutional (large-scale) kitchens. PCBs can also be found in sealed insulating glass units (consisting of two glass panes with a separating profile sealed with a jointing compound) and in capacitors used in electric fittings.

When undertaking a PCB survey, the surveyor should use adequate personal safety equipment (such as disposable gloves) and be aware that PCBs are highly contaminating. All tools used for removing materials must be carefully cleaned with acetone after each sample has been collected and the gloves disposed of. The samples must be completely separated from each other using an aluminium foil wrapping and each sample should then be placed in a plastic bag and properly marked before being sent for analysis. Before undertaking the survey, it is useful to make a plan of the building on which you can mark where the samples will be taken.

Initial PCB decontaminations were not always successful. For example, new jointing material was found to have been contaminated by PCBs from materials surrounding the new jointing compound. In Scandinavian countries this led to the development of extensive guidelines on decontaminating joints. The guidelines describe, for example, how surrounding materials, such as concrete facade elements, have to be partly ground down to remove the PCB.

Disposal

To minimise the spread of PCBs in the environment it is important that all disposals arising from decontamination works are carefully handled (including protective clothing). EC Directive 96/59/EC contains further requirements regarding the elimination of PCBs.

The biggest issue for surveyors is to undertake PCB surveys in a structured way (including testing) and to avoid contamination between samples.

Further information

❖ www.environment-agency.co.uk/business/topics/hazsubstances/ 32000.aspz

❖ Ospar Commission: www.ospar.org/

Contributed by Trevor Rushton, trevor.rushton@watts.co.uk

High Alumina Cement concrete (Calcium Aluminate Cement)

In 1925, Cement producer Lafarge commenced the UK manufacture of High Alumina Cement (HAC) to provide concrete that would resist chemical attack, particularly for marine applications. This cement developed high early strength, although its relatively high cost prevented extensive use.

During the late 1950s and 1960s the main use of HAC was for the manufacture of precast prestressed components which could be manufactured quickly, therefore offsetting the additional cost of the material. However, HAC loses strength with age and can become vulnerable to chemical attack.

The earliest UK failures were experienced during 1973–74 when several school roofs collapsed. In 1976 HAC concrete was banned for structural use, although new uses are now becoming established under the name Calcium Aluminate Cement.

Problems with HAC

HAC concrete undergoes a mineralogical change known as conversion. During this process the concrete increases in porosity, which in turn results in a loss of strength and a reduction in resistance to chemical attack. The higher the temperature during the casting of the concrete, the more quickly conversion takes place.

The relationship between conversion and strength is complex, however the strength of highly converted concrete is very variable and is substantially less than its initial strength. Typically the original design strength of $60N/mm^2$ may be reduced to $21N/mm^2$.

Highly converted HAC concrete is vulnerable to acid, alkaline and sulphate attack. For this to take place, water as well as the chemicals must have been present persistently over a long period of time at normal temperatures. Chemical attack is usually very localised in nature and the concrete typically degenerates to a chocolate brown colour and becomes very friable, often due to sulphate attack.

Given the sensitivity to moisture the greatest risk therefore lies in the use of HAC concrete in roof members. It is therefore important to appraise the condition of the concrete and any waterproof coverings before making any formal judgment as to the remedial work required.

In a warm and moist environment there is the possibility of a serious reaction known as alkaline hydrolosis occurring where high alkali levels may be present as a consequence of the use of certain types of aggregate or where alkalis may have ingressed from plasters, screeds and woodwool slabs. Alkaline hydrolysis is characterised by white powdery deposits and a severe loss of strength and integrity.

Investigation

There are three generic stages in an investigation, namely:

- ❖ **Stage 1**: identification.
- ❖ **Stage 2**: strength assessment.
- ❖ **Stage 3**: durability assessment.

A document known as the BRAC (Building Regulations Advisory Committee) rules is often used in the assessment of HAC components of certain standard types. The rules were first produced in 1975 and were reviewed recently; they are now published by the Building Research Establishment (BRE), albeit the guidance is essentially the same.

A Stage 2 strength assessment is required to determine if the precast concrete members have sufficient structural capacity, even at the reduced fully converted strength, to safely withstand the applied loading. The BRAC rules recommend that the assessment be based upon an assumed concrete strength of $21N/mm^2$. In other words there is no need to work out the degree of conversion that has taken place. The strength assessment requires the section properties of the beam to be established. Thereafter the structural strength of the element can be calculated. In cases where the section properties are unknown, or cannot be determined by investigation, then assessments are limited to determining the concrete strength using near-to-surface tests. The analysis will only work if the concrete is unaffected by alkaline hydrolysis, since the strength of the concrete could be below the $21N/mm^2$ assumed value.

Note that the calculation methods outlined in the BRAC guidance will only give accurate results for specific types of construction. Floors constructed using composite methods may seemingly fail to satisfy the calculations and yet perform perfectly well. In these circumstances in-situ load testing may give a more reliable result.

A Stage 3 durability assessment is required to determine the long-term durability where affected by chemical attack and reinforcement corrosion. Testing can be undertaken to determine the presence of alkalis and sulphates. Laboratory testing may be supplemented by a detailed visual inspection and the removal of lump samples for petrographic examination. A durability assessment should also include a visual examination of the reinforcing steel where lump samples are removed. In recent years it has been found that HAC is less durable than members containing ordinary Portland cement.

Loss of strength is only one of the issues that affects HAC concrete, and to conduct a full appraisal of an HAC structure it is necessary to consider durability as well. Essentially there are three areas to examine:

- ❖ loss of strength associated with the process of conversion;
- ❖ carbonation; and
- ❖ damage by chemical attack – mainly sulphates or alkalis.

Assessment

Putting all of this in context, however, there have been no recorded instances in the UK of a failure of a floor incorporating HAC concrete. It is important to know that in the case of the original historic failures, manufacturing faults were eventually discovered. The greatest reduction in strength occurred where a high water content was present during the period of mixing and there were high temperatures during curing.

Of the five failures or new failures of roof constructions, two did not directly involve the quality of the concrete, one was aggravated by chemical attack and two were apparently due to defective concrete which should have been rejected at the time of casting. On no occasion has weakening of the concrete due to conversion been the sole cause of failure.

Recent moves to rehabilitate HAC have involved subtle changes in the Approved Documents to the Building Regulations, while BS EN 14647: 2005 contains an appendix listing the principles for the correct use of calcium aluminate cements (formerly known as HAC).

Contributed by Trevor Rushton, trevor.rushton@watts.co.uk

Calcium chloride

Calcium chloride may be present in reinforced concrete as a result of its inclusion as an accelerator, by contamination from de-icing salts, or from the use of unwashed or poorly washed marine aggregate. Sufficient levels of chloride may result in 'chloride-induced corrosion' which can be more difficult to deal with than corrosion caused purely by carbonation. When chloride corrosion does occur, its effects may be wide-ranging, including a reduction in structural capacity.

Natural alkalinity of concrete

Steel does not corrode when embedded in highly alkaline concrete, despite high moisture levels in the concrete, because a passive film forms on the steel and remains intact as long as the concrete surrounding the bar remains highly alkaline (ph above 12.6).

Chloride-induced corrosion

The use of calcium chloride as an accelerating additive at the time of mixing was popular during the 1950s and 1960s. It was used in precasting yards to speed up the reuse of expensive moulds and was used on site during cold weather to increase the rate of gain in strength. The use of calcium chloride additive was banned in 1977. Corrosion may occur in concrete that contains sufficient chlorides even if it is not carbonated or showing visible signs of deterioration.

Chloride ions exist in two forms in concrete, namely free chloride ions, mainly found in the capillary pore water, and combined chloride ions which result from the reaction between chloride and the cement hydration process. These occur in proportions that depend on when the chloride entered the concrete. If chloride was introduced at mixing, for example, as an accelerator, approximately 90% may form harmless complexes leaving only 10% as free chloride ions. If, on the other hand, seawater or de-icing salts penetrate the surface of the concrete, the ratio of free to combined chloride may be 50:50.

All aggregates used commonly for concrete mixing contain a background level of chlorides, usually less than 0.06% by weight of cement. The presence of calcium chloride cast-in within the mix usually attracts a chloride level significantly greater than 0.4% by weight of cement. Ingressed chlorides through the outer surface of the concrete are variable in nature. However, the use of de-icing salts on, for example, external staircases and balconies is popular and may result in localised high concentrations of chlorides in excess of 1.0% by weight of cement. Concentrations of ingressed chlorides on the top surface of a car park deck may typically occur up to 3 or 4%.

The presence of free chloride ions within the pore structure of the concrete interferes with the passive protective film formed naturally on reinforcing steel.

The corrosive effect of chlorides is significantly affected therefore by the presence of free chlorides. The effects of chlorides are classified in terms of risk of corrosion because in certain conditions even low levels of chloride may pose some risk. The permissible level of chloride added at mixing specified in BS 8110 is 0.4% by weight of cement. For prestressed concrete the level is lower at 0.06%. The overall effect of reinforcement corrosion caused by chlorides must therefore be considered with the depth of reinforcement and the depth of carbonation.

Chloride-induced corrosion results in localised breakdown of the passive film rather than the widespread deterioration that occurs with carbonation. The result is rapid corrosion of the metal at the anode, leading to the formation of a 'pit' in the bar surface and significant loss of cross sectional area. This is known as 'pitting corrosion'. Occasionally a bar may be completely eaten through.

Chloride-induced corrosion may occur even in apparently benign conditions where the concrete quality appears to be satisfactory. Even if there is poor oxygen supply, reinforcement corrosion may still take place. Failure of reinforcement may therefore occur without any visual sign of cracking or spalling that would otherwise occur following the formation of expansive rust.

The presence of calcium chloride is further exaggerated by the presence of deep carbonation. Carbonation releases combined chlorides into solution to form free chloride ions, thus increasing the likelihood of corrosion. For this reason, many properties built approximately 20–30 years ago may only now start causing problems.

Risk assessment

Guidance on assessing the risk of reinforcement corrosion is provided by the Building Research Establishment (BRE) in Digest 444 Part 2. Here the risk of corrosion for structures of various ages is presented in a range from negligible to extremely high risk. Factors affecting the risk assessment are either a dry or damp environment, the depth of carbonation and of course the level of chlorides present. The digest includes risk assessment tables indicating the risk of corrosion activity according to the age of the building, whether in a wet or dry environment and whether the concrete is carbonated or uncarbonated.

Repair

The successful repair of chloride-induced corrosion is notoriously difficult because of the tendency for new corrosion cells to form at the boundary of the repair. This mechanism is called 'incipient anode effect' and should be minimised by removing, wherever possible, all concrete with significant chloride contamination. In recent years the introduction of proprietary sacrificial zinc anodes embedded within the patch repair and attached to the reinforcement can help to reduce this effect. For high levels of chlorides and long-term protection this may not be sufficient.

For heavily chloride-contaminated structures, particularly car parks, the only tried and tested long-term solution is cathodic protection. Cathodic protection is a means of corrosion protection whereby the potential of a metal structure is made more negative in order to decrease corrosion rates. The cost and complexity of installing cathodic protection is not usually warranted within building structures. A variation of cathodic protection is desalination – a short-term process using higher current densities than cathodic protection. Desalination gained some popularity in the 1990s but its use has since declined.

An alternative treatment is the application of surface-applied coatings that then migrate into the concrete. Migrating corrosion inhibitors have found some success, but there is some nervousness about their effectiveness in view of the difficulty of checking site work; the inhibitors must be applied under strict conditions.

Repair of concrete is now covered by BS EN 1504. See also Concrete Society Technical Report 69.

Further information

- ❖ *Corrosion of steel in concrete*, BRE Digest 444 Part 2, BRE, 1997
- ❖ *Investigating Hazardous and Deleterious Building Materials*, Rushton, T., RICS Books, 2006

Contributed by Trevor Rushton, trevor.rushton@watts.co.uk

Alkali aggregate reactions

Alkali aggregate reactions (AAR), of which alkali silica reactions (ASR) are only one variant, are relatively uncommon in building construction in the UK and tend to occur in civil engineering structures rather than conventional buildings. The other, even rarer form is alkali-carbonate reaction (ACR).

Alkali silica reactions – the problem

ASR in concrete can be very damaging, sometimes resulting in structural failure and the need to demolish a building or to undertake significant structural repair works.

Concrete is a highly alkaline material: it follows that pore water contained within the concrete will also be highly alkaline. ASR occurs when, given the correct combination of conditions, the pore water can react with certain types of aggregate to produce a gel.

The gel absorbs water, expands and can cause the concrete to crack or disrupt. Sometimes a pattern of 'map' cracking occurs but in others small 'pop-outs' can occur – rather like concrete with acne. The durability of the concrete can thus be compromised and in extreme cases the tensile strength of the concrete component can be reduced.

For ASR to occur, three factors must be present. Remove one and ASR will not take place:

- ❖ critical silica in the aggregate – the level of silica will affect reactivity, aggregates such as chert can be problematic;
- ❖ sufficient moisture – water being a critical component; and
- ❖ high alkalinity, either from the cement or from other external sources.

Most of the aggregates used in the UK are considered to be of 'normal' reactivity rather than high reactivity, although there are some troublesome types in the South West.

The Building Research Establishment (BRE) and the Concrete Society have prepared guidelines and flow charts to assist the designer in the selection of appropriate measures to reduce the risk of ASR.

In order to check whether the alkali content of the cement is above the critical level, chemical tests are needed. When dealing with the total alkali content of concrete it is usual to consider the equivalent sodium oxide in the concrete expressed as kilogrammes per cubic metre (kg/m^3). By adopting this 'sodium oxide equivalent' scale, cement can be classified according to low, moderate or high alkalinity. High alkalinity cement means a 0.75% sodium oxide equivalent or greater.

A combination of normal reactivity aggregate with high alkalinity cement is permissible, if the total alkalinity of the concrete is kept within certain limits. However, good construction practice dictates that for normally reactive aggregates, the total alkali content of the concrete should not exceed $3.0kg/m^3$.

What if ASR occurs?

A popular technique for the identification of ASR is the examination of thin sections of concrete, using a petrographic microscope. Polished sections of concrete can, in the alternative, be examined by scanning electron microscopy (SEM).

Concrete Society Report 30 and Part 4 of BRE Digest 330 are mainly concerned with the selection of materials to reduce the risk of ASR occurring. The available records seem to point to a low risk of the development of ASR, but remember that the third component necessary for the formation of a reaction is sufficient moisture.

If the concrete was reinforced, then any potentially expansive reactions in the concrete could be restrained (the degree of restraint depending upon the arrangement of the reinforcement).

A risk assessment based approach to analysis is advocated – this should take into account not only whether the concrete is wet or dry, or is restrained with reinforcement or not, but also the consequences of failure – the structural significance of a component. The structural significance of an element is a function of the consequences of its failure. These are judged to be slight or significant as defined below:

❖ **slight**: the consequences of structural failure are either not serious or are localised to the extent that a serious situation is not anticipated; and

❖ **significant**: if there is risk to life and limb or a considerable risk of serious damage to property.

Further information

❖ BRE Digest 330, *Alkali-silica reaction in concrete*

❖ *Structural effects of alkali-silica reaction: Technical guidance on the appraisal of existing structures*, Institute of Structural Engineers, 1992

❖ Concrete Society Report 30, *Alkali-silica reaction – Minimizing the risk of damage* (3rd edition), TR30, 1999

❖ *Investigating Hazardous and Deleterious Building Materials*, Rushton, T., RICS Books, 2006

❖ *Alkali Silica Reaction*, Fact Sheet 4, British Cement Association, 2006

Contributed by Trevor Rushton, trevor.rushton@watts.co.uk

Concrete repair

Concrete is generally a durable material, but poorly designed or constructed concrete structures can require extensive repair. In particular, many concrete buildings constructed in the 1960s and 1970s are now in poor condition. Deterioration can occur to both the concrete and the embedded reinforcement.

Deterioration of reinforcement due to carbonation can often be identified by visible rust staining or spalling of concrete. However, concrete containing excessive chlorides can lead to severe corrosion of reinforcement without any corresponding visual indication of the problem on the surface. Chloride-induced corrosion can occur where the original concrete mix included chloride containing additives. However, it is also particularly prevalent in car park structures where de-icing salts from vehicles are present. The correct choice of repair technique for each type of corrosion is important; there is the possibility of inappropriate repair actually accelerating the corrosion process.

Concrete repair work is now covered by the new, ten-part British Standard EN 1504 *Products and systems for the protection and repair of concrete structures – Definitions requirements, quality control and evaluation of conformity*.

The Standard is comprehensive and includes guidance on assessment of condition, identification of causes of deterioration, options for protection and repair, and specification of maintenance requirements following protection and repair.

The Standard introduces in Table 1 of Part 9, the concept of 'Principles and methods for protection and repair of concrete structures'. There are 11 principles and these are set out in detail in *Annex A: Guidance and background information*.

Before undertaking extensive repair of concrete structures, consideration should be given to the likely rate of ongoing deterioration and the required life of the structure, so that the cost effectiveness of different protection and repair strategies can be considered.

The possibility of adverse effects from repair methods and the consequences of interaction between them, should be considered before specifying repairs.

Many concrete repair techniques rely on the use of proprietary products or systems, and the work is often done by specialist contractors. The product manufacturers in particular can provide valuable advice in the correct use of their systems, but it is important to obtain independent advice so that the merits of different repair techniques can be compared.

Parts 9 and 10 of the Standard are the most relevant to specification and execution of repair work on site. Part 9: *General principles for use of products and systems* sets out common causes of deterioration which should be considered before investigating or treating deteriorated concrete.

Section A.6.2 of the Standard also draws attention to the possibility of adverse effects of chosen repair methods and the consequences of interaction between them.

Note: BS EN 1504 does not deal with all concrete repair methods, for example, electrochemical chloride extraction and electrochemical re-alkalisation of carbonated concrete are not covered.

Contributed by Graeme Lees, graeme.lees@watts.co.uk

Multi-storey car parks

There are over 4,500 multi-storey car parks in the UK, many having been poorly constructed and equally poorly maintained. Too often, car parks are treated with little respect for the serious potential problems that they may exhibit.

Multi-storey car parks (MSCPs) must be treated with the same level of caution as bridge structures; both are exposed elements subjected not only to the weather but to aggressive forms of deterioration from chlorides in road salts and other de-icing chemicals, such as urea. Being, in the main, open-sided and unheated structures, car parks are also subject to frequent wetting and drying, with the attendant risks of frost action and concentration of aggressive chemicals.

Until 1977, calcium chloride was routinely added to in-situ and precast concrete as an accelerator, thus, older structures could be at risk of corrosion damage arising from cast-in chlorides coupled with increasing carbonation. However, the structures are also at risk from chloride salts brought into the car park on vehicles and pedestrians during cold weather. High risk areas are ramps and traffic routes, as well as the wheel positions in car parking bays. Ramps leading up (or down) to the first two levels of the car park are most at risk of salt or other contaminants being brought in. On the top level of a car park, the effects of rainfall will wash the structure and dilute some of the salt. At lower levels, where there is no washing effect and water dries by evaporation, chlorides can become concentrated leading to a greater risk of corrosion damage.

Do not underestimate the effects of water ingress into a structure. The areas that are most likely to leak are those either at mid-span or at, or close to, the perimeter. At the perimeter will be found bearing conditions for precast structures, prestressing anchorages, reinforcement for edge beam and vehicle protection balustrades, structural joints and so on – precisely the details that need to be protected against corrosion.

Thermal movements, particularly in clear span structures, can be severe and must be accommodated in joint design. Sliding joints in precast structures are often very problematic and quite regularly lead to weeping.

Deflection of structures leads to ponding and difficulties with rainwater disposal. In turn, water then works its way into the structure via poorly designed or maintained movement joints (or cracks arising through lack of movement joints) where it may assist in the corrosion of reinforcement. Often leaks occur in the areas that are structurally most vulnerable, such as around balustrade fixings, half joints, etc.

Following the collapse of a car park floor slab at Pipers Row, Wolverhampton in 1997, the then Office of the Deputy Prime Minister (now Department for

Communities and Local Government (DCLG)) sponsored, in 2002, a publication *Enhancing the Whole Life Structural Performance of Multi-Storey Car Parks. Recommendations for the inspection and maintenance of car park structures* was published by the Institution of Civil Engineers in the same year. Both documents provide invaluable points of reference for both the design and the analysis of the performance of MSCPs.

In its tenth Annual Report (October 1994), the Standing Committee on Structural Safety (SCOSS) warned of a threat to structural safety as a result of neglected corrosion, especially of bonded or unbonded prestressing tendons or of reinforcement to cantilevers. SCOSS went on to draw attention to the potential lack of precautions against progressive collapse as this subject was not initially addressed by Building Regulations in buildings of less than five storeys in height. Early design codes for flat slab construction are now regarded as being suspect, as evidenced by the Pipers Row collapse. The simplified rules set out in BS 8110 do not necessarily ensure sufficient robustness with all forms of flat slab construction.

The Standing Committee on Structural Safety recommends that owners of car parks should:

- ❖ commission inspections by suitably experienced engineers before commissioning repairs – these inspections should go beyond those areas that are visibly defective;

- ❖ identify the risk of progressive collapse; and

- ❖ establish the suitability of edge barriers to resist accidental vehicle loads and to protect small children from falling.

Lift slabs

The Pipers Row car park collapse involved a building constructed using the lift slab method. Lift slab construction is a method of constructing buildings with repetitive floor layouts by casting them on the ground and jacking them into place. There are several different methods, but commonly a series of jacks are fitted to the top of precast columns, connected to threaded lifting rods and lifting collars cast within the floor slabs. After reaching a satisfactory strength the floors are jacked up into position and then fixed with wedges attached to the columns. The void between the floor and the column is then filled with fine aggregate concrete.

Flat slabs without thickening around the column heads, together with evidence of infill around the column head/floor slab should indicate the possibility of lift slab construction. It is sometimes possible to see footprints in a cast soffit with corresponding impressions on the slab beneath.

Early forms adopted columns at 4m centres across a bay width of 16m with a typical floor slab depth of 225mm. By the late 1960s, the method had changed to columns at 9.8m centres with cantilevers of 3.1m each side. In the early 1980s the same structural configuration was used, but with post-tensioned slabs of 250mm thickness. Car parks constructed using this method may not have waterproofing layers on the top level.

Pay particular attention to to the floor/column connections during any inspection of a lift slab car park. Shear reinforcement at this position was sometimes inadequate and was a significant factor in the Piper's Row collapse. Chloride attack in the post tensioning tendons could also be a matter of concern.

Contributed by Trevor Rushton, trevor.rushton@watts.co.uk

Corrosion of metals

Metals used in building are almost invariably the product of large amounts of energy used to transform raw materials (ores) into a finished product. The transformation from ore to metal creates an inherently metastable material which, under the influence of water and oxygen, will gradually revert (corrode) to its original form, releasing energy as it does so.

Corrosion is an electrochemical process in which a metal reacts with the environment in which it is located to form an oxide or other compound. Energy is released in the form of corrosion currents – these vary according to the metal.

Aside from gold, metals exposed to air develop an oxide film, a layer which is 30–100 Angstroms thick (about 15–50 atoms thick). The passive layer serves to protect the metal from corrosion; it greatly reduces the rate of passage of metal ions from the surface. In this condition the metal is described as being in a passive state.

If the metal is then exposed to an aqueous solution (electrolyte), the oxide film will tend to dissolve. Once this occurs, and the metal is exposed, it is termed active. In its active state, positively-charged ions tend to pass from the metal into the electrolyte. (An ion is an atom or group of atoms that carries a positive or negative charge as a result of having lost or gained one or more electrons. Ions with a positive charge are called cations; ions with a negative charge are called anions.)

Metallic ions, because they are formed from atoms that have lost electrons, are positively charged – when an atom or ion loses electrons it is said to have been oxidised.

The location of the oxidisation process is described as the anode. Here, the oxidisation of the metal is termed an anodic reaction. This flow creates an increase in the potential difference between the metal and the solution – the potential of the metal.

While the process of oxidisation continues, the deposition of dissolved metal ions from the solution occurs at the cathode. The corrosion current between the anode site and the cathode site consists of electrons flowing within the metal and ions flowing within the electrolyte. The electrolyte does not have to be liquid water – for example, the corrosion cells that form within reinforced concrete rely upon the small amount of moisture that remains in the pores of the concrete.

Corrosion is usually initiated by one or a combination of the following:

- ❖ a difference in the electrical potential of two metals in contact with an electrolyte – a galvanic couple;
- ❖ variations in the metallurgical state of the metal at different points on its surface; or
- ❖ local environmental differences, for example, variations in oxygen supply.

The following very broad categories of corrosion exist.

Uniform (general) corrosion	Accounts for about 30% of all corrosion-related failures. Occurs over the surface of the metal as a whole and is made up of a multitude of randomly positioned, microscopically-sized individual corrosion cells. This form of corrosion occurs when the passive layer has been damaged or dissolved, or where it ceases to offer protection. General corrosion can occur quite rapidly and is usually accompanied by the deposition of the products of corrosion on the surface – in the case of ferrous metals the deposition is rust. Rust does not protect the metal against corrosion, but other oxide forms can do, for example, the tarnishing of silver or the green patina associated with the corrosion of copper.

Atmospheric corrosion	Cycles of alternate wetting and drying can create conditions favourable to the corrosion of metals. When the atmosphere is contaminated with pollutants such as sulphur dioxide or chlorides, corrosion rates can be greater. Exposure to this form of corrosion is not confined to external situations; if the internal environment is favourable, corrosion can still occur.
Bimetallic or galvanic corrosion	A consequence of two metals in contact with an aqueous solution – see the following pages.
Microbiological corrosion	This term covers a variety of corrosion types initiated mainly by the presence of and/or activities of micro-organisms in biofilms that have formed on the surface of the corroding material. The formation of biofilms, sludge or other deposits can be particularly harmful as it can precipitate crevice corrosion, destroy corrosion inhibitors and directly influence a corrosion cell. A number of microbiological organisms have been associated with corrosion damage in water systems. These micro-organisms can influence corrosion by effects such as the creation of differential aeration cells, the production of corrosive mineral and organic acids, or ammonia, and chemical reductions. Four environmental conditions are required for this type of corrosion damage to occur: ❖ metals (the host location); ❖ nutrients; ❖ water; and ❖ oxygen (although some types of bacteria need only very small amounts of oxygen).
Localised corrosion – pitting corrosion, crevice corrosion, filiform corrosion	Likely to cause very serious effects. One form of localised corrosion is called pitting corrosion and can lead to the total or at least significant loss of section of plain and low alloy steel reinforcement without the formation of expansive rust and the tell-tale signs of concrete spalling. The problem often affects those metals that were selected because of their passive nature – for example, stainless steels, nickel alloys or aluminium alloys. Pitting corrosion penetrates perpendicular to the surface and is mainly associated with particularly aggressive ions such as chloride and fluoride, both of which can initiate in the absence of oxygen. Filiform corrosion can be found in the form of long filaments of growth between aluminium and its particular paint coating. The depth of penetration of this corrosion is generally found to be 10–20μm and is therefore considered to be cosmetic rather than structural. The deterioration process is primarily caused by a break or defect in the coating itself and is most commonly found in moist or wet environments (which may be internal or external) where sections of coated aluminium have been cut to form joints, or sections of cladding have been cut, drilled or damaged. Even the most microscopic of marks or breaks in the paint effectively cause the formation of a battery circuit between the exposed metal and adjoining sections which are protected from the air. The corrosion takes the appearance of a worm trail as the 'battery cell' moves along the surface of the aluminium underneath the paint.

Environment assisted cracking – hydrogen embrittlement, stress corrosion, liquid metal assisted cracking and fatigue	Environment assisted cracking can produce catastrophic failures in structural metals. The term is used to describe two prime methods of failure: stress corrosion cracking and hydrogen embrittlement.
Flow enhanced corrosion	The flow of a corrosive fluid across the surface of a metal (for example, the inside surface of a pipe), can lead to rapid erosion of the passive film in localised areas. A combination of erosion due to turbulent flow and corrosion can lead to extremely high pitting rates and pipe failure. The soft alloys of copper, aluminium and lead are particularly prone to this form of corrosion.

Bimetallic corrosion

Corrosion will often occur when two different metals are immersed in water containing an electrolyte such as salt or acid. Similar problems can also exist when dissimilar metals may not be in contact but are connected electrically. Metals submersed in seawater are particularly at risk. Detailed guidance on the subject may be found within BS PD 6484:1979, which contains a series of tables from which it is possible to identify the risk of additional corrosion of one metal in contact with another. However, the process of corrosion is complex and depends upon a number of variable factors and not just the presence of dissimilar metals: relative area, temperature and exposure to oxygen will all affect corrosion rates.

Some basic points: If a metal is immersed in a conducting liquid (the electrolyte), it will take up a conducting potential. Different metals assume a different potential – this is recorded in the electrolytic scale overleaf.

If two different metals are immersed in the electrolyte a current will flow from the more positive metal (the cathode) towards the more negative metal, the anode. This current flow arises because both metals have different electrical potentials. Standard texts often state that the further apart the metals are on the electrolytic scale, the greater risk of corrosion. The extent, or severity, of the corrosive action is proportional to the distance of separation of the metals in the list. This is an oversimplification of the position when it comes to the selection of metals during the design of buildings and services, as corrosion rates will also depend upon a number of other factors. For example, even metals that are potentially highly reactive can be used successfully together given the correct precautions.

Electrolytic scale

Anodic end (corrosion) –ve, (less noble metal)

Magnesium

Aluminium

Duralumin

Zinc

Cadmium

Chromium iron (active)

Chromium-nickel-iron (active)

Soft solder

Tin

Lead

Nickel

Brasses

Bronze

Copper

Chromium iron (passive)

Chromium-nickel-iron (passive)

Silver solder

Silver

Gold

Platinum

Cathodic end (protected to the detriment of the anodic metal) +ve, (more noble metal)

Seawater is highly conductive, and generally this will permit a greater electrical flow. A high flow produces more corrosion to the anode. By contrast, fresh water is generally less conductive. Rainwater, if polluted, can be moderately conductive and so exposure to a wet environment in an industrial area can be more damaging than in a rural area. Exposure to marine conditions can produce highly conductive conditions.

Surface contamination can absorb moisture from the atmosphere even when condensation does not form and so the fact that two metals are not immersed in water does not necessarily prevent corrosion from occurring. Metals buried in soil perform in much the same way as those that are immersed in water.

Corrosion rates can be affected by the area of the anode or cathode relative to the other. For example, a large cathode area and a small anodic area could result in a more severe condition.

Protection against bimetallic corrosion

Actions which may help prevent bimetallic corrosion include:

❖ insulating the metals from one another;

❖ applying a metallic coating;

❖ applying a non-metallic coating;

❖ using a jointing compound capable of excluding water;

❖ applying a paint coating; and

❖ applying sacrificial protection, e.g. cathodic protection.

The data within PD 6484 may be simplified and reproduced as in the following table, which should be treated as a guide only. If a particular combination is critical refer to the more complete information in PD 6484: 1979. The table shows the performance of each metal in contact. To determine whether or not corrosion is a problem, the performance of both metals must be checked. For example, to check the combination of cast iron with carbon steel, first check cast iron in the vertical columns – this shows no corrosion. However, now check carbon steel in the vertical column and it can be seen that in combination, the carbon steel will corrode in preference to the cast iron. The data does not apply to metals that are immersed in fresh water or seawater.

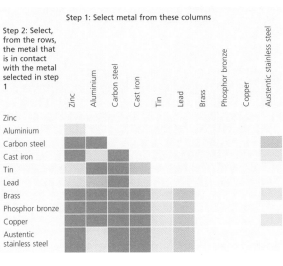

 Additional corrosion likely under all conditions

Additional corrosion likely under marine exposure

Additional corrosion likely under industrial or marine exposure

Additional corrosion unlikely under all conditions

References

BS PD 6484:1979, *Commentary on corrosion at bimetallic contacts and its alleviation*

Guides to Good Practice in Corrosion Control, National Physical Laboratory (NPL)

Further information

- ❖ Lifetime Management of Materials Service at the National Physical Laboratory: www.npl.co.uk/lmm
- ❖ Institute of Corrosion: www.icorr.org

There are also a number of trade and development organisations for metals such as zinc, aluminium, lead, copper, etc., who will provide information on the corrosion performance of metals.

Contributed by Trevor Rushton, trevor.rushton@watts.co.uk

Building defects

Materials and defects

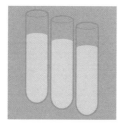

Common defects in buildings

It is easy to think of building defects as being a product of the 20th century. However, for as long as we have been building there have been building defects; it is simply that many defective buildings have long since passed out of our memory or knowledge. However, it is fair to say that the latter years of the 20th century saw an unprecedented period of innovation. No longer were traditional craft-based skills passed on from generation to generation; building had become a process of assembly.

Economies brought on by economic necessity, improved design and technology have all tended to make buildings lighter – and now more responsive to thermal and moisture movements.

Rather than look at typical problems associated with each style of building, the following table is intended to give a very brief introduction to a number of common or typical materials or construction faults. The list is not exhaustive.

Brief résumé of some problems

Key to common building types – these are indicative only:

> W = Warehouse or industrial
>
> O = Office or commercial developments
>
> H = Housing
>
> A = All types.

Period	Typical problem	Possible effects
Pre-1900	Alterations to trussed (loadbearing) partitions (H)	Removal of support gives rise to distortions in floors, reduction of loadbearing capacity and possible risk of collapse
	Damp penetration through 225mm brick walls (A)	Damage to plaster and finishes, decay to wall plates and bonding timbers
	Defective rainwater goods (A)	Risk of decay in built-in timbers
	Delamination of brick skins (A)	Bulging of brickwork
	Original facade concealed behind later finish of stone, brick or render (A)	Decay of original structure, delamination of skins
	Failed or lack of damp-proof course (A)	Rising dampness, penetrating damp, efflorescence on plaster, decay to skirtings, etc.
	Failure of brick arches and timber lintels (A)	Cracking and distortion of brickwork above window heads
	Insect attack, particularly in poorly ventilated and damp areas such as floor and roof voids (A)	Loss of strength if particularly badly affected

Period	Typical problem	Possible effects
Pre-1900 continued	Lack of restraint to flank walls (O, H)	Bulging or instability, associated cracking on front and rear elevations
	Lead lined parapet gutters – poor outlets and/or poor sizing of lead sheet, leading to splitting and water penetration (A)	Risk of water damage and decay
	Lead water mains (A)	Hazardous to health – partly depends on plumbsolvency (the degree to which the chemical content of local water supplies dissolves lead) of the water
	Over notching of floor joists for retrofit of services (O, H)	Deflection of floors, reduction in loadbearing capability
	Parapet gutters draining to lead secret gutters through roof voids (A)	Risk of blockage and subsequent water leakage/decay. Bird nesting causing blockage.
	Poor quality repairs to roofs and gutters (A)	Risk of timber decay
	Poor ventilation of floor voids (A)	Decay in wall plates, joists, etc.
	Poorly fitting sash windows, risk of decay within window reveals, water penetration beneath sub-sills (A)	Draughty or dangerous operation, decay in concealed areas, lack of security
	Roof covered with concrete interlocking tiles (H)	Overloading of roof structure, bowing of rafters and purlins, roof spread
	Settlement of bay windows (H)	Internal cosmetic damage, distortion in loadbearing elements
	Relaxation of torsional stair treads and landings (sometimes termed cantilevered stairs).	Serious loss of structural integrity; treads become loose and may fail.
	Settlement of internal partitions (H)	Plaster damage, distortion in floors and door openings
1900–1939	Boot lintels (A)	Rotation of lintel due to eccentric loading
	Corroded galvanised steel or steel windows (A)	Cracked glazing, high maintenance costs
	Corroded rainwater goods (A)	Risk of decay in built-in timbers, damp penetration
	Corrosion of roofing nails (A)	Slipping of tiles
	Delamination of render finishes to walls (A)	Cracking and bulging of render, detachment of same
	Lead water mains (A)	Possibly hazardous to health

Period	Typical problem	Possible effects
1900–1939 continued	Mundic concrete (H mainly)	Disintegration and expansion of blockwork leading to failure of rendering
	Outdated electrical services (H)	Possibly dangerous
	Timber joinery (A)	Decay to sills and softwood frames
	Wall tie failure in cavity brickwork (A)	Bulging of brickwork, horizontal cracking or 'pagoda effect'
1945–1979	Aluminum sash windows (O) A common type of window was the vertical sliding sash. Instead of the vision glazing being held in a frame, the glass ran in aluminium tracks, with horizontal top and bottom frame members clipped onto the glass. Spring balances were used to hold the windows open.	By now, these windows will be very worn. Defects in the springs or breakage of the glass can lead to the ejection of an entire sash window – clearly a health and safety issue. Treat these windows with caution.
	Asbestos (A) Very common in 1960s buildings. Chrysotile (white) for some insulation boards, roof sheets, water tanks, sill boards, etc. Artex, floor tiles, partition wall linings, fire doors, etc. may also contain some asbestos. Amosite (brown) used as insulating boards, fire protection or fire breaks, behind perimeter heaters, partitions, etc. Crocodilite (blue) often paste-applied friable material in boiler rooms, pipework, calorifiers, etc.	Major health risks depending on type, location and risk of disturbance. Deleterious material – detection, management and control are highly regulated. Ask for a copy of the asbestos register. (See also the *Asbestos* section, page 281.)
	Asphalt roofs (O) These could be of quite good quality and may have performed well if laid on a concrete deck.	The lack of insulation would have helped to reduce temperature ranges and so restrict thermal movements.
	Brick slips (O)	Risk of slips detaching from the structure owing to shrinkage of the frame and expansion of brick skin.
	Built-up-roof coverings (A)	Poor life expectancy of coverings, failure of BS 747 felts due to poor tensile strength.

Period	Typical problem	Possible effects
1945–1979 continued	Calcium chloride concrete additive (A) Often used by manufacturers of precast elements or for concreting in cold weather. Enables rapid set and removal of moulds. Can also be found in brickwork mortar. Use of unwashed sea-dredged aggregates may have led to chloride contamination, as may exposure to de-icing salt or a marine environment.	Corrosion of reinforcement. (See also the *Calcium chloride* section, page 293.)
	Calcium silicate bricks (A) Smooth, often creamy coloured bricks made from lime, sand and flint. Small particles of flint can sometimes be seen in cut bricks or weathered surfaces. Can be mistaken for concrete bricks (see page 311). Widespread use in 1960s and 1970s, still manufactured and gaining popularity again. Flank wall of calcium silicate bricks – shrinkage cracking.	Prone to shrinkage (unlike clay bricks which expand after laying). If movement control joints are missed or badly spaced (which they often were), diagonal cracking can occur. Thermal or moisture cracking often visible at changes in the size of panels, e.g. long runs below windows coinciding with short sections between windows. Look out for thin bed cracks and wider cracks to vertical joints. Do not confuse with subsidence cracking or corrosion of steel frame. Its use as a backing to clay brickwork is likely to cause problems as a result of expansion of clay brick and contraction of calcium silicate brick.
	Cladding systems (O, W) Early curtain walling systems relied upon the use of galvanised steel window components coupled together or fixed within framed openings. These systems were often single glazed and incorporated Vitrilite spandrel panels. In the early 1970s more aluminium curtain walling systems were developed. Early systems were single glazed and face-sealed but, latterly, drained systems were installed, incorporating double-glazed units.	Inspect opening sashes for signs of distortion – usually due to paint build up. Window fittings are usually worn or inoperable. Pay particular attention to the security of fanlight fixings. Early double-glazed systems were fully bedded. Deterioration of sealants is common, leading to voiding, leakage and deterioration of edge seals. Be suspicious of early face-sealed systems in terms of future durability.

Period	Typical problem	Possible effects
1945–1979 continued	Cold bridging and condensation (A) Poor insulation standards led to problems with severe cold bridging, particularly in housing with higher humidity levels. Polystyrene insulation was sometimes used but this was usually no more than 25mm thick. In the mid to late 1970s, thermal insulation standards were increased, particularly in industrial buildings.	Watch out for cold bridging around balcony structures and precast lintels. Provision of insulation within industrial buildings resulted in a spate of condensation problems within roofs. Cold night sky radiation gave rise to condensation on the underside of metal roofing, while poor application of vapour control layers meant that problems were exacerbated.
	Cold flat roof construction (A) Little thought was given to vapour control or, for that matter, roof insulation. It was common to provide sealed flat roof construction with minimal insulation and sometimes a foil-backed plasterboard ceiling lining. Ventilation to the roof void was often ignored. Built-up felt roofs were often asbestos based, but had a life of around 15 years and no more. For this reason most felt roofs would have been replaced by now.	Risk of condensation occurring, with subsequent risk of decay to roof decking or to structure.
	Concrete (A) Can be of mixed quality, sometimes poorly compacted and with lack of cover to steel reinforcement. Under codes, depth of cover for external work should have been c40mm.	Sometimes poor durability, corrosion due to the effects of carbonation or chloride content. Tests should be recommended. Poor curing methods could mean lack of durability. Calcium chloride added as an accelerator either in precast or in-situ work.
	Concrete boot lintels (A) Concrete lintels designed to have a projecting nib to support the outer leaf, and built only into the inner leaf, to provide a neat appearance externally.	Rotation of the lintel under eccentric load, creating diagonal cracking to the brickwork above the window. Other signs are opening of the bed joint immediately above lintels and splitting of the reveal brickwork immediately beneath. Once rotation has taken place, brickwork will tend to arch over the opening, thus relieving some of the load on the lintel. Cracks can then be repointed.

Period	Typical problem	Possible effects
1945–1979 continued	Concrete bricks (A) Similar in appearance to calcium silicate brick but often used in dark brown, dark red or dark grey variants. Harder and coarser texture than calcium silicate bricks.	Suffer from similar shrinkage-related problems. Can be hard to differentiate between these and calcium silicate bricks, but may be harder and contain small particles of visible aggregate.
	Concrete frame (W, O) Expressed concrete frames were common in the 1960s, often with brick infill panels. In the 1970s there was a move away from this form of construction to brick cladding, with the frame concealed either by brick slips or by a brick outer leaf supported on steel angles.	In both cases, there is a risk that the brick panels can become stressed as a result of the normal shrinkage (axial foreshortening) of the concrete frame. A failure to provide movement joints means that loads can be transferred to the panels with the result that the brickwork is disrupted.
	Corrugated 'big six' asbestos cement sheet (W) Often found on industrial buildings and warehouses well into the 1970s. Name given as a result of the 6-inch profile, but in fact 'big six' was one of several different profiles of sheet. Often based on an asbestos content of around 12–15% chrysotile (white asbestos), with profiled eaves and ridge pieces and hook bolt fastenings. By the end of the 1970s insulation was being added to the roof construction and this brought about condensation problems.	Obvious health risks from fibre release. Friable surface, and very fragile – never walk on such a covering without crawling boards. Corrosion of hook bolts will cause sheeting to split. Often coated with bitumen or rubber solutions as a remedial treatment. Be very cautious of the effectiveness of these treatments. Rigid foam spacers were sometimes used below cement fibre sheeting in order to create a void into which insulation could be placed. The rigid foam compresses with time and occasional traffic loads, leading to 'chattering' of the roof sheets and possible water ingress.
	Cracking of brickwork outer skins (A)	Failure to provide for movement resulting from thermal change and/or moisture. Shrinkage of concrete frames coupled with expansion of clay brickwork producing internal stress in the brickwork.
	Cut edge corrosion of Plastisol covered sheet steel roofing (W)	Deterioration of protective covering, corrosion of steel sheet leading to perforation of the base metal.
	Deleterious materials such as HAC, chloride, asbestos, woodwool as permanent shuttering (A)	See the section on deleterious materials, page 278.

Materials and defects

Period	Typical problem	Possible effects
1945–1979 continued	External ceramic tiling (O) See 'mosaic tesserae'. Tiles were often prism shaped or ridged in some way.	Similar problems to mosaic tesserae in terms of delamination of background materials.
	Failure of dark coloured Plastisol coatings (W)	Unsuitable colours for roofing lead to high temperature build-up and subsequent deterioration of coating, often large areas of coating flaking away.
	Flat concrete floor slabs (Plate floors) (O, W) Fairly thin slabs with mushroom head thickening around column heads.	Very high shear stress around column head has been found to be cause of structural failure. Beware of flat slab car park construction – e.g. 1997 major collapse of car park of flat slab construction at Pipers Row.
	Fully bedded glazing methods for thermally insulating glass units (A)	Water leakage, deterioration of edge seals and subsequent misting of glass panels.
	Glass reinforced concrete (GRC) (A) Lightweight cladding panels, balustrade panels, permanent shutters, planters.	Early forms of GRC contained fibres that deteriorated in alkaline conditions. Loss of strength, cracking and bowing can result. Later alkaline resistant types (Cem-fil) perform better.
	High Alumina Cement (HAC) concrete (O, W) Often used in precast and prestressed work rather than in-situ work, mainly (but not exclusively) for roof and floor beams. X and I profiles were common. Some variants for precast factory units (portals and purlins). Sometimes used to form an in-situ stitch between two precast beam members or column to beam connections. Developed high early strength. Can have a brownish tinge.	Loses strength with age. Susceptible to chemical attack in damp conditions and contact with gypsum plaster. (See also the HAC section, page 291.)
	Hollow clay pot floors (O) Quite common during the 1960s. Concrete poured between pots and in the form of a topping. Sometimes screed could be structural. In other cases, non-structural screeds may have been removed to gain additional load or headroom.	Watch out for clay spacer tiles between the pots. These can conceal honeycombing of the concrete rib, lack of fire protection, durability or strength. Removal of tiles and Gunnite repairs may be necessary.

Period	Typical problem	Possible effects
1945–1979 continued	Lack of movement control joints (A) Cement masonry walls are prone to thermal and moisture movements. Cement mortar is less flexible than older lime mortars, and the stresses induced by thermal movement are relieved by cracking. Centres of joints depend on nature of brick, size and shape of panel, etc. Lack of joints was common in 1960s buildings.	Oversailing of brickwork on dpc, particularly in warehouses. Also watch out for joints that have been filled with Flexcell impregnated board, as this is not very compressible and can reduce the benefit of a joint. Early sealants were also resinous and could lead to staining of adjoining surfaces. Hardening and embrittlement of joint sealants is to be expected now.
	Large panel buildings (H) A number of different systems were constructed. Large panels formed the external enclosure and also supported precast floor planks or slabs. Connection details were made on site with wire hoops and in-situ work. The design of joints in panel systems was critical in the success or failure of the system. A variety of types were often employed, in some cases using baffles in the form of open drained joints or face sealed joints using mastic or neoprene gaskets. The success of the building from a structural point of view relies on the connection between the individual panels. The ability to withstand local damage by means of alternative load paths is critical.	Risk of disproportionate collapse, e.g. the Ronan Point disaster. Following this, high-rise blocks were strengthened. Some low-rise blocks may not have been checked. Poor quality control of structural connections led to weakness, poor fire stopping or corrosion risk. Possible lack of tying-in of precast components. See 'Tying-in' later in this table. Large panel systems suffer from many of the defects described previously; the more important being rain penetration, corrosion of reinforcement, poor thermal insulation, distortion or physical damage to panels. Calcium chloride was not used in most precast systems, although in some types it was added on a batch-by-batch basis to aid manufacture, perhaps where there were particular programming problems. Thus the inclusion of the material is unpredictable. The most common faults with these systems relates to the gradual deterioration of the baffle (particularly where butyl rubber was used), ageing of sealants, or ageing of gaskets in face sealed joints.

Period	Typical problem	Possible effects
1945–1979 continued	*Large panel buildings continued*	Misplacement of baffles or insufficiently sized baffles in wide joints can lead to water penetration. It is quite common to find that quality control standards during manufacture were not up to scratch, with the result that reinforcement was commonly misplaced in the fabrication of the concrete panels. This later led to corrosion of the reinforcement and spalling of the concrete. In many cases dry packing used between infill concrete and the panel above is missing or poorly compacted, so that vertical loads are transferred only on the bolt fastenings, resulting in localised cracking around fixing positions. In the long term, panels can distort generally as a result of shrinkage in the concrete structure behind and as a result of normal thermal movements in the building as a whole. This can lead to damage at joints, displacement of seals and baffles and subsequent water penetration. Furthermore, smoke stopping between floors and compartments can be damaged with the result that in a fire, smoke can transfer rapidly between occupancies or zones.
	Lift slab construction (O) A method of multi-storey concrete frame construction where floors are cast on the ground and jacked up into position.	Risk of collapse of structures (e.g. car parks) where corrosion of reinforcement and other factors, such as lack of shear reinforcement at column/floor connections, gives rise to weakness.
	Mineralite render (O) A thin (2–5mm) coating of fine-grained minerals with a textured surface. Often applied to exposed concrete columns and beams or in larger areas, such as spandrel panels. Variety of colours available.	Beware of adhesion failure – can be widespread. Difficult to match repairs.

Period	Typical problem	Possible effects
1945–1979 continued	Mosaic tesserae (O) A common finish comprising small (25mm²) ceramic or glass tiles applied to a render background. Often supplied in paper-backed sheets of around 300 x 300mm to facilitate laying.	Adhesion failure of tiles leads to individual tiles falling off. Render loses adhesion to the concrete or brick substrate. This is potentially more serious as larger and heavier sections could collapse. A hammer survey is to be recommended to check for soundness and to identify hollow areas. Repairs are possible using vacuum injection techniques, but hacking off and repair of spalled areas can lead to peel back and cracking of adjoining surfaces and deterioration due to water ingress and freeze/thaw cycles.
	Mosaic tesserae in overhead situations (O) Often used as a soffit finish to projecting balconies, shopping mall covered ways, etc. Tiles would be bedded on render or possibly applied over expanded metal lathing.	Watch out for corrosion of the metal lathing or fixing screws as these may not have been protected against corrosion. Timber fixing battens behind the lathing can also be a problem. In severe cases, large sections of render and tile finish can collapse. If water penetration is suspected, recommend further intrusive investigation.
	No fines concrete (H) Used in the manufacture of large panels for housing and similar structures, intended to create slightly better insulation properties.	Very low level of resistance to carbonation, hence risk of carbonation and corrosion.
	Panel joints (O, H) Panel joints in large panel systems often comprised a plastic or metal baffle sprung into grooves in the edge of each panel. To prevent leakage, it was common to provide a tape back seal to the rear face of the joint.	Baffles may be missing or dislodged. Back seals often missing with consequent risk of water penetration. Flat roof abutments often dressed under the bottom edge of panels, which makes them very difficult to repair. Often necessary to modify the drained joint into a face-sealed joint.
	Poor cavity tray details (A)	Water ingress
	Poor installation of lateral bracing to trussed rafters (O, H)	Lack of restraint to gables, lateral buckling of trusses.
	Poor quality joinery (A)	Decay of external joinery
	Portland cement based render (A)	Cracking of finish, water penetration into wall, delamination of render.

Period	Typical problem	Possible effects
1945–1979 continued	Reconstituted stone (A) Often used as window sills or window surrounds, string courses or other projecting features in all types of buildings. Sometimes fixed with ferrous cramps rather than phosphor bronze. Contain light reinforcement.	Propensity to carbonate fairly rapidly with the result that reinforcement corrodes, causing the features to spall. Corrosion of cramps can lead to displacement of features such as projecting window surrounds.
	Reinforced aerated autoclaved planks (W, O) Often used as roof decks – 'Sipporex' or 'Durox' or sometimes as vertical walling. Thin reinforcement, 300–750mm width. Made from a mixture of cement, blast furnace slag, pfa plus aluminium.	If designed before 1980 may deflect excessively, evidenced by transverse cracking on soffit. Some concerns over durability of reinforcement.
	Reinforced concrete frames, carbonation and chloride attack (A)	Mechanisms of deterioration in concrete, spalling and corrosion of reinforcement, often compounded by poor cover, poor quality concrete and consequent lack of durability.
	Reliance on mastic sealant (A)	Poor durability, over-optimistic expectation of longevity.
	Render backgrounds (A) Used in conjunction with tile finishes and mosaic tesserae. Often very strong Portland cement based mixes were used.	Possible adhesion failures on concrete due to presence of traces of mould oil on the surface. Sometimes used water-based bonding agents (giving a white milky appearance when render is removed) when there was a poor mechanical key. Later bonding agents were of SBR, which were more durable. Inflexible renders, high vapour resistance and risk of water entrapment.

Period	Typical problem	Possible effects
1945–1979 continued	Sand-faced fletton bricks (A) These were a popular and cheap brick type manufactured by the London Brick Company near Peterborough. Often found in 1960s housing or industrial applications. Often, but not always, a red/pink colour with a heavy textured wire cut type of surface. Rear face of brick is smooth with colour bands or 'kiss marks' arising from the burning process.	No problem in sheltered applications but, in exposed situations (such as parapets, chimney stacks and freestanding walls) where saturation is common, bricks are at risk of sulphate attack. The bricks have a very high sulphate content. When wet, soluble sulphates react with Portland cement bedding mortars, causing the mortar to expand and so disrupting the brickwork. Once this occurs, the damage is terminal. Often rendered in the mistaken belief that this will cure the problem, but this very short-lived solution will only make matters worse.
	Softwood joinery (A) External joinery was often of poorly seasoned sapwood with a low life expectancy.	Very poor durability, especially glazing beads, sills and horizontal rails. Further decay where timber has been pieced-in during repair.
	Spontaneous failure of toughened glass (O mainly)	Often caused by nickel sulphide inclusions in toughened glass. Annealed glass not affected.
	Steel windows and cladding (O, W) Typical single glazed windows were manufactured using a section known as W20 by Crittal Windows. Either casements or tilt and turn varieties. Larger curtain walled sections were manufactured by coupling window units together with galvanised steel tee bars.	By now, early windows may be paint bound or distorted. Ironmongery may be defective. Timber subframes were common and may be decayed.

Period	Typical problem	Possible effects
1945–1979 continued	Stramit roof decking (A) An insulation board often used as a roof decking. It comprises a rigid board about 50mm thickness of compressed straw sandwiched between two layers of building paper. The boards were about 1200 x 450mm width and had a brown paper finish. Check in plant rooms, lift motor rooms, roof access housings, etc. Used in some domestic applications.	The material had a very low resistance to water and would decay easily. For that reason it is less usual to find it nowadays. The boards had a grain and needed to be laid correctly, with support perpendicular to the grain. Failure to do this could lead to distortion of the board and subsequent 'wave' effects in the roof line. This in turn could stress the covering and cause failure. Saturated Stramit board would turn into a brown silage-like mess. Beware of safety issues (risk of collapse) when walking on Stramit roofs.
	System built housing (H) In general terms these types of buildings were prefabricated, based on either steel or concrete construction. Examples would be the British Iron and Steel Federation properties or, if concrete, Woollaway, Unity, Airey, etc. The form of construction was generally based upon the erection of a frame with cladding fitted to it or alternatively a panel system.	Problems have occurred as a result of carbonation in the concrete and initial lack of cover, use of unsatisfactory materials (such as thin steel tube used as reinforcement), problems of interstitial condensation, damage to sealants, etc. In some cases the decay of structural parts has reached severe proportions and it has been necessary to contrive methods of reinforcing the frame or alternatively providing a new cladding system, possibly based on conventional brick and block cavity walling systems.

Period	Typical problem	Possible effects
1945–1979 continued	Trussed roof construction (H, O) Trusses were introduced into the UK during the mid-1960s and were primarily intended for the housing market, although gradual improvements in stress grading and timber engineering have now taken them into commercial, educational and leisure buildings. Commonly designed to pitches of between 20°–35°, with a span of around 3–10m, trussed rafters are usually jointed with factory-fixed galvanised steel fasteners, although plywood gussets are sometimes used. With the use of stress graded timber, sizes can be reduced to as little as 35mm in width, with trusses arranged at 450mm or more (usually 600mm) centres. Spans of greater than 10m can be achieved, although buckling of compression members can become a problem – and transport to site may be uneconomic.	The correct positioning of the connector plates is essential so that sufficient teeth engage in the timber to prevent the joint, particularly at the apex, from pulling apart. If this happens the truss will settle, or fail. The signs of this may be hogging in the roof and damage to internal finishes. Shrinkage of timber after fabrication can affect the adequacy of the truss as a whole. If the timber members cannot meet, all the joint forces will be taken up by the metal connections, which could buckle or pull out. Corrosion of gang nails used in the manufacture of trussed rafters due to interaction with certain timber preservatives. Compression members may be subject to sideways buckling under load. Bracing is also needed to prevent buckling. Roofs are vulnerable to long-term vibrations which, in an inadequately braced roof, can lead to lateral buckling either in one or two directions towards gable walls. The structure will also be expected to afford support to gable walls and this is usually achieved by the use of galvanised steel straps turned down into the cavity and fixed to at least two adjacent trusses. Lack of adequate restraint to gable walls or other unrestrained elements could allow an unacceptable degree of movement to take place.
	Tying-in of precast concrete floor and roof slabs (O, H) Prior to 1972 (CP110) tying-in was left to engineering judgment. There is a need to form a connection between wall structures and internal precast floor planks. This can be achieved with continuous metal straps or structural toppings to prevent planks from gradually moving apart.	Failure to tie-in properly can lead to the elevation gradually parting company from the floors. Evidenced by a series of parallel cracks in the floors, gradually increasing in severity higher up the building. If neglected, collapse could occur under accidental loads.

Period	Typical problem	Possible effects
1945–1979 continued	Vitrilite panels (O) Used in conjunction with steel windows (see earlier), these single glazed spandrel panels were made from annealed glass with a powder coating fused into the rear surface during manufacture.	Risk of failure due to heat build-up in spandrel panels, bird strikes or mechanical damage from cradles. Water penetration can cause staining and deterioration of rear surfaces. Replacement panels no longer available and may have been made from painted glass with less life expectancy.
	Wall ties (A) Often wire butterfly ties. Thin steel sections and poor galvanising standards. Cavity walls were rarely insulated and cavity tray detailing may be poor. During the 1960s it was common to use galvanised wire ties and, in some cases, vertical twist ties with substandard protection coatings. The life expectancy of bitumen and zinc coatings on these ties is frequently well under the 60 years that was originally predicted. In fact, in 1981, BS 1243 tripled the minimum allowed zinc coating thickness on wire ties.	Factors which could influence the life of the tie are the steel alloy used, the quality of the protective coating and the mortar type – particularly if this was contaminated with chlorides or if the building was in an exposed location. Research by BRE suggests that average zinc loss is about 2.1 microns a year. For pre-1981 ties, this results in a predicted coating life of 12–26 years for wire ties and 25–46 years for vertical twist ties. On the inner leaf, where the circumstances are less aggressive, the zinc coating can be expected to last much longer. If wire ties have been used, they tend to corrode away without any substantial physical disruption to the brickwork. Damage becomes manifest by the sudden collapse of an outer leaf, particularly in conditions of high wind. With the thicker, vertical twist ties the amount of metal is significantly more and if corrosion occurs it is likely that the thickness could increase by as much as four times. The cumulative effect of this corrosion will be the creation of horizontal cracks in the brickwork and eventually the lifting of the roof covering at eaves level to give the so-called pagoda effect.
	Woodwool as permanent shuttering (W, O) Often used in basement car parks where additional insulation was required, or in some office buildings.	Risk of poor compaction of concrete during placing, or grout loss leading to honeycombing around rebars. This could prejudice fire protection, durability or in extreme cases strength. Intrusive investigation required to determine if steel is covered properly.

Period	Typical problem	Possible effects
1945–1979 continued	Woodwool slab roof decks (A) Often with galvanised steel tongue and grooved edge strips and with a pre-screeded finish, or an applied finish reinforced with chicken wire. Size about 1200 x 450mm or 600mm. (See above for use in permanent shuttering.) The material offered some thermal insulation qualities. Often used in plant room roofs, access housings, etc.	Reasonably durable and, contrary to popular belief, does not degrade rapidly when wet. However, failure of screed is probable during re-roofing operations, leading to need to renew the deck.
1980– present	Composite panels (W)	See page 346. Use of expanded foam insulation in insulated panels and (pre-2000 especially) use of rigid polyurethane foam (PUR) can give rise to total loss in the event of a fire. Fire in a building can spread to the insulation, leading to (in some cases) explosive delamination and rapid fire spread. Polyisocyanurate (PIR) types of foam are now almost universally used for industrial buildings owing to insurance restrictions. Testing of foam type will not necessarily confirm if the panel type is Loss Prevention Standard (LPS) approved but should distinguish between PUR and PIR.
	External rainscreen systems and external wall insulation systems (A)	Possible defects in fire stopping within cavity leading to rapid fire spread. Risks of detachment or water penetration behind external wall insulation systems, particularly in high-rise buildings where the system may be applied without a drained and ventilated cavity.
	Insulated spacers in insulated glass units (O)	Risk of debonding of the spacer and gradual creeping of the spacer into the sight line.
	Liquid roofing systems (A)	Hot applied (generally in new work) and cold applied (for repairs and alterations). Risks of failure due to poor preparation and detailing, contamination of surfaces, etc.

Period	Typical problem	Possible effects
	Syphonic drainage systems (W)	A method of water disposal from roofs (particularly to industrial buildings) that relys upon syphonic conditions being created at the outlets and in collector pipes. The system can be very efficient if designed properly, but early systems were not always reliable owing to poor specification, lack of underground drainage capacity and too much time needed for syphonic action to occur. The outlets are vulnerable to blockage and must be well maintained.
	Thin marble facings (O) New methods of cutting enabled the use of thinner stone as a facing material. Used as a rainscreen cladding or in 'handplaced' situations.	Marbles can be prone to curling as a result of isotropic thermal expansion. The effects can be profound, leading to visible distortions and damage to fixings, loosening or cracking of stone and detachment of panels. There is no cure for this type of movement. Calcitic marbles are particularly prone to this form of deterioration.
	Toughened glass, use in overhead situations and in cladding systems (A)	Risk of spontaneous fracture due to nickel sulphide inclusions (see page 353). Overhead glazing particularly vulnerable in shopping centres, concourses, etc. where failure could result in collapse. Laminated safety glass preferred in these locations.
All periods	Blocking of airbricks (W, O, H, A)	Lack of ventilation, risk of decay
	Over notching of floor joists (W, O, H, A)	Reduction in strength, sagging
	Provision of insulation, blocking ventilation paths (W, O, H, A)	Condensation
	Removal of chimney breasts (W, O, H, A)	Possible lack of support
	Removal of loadbearing walls or walls affording stability (W, O, H, A)	Possible long-term structural consequences
	Removal of, or planting of, trees or large shrubs (W, O, H, A)	Possible desiccation or rehydration of subsoil, damage to drains or foundations

Period	Typical problem	Possible effects
	Replacement windows (W, O, H, A)	Poor support to bay windows, distortion of brickwork. Poor sealing of new windows to existing fabric leading to loss of airtightness and water penetration.

Contributed by Trevor Rushton, trevor.rushton@watts.co.uk

Steel frame corrosion (Regent Street disease)

Until the early part of the 20th century, substantial buildings tended to be constructed using load-bearing masonry – at least for the external walls. Because of the massive nature of these forms of construction, the walls were able to accommodate movements due to temperature and moisture, as well as small building movements, without significant harm. With the advent of steel as a versatile construction material, the position changed dramatically. By 1910, steel framing was becoming very popular, and this meant that walls could be reduced in thickness, with obvious benefits in terms of economy of material, weight and cost. The use of these construction methods in London's Regent Street has given rise to the common description of Regent Street disease, but it is a problem that is by no means confined to this location.

Typically of many new construction materials, the properties of steel were not fully understood, or at least if understood, ignored. From the early part of the 20th century up to the Second World War, it became common practice to construct load-bearing frames of steel, clad on the external faces with stone, brick or terracotta. The external cladding would be notched around the steel frame, with the void between the two filled with low-grade mortar.

As we now know, moisture, oxygen and steel do not make good bedfellows: corrosion cells are set up which can cause significant delamination and loss of strength. The main problem is that corroded steel has the propensity to expand to at least four times its original volume (some sources suggest up to ten times). Given that the voids around the steel were filled, the expansion of the steel would inevitably result in cracking of the stone, and in extreme cases the loosening or loss of support to horizontal stonework, which could then collapse. Such problems could occur long before the corrosion has compromised the ability of the structural member to perform properly.

While some corrosion protection was common after about 1930, the methods used were unlikely to offer a long-term benefit, and so it is now very common to find evidence of corrosion in many steel-framed, brick or stone-clad buildings. Evidence will take the form of vertical or horizontal cracks reflecting the location of the steel frame. Parallel cracks indicating a column position may be less serious than horizontal cracks to a beam location, but nevertheless investigations are needed to determine the condition of the steel. While early evidence of corrosion is reflected by hairline cracks, more significant problems (particularly in glazed brickwork) can indicate advanced corrosion or loss of section.

Dealing with corrosion using traditional methods is expensive and disruptive. The steel must be exposed, cleaned and protected – not an attractive proposition when dealing with a listed building or an important facade. It is usual to provide a corrosion barrier to the steel and then to create a void around it so that if further corrosion does occur, it will not result in cracking.

Because of the cost and disturbance of these forms of treatment, more attention is now being paid to the application of cathodic protection systems, which rely upon the concealment of discrete anodes into the stone joints, and electrical connection to the steel frame and the introduction of an electric current to reverse the corrosion current. These systems require very careful design and installation and it is imperative that the entire frame is protected in this way to prevent stray currents from having a harmful effect.

Further information

❖ Gibbs, P., *Cathodic protection of early steel framed buildings*, Monograph No. 7, Corrosion Prevention Association

❖ *Corrosion in masonry clad early 20th century steel framed buildings*, Technical Advice Note 20, Historic Scotland Technical Conservation Research and Education Division

❖ Warland, E. G., *Modern Practical Masonry*, London, Sir Isaac Pitman & Sons Ltd, 1929

Contributed by Trevor Rushton, trevor.rushton@watts.co.uk

Fungi and timber infestation in the UK

Fungi and moulds

Mould growths and wood rotting fungi are possibly the most common defects that will be encountered in buildings, particularly when inspecting domestic accommodation. Mould and fungi are effectively base plant forms: moulds draw nourishment from air and fungi from within host materials.

Wood rotting fungi are familiarly categorised as wet or dry rot. While there are numerous forms of wet rot, there is a single true dry rot, Latin name *Serpula Lacrymans*.

Fungi require both a source of nutriment and appropriate levels of moisture. Dry rot characteristically requires a lower average moisture content within the host timber than wet rots, though to some extent dry rot is able to manipulate its environment to create more favourable conditions. Dry rot is known to grow through plaster and masonry in a search of fresh sources of nutriment, but takes no nutriment from the plaster or masonry itself.

The *Fungi identification table* on the following pages provides an overview of the most commonly encountered wood rotting fungi in the UK. Hyphae (thin strands often mistaken for cobwebs, that make up the mycelium) spread out from the germinated spores, however it is often the sporophores (fruiting bodies) that are the first recognised indication of an infestation.

Numerous companies offer rot treatment works within the UK, many being members of the British Wood Preserving and Damp-proofing Association (BWPDA). However, beware of recommending so-called 'specialist surveys' as the specialists will have a vested interest in any repair recommendations that they may make.

Traditionally, treatment of dry rot included:

❖ stripping off of plaster to 1m beyond the last identified point of infection;

❖ removal of visible indications of the fungi;

❖ cutting back of affected timbers to 500mm beyond the last recognised point of infection;

❖ surface spraying of an approved fungicide; and

❖ irrigation of the surrounding walling.

Any new timber introduced to the area should be pre-treated in accordance with BS 5268-5:1989, remaining timbers being cleaned and then treated, to BS 5707:1997, with a solvent preservative, and possibly with application of a preservative paste.

In recent years irrigation has come to be considered of limited benefit, not least because of the amounts of liquid required and the potential for resultant damage. It is currently considered more important to reduce the moisture ingress in the area concerned and promote rapid drying in order to deprive the fungus of one of its essential life sources. Any remaining fungus within the masonry should then remain dormant, if it does not die off completely. Such forms of treatment are to be commended, particularly where historic buildings are concerned.

Wet rots are potentially less destructive and easier to treat than dry rots, though again stopping the source of the moisture should be a significant concern.

With regard to remedial works, developments in resin systems in recent years have allowed less intrusive repairs and a reduction in the need for significant timber replacement. This is particularly beneficial when dealing with historic buildings or significant structural timbers.

However the works are undertaken, the assurance of an insurance-backed guarantee should be sought, rather than reliance on the treatment company's own certificate.

On a cautionary note, remember that the treatment systems utilise powerful chemicals. Safety procedures must be followed and current safety legislation must be adhered to, in particular the *Control of Pesticides Regulations* 1986 (COPR), as amended in 1997, and the *Control of Substances Hazardous to Health Regulations* 2002 (COSHH), as amended.

Consideration must be given to any wildlife that may come into contact with the works. Under the *Wildlife and Countryside Act* 1981, the *Wildlife and Countryside (Service of Notices) Act* 1985, and the *[European Community] Conservation (Natural Habitats, etc.) Regulations* 1994 (as amended in 2007), treatment may require approval by one of the conservation agencies forming the Joint Nature Conservation Committee (JNCC), or indeed other appointed agencies.

Moulds are an increasing problem within the carefully controlled atmospheres of modern buildings. The advent of double glazing systems, and other modern building techniques, has often restricted air flow within properties and resulted in ideal environments for these microscopic plant forms to grow.

Mould has been a significant concern in the USA for some time, with black mould, *Strachybotrys Chartarum*, being blamed for various symptoms, including aggravation of asthma and rashes. Site operatives may display flu-like symptoms, as a result of Organic Dust Toxic Syndrome, when working in areas where widespread fungal contamination exists.

More seriously there is some evidence to suggest that black mould may also lead to bleeding in the lungs of infants exposed over long periods, and in turn to pulmonary hemosiderosis – a lung disorder in which bleeding (haemorrhaging) into the lungs leads to an abnormal accumulation of iron.

As well as reduction in moisture levels, improved ventilation is important in the fight against mould growth. Various proprietary chemical mould treatments are available and will help in the short term, though without solving the root cause the problem will reoccur. As with rot treatment, appropriate precautions and legislation will need to be considered.

Fungi identification table

Type	Usually found	Effect on timber	Mycelium	Fruiting body	Conditions for growth
Wood rotting fungi *Dry rot*					
Serpula Lacrymens	Inside buildings, mines, boats – never attacks timber outside	Large cuboidal cracking (brown rot)	Cotton-wool-like if damp; greyish white with purple/yellow and lilac patches if dry	Reddish brown centre, white margins; flat plate or bracket shape; possibly red spore dust nearby	Timber MC 20–40% (slightly damp) Temperature 0–26°C
Wet rots					
Coniophora Puteana (cellar fungus)	Most common of wet rots in buildings; associated with serious leaks – failed plumbing, etc.; also decays exterior	Cuboidal cracking – small cubes (brown rot); may leave thin veneer of sound timber; affected wood becomes dark brown	Brown branching strands on wood and masonry or brickwork; usually not in daylight areas	Rarely found inside; flat plate-like; greenish brown centre, yellow margin; knobbly surface	Timber MC 45–60% (very damp) Temperature –30°C to +40°C
Fibrioporia Vaillanti (mine or pore fungus)	Associated with water leaks; most common species of poria group	Cubodial cracking – large cubes (brown rot); affected wood darkens	Strands flexible when dry; white	Plate-shaped; white pores; rare	Timber MC 45–60% (very damp) Temperature up to 35°C
Phillinus Contiguous	Decay of external joinery (softwood)	Timber becomes soft (a white rot) Wood becomes fibrous	Light brown masses	Plate-like with pores; dull brown	Timber MC 22%+ Temperature 0–31°C
Phillinus Megaloporous	Attacks oak heartwood; presence often associated with death-watch beetle		Yellow	Large, plate-like, hard; various browns in colour	Timber MC 20–35% Temperature 20–35°C

Type	Usually found	Effect on timber	Mycelium	Fruiting body	Conditions for growth
Coriolus Versicolor (Polystictus)	Most common white rot decay of external hardwood	No splitting or decay but much weight loss	Rarely seen	Up to 25mm across; hairy ringed zones to pores to underside	
Lentinus Lepideus (Stag's Horn fungus)	Rare, but sometimes in flat roofs	Cuboidal cracking Darkens woods; wood feels sticky	Soft whitish needle-shaped crystals on surface	Some resemble stags horns, others are inverted mushrooms on stalk; brown	Timber MC 26–44% Temperature 25–37°C
Non-wood rotting fungi					
Peziza (Elf-Cup)	Occurs on saturated masonry or plaster, internally and externally; associated with leaks			Buff coloured and fleshy; distinctive	
Moulds					
Aspergillus Penicillium Pullularia	Almost any damp surface in humid conditions	Superficial – easily removed	Like coconut matting	Toadstool; white head; spores released in black ink type liquid Microscopic but spores show up as various colours: black, green, white, brown, yellow, pink	Very humid conditions
Strachybotrys Chartarum (Toxic mould)	On high cellulose content materials	Superficial to timber – various possible health risks	Green or black spots/mats		Elevated humidity

Insect infestation

Within the UK, wood-boring beetles are the major group of timber attacking insects. Wood-boring beetles are often erroneously referred to as 'woodworm', possibly because it is the larval stage of the insect's life cycle that eats into the wood before emerging as adults to start the breeding process over again.

The female beetles lay eggs within cracks or end grain of timber, and from there the eggs hatch and feed on the nutriments contained within the wood, leaving frass (digested waste) in the tunnels they form. The maturation can take up to 11 years (depending on the species of insect) before the adult beetle emerges from the timber. The common furniture beetle (Anobium Punctatum) has a life cycle of three years, and is (as its name suggests) the most commonly encountered of the beetles in the UK. The *Beetle identification table* on the following pages details the commonly found wood-boring beetles within the UK.

It is often the adult beetle's flight holes that are the first indication of infestation, by which time the damage has been done. The extent of damage will however depend on the type of beetle and the number of life cycles that have occurred before the damage has been observed.

Treatment with low odour insecticidal fluids can take the form of spray or brush application or gel or injection treatments. Fumigation may also be considered in certain buildings, though it is less effective as it does not directly target the infestation.

As with rot and mould, treatments utilise strong chemicals and the correct safety procedures and legislation must be adhered to (see the previous pages on fungi and moulds).

Termite problems in Europe are increasing and have been reported in the UK, though as yet not in significant quantities. Broadly speaking, treatment and eradication methods are similar to those for wood-boring beetles, although there are some significant differences. Unlike our common wood-boring beetles, termites are social insects living in colonies. The time span for damage caused by an infestation can therefore be significantly less than that of the more widely encountered wood-borers.

Contributed by Trevor Rushton, trevor.rushton@watts.co.uk

Beetle identification table

Species	Identification	Flight hole	Adult (not actual size)	Grub (not actual size)
Common furniture beetle	Very common, estimated that up to 80% of houses over 40 years old in rural areas are affected. Infestation often in damp areas of house, for example, beneath WC. Beetles are around 3mm long. Adult beetles emerge May to September.	1.5-2.0mm diameter		
Death-watch beetle	Infestation uncommon, often found in ancient buildings and therefore more expensive to eradicate. Confined to south and central parts of England and Wales. Attacks elm, chestnut and oak. Presence may indicate fungal attack. Adult beetles up to 8mm long emerge in spring.	Up to 4mm wide		
Waney edge borer	Found in timber where bark not completely removed. Larvae confined to bark areas and hence damage caused is superficial.	2mm		
House longhorn beetle	Only found in Surrey, Berkshire and Hampshire. Beetles are up to 25mm long. Regulations now require new timber to be treated prior to use. This is a very large borer.	Oval flight holes up to 9mm x 6mm		

Species	Identification	Flight hole	Adult (not actual size)	Grub (not actual size)
Forest longhorn beetle	Will attack softwoods and hardwoods in freshly felled lumber or standing trees; will not attack seasoned wood. Life cycle varies according to species. Treatment is usually unnecessary.	Oval, up to 10mm across. May be plugged with coarse fibres.		
Wood-boring weevils	Several species – only attack partially decayed timber, cause considerable damage. Beetles are 3.5mm long.	1mm		
Powder post beetle	Beetle 5mm long, few flight holes, convert timber to powder veneer of 'sound' timber.	1–2mm		
Termites	Varying in size from 4–15mm long and in color from white to tan and black, termite infestations are usually obvious by the presence of characteristic dry pellets in wood or on horizontal surfaces beneath infested wood. Darkening or blistering of wood in structures is another indication of an infestation.	n/a		n/a

Condensation

What is condensation?

In its gaseous form, water exists in air as water vapour. The warmer the air the greater the percentage of moisture vapour it can contain. Air itself is a mixture of gases of which water vapour is one; air does not carry water as such.

Condensation arises when moisture vapour comes into contact with cold surfaces and then cools to the point at which some of the vapour turns to liquid water on the cold surface.

The amount of water vapour in the air depends upon its temperature and pressure. The maximum amount of water that can be held at a given temperature occurs when air is said to be saturated. A measure of the amount of water vapour is 'Relative Humidity' which is expressed as a percentage of actual vapour against saturated air at the same temperature.

For a given amount of water in a given amount of air, there is a temperature at which the air will become saturated. The temperature at this point is called the 'dew point'. It follows therefore that for condensation to form on a surface, that surface must be at or below the dew point temperature.

Freely available psychrometric charts enable one to determine the relationship between the moisture content of air, the temperature, the partial vapour pressure and the dew point to seek to determine whether condensation is occuring.

An average household will generate about 12 litres of moisture per day through bathing, washing clothing and cooking. If paraffin or bottled gas heaters are used this will rise to over 20 litres a day, and will increase further if clothes are dried indoors.

Additionally, each person exhales approximately 1 litre of moisture per 24 hours.

In kitchens and bathrooms on inherently cooler tiled and ceramic/enamel surfaces, condensed-out moisture can be wiped away and does not usually offer a place where atmospheric moulds and fungal spores can propagate.

On slightly warmer surfaces, such as papered walls and ceilings, and woodwork, the mould and fungal spores have a far greater chance of propagating and growing to form both toxic and non-toxic growths that can both discolour decorations and, through mycotoxins, affect the health of inhabitants.

In modern, highly insulated and airtight homes, condensation risk must be mitigated by good design and by maintaining an efficient mechanical extraction and heat recovery system. Given the probability that these systems will not be maintained properly during their life and that users may be ignorant of the correct operating methods, there exists a significant risk that indoor air quality (of which condensation is a major factor) will deteriorate, leading to various health-related problems and damage to the building fabric.

Mechanisms for reducing condensation include:

❖ Have adequate natural permanent ventilation and temporarily ventilate rooms (to the outside) after cooking or bathing, or whenever you see condensation forming on cold surfaces such as glass to windows and doors.

❖ Avoid drying washing indoors or do so only on rooms with open windows and closed internal doors.

❖ Avoid using flueless gas and oil, especially paraffin heaters.

❖ Maintain natural 'wind tower' air movement paths in habitable buildings.

❖ Rooms that are mechanically ventilated (such as bathrooms and toilets) should be fitted with 'humidistat-controlled' extract fans.

❖ In bedrooms ensure that (at the very least) there are trickle ventilators to remove exhaled water vapour from sleeping persons.

❖ Maintain adequate working and operable windows to all habitable rooms.

❖ Improve the overall level of insulation to the property and install appropriate double or triple glazed openable window systems.

❖ Provide adequate background central heating, especially to bedrooms but without doubt to all habitable rooms, to bring the overall building up to a general fabric temperature that will mitigate against condensation formation. There should be low levels of background heating throughout the day and night in cold weather even when no one is at home. It is important not to rely on sudden bursts of high heating levels for short periods. Ideally a thermostatically-controlled system should be in place to maintain the habitable rooms at a minimum air temperature of 10°C with the ability to rapidly increase individual rooms or the whole system to between 17–21°C when the room or property is occupied.

See the following section on *Toxic moulds* for some of the negative consequences of condensation.

Contributed by Trevor Rushton, trevor.rushton@watts.co.uk

Toxic moulds

Surveyors may encounter black and green (or indeed other coloured) moulds, found on the walls, ceilings, floors, furnishings and fittings of buildings. It is therefore useful to have an appreciation of mould characteristics and problems.

There are many thousands of different moulds and they all occur naturally in our environment.

Fungal mould spores in the air will develop when they alight on parts of the building that provide the right substrate and conditions for growth.

Dry rot is the product of one family of mould spores.

Condensation mould describes not a 'mould' but a set of environmental conditions in which various moulds can propagate. Key requirements for propagation are:

❖ oxygen (although some moulds are obligate aerobes, which means they can grow in low concentrations of oxygen);

❖ moisture; and

❖ surfaces on which the moisture can condense.

'Toxic mould' is a serious concern for the health of a building's occupiers. The term is used in relation to either *Strachybotrys chartarum* or *Aspergillus fumigatus* in buildings, both of which can affect the health of people living or working in individual properties. Particular concerns originated in the United States.

Key toxic moulds in the UK are:

❖ *Strachybotrys chartarum* – a black or greenish-black mould that grows on material with a high cellulose content, including building materials, such as the paper facings of plasterboard, or chip and particle boards, when these materials become water damaged. This mould requires very wet or high humidity conditions for days or weeks in order to grow.

❖ *Aspergillus* – this comprises a family of some 185 subspecies, of which some 20 or so are presently considered dangerous; including fumigatus, flavus and niger. It is usually black, green or grey, although other light colours are known. Excessive indoor humidity from water vapour condensing on walls, plumbing failures, splashes from bathing or taking showers or water ingress from outside may lead to the growth of many mould varieties, including *Aspergillus*, *Blastomyces*, *Coccidioides*, *Cryptococcus* and *Histoplasma*, as well as *Strachybotrys*.

If you do observe black or green or grey moulds that you believe might be toxic, then there are UK laboratories that can identify whether they are present by means of testing from swabs taken from the moulds. Searching the web with keywords such as 'toxic mould analysis' will lead to appropriate organisations.

The best option for buildings and their occupants is to ensure that conditions do not exist whereby moulds of any variants can propagate. This is best achieved by keeping the buildings warm, dry and free from external water ingress into the fabric of the building. The following extract explains.

> 'Mould growth requires sustained high relative humidity but is unlikely to start unless surface water is present. Persistent surface condensation is the commonest, though not the only, cause of such conditions ... This occurrence of surface condensation depends on the relationship between, on the one hand, heating, ventilation, insulation, etc. and, on the other, the pattern of occupants' activities. The predominant cause can therefore either be in the design provisions or in the occupants' usage. There is no point in treating the symptoms unless the predominant causes have been identified and cured, since mould growth will otherwise recur.'

> (from *Walls and ceilings: remedying recurrent mould growth*, BRE Defect Action Sheet (DAS) 16, 1983)

BRE material is reproduced with permission from Building Research Establishment Ltd. BRE publications are available from www.brebookshop.com

See also the preceding section, *Condensation*.

Further information

* BRE publications DG85 and DG297 (both 1985), DG370 (1992) and IP12/95 (1995) are all worthy of consultation.

* *Toxic Moulds and Indoor Air Quality* by Jagjit Singh of Environmental Building Solutions Ltd, describes the relationship between toxic mould and indoor air quality, and may be found at www.aspergillus.org.uk/secure/articles/pdfs/singh.pdf (Indoor Built Environment Review Paper, 2005, 14;3–4:229–234, accepted 21 February 2005).

* *Research into mould and the implications for chartered surveyors*, RICS, November 2004, has most useful and thought-provoking lines of enquiry and research data into such moulds.

* *WHO guidelines for indoor air quality: dampness and mould*, published by the World Health Organisation Regional Office for Europe in July 2009 (ISBN 978 92 890 4168 3) is a most useful document and contains what are effectively their considered guidelines for the protection of public health from health risks due to dampness, associated microbial growth and contamination of indoor spaces. Available at: www.euro.who.int/document/E92645.pdf

* The City of New York has an excellent website which gives useful guidance and advice, see www.nyc.gov/html/doh/html/epi/moldrpt1.shtml. Please ensure that you refer to the enlarged 2007 edition of the document.

* the Australian websites www.abis.com.au/toxic-mould and www.mould.com.au

* RICS Factsheet 02 *Condensation* and the RICS Foundation *The risk of mould damage over the whole life of a building* available at: www.rics.org/site/download_feed.aspx?fileID=2915&fileExtensionPDF

Contributed by Allen Gilham, allen.gilham@watts.co.uk

Troublesome plant growth – Japanese Knotweed

Japanese Knotweed was introduced into the UK in the 19th century. It grows vigorously and can cover large areas to the exclusion of most other plant species. It has been known to grow through bitumen macadam, house floors and sometimes through foundations.

Japanese Knotweed is a highly invasive plant and is not easy to control due to its extensive underground rhizome system, which enables the plant to survive when all above ground parts of the plant are removed. It grows to a height of about 3m and is formed from stiff purple speckled stems or canes resembling bamboo. The canes grow densely in the summer and die back in the autumn with white flowers appearing late in the season. The cost incurred in control of the plant at the London Olympic Village is estimated to be £70m.

Spring shoots   Autumn leaf   Summer foliage

In the UK it is a criminal offence under section 14 of the *Wildlife and Countryside Act* 1981 to cause the growth in the wild of, among other things, Japanese Knotweed (other plants include Giant Hogweed, Japanese Seaweed and Giant Kelp). (In April 2010 **a further 36 plants were added to Schedule 9 of the Act**.) In Scotland, a new *Wildlife and Natural Environment Bill* was passed in the third reading at the beginning of March 2011. When it comes into force it will be **illegal to plant any non-native plant in the wild in Scotland**.

Anyone found guilty of an offence can face up to two years in prison and/or an unlimited fine. Any waste material arising from attempts to control this plant should be disposed of in accordance with the *Environmental Protection (Duty of Care) Regulations* 1991 as controlled waste. Landowners can also face civil actions for allowing the weed to spread to neighbouring land if it can be shown that the owner knew or ought to have known of the weed and the problems that it can cause.

Soil from a site contaminated with knotweed must be disposed of at a suitably licensed landfill site at a depth of at least 5m. On-site treatment is an alternative, but this is not an easy option. Detailed guidance has been published by the Environment Agency (see www.environment-agency.gov.uk).

Two natural but non-native predators have been identified to tackle the problem of knotweed growth. The proposals will raise concerns over the risk of unforeseen damage to the environment and will no doubt be controversial. The first predator is *Mycosphaerella* or leaf-spot fungus, the second being a small sap-sucking psyllid insect known as *Aphalara itadori* or jumping plant lice. Both species are native in Japan but are thought by the Centre for Agricultural Bioscience (Cabi) to be unlikely to harm the UK's ecosystem.

On 9 March 2010, the government announced approval to release *Aphalara itadori* for use as a biological control against Japanese Knotweed. Tests focussed on closely-related native species as well as important crops and ornamental species to ensure it does not attack other plants. If the first phase (controlled release at a few specific sites) is successful, the psyllid will be released at further sites where it will continue to be monitored.

Key issues

❖ Typical habitats include brownfield sites (which may be contaminated as a result of tipping of contaminated soil or knotweed cuttings), railway land, riverbanks, verges, etc.

❖ In winter, the leaves of the plant die off to leave tall, antler-like hollow stems with regular nodes in dense strands.

❖ In summer, the plants have green elongated heart shaped leaves with clusters of small white flowers. Young plants are often red stemmed with flower shoots spreading from the tip (not dissimilar to the appearance of bamboo, but more red than green).

❖ The rhizomes are yellow/orange when cut and snap rather like a carrot.

❖ The plant can be killed with the correct herbicides, but this is not a one-off treatment and can take up to three years.

❖ Controlled burning may destroy the plant at ground level, but the rhizomes can extend to 3m and may not be killed.

❖ Burial and covering with geotextile matting at a depth of at least 5m is possible, but very great care must be taken to avoid the spread of small fragments by mechanical diggers.

❖ Similarly, removal of contaminated soil carries the risk of spreading the plant; disposal must be under controlled conditions and transport off site could cost between £30 and £80 per tonne.

Contributed by Trevor Rushton, trevor.rushton@watts.co.uk

Troublesome plant growth – Giant Hogweed

In contrast to the equally vilified Japanese Knotweed, Giant Hogweed not only creates serious environmental problems but can also cause very unpleasant skin conditions in humans.

Like knotweed, it is not a native species, having been originally introduced as an ornamental plant in the 1890s. Needless to say, the plant 'escaped captivity' to become common within the UK. Once established, it can dominate other plants rapidly and damage the natural habitats of insects and other animals. It is often found growing along railway land, footpaths, roads, rivers and wasteland. Seeds can be transported along waterways to infect areas further downstream.

During the winter, the plant dies down, leaving bare patches which can result in soil erosion. Carrot fly can inhabit Giant Hogweed infestations making it a very undesirable plant to have around.

Identification

As its name suggests, Giant Hogweed is characterised by its size, often growing to 3–5m over four years or so. The plant has a purple to red stem and furry, spotted leaf stalks. Leaf and flower growth is also large, 1.5m width is not unknown for leaves, while the flower heads (which resemble Cow Parsley) can be around 250mm wide.

Flower heads   Leaf arrangement

Aside from the environmental problems associated with Giant Hogweed, it is also a risk to health. Brushing against the leaves or breaking the stem releases sap. The sap contains a substance that reduces the ability of the skin to resist ultraviolet light. Burns can result: these often develop into large watery blisters after 20 hours or so of contact and exposure to sunlight. The condition can lead to a more serious and difficult to treat form of dermatitis called Phytophotodermatitis, a reoccurring skin condition that can persist for many years.

Under the *Wildlife and Countryside Act* 1981 and the *Wildlife (Northern Ireland) Order* 1985, it is an offence to 'plant or otherwise cause Giant Hogweed to grow' in the wild. Thus, a landowner could commit an offence by moving contaminated soil from one location to another rather than treating it as controlled waste.

The control of Giant Hogweed is difficult. Unlike knotweed, plant propagation is by seed, with a single flower head producing upwards of 1,500 seeds and a large plant producing up to 50,000 seeds. Treating the active plant growth with the herbicide Glyphosate is effective, but unless retreatment is undertaken regularly, and over a period of several years, it is unlikely to be effective as the seeds can remain dormant for up to seven years. If spraying is to be undertaken it is vital that this is done early in the growing season, before the flower heads have time to develop and produce new seeds.

The alternative treatment is to dig up the plants and dispose of them as controlled waste. This treatment will often be coupled with spraying, although because of the health effects outlined above, great care is needed to minimise the risk of exposure to sap. If this does occur, the affected area must be well washed and protected immediately after contact.

When removing specimens, some of the seeds will fall to the ground, usually within a 4m radius of the plant. Care is needed not to distribute these seeds, particularly where tracked or wheeled equipment is likely to be used.

Further information

❖   Natural Environment Research Council: www.ceh.ac.uk

❖   NetRegs: www.netregs.gov.uk

❖   Royal Horticultural Society: www.rhs.org.uk

Contributed by Trevor Rushton, trevor.rushton@watts.co.uk

Rising damp

Research by the Building Research Establishment (BRE) and others suggests that rising dampness is often misdiagnosed by surveyors and so-called damp specialists, with the result that costly and unnecessary remedial treatments are specified.

In many cases, diagnosis is undertaken by means of electrical resistance or capacitance meters, but these can give very misleading and unreliable results in materials other than timber. It is fair to say that if the meter reveals the wall to be dry, then it probably is dry; the problem comes when a meter records something as damp. Surveyors should not diagnose rising damp without first having undertaken a proper study. When rising dampness is suspected, do not automatically recommend a specialist inspection – more often than not the specialist will use exactly the same resistance equipment to make his or her diagnosis. A more reliable method has been prepared by the BRE and may be found in BRE Digest 245, 2007.

Symptoms

Typically symptoms may include:

- ❖ damp patches;
- ❖ peeling and blistering of wall finishes;
- ❖ a tide mark 1m or so above floor level;
- ❖ sulphate action;
- ❖ corrosion of metals, for example, edge beads;
- ❖ musty smells;
- ❖ condensation; and
- ❖ rotting of timber.

The above symptoms do not of themselves indicate the cause of dampness. Common causes could be lateral rain penetration, condensation or entrapped moisture, hygroscopic salts such as nitrates and chlorides may also reveal themselves as damp patches. High external ground levels, bridging of damp-proof courses, defective rainwater goods, etc. should all be self-evident and could give rise to similar symptoms.

Other possible sources of salt contamination include chemical spillage, splashing from road salt, etc.

Equilibrium moisture content

Many building materials absorb moisture, and when exposed to damp air will attain equilibrium moisture content. This hygroscopic moisture content (HMC) will vary according to relative humidity. Typical relationship curves can be plotted for different materials and, although these can only establish general indications, it is possible to compare readings from different materials in the construction of a wall. For example, at 75% relative humidity (RH) the moisture content (MC) of yellow pine would be 13%, while the MC of lime mortar would be 2% and 0.5% in brick.

Some materials possess an HMC of as much as 5% without the introduction of salts from external sources. This figure should be regarded as an appropriate threshold as to whether or not remedial action is likely to be required.

Measurement of moisture content

Resistance or capacitance meters can give misleading results.

The presence of soluble salts on the surface of a wall will cause an electrical resistance meter to indicate a high reading, even if the wall were otherwise dry. Deep wall probes may give a more accurate picture, but will still be affected by soluble salts, as these are generally highly conductive.

A Speedy Moisture Meter (or carbide meter) will give a much more accurate reading of MC in all materials. (Resistance meters are usually calibrated for use in timber and can give an approximation of MC in that material.)

The Speedy meter comprises an aluminium flask fitted with a pressure gauge and a removable lid. Using a 9mm drill on slow speed, a sample of dust is taken from the brick, mortar or plaster. The sample is weighed and placed into the flask. A small quantity of carbide is then added and the flask sealed. Moisture in the sample reacts with the carbide to form acetylene gas. The pressure of that gas is then read off the pressure gauge, which is calibrated to read %MC. With care, the meter can give a very accurate reading, comparable with laboratory kiln dried tests. For brick and masonry, readings above 2% should be investigated, although the threshold can vary according to the nature of the material being tested.

Rising damp

In many cases, examination of facts will reveal that the source of damp is something other than simply 'rising damp' from the ground, i.e. a defective dpc. A leaking service pipe, for example, may produce similar symptoms. Rising dampness within a wall is in a sensitive equilibrium. There must be a supply of water at the base of a wall and the height to which that water will rise depends upon the pore structure, the brick, plaster or other finish. Water will also evaporate from the surface of the wall at a rate dependent upon temperature and humidity.

During wet weather, evaporation may decrease and groundwater tables may rise, giving rise to an increase in the severity of the dampness. The reverse may happen during dry spells, and evaporation will be increased by central heating.

Soluble salts are present in many building materials. The salts can be dissolved and moved to the surface of the element as evaporation takes place. Hygroscopic salts (typically, nitrates and chlorides from groundwater) can be present in some materials. These salts absorb moisture from the atmosphere, and can in certain circumstance cause extensive staining and disruption of finishes.

Salts will increase the surface tension of the water and so draw it further up a wall. Furthermore, as evaporation occurs, stronger salt solutions are drawn towards the surface and may eventually crystallise out. This process reduces the amount of evaporation and so may raise the height of the dampness. The soluble salts are often hygroscopic and absorb moisture from the atmosphere. If this occurs, the situation will appear worse during wet weather and better during dry.

As noted above, the presence of hygroscopic salts does not necessarily indicate rising dampness.

Diagnosis of rising damp

BRE Digest 245 sets out a method of diagnosis. The method involves drilling samples from the wall to measure both their moisture content (MC) and hygroscopicity (HMC). Samples are taken from mortar joints from 10mm to a depth of 80mm every two or three courses from floor level up to a level beyond that which damp is suspected. While the carbide meter can be used to measure MC it will be necessary to send samples to a laboratory to measure HMC – this is to see if the samples could have absorbed the quantity of moisture found from the atmosphere.

By subtracting HMC from total MC, it is possible to determine the value of 'excess' moisture, which could result from capillary action or water from other sources. The comparison of HMC and MC gives an indication as to which is controlling the dampness at any position. If MC is greater than HMC, then moisture is coming from some other source. If the reverse applies, then moisture is coming from the air. Plotting the results graphically can then assist in gaining an accurate picture of what is happening.

Surface damage arising from hygroscopic salts can be significant. The HMC of contaminated wallpaper or plaster can be as much as 20%. It follows, therefore, that contaminated plaster will need to be removed. BS 6576: 2005 deals with this subject in more detail.

Treatment of rising damp

Assuming that the source of the dampness is confirmed as rising as opposed to penetrating dampness, the most likely solution will be the insertion of a new damp-proof course (dpc), either by physical insertion or by chemical injection.

Physical insertion will provide a reliable barrier and will be appropriate in conditions where total certainty is required and possibly where it is necessary to extend an inner damp-proof membrane up to the dpc level and to make a physical connection with it. Care is needed during the insertion process, both from a health and safety point of view (the method uses a carbide tipped chainsaw) but also to ensure that the formed slot is properly wedged and packed upon completion to prevent settlement cracking.

Chemical insertion is used widely; there are a variety of aqueous and solvent-based systems, as well as injection mortars and thixotropic systems. Such treatments may be introduced using pressure or gravity. The BRE do not favour the use of alternative treatment systems such as siphons or electro-osmosis as these can be unreliable.

In certain circumstances, improvements can be made by simply reducing ground levels and or by controlling external water systems. The provision of perimeter land drainage may be more appropriate for older or listed buildings, where physical works may not be desirable or even practicable.

Replastering is often necessary as the existing plaster finishes may be contaminated with salt or in a deteriorated condition. In ideal circumstances, use plaster that is highly vapour permeable while at the same time able to act as a barrier to hygroscopic salts and moisture. Gypsum-based undercoats are unsuitable, while renovation plasters are effective at dealing with salt but not moisture. Sand and cement renders are effective barriers but may not be appropriate in all conditions – especially when dealing with buildings of historic importance.

Further information

❖ BS 6576:2005, *Code of practice for diagnosis of rising damp in walls of buildings and installation of chemical damp-proof courses.*

❖ Property Care Association, *Code of practice for the installation of remedial damp proof courses in masonry walls*, 2008.

❖ BRE Digest 245, *Rising damp in walls – diagnosis and treatment* (published 2007)

Contributed by Trevor Rushton, trevor.rushton@watts.co.uk

Subsidence

Many houses built on what are known as shrinkable clays have quite shallow foundations, usually less than 1m deep. Shrinkable clays are generally strong and able to support a building of four storeys on a single strip or trench-fill foundation. These soils shrink when their moisture content decreases and then swell when it increases. Slight movement of houses on foundations is therefore inevitable as a result of seasonal changes in moisture content resulting in downward movement or subsidence occurring during the summer and upward movement or heave during the winter.

Greater movements may occur during long periods of dry weather and may lead to sticking of doors and windows. Severe movements are almost always associated with localised subsidence caused by trees whose roots extract moisture from the soil. Conversely, removing a tree tends to cause heave as moisture gradually returns to the soil. Large broad-leaved trees of high water demand are notorious for causing damage.

Before World War II, it was common practice to use shallow foundations no more than 0.45m deep. Houses built within the past 25 years should comply with guidelines issued by the National House Building Council (NHBC) and the British Standards Institution (BSI). The former requires foundation depths often well in excess of 1m, while the latter requires a minimum depth of 0.9m for any buildings founded on clay and deeper foundations where there are trees nearby.

Because of the link between clay shrinkage and the weather, insurance claims for subsidence damage increase in long dry periods. Analysis of insurance claims indicates that of those cases involving foundation movements caused by the shrinkage or expansion of clay soils, 75–80% are exacerbated by moisture abstraction by trees.

Subsidence may also be a consequence of mining activity. The extent of subsidence due to mineral extraction depends on the method used for winning the minerals from the ground, whether by mining, pumping or dredging. The main problems in the UK arise from coal mine workings.

In many coal fields in the UK, the presence of old workings remain as a constantly recurring problem in foundation design where new structures are to be built over them. If the depth of cover of soil and rock overburden is large, the additional load of the building structure is relatively insignificant and the risk of subsidence due to the new loading is negligible. If, however, the overburden is thin, and especially if it consists of weak crumbly material, there is a risk that the additional load imposed by the new structure will lead to local subsidence.

The risk of subsidence associated with coal workings may be obtained via a Coal Mining Report obtained from the Coal Authority.

It is important to differentiate between subsidence and settlement. In terms of foundation movement:

❖ subsidence is downward foundation movement caused by change in the site below the foundations, usually associated with volumetric changes of the subsoil; and

❖ settlement is downward foundation movement caused by an application of load.

Contributed by Graeme Lees, graeme.lees@watts.co.uk

Tree identification

The influence of trees on buildings

Broadly, there are two possible mechanisms by which trees can influence low-rise buildings:

❖ **direct action**: the physical disturbance of the structure by root growth; and

❖ **indirect action**: usually associated with the changes of moisture content in shrinkable clay subsoils.

Damage due to direct action is fairly rare in buildings, although disturbance of boundary walls, brick planters, etc. is more frequent. The damage is usually related to the growth of the main trunk and roots, and will diminish fairly rapidly with distance. The radial and longitudinal pressures exerted by roots are fairly weak and so roots will tend to grow around an obstruction rather than displace it.

Damage due to indirect action depends on a number of different factors such as the species of tree, the type of soil, proximity to the building, depth of foundations, availability of water supplies, climate, etc. The problem of clay heave or damage due to desiccation of clay soils can occur throughout the UK, although areas to the south east of a line joining Hull to Exeter appear to be worse affected as clay soils are very common there.

BRE Digest 298:1999 identifies four types of movement associated with clay soils and vegetation growth:

❖ normal seasonal movements such as would occur with a grassy area;

❖ enhanced seasonal movements resulting from increased moisture transpiration following the planting of trees;

❖ long-term subsidence occurring as a result of water deficit as trees develop; and

❖ long-term heave following the removal of trees and the dissipation of the water deficit.

Certain species of trees – notably oaks, poplar, elm and willow – have been known to cause damage to buildings. A very rough rule of thumb would be to limit the proximity of a tree to its maximum potential height at maturity (the 1H rule); in many cases this will result in an over-estimation of the 'safe distance' from a building. Using a safe distance for planning purposes is one thing, but deciding whether a tree has influenced a building (particularly if the tree and the building are in different ownership) requires better data. A detailed account of the various studies that have been conducted may be found within *Tree Roots in the Built Environment*, Research for Amenity Trees No. 8, published by DCLG, 2006.

Tree identification

The accurate identification of species is usually made by reference to the characteristics of features such as the petals and stamens of flowers, as these tend to be more constant than the shape of a tree, although some basic information on the shape of the leaves can give a good indication. There are several useful online guides to assist identification, for example:

❖ www.woodlands.co.uk/owning-a-wood/tree-identification/

❖ http://apps.kew.org/trees/?page_id=17

Since the shape and size of a tree can be influenced by numerous factors, its shape is not necessarily a reliable guide to identification. More useful information (particularly in winter) can be provided by an examination of the bark, the twigs and features such as buds.

If the identification cannot be made on site, record the approximate height of the specimen, and the characteristics of its bark, fruit and leaves. Look out not only for the shape of the leaf, but its texture, its margin (see below) and its arrangement on the stalk (petiole). Are the leaves arranged in groups on a single petiole, in pairs or singly?

Some definitions to assist identification:

❖ **Lamina**: the flat surface of the leaf.

❖ **Adaxial surface**: the top surface of the leaf.

❖ **Abaxial surface**: the under surface of the leaf.

❖ **Petiole**: the stalk which joins the leaf to the twig.

❖ **Margin**: the edge of the leaf; usually entire (smooth), ribbed or lobed.

❖ **Palmate compound leaf**: several leaflets connected to a common petiole rather like the palm of a hand.

❖ **Pinnate compound leaf**: several leaflets, often in pairs, connected to a common petiole.

❖ **Lenticels**: the small areas on a stem where gas exchange takes place; often small slits or round dots.

❖ **Axil**: the angle between the petioles of adjoining leaves.

As noted earlier in this section, the water demand of various species is difficult to predict with certainty, particularly due to conflicting data. The following list is in the general order of water demand but various studies show differing results and so the ranking should be treated as a rough guide only. All dimensions are approximate.

Oak
Max. height 23m. Radius of potential damage 13m. Strong root activity. Deeply fissured bark. Lobed, simple leaves, 5–7 lobes per side. Buds clustered near end of twig. Drooping catkins on male trees; acorns on female.

Poplar
Max. height 24m. Radius of potential damage 15m. Strong root activity. Simple palmate leaf with downy abaxial surface.

Elm
Max. height 25m. Radius of potential damage 12m. Strong root activity. Variable size simple leaf, some with shiny leaf and hairs on abaxial surface.

Ash
Max. height 23m. Radius of potential damage 10m. Medium root activity, fast growing – up to 500mm per year. Compound, pinnate leaf. Pale grey bark with ridges.

False acacia
Max. height 20m. Radius of potential damage 8.5m. Medium root activity. 13 leaflets. Dull brown bark, often deeply furrowed. Two spines at each bud.

Horse chestnut
Max. height 25m. Radius of potential damage 10m. Medium root activity. Compound palmate leaf. Bears fruit in late summer/autumn.

Hawthorn
Max. height 10m. Radius of potential damage 7m. Simple leaves with deep lobes. Thorns on twigs. White blossom in spring.

Lime
Max. height 24m. Radius of potential damage 8m. Medium root activity. Simple, broad leaves with prominent veins on abaxial side with tufts of white hair. Sticky residue produced by aphid attack.

Willow
Max. height 15m. Radius of potential damage 9m. Strong root activity.

Beech
Max. height 20m. Radius of potential damage 9m. Weak root activity. Simple leaves, pointed oval shape with 5–9 pairs of veins arranged alternately along twig. Long pointed buds. Smooth grey bark.

Plane
Max. height 30m. Radius of potential damage 6m. Medium root activity.

Sycamore
Max. height 24m. Radius of potential damage 9m. Simple, large leaves arranged in opposite pairs. Winged seeds when fertilised – a helicopter-like structure.

Birch
Max. height 14m. Radius of potential damage 7m. Root activity weak. Toothed, simple leaf, roughly triangular with rounded corners. Silvery bark on older trees with 'arrows and diamonds'.

Rowan, service tree
Max. height 12m. Radius of potential damage 7m. Root activity medium. Nine leaflets arranged on stem in opposite pairs; leaves have pointed lobes.

Contributed by Trevor Rushton, trevor.rushton@watts.co.uk

Cladding

Materials and defects

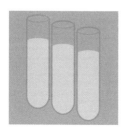

345

Mechanisms of water entry

There are several mechanisms by which rainwater can penetrate a building:

- ❖ kinetic energy;
- ❖ surface tension;
- ❖ gravity;
- ❖ capillarity;
- ❖ pressure differentials; and
- ❖ any combination of these.

Kinetic energy

This is the direct action of the wind carrying a droplet of rainwater with sufficient momentum to force it through a sealed joint. Prevention or drainage overcomes this. Prevention can be by baffles, by a durable seal or by a labyrinthine shape within the joint. Drainage collects the penetrating water and diverts it back to the outside.

Surface tension

This can cause water to adhere to and move across surfaces. It is guarded against by drip edges or throatings along leading edges, and horizontal surfaces should slope down and out. Connecting components can also have appropriate grooves or ridges.

Gravity

This can take water through open joints that lead inwards and downwards. Reversing the slope overcomes this.

Capillarity

This occurs in fine joints between wettable surfaces. It is only severe when other mechanisms persist, for example, wind-assisted capillarity. In metal components it is resolved by capillary breaks within the joint surfaces.

Pressure differential

This is a very important mechanism. Since air at high pressure will migrate to areas of low pressure, it follows that high pressure, moisture-laden air can transport moisture into an area of lower pressure. It is overcome by maximising the outer deterrent and minimising the pressure differentials. This is achieved by self-contained (compartmentalised) air spaces behind the outer skin, which are well ventilated to the outside thus enabling rapid equalisation of pressures.

Contributed by Trevor Rushton, trevor.rushton@watts.co.uk

Composite panels

After a series of major insurance losses in the late 1990s and the early part of the new millennium, insurers sought to limit their risks by insisting that composite panels, and particularly those with thermoplastic cores, be replaced with materials of known fire performance. Generally, materials containing polyurethane (PUR) cores were considered unsatisfactory, while polyisocyanurate cores (PIR) that complied with Loss Prevention and Factory Mutual standards were favoured. As an alternative to replacement, insurers charged inflated premiums or increased the level of deductibles. Even though materials complied with Building Regulations, the insurance conditions could be prohibitively expensive.

Sandwich panels are of a composite construction, comprising two outer layers of steel or aluminium sheet with an inner core of an adhesive bonded lightweight core material. The resulting product is lightweight yet strong and able to span greater distances than would be possible with the individual component parts in isolation. Flexural strength is attained by maintaining the bond between the layers. One side will be in tension, the other in compression. Remove the bond to one face and integrity is destroyed and the panel will fail.

Typical insulating cores and their properties are given below.

Insulating core	Properties
Foamglass (fairly rare)	Non-combustible
Thermosetting rigid foam – polyisocyanurate (PIR) and polyurethane (PUR)	Undergo localised charring, although flaming can take place if flammable vapours are released. The charred material will shrink and can lead to delamination of panels. While PIR is also a thermosetting foam, it performs better in fire than straight PUR. Many pre-2000 panels were of PUR while today PIR is the material of choice.
Thermoplastic polystyrene (EPS)	Polystyrene materials may burn fiercely, give off thick black smoke and allow burning droplets to fall.
Machine made mineral fibre (MMMF)	Generally non-combustible, but some of the adhesives used to bond the panels can be combustible.
Phenolic foam	Generally non-combustible, but some types may hold water and have a corrosive effect upon the metal outer skins.

Panel instability can affect composite panels that are not properly supported or restrained. In the case of roof and wall cladding, there are usually additional supports in the form of purlins and sheeting rails and primary fasteners, which serve to tie the two leaves together and prevent them from becoming detached. However, in internal situations (such as food processing plants, cold storage facilities, etc.) the quantity of insulation required will often lead to panels of 200mm thickness or more. Such panels require less support and so present a greater risk of delamination. It is these panels which cause the greatest levels of concern – particularly as the core materials are often no more than EPS.

There will be a conflict between the requirements of the Building Regulations and the requirements of insurers. Building Regulations are aimed essentially at ensuring the health of users and neighbours of the building (and of course visitors or the emergency services). Insurers may want higher standards of protection, fire suppression and/or more reliance upon non-combustible materials.

The relevant standards for composite panels were originally set by the Loss Prevention Council but are now administered by BRE Global under LPS 1181. Generally, materials with a PUR or EPS core will almost certainly not satisfy the requirements of LPS 1181, whereas PIR or MMMF products can be engineered to comply.

The Association of British Insurers has produced a report on the issue and it is hoped that insurers will now take a more relaxed view if buildings have been constructed using materials certified under LPS 1181 Part 1 (for external systems) or Part 2 (for internal applications). However, many buildings have been constructed (and still are constructed) using materials that do not satisfy these standards and, in these circumstances, it is important to consider the overall level of risk rather than the mere existence of the panels.

Whether or not sandwich panels constitute a risk is a matter of judgment and scientific fire risk assessment. A reasoned approach may involve the consideration of the following:

- ❖ Is there a sprinkler installation in the building?
- ❖ Are there any specific fire risks – use, storage of inflammable materials, arson, etc?
- ❖ Are the panels in the vicinity of battery charging areas?
- ❖ Are the panels perforated such that the cores are exposed?
- ❖ How are the panels fixed – are they properly restrained?
- ❖ What is the nature of the insulant?
- ❖ What is the extent of the material and to what extent could it contribute to fire load?

Many manufacturers keep records of consignments and can often, given the nature of the contractor, identify the nature of the material supplied to a specific site. More modern trends have included a small identifier that can be marked on the panels and revealed by exposure to a small UV light source.

Contributed by Trevor Rushton, trevor.rushton@watts.co.uk

Curtain walling systems

Curtain walling is a weatherproof and self-supporting enclosure of windows and spandrel panels in a light metal framework which is suspended right across the face of a building, being held back to the structure at widely spaced joints.

Types of curtain walling system

Stick systems

Stick construction is the traditional form of curtain walling, comprising a grid of mullions and transoms into which various types of glass and/or insulated panels can be fitted. Most of the grid assembly work is done on site. The advantages include relatively low cost and the ability to provide some dimensional adjustment. The disadvantage is that performance is workmanship sensitive. It is not unusual to find systems failing initial waterproofing tests during erection.

Unitised systems

Unitised systems comprise narrow-width storey-height units of aluminium framework containing glazed and/or opaque panels. The entire system is pre-assembled under factory-controlled conditions. Mechanical handling is required to position, align and fix units on site onto pre-positioned brackets attached to the floor slab or the structural frame. Modern installation techniques increase the speed of erection and often minimise the requirement for scaffolding. Unitised systems have higher direct costs and are less common than stick systems. Nowadays the curtain walling to most prestige buildings is of this type.

Panellised systems

Panellised curtain walling comprises large prefabricated panels of bay width and storey height which are connected back to the primary structural columns or to the floor slabs. Panels may be of precast concrete or comprise a structural steel framework which can be used to support a variety of stone, metal and masonry cladding materials. The advantages of these systems are improved workmanship as a consequence of factory prefabrication, allowing improved control of quality and rapid installation with the minimum number of site sealed joints. Panellised systems are less common and more expensive than unitised construction, however, they often appear similar to unitised systems.

Variations

Structural sealant glazing: this is a form of glazing that can be applied to stick or unitised curtain walling systems. With structural sealant glazing, the double-glazed units are attached to the grid framework preferably with factory-applied structural silicone sealant rather than by pressure plates and gaskets in a more traditional system. The attraction of this form of glazing is that it provides relatively smooth facades which are visually attractive. Some systems involved bonding the glass to a metal carrier system that is itself fixed mechanically to the supporting framework. It is usual for structural sealant glazing to be bonded on two sides and mechanically fixed on the top and bottom edges – 'two-sided' although some systems involves 'four-sided' fixing.

Structural glazing: this typically comprises large, thick, single panes of toughened glass assembled with special bolts and brackets that are supported by a secondary steel structure. This form of glazing is often referred to as 'planar' glazing and is commonly used to form the enclosure to atriums and entrances.

Weather tightness

There are various methods of preventing rainwater ingress.

Face sealed systems

Early curtain walling systems tended to be face sealed, relying on a weatherproof outer seal to prevent water penetration. The seal must remain completely free of defects to prevent leakage paths occurring. Where there is no provision for drainage, any water that bypasses the outer seal could result in internal water ingress. With drained systems, any water within the glazing rebate can then drain away within the framing system. There are also a small number of proprietary systems incorporating front zipper gaskets containing a large rubber gasket with a central press-in segment or zip which, when pressed into place, forces the gasket out onto the surface of the glass. This system does not normally have provision for water drainage.

Fully bedded systems

These systems are now largely obsolete and were used on early forms of curtain walling. Fully bedded glazing is a face sealed system relying on the glazing rebate being completely filled with glazing compound to prevent the passage of water. They are therefore 'undrained'. Any voids within the bedding are a potential weak link for water ingress and early failure of the double-glazed units.

Drained and ventilated systems

Most cladding designers now accept that it is difficult to exclude water and therefore provision for a small amount of leakage can be made within a drained system. Typically these dry glazed systems comprise an outer decorative cover plate, and an aluminium pressure plate with two narrow rubber oyster gaskets either side clamped against the glass or insulated infill panel. The pressure plates are screw fixed through a thermal break into the mullion or transom member. A further inner gasket between the glass and the mullion or transom provides a further seal.

In drained and ventilated systems, the front gaskets provide an initial barrier. The rebates and cavities are drained and ventilated to the exterior to prevent the accumulation of any water that bypasses the outer seals. Drainage is usually via small holes or slots in the underside of transoms that drain water down through the mullions.

Some systems also incorporate a foil-faced butyl adhesive tape applied over the transom and mullion nosings directly beneath the pressure plate to serve as a secondary line of defence.

While these systems will accommodate a small quantity of water within the glazing rebates, it is important that the pressure plate is fixed to the correct torque so that the gasket seals form a good seal against the glass.

While structurally bonded systems appear to rely on silicone seals between the glass, they will often contain drainage and ventilation systems in the same way as conventional curtain walls.

Pressure equalised systems

Pressure equalised systems are an improved variation of drained and ventilated systems. Here the ventilation openings in the pressure plates are of an increased size to permit rapid equalisation of pressure in the glazing rebates with the external pressure thereby preventing water penetration of the outer face. Consider the following diagram.

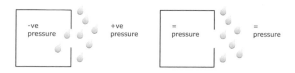

The rectangular box may be considered as the area around the glazing in a cladding system. If the pressure inside the box is less than the pressure outside, the water will be drawn in. If we can equalise the pressure in the box then the probability is that water will stay on the outside. In curtain walling systems we must provide a perfect seal around the inside of the window and must also provide the number of slots around the perimeter of the glass to enable pressure within the glazing rebate to equal that of the external air pressures almost instantaneously. Fundamentally therefore, with pressure equalised systems the outer face is sealed as tight as possible against rainwater while the inner face is sealed as tight as possible against air inflow. Nearly all modern curtain walling systems are designed utilising the principles of pressure equalisation.

It is very difficult to identify the differences between a drained and ventilated system and a pressure equalised system. However, for pressure equalisation to work properly, the various zones of pressure must not be too large. Thus it is common to consider the area around one glass pane as one zone and therefore drainage must be made from the transom members and not from the mullions. In practice it is very difficult to provide full pressure equalisation and there is some doubt in the industry as to whether it is fully effective.

Double-glazed units (insulating glass units) (DGUs and IGUs)

Double-glazed units comprise two or more panes of glass spaced apart and hermetically factory-sealed with dry air or other gases in the unit cavity.

The perimeter edge sealant prevents moisture from entering the unit cavity and holds the unit together. Two forms of edge seal configuration are single seal systems and dual seal systems. Single seal systems rely on the edge sealant to act both as the vapour barrier and as an adhesive bond to hold the panes of glass together. Dual seal glazing units rely on two seals, an inner seal to control water vapour transmission and an outer secondary seal to hold the glass tightly against the spacer bar. The combined properties of primary and secondary sealant provide high quality glass units. Nearly all units are now of this type.

The appropriate British Standard for dual seal systems was BS 5713: 1979 and although this remains current it is now obsolescent.

Types of glass

✦ **Annealed glass**: this is untreated glass manufactured from soda lime silicates. It is the least expensive and most readily available type of glass. Annealed glass breaks into sharp edged shards and is therefore considered to be unsafe in all fire and breakage situations.

❖ **Low-e coatings**: these reduce the emission of long-wave thermal radiation from the glazing and increase the reflection of this radiation. In the winter, solar radiation can be trapped within a room and reduce the need for heating. In the summer however heating can also occur and so Low-e glass needs to be used in conjunction with adequate provision for ventilation. Most Low-e glass can be toughened and laminated. The coatings can either be 'soft' or 'hard' (pyrolytic) coatings – the latter generally being more robust.

❖ **Thermally toughened glass**: this is formed by heating and then rapidly cooling or quenching annealed glass. Differential cooling and hardening across the thickness of the glass generates a compressive stress in the surface layer of the glass. Toughened glass is always a safety glass and compared with annealed glass is four to five times stronger in compression and bending. In failure, toughened glass shatters into small, relatively safe fragments. See page 353 for information on the spontaneous fracture of toughened glass due to nickel sulphide inclusions.

Toughened glass can suffer from a problem known as roller wave – this produces optical distortions that can be particularly noticeable in mirrored glass claddings.

❖ **Heat strengthened glass**: this is formed by heating annealed glass and then cooling it under controlled conditions. Heat strengthened glass offers some of the strength of toughened glass but a reduced risk of failure due to nickel sulphide inclusions because of the reduced tensile stress in the glass. This glass is often also referred to as 'partially toughened'. Heat strengthened glass is also less likely to display roller wave distortions.

❖ **Laminated glass**: this is formed by bonding together two or more panes of glass using a plastic (PIB) interlayer. Any of the above forms of glass may be used in any combination. Upon failure, laminated annealed glass breaks into shards which are held together by the interlayer. Laminated glass may include one or more panes of toughened glass. If all panes are of toughened glass then the broken glazing will lose all structural integrity and may pull free from the pane unless properly secured. Laminated glass is recommended for the inner pane of overhead glazing and is considered to be safety glazing.

Surface finishes

The metal components of a curtain walling system will nearly always require finishes to provide protection against corrosion or for appearance.

To preserve the decorative and protective properties of any metal finishing, it is essential that atmospheric deposits are removed at frequent intervals, particularly those surfaces which are not exposed to the washing effects of the rain. If the finish becomes chalky, specialist cleaning systems can be used, but these are very expensive.

Beware of spray applied repairs to site damage during installation; these areas will weather at a different rate and become visually apparent within a few years.

Quality of workmanship is particularly important and it is therefore essential to choose a reputable applicator preferably covered by a quality insurance scheme. Independent acceptance inspection testing can be undertaken to ensure compliance with the specification.

Organic coatings (carbon based coatings)

Organic coatings are normally applied to either steel or aluminium and include polyester powder, PVDF, PVC, Plastisol, and polyester. The most common organic finish for windows and curtain walling is polyester powder coating, however, a range of wet applied finishes is widely used for opaque cladding panels. Polyester powder coatings may be applied to either galvanised steel or aluminium and are available in a wide range of colours. They are tough and abrasion resistant. Manufacturers often provide a guarantee for 15–20 years.

Anodising

Anodising is an electrolytic process that produces a dense, hard and durable oxide layer on the surface of aluminium. The oxide layer is porous and must be sealed to prevent staining but can be coloured by introducing dyes or chemical treatment before sealing. Anodised finishes are generally harder and more abrasion-resistant than organic coatings, with an expected life of 50 years or more. However, anodised surfaces are susceptible to alkaline corrosion from contact with fresh concrete or mortar and rainwater run-off from concrete surfaces.

Testing

Many standard and bespoke curtain walling systems are tested in laboratory conditions to determine the resistance to wind load, airtightness and water tightness. These tests are undertaken on a very small number of test panels assembled in factory conditions. By necessity they are a test of the design rather than on-site workmanship.

It is therefore critical that all installed curtain walling systems are subject to on-site testing to establish that the fabrication and installation has been undertaken to a satisfactory standard.

Water tightness on site is typically assessed using the methods outlined in the following documents:

- ❖ Pressure spray in accordance with AAMA standard 501-94, *Methods of test for exterior walls*, Architectural Aluminium Manufacturers Association, USA;

- ❖ CWCT, *Test methods for curtain walling*, 1996;

- ❖ BS EN 13051, *Curtain walling. Watertightness – Field test without air pressure using a water spray bar*;

- ❖ BS 5368-2: 1980, *Methods of testing windows. Watertightness test under static pressure*; and

- ❖ ASTM E1105-96, *Standard Test Method for Field Determination of Water Penetration of Installed Exterior Windows, Curtain Walls and Doors by Uniform and Cyclic Static Air Pressure Difference*.

The CWCT and AAMA test regime is essentially similar.

Ideally, the first areas to be tested should be among the first areas of each type of curtain wall to be constructed on site. Typically, the test areas are at least one structural bay wide and one storey in height, providing that all horizontal and structural joints or other conditions where leakage could occur are included.

Under the CWCT and AAMA methods, water is applied via a brass nozzle on the end of a hose that produces a solid cone of water droplets with a spread of 88°. The nozzle is provided with a control valve and a pressure gauge between the valve and nozzle. The water flow to the nozzle is adjusted to produce 22 +/– 2 litres per minute, producing a water pressure at the nozzle of 220 +/– 200 Kpa (Kpa = 1000 pascals). Water is directed at the joint perpendicular to the face of the wall and moved slowly back and forth over the joint at a distance of 0.3m from it for a period of five minutes for each 1.5m of joint. There should be an observer of the inside of the wall, using a torch if necessary, to check for any leakage.

Contributed by Trevor Rushton, trevor.rushton@watts.co.uk

Spontaneous glass fracturing due to nickel sulphide inclusions

Nickel sulphide is one of several chemical contaminants that can occur during the manufacture of glass. There is some debate as to its origin, but it is thought that it is due to the mix of nickel and sulphate impurities within the glass batch materials, the fuels or even the furnace equipment, and this creates polycrystalline spheres which vary from microscopic to 2mm in diameter.

All glass has some of these inclusions present; they are impossible to eliminate entirely and therefore they are not considered a product defect.

In untreated (annealed) glass they are not a problem. But when glass is heat treated (toughened or tempered), the inclusions are modified into a metastable state. The particles initially decrease in volume, but over a period of time (sometimes years) gradually revert to their original volume; this expansive force acts on the glass around the particle.

In a majority of cases this has little effect but, dependent on size and proximity to the centre of the pane where the forces are greatest, this can eventually cause the glass to break. Failures can occur with inclusion sizes in the 100–200 micron range, but sizes above this are far more likely to cause failures.

There is a theory that for an initial period of approximately one year after manufacture there are relatively few breakages. After this, the number increases for up to several years, thereafter decreasing in frequency. There have been reported incidences where fractures have occurred more than 20 years after the installation of glass.

Prior to pr EN 14179, a breakage rate of 1 per 5 tonnes of glass was thought an average level. However, this corresponds to only 200m² of 10mm glass and so a glazed roof of say 6,000m² could be expected to have 30 breakages.

Panes in external situations are at greater risk. However, there have been a small number of cases where spontaneous breakage has occurred in internal glazing, remote from external influences, for example, panels to a staircase balustrade or an internal partition.

Because of the risk of falling debris some toughened glass should be avoided in sloped overhead applications where it is used either as a single pane or as the inner leaf of a sealed unit. If laminated toughened glass is used, the polyisobutylene (PIB) interlayer and the intact sheet may be more likely to hold the glazing in place.

In 'heat strengthened' glass, nickel sulphide inclusion is not generally regarded as a source of fracture. The difference between this and toughened glass is the rate of cooling. In the former this is less rapid, reducing surface compressive strength and making it much less susceptible to the transformation of nickel sulphide inclusions. Offering 5.5 times the strength of annealed glass, in many circumstances it is a useful replacement for tempered glass. However, it is not a suitable substitute where safety glass is required.

'Heat soaking' is a quality controlled process which gives increased reassurance against the presence of critical nickel sulphide inclusions by subjecting the glass panels to accelerated elevated temperatures to stimulate the transformation of the crystals and thus initiate immediate failure. It is thought that this process identifies 90% or more of the glass which might have subsequently failed after installation. The heat soaking process could be used either as a sampling method or as an additional treatment, which in the case of clear toughened glass could add up to 20% to the cost.

Heat soaking does not change any of the physical properties of toughened glass and therefore there is no means of distinguishing whether or not this process has been carried out. Current best practice dictates that specifiers should ensure that they specify 'heat soaked toughened glass to pr EN 14179'. This standard reduces the anticipated failure rate to 1 per 400 tonnes of glass used. Prior to EN 14179, heat soaking standards were less rigorous, leading to unreliable results.

Materials and defects

It is generally accepted that nickel sulphide contamination is a problem that can affect batches of glass – some batches may perform perfectly well, while others suffer a high proportion of breakages. Examination of the edge spacers of double-glazed units may reveal information as to the age of the glass panel (usually month and year of manufacture) although it may not contain information as to the actual production run of the glass.

Identification

When toughened glass is broken, the tensile stress is spread out from the source causing the pane to crack into small fragments (dicing). These fragments tend to be slightly wedge-shaped, emanating from the source of the fracture and are often held into position wedged against the frame due to their increased volume.

If the fracture is as a result of expansion of the nickel sulphide inclusion, those fragments immediately adjacent are more hexagonal and at the epicentre of the breakage the two larger particles form a distinctive butterfly shape linked by a central straight line crack. If large enough, the inclusion may be seen in the form of a black spec, or its presence may be confirmed by optical microscopy.

When carrying out an investigation, all possible causes of failure should be considered, including poor glazing tolerances and insufficient allowance for subsequent movement of the frame and any supporting structures. Possible causes may include deflection or rusting of steel frame, shrinkage of concrete frame, thermal movement, normal air pressures and even sonic booms. If the fracture is a result of impact or of local point loading, there should be evidence of local crushing.

The chances of installing a toughened glass pane which may later fail due to the expansion of nickel sulphide inclusions are very small. Where it is essential, for reasons of accessibility or safety, that the pane should not fail, alternative forms of glass should be considered. One particular example would be in overhead situations – say in a shopping mall.

Testing

Visual testing of undamaged glass is not practicable; photographic examination has been shown to be possible but is not commercially viable.

Samples of fractured glass should be sent intact with the epicentre protected with clear film to a suitable testing laboratory. Microscopic analysis will be sufficient for an initial diagnosis, but a scanning electron microscope will yield more information.

Further information

❖ BS EN 14179-2: 2005 *Glass in building. Heat-soaked thermally-toughened soda lime silicate safety glass. Evaluation of conformity/product standard.*

Contributed by Trevor Rushton, trevor.rushton@watts.co.uk

Flooding

Materials and defects

355

Flooding and its impact on property

Floods are one of the most common and widespread of all natural disasters, and are growing in frequency and severity.

In England, around '2.1 million domestic and commercial properties in flood risk areas are at risk, corresponding to some 4-5 million people. Approximately £250 billion assets are at risk'. (*Flood And Coastal Erosion Risk Management*, Defra, Flood Management Division, November 2007).

© *Crown copyright material is reproduced under the Open Government Licence v1.0 for public sector information:* www.nationalarchives.gov.uk/doc/open-government-licence/

The government's *Foresight Future Flooding* report, (Flood and Coastal Defence Project, Foresight programme, DTi, 2004) predicted that 'climate change will be an important factor in increasing flood risk', and that 'both the number of people in danger from flooding and the costs of damage from floods will rise significantly'.

Who is responsible?

The Department for Environment, Food and Rural Affairs (Defra) has overall responsibility for policy and funding of the flood risk management service in England. Delivery of service is through a range of partners, principally the Environment Agency, but also to a lesser extent local authorities and internal drainage boards. The Environment Agency uses Defra funding to undertake a range of measures both to reduce the likelihood of flooding (e.g. through physical defences) and also to reduce the consequences of flooding (e.g. through flood forecasting and warning systems, public awareness campaigns and preparing for flooding emergencies).

Defra and the Environment Agency also seek to influence others to improve resilience to flooding of the national power, transport, etc. infrastructure. Taken together, these approaches help reduce flood risk overall (flood risk being defined as a combination of likelihood and consequences). For further information, see *The National Flood Emergency Framework for England* available at www.defra.gov.uk/publications/2011/06/08/pb13430-national-flood/

Managing the risk

Defra's policy is to reduce risks to people, property and the environment from flooding and coastal erosion through the provision of defences, flood forecasting and warning systems, increased flood resilience of property, beneficial land management changes and discouragement of inappropriate development in areas at risk of flooding. For more information, see *Appraisal of flood and coastal erosion risk management* available at www.defra.gov.uk/publications/2011/03/30/pb13278-erosion-management/

The devastating floods of summer 2007 caused 55,000 properties to be flooded and nearly 7,000 people to be rescued from flood waters.

The government commissioned a report by Sir Michael Pitt into these floods – *The Pitt Review: Learning lessons from the 2007 floods*, Defra. Published in June 2008, it recommended that a 25-year plan be drawn up on flooding and a new dedicated Cabinet Committee be created. It also recommended that:

❖ Building Regulations should be overhauled to protect new houses in flood risk areas from 2010;

❖ local authorities should create a definitive map of all drainage ditches and streams in their area, making it clear who is responsible for maintaining them;

❖ a nerve centre should be set up jointly by the Meteorological Office and the Environment Agency to pool information and issue more accurate flood warnings;

❖ a greater onus should be placed on utility companies to protect key infrastructure sites;

❖ central and local government should spend a minimum of £650 million in 2008–2009 on flood and coastal erosion risk management (Defra); and

❖ construction in flood risk areas should be kept to an absolute minimum, but a blanket ban was not realistic, given the large demand for housing.

In response to *The Pitt Review*, the increased risk of flooding, and new legal obligations such as those arising from the EU Floods Directive, a more integrated approach to the management of flood risk, water resources and water was proposed in the *Flood and Water Management Bill*.

The *Flood and Water Management Act* 2010 (covering England and Wales) received Royal Assent on 8 April 2010. The first commencement order came into force on 1 October 2010. This implemented definitions and statutory instrument making powers, and required the Environment Agency and Lead Local Flood Authorities to develop risk management strategies. The *Flood Risk Management Functions* Order 2010 and the *Water Use (Temporary Bans) Order* 2010 under s76A(2) of the *Water Industry Act* 1991 also came into force on this date. This additional legislation supports the *Flood and Water Management Act* although it is not specifically related to flooding.

The main points of the *Flood and Water Management Act* 2010 are:

❖ The Environment Agency is required to create a National Flood and Coastal Erosion Risk Management Strategy.

❖ Leading local flood authorities must create local flood risk management strategies.

❖ It allows the Environment Agency and local authorities to carry out flood risk management works.

❖ It introduces an improved risk-based approach to reservoir management.

❖ It allows the reduction of bad debt in the water industry through amendments to the *Water Industry Act* 1991.

❖ It widens the list of non-essential water uses that water companies can control during periods of water shortage.

❖ It allows water companies to offer concessions to community groups for surface water drainage charges.

❖ Sustainable drainage systems should be incorporated into certain new developments.

❖ A mandatory building standard for sewers is to be introduced.

The *Flood Risk Management (Scotland) Act* 2009 was enacted on 16 June 2009. It will be introduced in stages and current legislation will remain in place until section 70, which revokes the *Flood Prevention (Scotland) Act* 1961, has been instigated. This Act represents sustainable flood management taking into account climate change and the needs of the 21st century at a national and local level.

The *Flood Risk Management (Scotland) Act* establishes:

❖ a framework for coordination and cooperation between all organisations involved in flood risk management;

❖ assessment of flood risk and preparation of flood risk management plans;

❖ new responsibilities for SEPA, Scottish Water and local authorities for flood risk management;

❖ a revised, streamlined process;

> ❖ new methods to enable stakeholders and the public to contribute to managing flood risk; and
>
> ❖ a new single enforcement agency for the safe operation of Scotland's reservoirs.

The Defra publication *Making space for water*, published in 2004, aims to manage the risk from flooding. It sets out a portfolio of measures tailored to conditions in each location. These measures include the way in which land is used, what flood defences are built and the way in which flood warnings are given.

A five-year strategy for flood risk management is now in place, with the aim of reducing the risk of flooding to around 80,000 homes.

This is being achieved by:

> ❖ ensuring more residents in flood risk areas know they are at risk and are aware of the action they need to take to protect themselves;
>
> ❖ improving the coverage of flood warning services to reduce the number of properties exposed to a high risk of flooding; and
>
> ❖ planning flood defences based on how a whole area is affected, rather than individual locations.

Contributed by Watts' environmental team, contact Mark Wootton, mark.wootton@watts.co.uk

Forecasting floods and flood plans

Forecasting floods

We are still a long way from being able to forecast accurately, and a long way in advance, the risk of flooding events.

Short periods of intense rainfall can cause flash 'pluvial' flooding. Longer periods of widespread heavy rain can cause rivers to overflow, producing 'fluvial' flooding, with storm surges causing coastal flooding.

Fluvial flooding is easier to predict in advance, as it is possible to predict from rising water levels where water will breach its banks.

Pluvial flooding, in contrast, is more difficult. The location and extent of flooding depends on the heaviness and the duration of rainfall, as well as the suitability of drainage sytems. The localised heavy rainfall that often causes flooding is hard to provide accurate forecasts for. The Meteorological Office can predict showery airstreams days in advance, but to predict exactly where showers will fall is much harder.

The Meteorological Office is currently working with a number of agencies, including Ordance Survey and the British Geological Survey, to agree standards to improve flood modelling and forecasting. It is now trialling the National Severe Weather Warning Service (NSWWS) with local authorities and emergency services, so they receive more precise information about where heavy rainfall will fall further in advance.

Flood plans

The Environment Agency has recently developed 'Catchment Flood Management Plans' (CFMPs) and 'Shoreline Management Plans' (SMPs) that identify the main factors influencing flood flows and flood risk, and will assess how these may change over time.

CMPFs do not aim to provide detailed flood risk management solutions for individual flooding issues. Instead, they are intended as a guide to recommend the best ways of managing that risk during the next 50–100 years. They look at land use across a larger area, or 'catchment', to see if the water can be moved to where it will do least harm to people and the environment, taking into account climate change, land use and management, and sustainability. More information is available at www.environment-agency.gov.uk/research/planning

Contributed by Watts' environmental team, contact Mark Wootton, mark.wootton@watts.co.uk

Rising groundwater

During the latter part of the 20th century, the level of groundwater beneath major UK cities rose rapidly, leading to increasing concern that huge costs could be incurred from damage to buildings and infrastructure if preventative measures were not taken. The problem stemmed from the city-centre industries that populated the areas during the industrial revolution and their demand for water. Beneath London this led to a reduction in the level of up to 90m. The usage has declined significantly since the late 1960s as the industries relocated and, without this extraction, levels recovered, rising by 1.5m a year initially and by as much as 3m a year recently. By the late 1990s, water levels in central London recovered by 35m, close to the 1900 level.

It was therefore realised that action to minimise the damage was needed urgently to allow time for planning and implementation. A group was formed from interested parties and in March 1999 it announced that a five-stage plan had been developed to safeguard London from the effects of rising groundwater. The plan involved controlled increased abstraction from 50 or more existing and new boreholes, with the amount that could be used for drinking water maximised and the remainder to be used for industrial or agricultural processes.

In 2000 it was realised that early assessments had been too onerous and so water abstraction rates were reduced.

This revised, lower estimate of additional abstraction resulted in changes to the phasing of strategy and the distribution of the new abstraction boreholes.

From ongoing monitoring it is clear that groundwater levels are now broadly stable in the centre of the basin. In south west London groundwater levels are currently declining at rates of around 5m per year but still rising in north west London at rates of around 1m per year.

As there has been a more rapid decline in groundwater levels in central and south west London than expected, further licensing of abstractions has been restricted under the London Catchment Abstraction Management Strategy (CAMS). The London CAMS is one of a series of strategies for the management of water resources at a local level. They give information on water resources and licensing practice and allow the balance between the needs of abstractors, other water users and the aquatic environment to be considered in consultation with the local community and interested parties.

See also the UK Groundwater Forum: www.groundwateruk.org

Contributed by Trevor Rushton, trevor.rushton@watts.co.uk

Planning to avoid flooding

With the government's policy of localism under active debate, there is concern that the initiative has caused delays and in some cases undermined efforts to protect the UK from a recurrence of the devastation cause by the 2007 flooding. Under the Localism Act, local communities can champion creative and sustainable schemes for surface water management based on intimate local knowledge and, where only part-funding is available, help to identify potential finance streams.

Planning Policy Statement 25 (PPG25) sets out the government's spatial planning policy on development and flood risk. The latest guide was issued on 29 March 2010 and replaced the December 2006 version. The guide has been revised to clarify the definition of a functional floodplain, and to amend how the policy is applied to essential infrastructure, including water treatment works, emergency services facilities, installations requiring hazardous substances consent and wind turbines in flood risk areas.

The *Flood and Water Management Act* 2010 gives county and unitary councils new powers to manage local flood risk. The Act was designed to protect water supplies to consumers and protect community group from excessive charges for surface water drainage.

The Act's provisions include:

    ❖   requirements for unitary and county councils to bring together relevant bodies to develop local strategies for managing local flood risk;

    ❖   the ability for the Environment Agency, local authorities and internal drainage boards to ensure that private assets which help manage the risks of floods cannot be altered without consent;

    ❖   the ability for the Environment Agency, local authorities and internal drainage boards to manage water levels to deliver leisure, habitat and other environmental benefits;

    ❖   a requirement for all new developments to be in line with new National Standards to help manage and reduce the flow of surface water into the sewerage system;

    ❖   new sewer standards – all new sewers are to be built to agreed standards in future so that they are adopted and maintained by the relevant sewerage company; and

    ❖   a new risk-based regime for reservoir safety.

The *Flood Risk Regulations* 2009 have now come into force placing duties on the Environment Agency and local authorities to prepare flood risk assessments, flood risk maps and flood risk management plans.

The Environment Agency and Defra have developed a strategy and supporting documents to reflect government policy. This strategy describes what needs to be done by all organisations involved in flood and coastal erosion risk management. These include local authorities, internal drainage boards, water and sewerage companies, highways authorities, and the Environment Agency. The strategy sets out a statutory framework that will help communities, the public sector and other organisations to work together to manage flood and coastal erosion risk (FCERM). It will support local decision-making and engagement in FCERM, including the development of local flood risk management strategies by lead local flood authorities, as well as a strategic overview of all sources of flooding and coastal erosion.

Flood risk assessments

It is vital that checks are carried out at an early stage of all new developments to determine whether or not they are located in areas that fall within the Environment Agency's flood plain map (available at www.environment-agency.gov.uk/homeandleisure).

The Environment Agency requires a Flood Risk Assessment (FRA) to be submitted alongside planning applications for developments over one hectare in size, and areas that are known to be at flood risk.

A flood risk assessment (FRA) should include:

    ❖   the location of the development or redevelopment, showing streets, water courses, etc. with property clearly marked;

    ❖   a site plan showing existing and future floor levels;

    ❖   a cross section of the site showing floor levels and river banks;

    ❖   details of proposed flood alleviation measures;

    ❖   sources of possible flooding;

    ❖   existing information on flooding;

❖ assessment of the probability of flooding and the expected impact of climate change;

❖ assessment of rate and duration of flooding;

❖ assessment of the likely rate and speed with which flooding might occur;

❖ assessment of the potential impact of any development on fluvial morphology (ground movement as a result of the action of water);

❖ assessment of the need for preventative measures, such as internal flood barriers, raising of threshold levels, flood attenuation using SUDS (sustainable urban drainage);

❖ assessment of the impact of the development on drainage, i.e. will there be increased run-off and if so, how this could be remedied; and

❖ assessment of escape routes and evacuation procedures.

Contributed by Trevor Rushton, trevor.rushton@watts.co.uk

Protecting property from floods

Although it is not possible to prevent floods, there are a number of ways in which property owners can help safeguard their property from water damage. In addition to using specialist flood protection products, property owners living in high risk areas should address the following:

❖ Check that all buildings insurance policies include cover for flood damage and inform insurers as soon as possible after an event so that a claim can be assessed immediately.

❖ Protect people, data and equipment – make sure that records and other business information are archived and stored off the premises.

❖ Consider investing in a generator to maintain emergency power supplies.

❖ Move valuable items away from lower floors where possible.

After a flood:

❖ Open doors and windows to ventilate the building.

❖ Don't heat the building to more than 4°C until all the water is removed and expose as much damp timber as possible to accelerate the drying out process.

❖ Don't forget about security. Burglar alarms may not be working if the electricity supply has been affected by the high water level: if necessary cover open or broken windows with security mesh.

❖ Never attempt to move back into a property that still contains standing water: it is a potential health hazard and should be pumped or baled out. Open up all the floor voids to check there is no water there.

Effects of flood water on building materials and remedial repairs

Flood water can penetrate buildings rapidly, causing widespread damage to floors, walls, and finishes, with structural damage in more severe cases. The vulnerability of individual properties is dependent on building materials and construction methods.

Brickwork

Brickwork will inevitably allow some moisture penetration, so it is unlikely to remain waterproof if exposed to flood water for long periods. Generally, brickwork should be largely unaffected by flood water if it is allowed to properly dry out. However, as walls are wetter after a flood, there is a greater risk than normal that they will deteriorate from frost damage and may spall, flake or crack. The chemical action of salts in some flood water can also affect brickwork, particularly in older buildings, compromising the damp-proof course. This can cause long-term damp problems.

Walls are best dried by evaporation from the outer surface. The drying out process may take some time if the brickwork has been saturated. As a guide, RICS recommends one month for every inch of wall thickness to dry out completely.

If the brickwork fails to dry, then samples of the brickwork should be tested for moisture content. This will indicate if there is a rising damp problem, and if additional measures are required.

Concrete

Depending on its quality, concrete can sometimes absorb large amounts of water and take a long time to dry out. This can cause ongoing problems such as chemical reactions and fungal growths, which can affect both the structure and contents until it is completely dry.

The construction of concrete floors may influence the length of drying time required. If the damp-proof membrane (dpm) is between the slab and the screed, generally there will be less damage than if it is located beneath the slab – because of relative drying times.

Where concrete floors are finished with timber-based flooring on battens, water retained under the flooring, or in any insulation, will not dry efficiently. In this situation, the insulation and battens must be removed and replaced.

If there is a high chloride content in the flood water, reinforced concrete could become contaminated allowing reinforcement bars to corrode.

Timber

Decay of timber is unlikely if the timber dries out within a few weeks, but the longer it remains wet, the greater the risk of swelling, distortion or decay. This can result in loss of strength and cohesion potential and, in extreme cases, structural failure.

In timber-framed buildings, members that are immersed in water for prolonged periods could cause damage in other parts of the structure, for example, through stresses on external cladding.

Timber exposed in a well-ventilated space can dry to an acceptable moisture content of <20% in three weeks, although the bottom members may take longer. Concealed areas should be inspected for lingering moisture. Timber held at a moisture content of 20% and more is at risk of fungal decay.

Reducing moisture content will kill off rot, but if growth is rapid, replace any timber that shows signs of rot, and treat adjacent timber to reduce the risk of further spread.

Metals

Metals exposed to flood water will dry quickly, and a one-off flood event may not have any significant effect. Prolonged exposure can result in rusting. Powder-coated metal finishes are robust, and are unlikely to suffer long-term damage.

Render (external)

Undamaged renders containing cement are unlikely to suffer long-term damage, although they may be hard to clean and will be at risk from frost damage for several weeks.

Any significant damage (including cracking, spalled areas or hollowness) to an existing render finish should be repaired. The damaged render should be removed by hacking off to the masonry background. A consistent appearance between the original and repaired areas can be achieved by using a masonry paint finish.

Plaster and plasterboard

Gypsum plaster can be damaged in floods of significant duration, although very short-term duration floods are unlikely to cause significant damage. However, instances such as surface wetting, which may dry out relatively quickly, could still develop water stains or mould requiring remedial treatment/action at a later stage of the project.

If the flood stands for longer periods, gypsum-containing materials and components will absorb large quantities of water and begin to distort.

It is normal practice for gypsum plaster to be removed from the wall face, after flood water has subsided, to a level just above the flood tidemark.

Gypsum board that is exposed or in contact with water for longer than two hours will require replacement. This is necessary not only to remove the waterlogged and damaged gypsum board, but to open up the walls and expose the cavities of the walls so that the insides of the walls and the wood studs within can dry out. Delamination of the board can occur and damaged gypsum board may exhibit powder and mildew, causing unpleasant odours and an unacceptable base for paint if it is not removed. Furthermore, the risk of toxic moulds cannot be discounted.

Finishes

Internal decorations (e.g. wallpaper, paint, wall tiles) and floor coverings (e.g. linoleum and vinyl sheeting) may become debonded by wetting, as they will hold water and delay drying. The drying process can be speeded up by removing such coverings.

Gloss paint is fairly robust, however, it may bubble off and suffer from peeling after prolonged exposure to water.

Wash down and remove loose and flaking finishes. Remember also that moisture may be trapped beneath certain impervious finishes.

The drying of low permeability wall coverings, such as vinyl wallpaper, gloss paint and tiling, will slow down the drying of masonry, and could cause timber studs to rot.

The drying process can be speeded up if such coverings are removed from at least one side of the external walls.

Mould, blistering and peeling may occur if surfaces are painted or papered too soon. Once the repairs have finished, painting or papering should be left for at least three months to ensure the surface does not blister, mould or peel. Oil-based or stain block paint should be used before final painting to help stop emulsion staining from occurring.

The use of high permeability lime-based paints rather than oil-based paints or emulsion can allow walls to dry out more quickly following flooding.

Further information

❖ *Flood Products – using flood protection products – a guide for home owners*, Environment Agency, 2003

❖ *Design Guidance on Flood Damage to Dwellings*, The Scottish Office, 1996

❖ *Improving the flood resistance of your home*, Series of 8 advice sheets, CIRIA, 2003, available at: www.ciria.org/flooding

❖ *Planning and Building Standards Advice on Flooding*, Planning Advice Note PAN 69, 2004, Scottish Government Publications

❖ *Preparing for floods: interim guidance for improving the flood resistance of domestic and small business properties* (2003 reprint with amendments), ODPM (now Department for Communities and Local Government (DCLG)), 2003: see www.communities.gov.uk/publications/planningandbuilding/ preparingfloods

❖ *Repairing flood damage*, BRE Good Repair Guide 11 (series of 4 booklets), BRE, 1997

❖ *Repairing flooded buildings – An industry guide to investigation and repair*, Flood repairs forum, BRE, 2006

❖ Garvin, S., Reid, J., Scott, M., *Standards for the repair of buildings following flooding*, C623, CIRIA, 2005

❖ www.theconstructioncentre.co.uk/flood-advice

Contributed by Watts' environmental team, contact Mark Wootton, mark.wootton@watts.co.uk

The surveyor's role in flooding

Construction professionals have an important role to play in advising clients about the impact of flooding. This applies both to those providing advice on proposed developments and to those inspecting and reporting on existing buildings that may have suffered flood damage.

RICS has a detailed information paper *Flooding: issues of concern to chartered surveyors* 2009 (available to RICS members at www.rics.org). This provides background information on the issues involved in flooding and flood defence, and provides useful guidance to help assess the consequences of changes in climate and rainfall patterns, along with government policies for property and land management.

CIRIA has produced a useful guide, *Standards for the repair of buildings following flooding*, published in 2005, which is aimed primarily at building professionals and insurers experienced in flood damage and repair.

Contributed by Watts' environmental team, contact Mark Wootton, mark.wootton@watts.co.uk

Compensation for flooding

It has been the policy of successive governments that individuals should not be compensated for any flood loss except in exceptional circumstances. The thinking behind this is that, as flooding is generally an insurable risk, government compensation for flood losses would disrupt the private insurance market.

However, limited emergency financial help in the form of non-repayable 'Community Care' Grants and interest free repayable 'Crisis Loans' can be claimed by people who have limited resources, for example, those receiving income support.

The Association of British Insurers' (ABI) has an agreement with the government on the provision of flood insurance, until 2013 when it will be reviewed. Provided that the government commits to reducing the risk of flood to an acceptable level, ABI members will continue to provide insurance where there is no more than 1 in 75 annual risk.

ABI tends to deal with flooding risks as follows:

❖ for existing customers in higher risk flood areas, premiums may be higher or the customer may be asked to pay a higher excess to reflect the increased frequency of flood claims;

❖ for new customers in high risk areas, all cases are considered on an individual basis; and

❖ in exceptional cases, where flooding has occurred frequently and where no flood defences are planned 'within a reasonable timescale', flood cover may be withdrawn completely.

In all cases, premiums are set by the insurer and will reflect differing degrees of risk.

Further information

❖ www.defra.gov.uk

❖ www.environment-agency.gov.uk

❖ www.abi.org.uk

❖ www.ciria.org

❖ www.communities.gov.uk

❖ www.floodforum.org.uk

Contributed by Watts' environmental team, contact Mark Wootton, mark.wootton@watts.co.uk

Environmental

Sustainability

Contaminated land

Environmental due diligence is now commonplace in property transactions. The presence of contaminated land can adversely affect site value and rental income and can hinder transactions if not properly managed. With an increasing move away from greenfield development, it is no longer possible for the majority of investors or tenants to avoid owning or occupying some land affected by contamination, whether as a city-centre property that has had a variety of past uses, or a new out-of-town development constructed on an old industrial site.

Statutory definition of contaminated land

Under Part IIA of the *Environmental Protection Act* 1990 'contaminated land' is defined as:

> 'land which appears to the Local Authority in whose area it is situated to be in such a condition, by reason of substances in, on or under the land, that:
> (a) significant harm is being caused or there is the significant possibility of such harm being caused; or
> (b) pollution of controlled waters is being, or is likely to be, caused'.

Many sites that are contaminated will not fall within the definition and will not be classified as 'contaminated land' under Part IIA. However, such contamination could still have implications for owners and occupiers (e.g. in terms of liability affecting the saleability and marketability of a site) and may still require a Phase II investigation.

Land is only defined as 'contaminated land' if there is a 'significant pollutant linkage' present. There must be evidence of a 'source – pathway – target' relationship. This means there should be a source present, a receptor that could be harmed by the source (e.g. humans), and a pathway linking the two.

Documentation

Documentation is the key to ensuring a smooth property transaction. Documentation should be in place to demonstrate that the site condition has been adequately assessed. This can be undertaken by commissioning an Environmental Audit and/or an intrusive ground/groundwater investigation. These assessments, which are discussed in further detail below, should ascertain:

❖   whether the site condition has been adequately assessed by an environmental assessment or review (commonly known as either an Environmental Audit or Phase I) and/or an intrusive site investigation (Phase II) and there are no significant information gaps;

❖   whether contamination is present (or is likely to be present), and the types of contaminants;

❖   where contamination has been identified, it does not represent a risk to the existing or proposed use of the site;

❖   that contamination is not migrating off site within groundwater;

❖   that contamination does not represent a significant risk to groundwater and surface water resources or other sensitive receptors (e.g. sites of special scientific interest);

❖   that contamination does not represent a risk of regulatory authority action (e.g. under Part IIA of the *Environmental Protection Act* 1990);

❖ that contamination does not represent a risk of third party action (e.g. from adjoining land owners); and

❖ whether any potential liabilities may exist from any forthcoming business transaction.

Environmental Audit

While an Environmental Audit desktop study does not include a site visit, an Environmental Audit (also known as a Phase I or an Environmental Assessment) is based on background research and should include a site inspection or walkover. A walkover would normally be advised to ensure all present day site issues are appropriately assessed. The research will normally include a review of:

❖ current site uses;

❖ historical site activities;

❖ environmental sensitivity;

❖ regulatory authority records; and

❖ a risk assessment and environmental risk rating.

Intrusive ground/groundwater investigation

An intrusive ground/groundwater investigation (also known as a Phase II) is based on a physical assessment of the underlying site conditions, and usually comprises chemical analysis and/or monitoring of soil, groundwater and ground gas.

If an Environmental Audit or existing knowledge identifies a potentially significant contamination issue, then it may be necessary to conduct a Phase II investigation to gain an understanding of whether contamination is actually present and whether it is likely to represent a significant risk or liability.

A Phase II investigation will normally include:

❖ a summary of the Environmental Audit findings;

❖ a description of the Phase II investigation methods;

❖ data and observations recorded during the site work, including field evidence of contamination;

❖ data from chemical analysis of ground/groundwater/ground gas samples;

❖ interpretation of the results and an assessment of risk; and

❖ recommendations for remediation (if required) of the underlying ground and/or groundwater.

The Phase II investigation should be designed to address the specific issues raised by the Environmental Audit, such as the range of contaminants highlighted as possibly being present (e.g. hydrocarbons at a petrol station, ground gas from a landfill site, etc.).

Typical sampling methodologies are:

❖ **Soil sampling:** Soil samples are required for chemical analysis to determine the presence of any contamination. Methods of soil sampling differ depending on the contaminants being tested. Usually disturbed samples are adequate for testing most chemicals. These can be obtained from the excavator bucket when trial pits are being used, from the cuttings from boreholes or from the window within a window sampler.

Samples are analysed in the laboratory for a wide range of 'baseline' contaminant chemicals, often supplemented by further specialist testing depending upon the type of contamination present.

❖ **Water sampling:** Water samples can be obtained by inserting a standpipe into a completed borehole. Water samples will be taken after insertion for further chemical analysis. The well may also be used for the monitoring of gas. Installation can be permanent or semi-permanent to facilitate further sampling at a later date. Laboratory analysis is similar to soil samples.

❖ **Gas sampling:** The presence of methane and carbon dioxide may be established on sites which are landfills or close to neighbouring landfills. Monitoring wells constructed for water sampling may also be used to sample the presence of land gas. In-situ measurements of gas concentrations and flow are taken at ground level on the head of the monitoring well using an infrared gas analyser. Wells may be constructed to measure gas concentrations and flow at different depths.

The majority of sites undergoing development will require a Phase II investigation, particularly where the previous use was industrial. Phase II investigations can often be combined with geotechnical investigations for foundation design. Sites that are not being developed may also require Phase II investigations (e.g. during transactions). This may depend on whether a significant pollutant linkage has been identified or if the local authority may investigate the site as part of their Part IIA inspection strategy in the near future.

Remediation

Remediation of sites can be achieved by removing sources of contamination, reducing levels of contamination or modifying the 'pathways' between the source and the identified sensitive receptors. The main approaches include:

❖ excavating and removing contaminated material off site to landfill (dig and dump);

❖ encapsulating or separating contaminated material on site, by severing contaminant pathways with barriers (e.g. underground bentonite walls); and

❖ treating the contaminated material, either in situ or after removal (e.g. bioremediation or soil washing).

Remediation can often be combined with the redevelopment of the site. Remediation strategies should be approved in advance by the local authority and the Environment Agency. Post-remediation validation sampling (e.g. of soil or groundwater) should be undertaken to document that the remediation has been effective.

Environmental insurance

Environmental insurance is increasingly being used in property transactions to cover risks associated with contaminated land. Environmental insurance can be obtained directly from specialist underwriters or through an insurance broker. A broker will normally obtain quotations from a number of different underwriters in order to negotiate the best insurance cover and premium for a client.

The most common type of environmental insurance covers regulatory and third party claims due to land contamination. Other types of insurance can provide protection against unpredictable costs should site remediation expenses prove difficult to quantify at the planning stage.

When taking out environmental insurance, one of the most important aspects is to understand what circumstances the policy would cover. Furthermore, as with many insurance policies, environmental insurance policies are often written in a language that is sometimes unclear.

Common exclusions from policies are:

❖ known contamination;

❖ business disruption costs;

❖ remediation costs on change of land use; and

❖ loss in value.

Key contaminated land legislation

The government believes that the planning process provides the best means of remediating sites. In most cases the planning system is capable of handling such issues, for example by requiring Phase II investigations or by requiring remediation to be approved by the local authority prior to development. A new contaminated land regime was introduced in 2000 in the UK (as Part IIA of the *Environmental Protection Act* 1990). This is intended to deal with problem contaminated sites that are not being developed and which would therefore not be dealt with under the planning system.

Enforcing authorities

The local authority is duty bound to provide a public register containing information about land that has formally been identified as potentially contaminated, and the action which has been taken to remediate it. Any land that has satisfactorily been remediated prior to a remediation notice being served will not appear on the public register. Furthermore, if land is to be redeveloped in the near future it is unlikely that a notice will be served.

The cost of any clean up will normally lie with the person (or 'appropriate persons') who knowingly caused the contamination. The local authority will ensure the clean up is carried out either through the planning process, via voluntary remediation, or if necessary by serving a remediation notice requiring them to clean up the site. In the case of an emergency the council will remediate the site and recover the costs afterwards.

Local authorities have primary responsibility for the identification of contaminated land, although the Environment Agency (EA) will respond to requests from a local authority for information on land that it is considering prioritising for inspection. Where a site has been determined as contaminated land, local authorities must take into account any information held by the Environment Agency on issues of water pollution.

Special sites

Land may also be categorised by a local authority as a 'special site'. This definition includes sites which may be affecting underlying water supplies or major aquifers, such as military land, oil refineries and nuclear plants.

Once the local authority has made this designation then the Environment Agency takes over the enforcing role. The Environment Agency would then maintain full responsibility for the site including both the cost of enforcement and also any testing and monitoring required. Should the site become an 'orphan site' (when no knowing polluter is found) then the Environment Agency will also be responsible for the cost of remediation. The disadvantage from the local authorities' perspective is that they do lose control of what can be politically sensitive sites. If there is a dispute as to whether or not the site is a special site, the matter can be referred to the Secretary of State for determination.

Remediation notice

The local authority cannot serve a remediation notice until three months have elapsed since the person or persons were notified of the designation of their land as contaminated. If the local authority, in the course of the consultation period, finds additional appropriate persons, it must notify them of the designation of the land as contaminated, and then wait a further three months before serving any remediation notice on them.

Although the local authority is under a duty to serve a remediation notice, it may wait for more than three months before doing so. This may well be the case where discussions about voluntary remediation are ongoing. It is vital that time limits be set for the actions that are going to be required otherwise it will not be possible for the local authority to initiate enforcement proceedings on the basis that the action has not been carried out. Any remediation notice must effectively be justified with reference to the statutory *Contaminated Land (England) Regulations* 2006 (SI 2006/1380) guidance by including:

- ❖ the remediation scheme proposed;
- ❖ any exclusion from liability; and
- ❖ any apportionment of costs.

The remediation notice may, therefore, have to be a fairly lengthy document. It should be carefully drafted, so as to attempt to avoid an appeal being made against it. Remember that there might be several remediation notices for each site. Copies should be provided to all the parties that were consulted about remediation, and to the Environment Agency. Where there are several appropriate persons for a given action, a single remediation notice may be served on all of them. Details of the notice must be included in the register.

Appeals

There is a right of appeal against a remediation notice. Where the local authority serves a remediation notice the appeal is heard in the local Magistrates' Court. An appeal is made by way of a summary application to the Court. If the Environment Agency serves the remediation notice because it has taken over regulation of a site and it is now the appropriate authority, an appeal will be heard by an inspector appointed by the Secretary of State.

The time limit for bringing an appeal is 21 days, beginning with the first day of service. A remediation notice, on appeal, can be modified, confirmed or quashed. The remediation notice may be quashed if there is 'a material defect' in the notice. The grounds for appeal are set out in the *Contaminated Land (England) Regulations* 2006. There are a large number of grounds of appeal including:

- ❖ the appellant is not the appropriate person;
- ❖ the authority failed to exclude the appellant;
- ❖ there has been an improper apportionment of costs;
- ❖ there is some error with the notice;
- ❖ the requirements of the notice are unreasonable having regard to the costs and benefits; and
- ❖ the period of time for compliance is insufficient.

Who is liable under Part IIA?

- ❖ Remediation notices are served in the first instance on 'Class A' persons, i.e. polluters or knowing permitters of contamination. If these responsible parties cannot be found, the current owner or occupier may be responsible (although for a more limited range of liabilities) – 'Class B' persons. Several parties may be implicated.

- ❖ Sellers can avoid liability where there are payments for remediation, with an explicit statement in the sale contract that a purchaser is being paid to clean up land or that the purchase price is being reduced to reflect the contaminated state of the land.

- ❖ Sellers/landlords can also avoid liability by selling with information – giving the purchaser (or tenant under a long lease) the necessary information to identify contamination before buying. Where transactions have occurred since 1990 between large commercial organisations, the granting of permission by the seller for the buyer to carry out its own investigations as to the condition of the land, is normally sufficient to indicate that the buyer had the necessary information.

Contributed by Janette Stevens, janette.stevens@watts.co.uk

Ground gas including radon

Methane and carbon dioxide

The occurrence and associated dangers of methane and carbon dioxide within the construction industry are well understood. Both gases occur naturally, although prominence of issues arises around areas of made ground, i.e. landfills.

Methane (chemical formula CH_4) is a basic hydrocarbon and is explosive in air at concentrations of between 5–15%. Methane is generated by the anaerobic (absence of oxygen) degradation of organic material.

Carbon dioxide (chemical formula CO_2) is a product of aerobic (presence of oxygen) organic degradation. Carbon dioxide is classed as highly toxic. Where 3%v/v carbon dioxide is present, this can result in headaches and shortness of breath, with increasing severity up to 5%v/v or 6%v/v. (Source: *Guidance on evaluation of Development proposals on site where Methane and Carbon Dioxide are present*, National House Building Council (NHBC), March 2007.)

Both methane and carbon dioxide are asphyxiants (methane by its capability to displace oxygen). Numerous studies have identified the risk presented by the entry of these gases into building voids and other confined spaces.

Perhaps the best known UK incident concerning landfill gas was at Loscoe, Derbyshire in March 1986, when a bungalow adjacent to a landfill site was destroyed by an explosion of accumulated methane. A subsequent investigation attributed a rapid drop in atmospheric pressure (27 millibars over seven hours) resulting in gas being drawn in towards the property through the permeable underlying geology.

Another well-documented incident at Abbeystead in March 1984 resulted in 16 fatalities. Natural dissolved methane in water passing through a valve house at the Lune/Wyre water transfer scheme was released and allowed to accumulate during a period of inactivity. An unknown source (thought to be either an electrical fault or cigarette lighter) triggered the subsequent explosion, occurring at a time of an organised tour and demonstration of the valve house.

Sources

Natural sources of ground gas include:

- ❖ peat bogs and mosslands;
- ❖ limestone and chalk;
- ❖ coal measures;
- ❖ river and lake sediments;
- ❖ made ground;
- ❖ farmland; and
- ❖ sewers.

Detection and control

The assessment of risk from ground gas within new developments is a material consideration in local authority building control, planning and environmental health legislation.

- ❖ The *Town and County Planning Act* 1990 requires that the potential for contamination and risk from landfill and ground gases must be considered during development. If the development is within an area of potential risk, a planning condition will be likely to be attached to any permitted application, requiring satisfactory assessment and mitigation. The duty of the developer to maintain any gas protection systems may be a condition of the planning consent.

❖ Ground gas is also dealt with under Part IIA of the *Environmental Protection Act* 1990. Where a significant potential of significant harm exists to a development (either existing or being developed), the local authority can enforce appropriate remediation or mitigation.

❖ Approved guidance to the Building Regulations (Approved Document C, 2006 edition) states that where there is a potential risk, further investigation is required to determine whether gas measures are required and what level of protection is necessary.

A number of measures can be undertaken to reduce the risk of ground gas.

A desk study may be undertaken to determine the probability of ground gas affecting the site. This includes a desk-based study of the history and geology of the area and any additional information such as mining or landfill activities. If a source of gas is identified, gas monitoring installations and monitoring may be recommended.

British Standard 1017:2001 *Investigation of potentially contaminated sites – Code of Practice* and BS 5930:1999 *Code of Practice for site investigations* recommend a minimum of 12 months' monitoring.

The most common method of detection is a standard landfill gas analyser and flow meter, which measure methane, carbon dioxide and oxygen concentrations. Photo ionisation detectors (PID) and flame ionisation detectors (FID) can be used where other gases, such as organic volatiles, are suspected.

Protection measures

The type of mitigation measures required depend on the type of development, gas type, volume, source and emission rate.

In ground barriers

These are physical barriers to block gas migration and usually comprise compacted clay, bentonite or polyethylene. This method is often used for large areas, such as closed landfill sites. However, it is a relatively expensive protection measure.

Ventilation

Ventilation (either active or passive) is the most commonly used gas protection measure. A secondary level of protection is often required, as ventilation is influenced by factors such as wind speed and direction, and atmospheric pressure.

Ventilation can comprise underfloor venting or trench venting. Underfloor venting uses an open void space with connection to the atmosphere, such as air bricks, pipe riser and gravel filled trenches. Trench venting involves excavating a trench or series of columns and backfilling with a permeable infill such as gravel. Gas permeates freely to the open atmosphere rather than migrating laterally. This method is commonly used at the boundaries of landfill sites.

Gas resistant membranes

Membranes are often used in conjunction with other measures. A number of different types of membrane are available depending on the volatility and density of the gas. The effectiveness of a membrane is dependent on techniques of sealing the membrane to the building fabric, ensuring that gas cannot leak through to occupied areas or accumulate in voids.

Alarm systems

Alarm systems are designed to trigger when gas concentrations reach a certain level. Gas probes are situated around the building and feed data into a central system. These are mainly used as additional protection for high risk sites or existing buildings where it is not possible to use other protection measures. They are, however, costly and require regular maintenance.

Radon

Radon is a colourless, odourless gas that is radioactive. It is formed where uranium and radium are present and can move through cracks and fissures in the subsoil, and so into the atmosphere or into spaces under and in dwellings. Where it occurs in high concentrations it can pose a risk to health. (Source: *Radon: guidance on protective measures for new dwellings*, Building Research Establishment, 1999.)

Radon is everywhere but usually in insignificant, variable concentrations. Problems occur when it enters enclosed spaces, such as basements, where concentrations can accumulate. Some areas in the UK are more exposed to radon due to localised geology.

The Health Protection Agency (HPA) publishes maps of radon affected areas across England and Wales, Scotland, and areas of Northern Ireland. The HPA has set threshold levels for both commercial and residential properties. Where potential health risk may exist, detectors should be installed and remedial work be undertaken to reduce exposure.

The HPA offer a search service and report, specifying whether a property is in a radon affected area. The British Geological Survey (www.bgs.ac.uk) also states whether radon is likely within a particular area as part of its Address-Linked Geological Inventory.

Identification of radon

Radon levels can vary substantially with time, so prolonged measurements are required for reliable results. Short measurements can be misleading, low or alarmingly high. The government recommends that people in affected areas test their property for a period of three months using passive monitors in order to provide a reliable estimate of the average radon level. Passive monitors are easy to use, inexpensive and available from the Department for Environment, Food and Rural Affairs (Defra).

Remedial action for high radon levels can be quite straightforward. The best approach is to prevent radon entering the building from the ground by altering the balance of pressure between the inside and outside.

This can be achieved by carrying out the following:

❖ Install a small sump pump below the floor and connect to a low power fan in order to extract the air and reduce the pressure under the floor. Multiple sumps can be used in large buildings.

❖ Improved ventilation under suspended timber and concrete floors. New airbricks are installed, sometimes together with a fan.

❖ Increase the pressure in the building by blowing air (called positive pressurisation) from the roof space with a small fan. Best results are in buildings with low natural ventilation. Secondary benefits may include a reduction of other indoor pollutants such as carbon dioxide, reduced condensation and a 'fresher' indoor environment.

❖ Alternatively, one may seal ducts, joints and cracks in the floors, although this is rarely effective by itself and always laborious. It is helpful to close large openings when a sump is used.

❖ Install a membrane barrier. This is very difficult to successfully achieve in an existing building.

Radon and the Building Regulations

With the new understanding of radon risk, the government legislated that houses built since 1988 in parts of Devon and Cornwall and 1992 in parts of Somerset, Derbyshire and Northamptonshire had to have radon protection measures built in. Additionally, the precise areas where radon protective measures should be taken are periodically reviewed by Defra as new data is provided by the Health Protection Agency.

Two zones of risk were allowed for. First the primary zone (the area with the highest risk). Requirement C2 of Schedule 1 of the Building Regulations requires that each house has a radon proof area, together with other precautionary measures that can be upgraded if a risk shows high radon levels. In the secondary zone (where the risk is lower) only precautionary measures must be built in. If a house has precautionary measures, upgrading them (e.g. adding a fan to a sump and pipe system) could solve the radon problem quickly and simply. The Building Research Establishment (BRE) has published guidance on protective measures for new dwellings in support of the Building Regulations entitled BRE Report *Radon: Guidance on Protective Measures for New Dwellings*. Equivalent advice has been prepared by the Health and Safety Executive (HSE) within a document entitled *Radon in the workplace*. The document recommends many similar measures are applicable for non-domestic buildings.

Contributed by Janette Stevens, janette.stevens@watts.co.uk

Environmental Liability Directive

The *Environmental Liability Directive* (ELD) came into force in all European Union (EU) member states in April 2004. In the UK, although existing legislation already applies to many of the areas covered, the ELD enforces some important changes, particularly in the area of remediation. After a number of delays, the ELD was finally implemented in England in March 2009 through the *Environmental Damage (Prevention and Remediation) Regulations* 2009.

The ELD aims to establish a framework that would prevent 'significant environmental damage' or rectify damage after it has occurred, by forcing industrial polluters (or 'operators') to pay prevention and remediation costs. In this respect it is no different to the *Environmental Protection Act* 1990 and its accompanying Part IIA legislation dealing specifically with contaminated land, which was introduced in 2000.

For this reason, it is thought unlikely that the ELD will lead to an increase in the number of contaminated sites for which UK operators find themselves liable. However, at a more detailed level it does introduce a number of key changes. There are new, specific criteria for determining environmental damage, as well as the two new categories of complementary and compensatory remediation, which will have implications for UK businesses.

Determining damage

As described in the ELD, 'significant environmental damage' is defined by reference to:

- ❖ biodiversity, whether protected at EU or national levels;
- ❖ waters covered by the *Water Framework Directive*; and
- ❖ human health (including land contamination when it is a threat to human health).

The ELD provides specific criteria to assess when damage is 'significant'. Member states will be under a duty to ensure that the necessary preventive or restorative measures are actually taken but will have the flexibility to decide when measures should be taken by:

- ❖ the relevant operator;
- ❖ the competent authorities; or
- ❖ a third party.

What are the implications?

Operators carrying out 'hazardous' activities will be held strictly liable (i.e. no need to show fault or negligence) for preventing or restoring any damage caused by those activities to land, water and protected habitats and species. In addition, operators carrying out other less harmful activities will be held liable when damage to protected habitats and species has been caused by their fault or negligence.

For UK businesses, the most significant changes that will be introduced by the ELD are the two new categories of 'complementary' and 'compensatory' remediation. Under previous UK legislation, operators were only held liable for what the ELD calls 'primary remediation'. This meant remedying the particular damage caused in order to return the damaged natural resources and/or impaired services to or towards 'baseline' condition (or that which would have existed had the damage not occurred). However, liability has now been extended to include:

    ❖   **complementary remediation**: any remedial measure taken to compensate for the fact that primary remediation does not result in fully restoring the damaged resources and/or services; and

    ❖   **compensatory remediation**: any action taken to compensate for interim losses of natural resources and/or services that occur from the date of damage occurring until primary remediation has achieved its full effect.

Operators are now automatically exempt from having to compensate for damage caused:

    ❖   by emissions within the terms of permits;

    ❖   despite the use of best practice;

    ❖   by war or an act of God; or

    ❖   by a third party, despite having taken all safety measures.

Damage from nuclear and maritime accidents falls outside the regime's scope and remains subject to existing treaties.

Opportunities

The ELD is expected to provide opportunities for environmental and property consultants to advise their clients on:

    ❖   whether or not significant damage has occurred to the environment as a result of their business activities;

    ❖   whether or not they can be held liable;

    ❖   what type of remediation will be required and at what cost; and

    ❖   when successful remediation of the site has been achieved.

Contributed by Janette Stevens, janette.stevens@watts.co.uk

Water Framework Directive

Water quality in England and Wales has improved dramatically in recent years. Building on progress to date, the *Water Framework Directive* (WFD) sets out to enforce sustainable water use and promote a range of ecological objectives.

The WFD is the most substantial piece of EC water legislation to date. The Directive came into force on 22 December 2000 and was transposed into law in England and Wales in 2003, with implementation from December 2006 (by the *Water Environment (Water Framework Directive) (England and Wales) Regulations* 2003). The WFD requires all inland and coastal waters to reach 'good status' by 2015. This standard is far more rigorous than previous water quality measures, with an estimated 95% of water courses at risk of failing to meet the criteria set out by the Directive. The Environment Agency has statutory duties in England and Wales to implement the Directive and ensure the environmental objectives are met by the 2015 deadline.

The key environmental aims of the WFD are to:

    ❖   prevent deterioration of aquatic ecosystems;

- ❖ protect, enhance and restore polluted waters and groundwater to 'good status', which is based on ecological and chemical factors for surface water and water quantity and chemical status for groundwater;

- ❖ comply with water-related standards and objectives for environmentally protected areas established under other EU legislation;

- ❖ progressively reduce pollution from priority substances (pollutants that represent a significant risk to the aquatic environment) and cease or phase out discharges from priority hazardous substances (those that are the most polluting); and

- ❖ prevent or limit input of pollutants into groundwater and reverse any significant or sustained upward trends in the concentration of groundwater pollution.

These demanding new environmental objectives will be set within an integrated river basin district structure. Each river basin will have its own management plan (RBMP) for surface and groundwater; all with common objectives and principles. RBMPs were submitted to the Secretary of State for Environment, Food and Rural Affairs and Welsh Ministers for approval on 22 September 2008. These were eventually published on 22 December 2009 and are available on the Environment Agency's website. For planners and developers the WFD has far-reaching implications. However, according to the Royal Town Planning Institute (RTPI) many planners remain unaware of the impact it will have on the planning process. As a result, a report has been produced jointly by the RTPI, the Environment Agency, the Local Government Association and the Welsh Local Government Association, to provide advice for planners in advance of the final details of the WFD. The report, *The Water Framework Directive and Planning: Initial advice to planning authorities in England and Wales*, outlines the key elements of the Directive and focuses strongly on its future ramifications.

Spatial planners are increasingly aware of the fundamental need to manage development pressure against a background of challenging water-related issues and constraints. The report recognises the additional requirement on planners, who now need to balance the need to provide water and to treat waste water with a requirement to maintain/improve the water environment.

In some parts of England, major growth is proposed in places where water resources and the ability to handle increased volumes of sewage are already stretched. Implementation of the WFD means that future development will have to be carefully planned so that it does not result in further pressure on the water environment.

However, new development can provide an opportunity to tackle existing pressures on water, through imaginative, high-quality project design and planning, as well as the use of planning conditions and obligations attached to planning permissions. The RTPI makes the point that these positive impacts can be linked to the remediation of contaminated land and hence improvements to ground and surface water quality, river habitat restoration, water-use efficiency and protection of natural ecosystems. Where waste or a legacy of contaminated land or mine water is causing pollution, intervention by a range of authorities and agencies will be needed to clean up or at least mitigate these problems. All this will add a new element to both the planning and development processes and therefore it is important that client organisations are aware of the implications for their future projects.

It is not only at planning stage that property and construction will be affected by the Directive, there may be more technical issues to deal with. For example, the Building Research Establishment (BRE) is in the process of undertaking research into the use of recycled and secondary aggregates (RSA) in structural concrete in the context of the WFD. There is a perception in the construction industry that use of RSA may lead to hazardous materials leaching into the soil from foundations and resulting in drinking water or groundwater pollution. BRE is keen to determine whether or not this is the case and is working with the Waste & Resources Action Programme (WRAP) to research the issue. It seems inevitable that other building materials and techniques will also be called into question in future.

The implementation of the Directive will take place in a number of planning cycles with reviews every six years. This will allow a better understanding of basin characteristics and long-term trends, such as climate change, to be taken into account. The first cycle is due to be completed in 2015.

Contributed by Janette Stevens, janette.stevens@watts.co.uk

Electromagnetic fields

Electromagnetic fields (EMFs) are a combination of electric fields and magnetic fields.

Electric fields are produced as a result of voltage within wiring. The higher the voltage, the stronger the field. They exist even when an electrical appliance is not in use as voltage is always present. Electric fields can be blocked by objects such as buildings and trees. They are measured in volts per metre (Vm^{-1}) or kilovolts per metre (kVm^{-1}).

Magnetic fields are created when electric currents flow and therefore are not present unless an appliance is turned on. Magnetic fields are measured in nanotesla (nT), microtesla (μT), millitesla (mT) or tesla (T). Magnetic fields are not usually blocked by objects, although certain types of metal can shield against them.

Awareness of the health effects of electromagnetic fields (also known as electromagnetic radiation) has been steadily increasing since the 1970s as exposure to human-induced EMFs has increased both in the home and in the workplace, according to the World Health Organisation (WHO) 2007.

The Radiation Protection Division of the Health Protection Agency currently has the responsibility for providing advice on limiting exposure of the general public to EMFs. Following the government spending review in October 2010, it is understood that the Health Protection Agency will be abolished and these functions are to be transferred to the new Public Health Service by 2012.

What are the common sources of electromagnetic radiation?

EMFs are present everywhere in the environment, existing through the generation and transmission of electricity, the use of electrical appliances and telecommunications (WHO, 2007). Of particular concern have been the effects of overhead and underground power lines, electricity substations, microwave ovens, computer and television screens, security devices, radars and the use of mobile phones.

Transmission power lines in the UK operate at 275 and 400 kilovolts (kV) and distribution lines at 440V, 11kV, 33kV, 66kV and 132kV. The strength of EMFs decreases rapidly with increased distance from the source. Human epidemiology studies of magnetic fields have tended to use a field of 0.4 microtesla (μT) or above to identify potential risks. For high voltage power lines at 132kV and above, average field levels of 0.4μT or above may exist at ground level at distances greater than 100 metres. For lower voltage lines, a field of 0.4μT or above may occur up to a few tens of metres away.

EMFs can also occur naturally within the environment through the build up of electrical charges associated with thunderstorms within the atmosphere.

What are the health effects associated with exposure to electromagnetic radiation?

A wide variety of symptoms and illnesses have been associated with exposure to EMFs, although these are not scientifically proven. These include:

❖ headaches;

❖ anxiety;

- ❖ suicide and depression;
- ❖ nausea;
- ❖ fatigue;
- ❖ premature pregnancies and low birth weight;
- ❖ cataracts;
- ❖ cardiovascular disorders;
- ❖ neurobehavioral effects and neurodegenerative disease;
- ❖ cancer, including childhood leukaemia;
- ❖ sleeping disorders; and
- ❖ convulsions and epilepsy.

Research and current knowledge

A large number of epidemiological studies have been undertaken across the world on the effects of exposure to EMF on human health. One of the most highly publicised issues is whether there is an increased risk of cancer within populations living near power lines or other sources of EMF. A great deal of research has been focused upon the risk of childhood cancer, in particular leukaemia.

Analysis of several studies has indicated 'the possibility exists of a doubling of the risk of leukaemia in children in homes at high levels of exposure to extremely low frequency (ELF) magnetic fields' (Health Protection Agency – Pooled Analysis, 2000). A task group set up by the WHO in October 2005 to assess risks to human health as a result of exposure to ELF EMFs concluded that additional studies since 2000 do not alter this view on the risk of childhood leukaemia.

The WHO task group in 2005 also assessed whether there was an association with ELF EMF exposure and the aforementioned associated health effects. It was concluded that 'scientific evidence supporting an association between ELF magnetic field exposure and all of these health effects is much weaker than for childhood leukaemia' (WHO, 2007).

The advisory group to the Health Protection Agency on non-ionising radiation has stated in relation to adults 'there is no reason to believe that residential exposure to EMFs is involved in the development of cancer'. However, it should be noted that there have been far fewer studies on the health effects on adults than on children.

What guidelines exist within the UK relating to EMFs?

A report published in 2004 by the former National Radiological Protection Board recommended the adoption in the UK of the guidelines produced by the International Commission on Non-Ionizing Radiation Protection (ICNIRP) for limiting exposures to EMFs having a frequency less than 300 GHz. The ICNIRP exposure guidelines relate to occupational and public exposure to EMFs.

Research into the effects of EMFs is under constant review by the Health Protection Agency to ensure guidelines are in line with the most up to date information. Guidelines are therefore susceptible to change. For the most up to date guidelines and information, the Health Protection Agency (while still in existence) and ICNIRP websites should be consulted.

Further information

- ❖ World Health Organisation, June 2007, *Electromagnetic fields and public health – Exposure to extremely low frequency fields*, Fact Sheet No. 322 from www.who.int/mediacentre/factsheets/fs322/en/index.html

- ❖ National Radiological Protection Board, 2004, *Advice on Limiting Exposure to Electromagnetic Fields (0–300 GHz)*, Documents of the NRPB, Volume 15 No. 2

- ❖ Health Protection Agency website: www.hpa.org.uk

❖ International Commission on Non-Ionizing Radiation Protection
   website: www.icnirp.de

Contributed by Janette Stevens, janette.stevens@watts.co.uk

Ecology and bat surveys

Consideration of ecology and biodiversity in development or demolition

Some animal species are protected from disturbance by virtue of their vulnerability such as bats. However, legislation also exists to protect, maintain and encourage biodiversity and this will inevitably encompass many different species of plants or animals.

Proposed developments that require planning permission, particularly larger schemes, are more likely to require consideration for the protection of any existing animal inhabitants in and around a building.

Protected species include bats and protected birds, such as peregrine falcons, owls and the black redstart. Bats are the most common inhabitants of our buildings and as such are covered in more detail within the next subsection.

Bats

Bats make up between a quarter and third of the mammal population in the UK and their existence is protected by law. The reduction in the number of natural roosting sites across the country has led to more and more bats forming roosts in the man-made structures which, when maintained or refurbished, can threaten the security of roosts.

It is a criminal offence to kill or injure a bat, or to destroy or disturb their roosts and the offences attract fines of up to £5,000 or six months in jail per bat. The overriding legislation protecting bats is the *Wildlife and Countryside Act 1981* (as amended).

Prior to any major refurbishment or demolition, surveyors need to be aware of the implications of finding bats or other species within these structures. Changes such as upgrading or providing artificial lighting can affect bats' navigation senses and could cause bats to avoid or desert a roost and/or affect their emergence times.

Bat surveys

Surveyors involved with the management, maintenance and refurbishment of properties and should be aware of the obligations in relation to bats or other species that may be present. The following steps may help the surveyor to comply with legislation:

❖ Contact your local SNCO (Statutory Nature Conservation Organisation) Natural England, for example, if a bat or roost is found within a property considered for refurbishment. The SNCO can arrange for a roost visit or for commercial development advice on a local ecology or bat survey from a specialist who will be able to assist.

❖ The specialist can advise on the roosting potential of the building (for example, open eaves or accessible roof voids) and assess the surrounding area for foraging sources and suitable fauna.

❖ The specialist will carry out daylight surveys and, if considered necessary, emergence surveys during dusk, to establish whether or not roosts are active.

❖ Experts can assist in the granting of licences to enable roosts to be disturbed or moved. However, this is only if it is considered absolutely necessary, within the public interest, and not likely to be detrimental to the species as a whole.

Further information

❖ The Bat Conservation Trust website contains useful information on bats and free pdf publications on *Bat surveys – Good practice guidelines, Bats and Lighting in the UK*: www.bats.org.uk

❖ BRE Good Repair Guide GRG 36: *Bats and refurbishment*, BRE, May 2009

❖ National Building Specification Shortcuts: NBS Shortcut 76, *Do not Disturb: Bats in buildings*, June 2009

❖ *Planning Policy Statement 9: Biodiversity and Geological Conservation* (PPS9), 2005. Bats and other species are given material consideration during the planning process. Measures to promote or protect species (such as bat or bird boxes) may be specified by authorities.

❖ *Biodiversity for Low and Zero Carbon Buildings: A Technical Guide for New Build*, RIBA Publishing, 2010, provides guidance on all relevant protected species likely to be found in and around existing buildings and some good product information on bat boxes, artificial nests, etc.

Contributed by Phil O'Brien, phil.o'brien@watts.co.uk

Carbon reduction

Sustainability

383

Energy conservation

Some of the ways in which energy efficiency can be enhanced are outlined below:

❖ **Greater thermal insulation**: One of the most cost-effective ways of increasing a building's energy efficiency. With new buildings, the starting point is to meet the standards of thermal insulation set out in the current Building Regulations. However, there is a strong argument for further increasing thermal insulation – the level chosen will depend upon a variety of factors including the payback period required, the user's pattern of occupation and whether environmental concern outweighs strictly financial considerations. Our existing buildings offer great scope to increase insulation and this can be carried out during refurbishment or maintenance periods when better use can be made of access equipment and other site overheads. Over the next few years we can expect to see significant developments in the use of nanotechnology to create new, highly-insulating materials, for example, aerogels in which the water component of a gel is replaced with gas.

❖ **Efficient lighting**: In commercial buildings, lighting costs usually run between 40% and 50% of total energy costs. Highly efficient lighting that can significantly reduce running costs is now available for both new and existing installations.

❖ **Efficient services**: Services need preventative maintenance to ensure that all plant is operating at maximum efficiency. When plant requires renewal, alternatives (such as condensing boilers or combined heat and power plant, or even natural cooling) should be considered.

❖ **Building management systems**: These monitor and control all service installations. Due to recent technological advances, these systems are becoming less expensive and can therefore be installed on smaller properties. Even where a full BMS is inappropriate, simple systems are available which control single services, such as lighting.

❖ **Using locally-sourced materials**: This minimises energy consumption when transporting materials to site.

❖ **Building materials**: Those with a long life expectancy imply energy efficiency because they make good use of resources. The manufacture of building materials entails energy consumption and this varies widely depending on the product. Data can be unreliable, but as a rule of thumb assume that the greater the degree of processing, the more energy consumed during manufacture.

❖ **Making use of solar gain**: Even with their humblest dwellings, our ancestors frequently designed their buildings to make use of solar gain. Generally this entails the use of large areas of glazing on southern elevations and minimal openings to the north.

❖ **The use of soft landscaping**: Trees and other planting can conserve energy in buildings by minimising heat gains and losses. A screen of deciduous planting at the south of a building will filter strong summer sun but will allow for natural heat gain from weaker winter sun. Soft landscaping also has an important part to play in influencing the micro-climate around buildings by reducing wind speeds.

❖ **Out-of-town schemes**: Many of these schemes are built with high levels of thermal insulation and efficient building services. Nevertheless, because of the fuel used in transporting building users from their homes, the whole scheme may be very inefficient in energy terms.

Increased energy efficiency is available at little extra cost – it is just a matter of adopting an environmental train of thought. Increased public awareness of these issues and pressure of legislation should be seen as an opportunity to create more energy efficient buildings.

Contributed by Trevor Rushton, trevor.rushton@watts.co.uk

Air-conditioning inspections

Article 9 of the *Energy Performance of Buildings Directive* requires that all air-conditioning equipment with a rated output exceeding 12kW shall be inspected at intervals not exceeding five years.

The purpose of the inspection is to provide building owners/operators with information relating to the efficiency of the installed systems and to highlight areas where energy savings can be made, resulting in reduced operating costs.

The responsibility for ensuring that the inspection report is carried out rests with the building owner or operator or whoever is in control of the air-conditioning system. Failure to produce a report will result in a £300 fine enforced by Trading Standards Officers.

A full explanation of the purpose and scope, together with guidance on carrying out the inspections, is provided in TM44:2007 produced by the Chartered Institution of Building Services Engineers (CIBSE).

See also *Air-conditioning systems*, page 270.

Contributed by Tony Churchill, tony.churchill@watts.co.uk

Ozone depleting substances

Ozone depletion

Ozone (chemical formula O_3) is a triatomic gas consisting of three oxygen atoms. Ozone has a similar molecular structure to atmospheric diatomic oxygen (chemical formula O_2) but is much less stable.

Ozone can be both an air pollutant or an important atmospheric gas depending upon its location within the atmosphere. At ground level ozone is a hazardous pollutant, which can potentially cause respiratory problems in humans and animals. Ozone located in the upper atmosphere, in a zone known as the stratosphere, is essential for filtering and thus reducing the amount of ultraviolet (UV) radiation from the sun reaching the earth's surface. It is commonly understood that a group of man-made chemicals containing chlorine and bromine (known as halocarbons) have the potential to cause significant damage to this ozone layer.

The best-known group of halocarbons are chlorofluorocarbons (CFCs). The emission of CFCs to the atmosphere has largely been due to their use as refrigerants within air-cooling equipment, refrigerators and as aerosol propellants. This low reactivity of CFCs affords the gases enough time to disperse to the upper levels of the atmosphere where UV radiation from the sun breaks down the CFCs releasing chlorine atoms. The chlorine atoms act as highly reactive free radicals, which catalyse a number of reactions resulting in the breakdown of ozone into oxygen. As these reactions generally regenerate the chlorine atom, a single atom has the potential to destroy many thousands of ozone molecules.

The aforementioned reactions are widely believed to be the cause of the 'holes' in the ozone layer above the earth's polar regions. The first observation of an ozone hole was recorded in 1985 above Antarctica. Data published by NASA and the Royal Netherlands Meteorological Institute has suggested that in recent years the ozone hole has covered an area equivalent to the size of North America.

Protection of the ozone layer is considered vital to minimise the harmful effects of UV radiation on human health and other flora and fauna. Health problems such as increased rates of skin cancer, eye cataracts and reduction in human immunity to disease are all effects considered attributable to increased UV radiation.

In reaction to the issue of ozone depletion, an international agreement between world leaders was sanctioned in Montreal in 1987. The Montreal Protocol comprised an international treaty designed to protect the ozone layer by phasing out and banning certain substances known to deplete stratospheric ozone. Since its inception the Protocol has undergone five revisions, most recently in Beijing in 1999. The Protocol concentrates on several groups of ozone depleting chemicals and provides a timetable for their phasing out and eventual elimination. Overall, this has been regarded as one of the most successful pieces of international legislation to date, resulting in a recorded 95% reduction in ozone depleting substance consumption by developed countries and a 50–75% reduction by developing countries (Defra, 2004). The extent of the recovery of stratospheric ozone remains uncertain. However, providing the provisions of the Montreal Protocol are adhered to, some predictions state the ozone layer could be replenished by 2100.

Existing plant

Where CFCs or hydrochlorofluorocarbons (HCFCs) are identified as being contained within existing air conditioning or refrigeration plant, the contract administrator is to be informed immediately and instructions obtained.

Where the plant is scheduled, or instructed subsequently, for removal then under no circumstances is the gas to be dumped by venting into the atmosphere. The gas is to be collected for recovery/destruction by a specialist firm.

The contract administrator is to be informed in writing of the specialist undertaking the works and the date for removal, and is to be provided with a copy of the recovery/destruction certificate.

New plant

The contractor shall receive and transmit to the contract administrator documentary evidence from suppliers, subcontractors and designers of all new installations that no new or reused plant contains refrigerants with an ozone depletion potential of more than 0.06 (or with any ozone depleting potential). Furthermore, compounds with the lowest possible ozone depleting potential are to be selected where there is a choice.

As an alternative, consideration can be given to the use of absorption chillers or ammonia chillers.

Halon fire fighting systems

The general requirements for decommissioning these systems are the same as for CFCs and HCFCs in plant.

If the system is to be tested, then compressed air or some other non-ozone depleting gas shall be used.

If the system is to be recharged, a leak detection system should be installed. However, the preference is for some other form of fire extinguishing system wherever possible. Depending on the circumstances, options include inert gases (Inergen, Argonite, etc.), carbon dioxide and water fog/mist systems.

The use of halons in critical fire fighting systems (such as on aeroplanes, within the Channel Tunnel and in military vehicles) will be permitted.

Hand-held fire extinguishers

All fire extinguishers on site supplied by the contractor, or specified to be supplied in the Schedule of Works section, should be powder, foam, carbon dioxide, water spray or some other type without the use of halon.

Additional measures

CFCs and HCFCs are used in the manufacture of a variety of other products, including insulating materials, carpets, furnishings and aerosol sprays. They must not be used unless specifically instructed by the contract administrator.

Refrigerant phase out (F gases)

❖ R11/R12: CFC refrigerants banned from use due to ozone depletion potential; unlikely to be encountered.

❖ R22 is an ozone friendly HCFC refrigerant used in chillers, split and VRF/VRV systems up to 2001. These refrigerants have high global warming potential and will be prohibited from use at the end of 2014. See www.bis.gov.uk/files/file29101.pdf

❖ R22 'drop-in' replacements: alternatives do exist and are used successfully but each requires modification of the machine, which can be nearly as expensive as replacement. Consider also that the machines may be obsolete. See www.gas2010.com by BOC for details.

❖ R407c, R410a, R134a: Less damaging refrigerants, not currently restricted but use is regulated (see www.defra.gov.uk/environment/quality/air/Fgas)

Contributed by Janette Stevens, janette.stevens@watts.co.uk and Mark Rabbett, mark.rabbett@watts.co.uk

Energy Performance of Buildings Directive

The European Directive on the *Energy Performance of Buildings* (EPBD) took effect from 4 January 2006. A recasting of the requirements (www.communities.gov.uk/documents/planningandbuilding/pdf/1301240.pdf), which is significantly more demanding, was approved in May 2010 but will not apply in the UK until 2013/14.

Buildings account for more than 40% of UK carbon emissions. The Directive aims to promote the improvement of energy performance in buildings by encouraging owners and tenants to choose energy efficient buildings when seeking new premises and to improve the energy efficiency of existing buildings that they occupy. In the UK, the Directive was implemented through major changes to the Building Regulations 2006 and the introduction of energy certification legislation for both domestic and non-domestic properties. The *Building Regulations* 2010 clarified the requirements and introduced further requirements, primarily for new buildings.

The Regulations require energy certification be applied to new buildings and buildings being refurbished to any significant degree. This applies to both the building fabric and the services installations, e.g. upgrading of roof insulation is likely to be required when stripping and re-covering a roof. Further information can be found in Part L of the Building Regulations and the accompanying Approved Documents (ADs).

The Directive's key provisions are:

❖ minimum requirements for the energy performance of all new buildings (enforced through Building Regulations);

❖ minimum requirements for the energy performance of existing buildings more than 1,000m^2 that are subject to major renovation (also enforced through Building Regulations – improvements must be undertaken but only where they are technically and economically feasible and with a 15-year payback. Historic buildings are not exempt. Improvements are required on buildings less than 1,000m^2 where, for example, parts of the building envelope are renewed, such as windows and doors);

❖ energy certification of all buildings being traded (which on public buildings needs to be prominently displayed). Certification needs to be in place prior to sale or lease of buildings and needs to be renewed every ten years; and

❖ regular mandatory inspection of air-conditioning systems in buildings (see CIBSE publication TM44 for a practical inspection and assessment method).

Energy Performance Regulations

The *Energy Performance of Buildings (Certificates and Inspections) (England and Wales) Regulations* 2007 (the 'Energy Performance Regulations') came into force during 2008. These implement the EPBD in England and Wales. The *Energy Performance of Buildings (Certificates and Inspections) (England and Wales) (Amendment No. 2) Regulations* 2008 came into force in October 2008. See www.communities.gov.uk/planningandbuilding/sustainability/ energyperformance for details.

❖ **Energy Performance Certificates** (EPCs) are required when buildings over 50m^2 are constructed, sold or rented out and when existing buildings undergo major alterations. An EPC provides a property with an asset rating (A-G). Sellers and prospective landlords must make this available free of charge to prospective buyers or tenants at the earliest opportunity and no later than at exchange of contracts. This will be revised in April 2012 to require the EPC to be provided on marketing. EPCs are also required for all new construction work over 50m^2. The scrapping of home information packs (HIPS) did not remove the requirement to produce EPCs for dwellings.

❖ **Display Energy Certificates** (DECs) are required to be displayed in large buildings (over 1000m^2) that are partly or wholly occupied by public authorities and institutions that provide public services (such as public museums and swimming pools) even if privately operated. DECs are intended to show the public how well a building is performing and are based on actual metered energy usage. Consultation led to plans for DECs being required for commercial properties but the necessary amendment to the *Energy Bill* 2011 was dropped in September 2011.

❖ The Regulations require EPCs and DECs to be accompanied by recommendations on improving the energy performance of the building. There is no requirement to implement any of the recommendations.

❖ Exemptions from the duty to provide an EPC apply to places of worship, temporary buildings with a planned time of use of two years or less, certain buildings with low energy demand (as identified in AD L2A 2010), stand alone buildings less than 50m^2 and certain limited buildings that are to be demolished. An unheated building, or more correctly, a building that is not expected to be heated (e.g. a storage or distribution building under planning use class B8), does not require an EPC.

❖ EPCs are valid for ten years. DECs are valid for 12 months but must be renewed for a matching 12-month period each year.

❖ Regular inspection and reporting on the energy performance of air-conditioning systems is required where the collective cooling capacity is larger than 12kW. Inspection intervals are not to exceed five years. The report must contain advice on improving the efficiency of the system. There is no requirement to act on any advice given. For more information see *Air-conditioning inspections*, page 385.

❖ Qualified and/or accredited energy assessors are required to carry out the certification process in an independent manner. Accreditation bodies include construction professional institutions and a number of recognised trade associations. Assessors can qualify at level 3 (small simple buildings), level 4 (large commercial buildings) or level 5 (very large complex buildings requiring full simulation to properly represent their energy usage pattern).

❖ For commercial property, penalties for breaches of the Regulations depend on the rateable value of the property. The Regulations are enforced by Trading Standards Officers who have legal right to demand sight of certification at any time.

New guidance continues to emerge from DCLG, who have stiffened the enforcement regime significantly since EPCs were first required. Amendments have taken the form of revisions to the Regulations (September 2011 revisions apply from 6 April 2012) plus imposing conventions and increased auditing on assessors in order to make EPCs both accurate and repeatable. EPCs and DECs must be uploaded to the Landmark website to be legally valid. The requirement will also apply to Air Conditioning Inpection reports from April 2012. The website can also be used to check the validity of certification.

For more information visit www.communities.gov.uk

Scotland energy certification

The Scottish Building Standards Agency (SBSA) implements the EPBD on behalf of Scottish Ministers, through a new building standards system in Scotland, introduced on 1 May 2005. Energy certificates are required when buildings are constructed, sold or rented out – whether residential or commercial, public or private sector.

SBSA has entered into assessor accreditation protocols with recognised construction professional institutions and trade bodies to accredit members to deliver services required by the Regulations.

The assessment calculation in Scotland, while still using the Simplified Building Energy Model (SBEM), differs from the method used in England and Wales, and the ratings produced are not directly comparable. Scotland has also replaced DECs with displayed EPCs for public buildings.

Air Conditioning Inspections are required in Scotland. All systens over 250kW must now have reports in place. Systems over 12kW require reports to be in place by January 2013.

In Scotland, the exemption for places of worship does not apply.

For more information visit www.scotland.gov.uk/Topics/Built-Environment/Building/Building-standards

Northern Ireland energy certification

The EPBD is being implemented jointly by the Department of Finance and Personnel and the Department for Social Development.

The requirements are broadly similar to those for England and Wales, and energy assessors accredited in England and Wales can also practice in Northern Ireland.

See also www.dfpni.gov.uk/energy-performance-of-buildings

Contributed by Mark Rabbett, mark.rabbett@watts.co.uk

Renewable and low carbon energy

Renewable energy relates to naturally available sources that are constantly being replenished and are capable of being harnessed for human benefit, such as energy from the sun, the wind and tides, and energy from replaceable matter such as wood, domestic waste or industrial by-products.

Sustainability

Low or zero carbon energy (LZC), synonymous with renewables, is the term normally applied to renewable sources and to technologies which are more efficient than traditional solutions or emit less carbon. Common LZC technologies include:

- ❖ solar thermal systems;
- ❖ photovoltaics;
- ❖ district heating and cooling;
- ❖ combined heat and power;
- ❖ ground source cooling;
- ❖ ground and air source heat pumps;
- ❖ wind power;
- ❖ hydroelectric power;
- ❖ biofuels; and
- ❖ fuel cells.

These technologies can either be utilised on a 'micro' basis, to serve individual properties, or on a large scale where captured energy is fed straight to a common source, like the national grid.

Solar thermal systems

Solar air or water collectors absorb solar radiation, which is transferred directly into the interior space or to a storage system to be distributed to the building later. Contemporary 'evacuated tube' solar collectors are suitable for effective year-round operation within the northern hemisphere.

Photovoltaics

Photovoltaic (PV) systems use solar cells to convert sunlight into electricity. PV is usually installed in parallel with the grid, although stand-alone generation is not uncommon, particularly in isolated areas. Large-scale PV generation has been used to harness solar energy effectively in southern European countries, such as Spain, for commercial electricity generation.

District heating and cooling

District heating, also known as community heating, provides heat from a central source to more than one building or dwelling via a network of distribution mains. Heat may be generated from LZC sources such as combined heat and power (CHP) or biomass boilers, or heat that would otherwise be dumped into the atmosphere can be used. District heating is more prevalent in northern European and Scandinavian countries where waste energy from industrial activities is harnessed for the benefit of the local community.

Combined heat and power

Combined heat and power (CHP), or cogeneration, refers to the simultaneous generation of electricity and heat in the form of hot water or steam. Electricity is generated using an engine or turbine, and useful heat is recovered from the exhaust gases and cooling systems. Tri-generation is a term applied to a CHP system that produces electricity, heating and cooling. The cooling output is generated from the waste heat feeding an absorption chiller. Micro CHP technology is now available commercially for small-scale installation into individual buildings.

Ground source heat pumps

Fluctuations in ground temperature reduce with depth and stabilise to around 9°–12°C at about 12m below the surface in the UK. Ground source heat pumps (GSHPs) make use of refrigeration equipment to extract heat from the stabilised ground temperature and raise it to a more useful output temperature to heat the building. The depletion of the heat source is matched by the rate of heat flow back from the surrounding earth and under these circumstances the technology is a renewable source of energy. Because the ground is at a constant temperature the refrigeration process can be very energy efficient. GSHPs can also be used as a means of generating cooling in a building by utilising reverse cycle heat pumps, with the recovered waste heat dissipated to the ground.

Air source heat pumps

Air source heat pumps work in a similar manner to GSHPs and extract heat from the air surrounding a building. ASHP systems are considered an efficient alternative to 'electric heating' and are proving a popular means to satisfy contemporary Building Regulations requirements, particularly in situations where gas-burning appliances are not viable.

Wind power

Wind power is used to turn a turbine and generate electricity, which is distributed in much the same way as for photovoltaic systems. In order to generate worthwhile quantities of electricity, average wind speeds of more than 5–6m/s are typically required. It is estimated that 40% of Europe's wind energy passes over the UK. There are essentially two basic kinds of wind turbine in use, defined as horizontal axis and vertical axis. Horizontal axis turbines are the more common comprising a central hub with evenly-spaced blades, supported on a tower. Vertical axis systems can be installed without the need for a tower and may be easier to integrate with a building's structure.

Hydroelectric power

Hydroelectric power is widely regarded as the most reliable source of renewable energy. Large-scale hydroelectric generation has been in use for several decades in the UK and complements fossil fuel energy generation. Micro-hydroelectric generation is suitable for buildings located next to a source of running water. Generation is non-stop, assuming water levels are not subject to seasonal variation.

Biofuels

Energy from biomass is produced by burning organic matter such as trees, crops or animal dung. The biomass is carbon based so when used as a fuel it also generates carbon emissions. However, the carbon that is released during combustion is equivalent to the amount that was absorbed during growth, and so the technology is carbon neutral. The bio-energy created may be in the form of electricity, heat, steam, and solid fuels. To be most effective in terms of reduced carbon production, the point of use, or generation, needs to be close to a plentiful source of biofuels.

Fuel cells

Hydrogen fuel cell technology, although still at an early stage of development, is starting to be used as a means of storage as opposed to a source of energy. The hydrogen fuel cells can produce heat, power and pure water without releasing any greenhouse gases.

Contributed by Tony Churchill, tony.churchill@watts.co.uk

Carbon management

The need to tackle climate change and improve energy efficiency is now critical to both the business and public sectors. This is due to:

- ❖ the need to comply with environmental legislation and regulation;

- ❖ increasing energy prices and the future prospect of fossil fuel shortages;

- ❖ the opportunity to reduce overheads and increase operational efficiency;

- ❖ brand enhancement via improvement of corporate environmental credentials; and

- ❖ consumer pressure.

Carbon management provides a framework within which organisations can take a structured approach to these challenges and opportunities. By dealing in a systematic and comprehensive way with the issue of climate change, businesses and other organisations can reap the benefits, even if attention is already being paid to reducing carbon emissions. Carbon management means taking the organisation as a whole and determining where improvements can be made across all aspects of the operation.

In 2001, the UK Government established the Carbon Trust as an independent company to promote energy efficiency to business and the public sector through its carbon management programme. The programme encourages organisations to take a holistic view of their operation, from revenue and cost through to aspects that would not necessarily be included in an energy audit or operational efficiency review (such as research and development, procurement, and employee or community relations) and to consider them in terms of climate change. The Trust sees this as a way of:

- ❖ embedding consideration for carbon reduction into long-term strategy;

- ❖ documenting future measures to save energy; and

- ❖ ensuring that stakeholders can calculate accurately how much money such measures will save.

For small businesses, the Trust has developed a range of tools, services and information to enable them to reduce energy and make cost savings. User-friendly tools are available via the Trust's website to help businesses calculate their carbon footprint: the first step towards cutting emissions. For medium-sized businesses, one-day on-site carbon surveys are available to identify low or no-cost energy efficiency measures and methods of implementation.

The Trust's carbon management programmes are also designed to meet the requirements of larger companies, helping them to understand and manage their carbon emissions using a methodical approach that provides a range of tools and capabilities to manage risks and identify existing and future opportunities. The Trust claims savings of £2.6bn for UK business since 2001, as a result of the direct cost savings made by reducing carbon emissions.

- ❖ **Step One – Diagnosis**

    Footprinting – organisation/value chain/product

    Carbon and cost reduction opportunity sizing

    Market and revenue opportunity assessment

    Risk analysis

    Capabilities and process diagnostics

- ❖ **Step Two – Strategy**

    Corporate sustainability strategy and target setting

    Low carbon revenue growth strategies

    Business case development and assessment

Supply chain strategy and targets

❖ **Step Three – Solution**

Process improvement and change management

Internal engagement and governance support

External engagement supportive – industry/suppliers/customers

Standards, tools and methodology development.

The above methodology is recommended for large businesses but the Trust also provides programmes tailored to suit small and medium sized businesses.

There are also bespoke programmes for the public sector, with individual guidance tailored to meet the needs and objectives of local authorities, higher education and the NHS.

With the use of energy in buildings producing an estimated 45% of UK carbon emissions, property professionals have a key role to play in carbon management. RICS actively promotes this aspect of property advice on behalf of members and has produced guidance for those advising clients or employers on the carbon management of their real estate in partnership with the Carbon Trust. The guidance highlights that carbon management 'can provide real commercial returns as well as making a significant contribution to climate change'. Tenants are already increasingly seeking out buildings with high levels of energy performance and, in future, RICS anticipates that buildings that do not perform to these standards will be harder to let and will not achieve rental levels as high as better-performing buildings. Businesses that follow energy-efficient practices benefit from financial savings as well as reducing their impact on the environment. As energy prices increase, the effect of energy savings is compounded, says RICS.

Further information

The RICS guidance note, *Carbon management of real estate*, 2008, is available from www.ricsbooks.com

For more information on the Carbon Trust go to: www.carbontrust.co.uk

Other sources of information are:

❖ www.energysavingtrust.org.uk

❖ http://envirowise.wrap.org.uk

❖ www.bpf.org.uk

❖ www.bre.co.uk

Contributed by Robert Staton, robert.staton@watts.co.uk and Lesley Davis, 01243 784054, lesley@davisaylingmedia.co.uk, of Davis Ayling Media, Genista Cottage, Stane Street, Westhampnett, Chichester, PO18 0PA.

Green legislation

The key drivers in green legislation include the *Energy Performance of Buildings Directive* (EPBD) (see below) and the stated desire to reach zero carbon for all new housing by 2016 and for all new non-domestic buildings by 2019. The focus so far has been on new buildings rather than the existing stock, however proposals currently out for consultation should address this.

Legislation which is already active or on the statute book (including EU directives)

A Code for Sustainable Homes (CSH)

This is the main documentation with legal status for setting the standards with regard to environmental performance for **new** homes (and has replaced BRE Ecohomes).

The Code's purpose is to establish minimum standards for energy and water use, surface water management, site waste management, household waste management and the use of construction materials on site.

All new builds are required to have a CSH certificate as part of a Home Report (even if nil rated) in Scotland, where Home Reports are still in operation. Registered Social Landlords and other organisations using Homes and Communities Agency funding will be required to meet particular code levels to receive grant funding.

For more detail see *Code for Sustainable Homes* on page 412.

Building Regulations Part L

Part L of the Building Regulations, entitled *Conservation of Fuel and Power*, has been operational since April 2006. Part L 2010 has now been issued.

The purpose of Part L is to establish energy standards for all types of buildings. It is under this section that new buildings particularly are required to be air pressure tested. Part L also advocates that compliance is calculated using the updated version of SAP 2009 for dwellings and Simplified Building Energy Model (SBEM) for non-dwellings.

For more detail see *Part L 2010 compliance* on page 183.

Energy certification of buildings

The *Energy Performance of Buildings Directive* (EPBD) (EU Directive 2002/92/EC), governs and controls energy certification of buildings. It came into force on 4 January 2003. The concept requires that energy performance of a building fabric is assessed each time the building is sold or rented and given an energy rating on an A to G scale – so that future occupiers are able to take into account a building's likely energy performance when deciding to either purchase or rent the property.

For more detail see the EPBD section, page 387.

Site-based management plans for waste

Since 6 April 2008 all construction projects in England worth more than £300,000 have had to have a site waste management plan (SWMP). These aim to help contractors to reduce construction waste and identify the by-products produced, then minimise them by using materials efficiently, using recycled products and ensuring waste is disposed of responsibly. On completion, the performance is checked against targets and lessons learned are carried through to the next job so that individual contractors can build up a portfolio of improvements.

There is, however, ongoing debate with regard to the depth behind some of these green initiatives, and the true carbon cost of recycling materials to a plant that may be some distance from the site.

Landfill Directive

The *Landfill Directive* (EEC/1999/31/EC) came into force on 16 July 1999. It is implemented in the UK through the *Landfill (England and Wales) Regulations* 2002, and through equivalent legislation in Scotland and Northern Ireland. It prohibits **all** businesses from sending non-hazardous waste to landfill without prior treatment. Landfill sites can no longer accept untreated waste. Since 30 October 2007 liquid wastes have been banned from landfill and waste must be treated before it can be land-filled.

For more information see www.environment-agency.gov.uk/business/topics/waste/32122.aspx

Waste Electrical and Electronic Equipment Directive

The *Waste Electrical and Electronic Equipment Directive* (WEEE Directive 2002/96/EC) came into force in January 2007. It aims to reduce the amount of electrical and electronic equipment being produced, and to encourage recycling of equipment. This directive especially affects mechanical and electrical equipment manufacturers and suppliers. It will benefit clients wishing to upgrade their equipment while minimising the disposal cost.

For more information see www.environment-agency.gov.uk/business/topics/waste/32084.aspx

Other

There are also directives that cover groundwater and wastewater protection, which affect extraction for heat pumping. Details can be found on the Environment Agency website: www.environment-agency.gov.uk

The Climate Change Act 2008

The *Climate Change Act* 2008 (enacted November 2008) puts in place a legally binding agreement target to reduce greenhouse gas emissions by at least 80% by 2050, and the government must report every five years on how it is achieving this target.

The Act also sets out the enabling powers for the carbon reduction commitment (see below) and the role of the Climate Change Committee (CCC) that will oversee much of the CRC scheme.

See www.legislation.gov.uk/ukpga/2008/27/contents

The carbon reduction commitment (CRC) Energy Efficiency Scheme

The CRC is a mandatory carbon trading system designed to incentivise organisations to reduce their emissions, thereby helping to meet the target of reducing carbon emissions by 80% by 2050. The scheme will work in tandem with the existing European Union Emissions Trading Scheme (EU ETS) and climate change agreements.

It will initially include organisations with one or more half-hourly electrical meter readings over 6,000mwh in 2008 (including all subsidiaries, except where large enough to qualify in their own right). The CRC is expected to gradually include all organisations.

Government policy based on public consultation was released in October 2009, a result of which is that the first year (April 2010–April 2011) of the Introductory Phase is a monitoring period.

For further information see www.decc.gov.uk and the CRC section on page 400.

Green Investment Bank (GIB)

The UK coalition government has backed plans for a Green Investment Bank, which would help fund projects such as railways, offshore wind power and waste management.

The original Labour proposal was to establish a £2 billion bank backed, with half of the funds coming from government asset sales and the other half from the private sector.

The coalition government has not yet revealed its own plans for how the bank would work, however, it is likely to be from the issuing of 'green' investment bonds, and probably would take control of most of the funding available for green technologies and carbon saving infrastructure and development.

Low Carbon Buildings Programme (LCBP)

Phase 1 of the Low Carbon Buildings Programme has now closed, and any new applications for Phase 2 are also closed. The Building Research Establishment (BRE), which manages Phase 2, will honour all applications but claimants must draw down their grant by the end of February 2011. The scheme ended on 1 April 2011.

This programme has effectively been replaced by the Feed in Tariff and the Renewable Heat Incentive.

For further information see:

❖   www.lowcarbonbuildings.org.uk/Microgeneration-for-your-home/Closure-of-the-Low-Carbon-Buildings-Programme; and

❖   www.lowcarbonbuildingsphase2.org.uk/

Renewables Obligation Certificates (ROCs)

A Renewables Obligation Certificate (ROC) is a green certificate set up under the Renewable Obligation Order (RO). It is issued to an accredited generator for eligible renewable electricity generated within the UK and supplied to customers within the UK by a licensed electricity supplier.

The scheme originally came into effect in April 2002 in England, Wales and Scotland and in April 2005 in Northern Ireland but is continually updated. The day-to-day functions are performed by Ofgem.

The RO places an obligation on UK electricity suppliers to source an increasing proportion of their electricity from renewable sources. The current obligation in England and Wales for 2010/11 is 0.111 ROCs per MWh, i.e. approximately 11% renewable electricity.

Suppliers meet their obligations by presenting sufficient ROCs. Where suppliers do not have sufficient ROCs to meet their obligations, they must pay an equivalent amount into a fund, the proceeds of which are paid back on a pro-rated basis to those suppliers that have presented ROCs.

For further information see www.ofgem.gov.uk/Sustainability/Environment/RenewablObl/Pages/RenewablObl.aspx

Feed in Tariff (FiT)

The FiT is paid by electricity generators directly to people that have installed an eligible renewable energy system. Eligibility criteria includes a requirement that the system generates under 5MW (which would be most non-industrial systems) and that the installation was by an approved installer.

Older systems that were installed before July 2009 but were registered for the Renewables Obligation scheme (ROCs) will also qualify, but at a reduced generation rate of 9p/kWh. Newer systems may qualify if they are a retrofit or a new build. Retrofit has a 41.3p/kWh generation FiT and new build has a 36.1p/kWh generation FiT.

The export tariff has a minimum rate of 3p/kWh (which is linked to the Retail Price Index). This export tariff can be negotiated, i.e. if you have a large generation system you might be able to get a better rate, but this is the minimum.

For example, a small domestic system of around 1.5kW might provide around 1,000kWh of electricity every year based on orientation, shading, etc. The average household consumption in the UK is around 3,300kWh per annum so a small domestic system might provide around a third of the electricity needs. Such a system would provide an income of around £360 p.a. (1,000kWh/yr x 36.1p/kWh for new build) and the householder would also be able to use that electricity to reduce its costs. If that electricity is then exported rather than used, there is an additional tariff income of £30 p.a. (1,000kWh/yr x 3p/kWh), based on the minimum rate.

Examples of eligible technologies include:

❖   photovoltaic;

❖   wind;

❖ anaerobic digestion; and

❖ hydroelectric.

Renewable Heat Incentive (RHI)

The RHI is similar to the FiT, but is used to encourage heat generation, such as solar hot water. The DECC planned to introduce this scheme in April 2011, but so far has only completed consultation (the government announced details on 10 March 2011). The regulations were originally expected to be approved during 2011 for the introduction of RHI in October 2012. The principle will be that you could get paid a set amount each year as an incentive for you to replace your existing fossil fuel heating system (e.g. gas, oil or coal) with a renewable technology (e.g. wood fuel).

The government does not propose to measure the heat generated from installations. Instead, an estimated figure will be used to work out payments. The estimated figure represents the amount of heat energy needed to warm the home and/or hot water and will vary by house age and size, as well as by technology. It is proposed that payments would be made annually to householders.

Eligible technologies include:

❖ air, water and ground source heat pumps;

❖ solar thermal;

❖ biomass boilers;

❖ renewable combined heat and power;

❖ use of biogas and bioliquids; and

❖ injection of biomethane into the natural gas grid.

For further information see www.decc.gov.uk/en/content/cms/what_we_do/ uk_supply/energy_mix/renewable/policy/renewable_heat/incentive/ incentive.aspx

Carbon Emissions Reduction Target (CERT)

Under CERT, energy suppliers will provide grants and offers to *help private owners* pay for energy efficiency measures and renewable energy technologies for the home. Grants and offers can be taken from any energy company, regardless of whether they supply your gas and electricity.

Community Sustainable Energy Programme (CSEP)

CSEP is an open grants programme run by BRE, an award partner of the Big Lottery Fund. Part of the Fund's Changing Spaces programme, CSEP has been set up to help *not-for-profit community-based organisations* in England to reduce their energy bills and environmental impact.

Both capital and project development grants are available under this scheme. Capital grants are available for the purchase and installation of a range of low carbon technologies (such as solar water heating, photovoltaics or wood-fuelled boilers), along with various energy efficiency measures (such as cavity wall insulation). Project Development Grants are available for feasibility studies.

For further information see www.communitysustainable.org.uk

Low Carbon Infrastructure Fund (LCIF)

Circa £20 million capital funding has been made available to support low carbon infrastructure exemplars in the Growth Points and Growth Areas, to reduce carbon emissions from housing.

Eligibility criteria include:

❖ exemplar status – for instance, size of scheme, support to new and existing homes, technologies deployed;

❖ affordable heat and power – provisions to protect the fuel poor;

❖ fuel diversity – use of renewables or extending the efficiency of fossil fuels;

❖ readiness – ability to allocate and spend the fund within two years; and

❖ leverage – commitment of funding or assets from other project partners.

For further information see www.homesandcommunities.co.uk/ourwork/low-carbon-infrastructure-0

Energy Saving Programme (ESP)

Circa £83 million additional funding was made available to help social landlords insulate hard-to-treat cavity walls that otherwise would not be filled under the Decent Homes programme.

Eligibility criteria included:

❖ must be Category 3 cavity wall insulation, or more than 80% Category 3;

❖ must be additional to works already planned;

❖ must be planned and delivered within agreed timeframe, and before end of 2010/11; and

❖ minimum bids considered – 1,000 properties. HCA will consider bids from consortia.

The programme concluded in March 2011, for further information see www.homesandcommunities.co.uk/ourwork/existing-stock

Retrofit for the Future

Currently £17 million of government funding is available to test low carbon building technology in the Retrofit for the Future programme (approx. £142k/unit).

For more information see www.innovateuk.org/competitions/retrofit-for-the-future.ashx

Energy efficiency loans for SMEs to replace equipment

Unsecured interest-free energy efficiency loans of up to £100,000 (£200,000 in Northern Ireland) are available for SMEs through the Carbon Trust when replacing or upgrading existing equipment with a more energy-efficient version (on projects such as lighting, boilers or insulation).

Details of the scheme and an online application form can be found at www.carbontrust.co.uk/cut-carbon-reduce-costs/products-services/business-loans/pages/loans.aspx

Planning Policy Guidance and Statements (PPGs and PPSs)

PPS1: Delivering Sustainable Development

This sets out the government's overarching policies on the delivery of sustainable development through the planning system.

PPS1 Supplement: Planning and Climate Change

This supplement sets out how planning policy should contribute to reducing emissions. Therefore planning authorities should take this supplement into consideration when drafting Local Development Frameworks by defining key planning objectives.

PPS1 Supplement: Eco-towns

In July 2009, the then Housing Minister, John Healey, announced the publication of the PPS supplement dealing with eco-towns. Eco-towns will be new towns, of a minimum of 5,000 homes, which are to be exemplar green developments. This PPS provides the standards any eco-town will have to adhere to.

The schemes considered are:

❖ Whitehill-Bordon in Hampshire;

❖ St Austell (China Clay Community) in Cornwall;

❖ Rackheath (Norwich) in Norfolk; and

❖ North West Bicester in Oxfordshire.

For related information see *Defining sustainability* on page 404.

PPS 22: Renewable Energy

This PPS enables local authorities to ensure that a significant percentage of buildings and energy requirements are generated from on-site renewables as a condition of planning. It links in with the future requirements of Part L as projected. Different councils vary their requirements. Typically 10% is requested but some authorities demand 20%. The initial running has been made primarily by the local authorities in the south-east, in particular Merton and Croydon, hence why this is often called the 'Merton Rule'.

For related information see *Renewable and low carbon energy* on page 389.

Selection of measures coming into force which may affect UK legislation

❖ **Evaluation and Revision of the Action Plan for Energy Efficiency**: European energy policy seeks to enable the EU to reduce greenhouse gases by at least 20%, to reduce energy consumption by 20% and to increase to 20% the share of renewable energies in energy consumption by 2020. A major mid-term review to evaluate its effectiveness and results is taking place.

❖ **Commission Green Paper, 22 June 2005, *Energy Efficiency – or Doing More With Less***: the EU is looking at ways to reward energy-saving behaviour.

Standard contractual changes

Joint Contracts Tribunal (JCT) changes to contract

Following a period of consultation with the construction industry, the JCT included contract clauses to enable greater controls on sustainable matters and selection of materials.

The clauses are located in the schedule of Supplemental Provisions, which is to apply unless the contract is amended to state that it does not, or unless there are some other contractual arrangements that deal with the same issues.

The sustainability wording encourages the contractor to suggest economically viable changes to the works, which might result in environmental benefits to the works or the life cycle of the building. For example, this could involve the contractor revisiting the specification and recommending the use of a particular clean technology (or 'cleantech') if appropriate. The wording also requires contractors to provide the employer with information on the environmental impact of the materials they select and use.

Contributed by Robert Burke, robert.burke@watts.co.uk

The carbon reduction commitment (CRC) Energy Efficiency Scheme

The CRC Energy Efficiency Scheme (formerly known as the Carbon Reduction Commitment) is the UK's mandatory climate change and energy saving scheme. It is designed to incentivise organisations to reduce their emissions and works in tandem with the existing European Union Emissions Trading Scheme (EU ETS) as well as the Climate Change Agreements.

The Department of Energy and Climate Change consider the scheme to be central to the strategy for reducing the UK's carbon dioxide (CO_2) emissions in accordance with the *Climate Change Act* 2008. The UK's goal is to reduce CO_2 emissions by 80% before 2050.

The CRC commenced on 1 April 2010, having been first outlined in an Energy White Paper published in May 2007. The scheme focuses on energy in use but at a corporate level. It became law via the *CRC Energy Efficiency Scheme Order* 2010, which came into force on 22 March 2010.

Prior to being laid before Parliament, the Order was subject to public consultation on the draft guidance for how UK organisations should measure and report their greenhouse gas emissions, with Watts Group PLC being one of the consultees.

The government response to the consultation was released in October 2009 and included a policy decision that the first year (April 2010–April 2011) of the Introductory Phase would be a monitoring period.

Initial participation in the Scheme is limited, however, it is expected to gradually include all organisations. Where a company's meter readings exceeded 6,000mwh in 2008 (including all subsidiaries, except where large enough to qualify in their own right), full participation in the Scheme is required. Where a company's energy usage is below the threshold, there is a general requirement for the organisation to disclose information on its half-hourly energy usage. It is estimated that initially 5,000 organisations will qualify for full participation, including supermarkets, banks, local authorities and all central government departments. A further 15,000 will have to make an information disclosure.

Where the landlord pays energy bills for areas occupied by a tenant, providing common services, this energy counts towards the total energy use of the landlord, i.e. a shopping centre or shared office.

For further information see: www.decc.gov.uk

Contributed by Robert Burke, robert.burke@watts.co.uk and Trevor Rushton, trevor.rushton@watts.co.uk

Green leases

Commercial buildings are estimated to contribute around 20% of UK carbon emissions. Property owners and occupiers are under increasing pressure to improve the energy efficiency of their buildings and to reduce their carbon footprint, not only to meet their environmental responsibilities but also to:

- ❖ reduce operating costs in the face of rising fuel costs and challenging market conditions;

- ❖ comply with environmental legislation such as the CRC Energy Efficiency Scheme and energy performance certification regime; and

- ❖ enhance their reputation with clients and employees.

For owner-occupiers, the motivation to improve the sustainability of commercial space is clear. In the commercial leasehold sector, the mismatch between the benefits of environmental improvements gained by landlords and tenants poses what has become known as the 'split incentive' problem. Both parties have something to gain but their financial incentives are different, as are the potential gains in terms of brand enhancement and other 'soft' benefits. And where a building is leased to more than one tenant the problem is exacerbated: those on short-term leases have no vested interest in long-term sustainability of the premises and are unlikely to willingly contribute upfront to environmental improvements that offer no benefit to them. Tenants on longer leases may be more inclined to make a contribution as they will reap the long-term benefits, but will not wish to pay for their fellow leaseholders' share of the cost.

One way to tackle this problem is to adopt a 'green lease' which enables the landlord and tenant to operate the building in as sustainable a way as is commercially viable for both parties. Green leases have been gaining momentum in the UK for a number of years, aiming to help owners and occupiers agree energy, water and waste reduction strategies that best fit the individual circumstances of their particular premises, while at the same time distributing the related costs and benefits more fairly between the parties.

The Investment Property Forum (IPF) defines a green lease as one 'which, within its terms or through an attached schedule, includes provisions that encourage either the landlord, tenant or both, to carry out their roles in a more sustainable way'. The details of these provisions and the way in which they encourage the parties to reduce their carbon footprint and take a responsible approach to the environmental aspects of building ownership/occupancy are negotiated between landlord and tenant. However, generally, these relate to setting, monitoring and/or achieving targets for energy and water use and managing waste. Emphasis may also be placed on using sustainable construction or refurbishment materials.

In order to 'green' a commercial lease, it is likely that the lease terms that will need to be closely scrutinised and appropriately worded will include those dealing with repair, user, outgoings, alienation/assignment, service charges, rent reviews and reinstatement. However, there is little mileage in drawing up a green lease that either or both of the parties find it hard to adhere to. It is key to the success of green leases that the lease terms are realistic and that both parties are in agreement. It is also important that the terms of a green lease are seen to be enforceable. According to the IPD, it is important that any elements, 'that might undermine enforceability are clearly established, including the means through which compliance is demonstrated, the penalties that non-compliance will bring and what rectification is available to each party'.

Green leases toolkits

The Better Buildings Partnership (BBP) has produced a comprehensive toolkit for green leases, aiming to help owners and occupiers of commercial buildings to work together to reduce the environmental impact of their premises.

The toolkit includes:

- ❖ best practice recommendations which are designed to help owners and occupiers agree appropriate lease terms;
- ❖ a model Memorandum of Understanding;
- ❖ model form green lease clauses, which the BBP believes are the minimum for inclusion in new and renewal leases depending on the particular circumstances.

Another useful resource for landlords and tenants interested in improving the energy efficiency of their buildings is the British Property Foundation (BPF) LES-TER project. The Landlord's Energy Statement (LES) is a free tool, accessed via the internet, that enables landlords to calculate the energy/CO_2 requirement of providing communal services in commercial buildings. LES then allows comparisons to be made against equivalent buildings and identifies areas for improvement. It can also be used to show year-on-year improvements. The Tenants Energy Review (TER) is an equivalent tool for tenants – calculating direct energy use and identifying occupancy features which influence energy demand and areas for improvement. By using both tools, users can also put together the information required for a Display Energy Certificate.

Good practice guide

The Centre for Research in the Built Environment (CRIBE), based at Cardiff University, has also produced a three-part good practice guide *Incorporating Environmental Best Practice into Commercial Tenant Lease Agreements*. The first part of the guide gives 15 model lease clauses, covering service charges, repairs, consents, financial aspects and communication, focusing on the benefits for landlords and tenants.

The aim is to encourage landlords and tenants to discuss the various clauses and pick those that are most appropriate for their circumstances. The second part of the guide looks at the legislative background to green leases and Part 3 sets out recommendations for best practice in existing, multi-tenanted commercial buildings, which CRIBE describes as, 'the biggest challenge for improvements in energy performance within the UK'.

Further information

- ❖ Better Buildings Partnership: www.betterbuildingspartnership.co.uk
- ❖ LES-TER: www.les-ter.org
- ❖ Investment Property Databank: www.ipd.com
- ❖ Royal Institution of Chartered Surveyors: www.rics.org
- ❖ British Property Federation: www.bpf.org.uk
- ❖ BCSC: www.bcsc.org.uk
- ❖ British Council for Offices: www.bco.org.uk

Contributed by Paul Lovelock, paul.lovelock@watts.co.uk and Lesley Davis, 01243 784054, lesley@davisaylingmedia.co.uk, of Davis Ayling Media, Genista Cottage, Stane Street, Westhampnett, Chichester, PO18 0PA.

Sustainable development

Defining sustainability

What is sustainability?

Sustainability is meeting 'the needs of the present without compromising the ability of future generations to meet their own need.' (Source: the 1987 Brundtland report on sustainable development)

Sustainability often means different things to different people but is commonly referred to in terms of the 'triple bottom line': optimising the three key elements of **economic**, **social** and **environmental** sustainability – living within environmental limits; ensuring a strong, healthy and equal society; and maintaining a sustainable economy. In industry it is often talked about in the same way as Corporate Social Responsibility (CSR).

Why do we need to be more sustainable?

Buildings are responsible for almost half of the UK's carbon emissions, half of our water consumption, about a third of landfill waste and one quarter of all raw materials used in the economy. The construction industry therefore has a central role in ensuring that the processes are refined and changed in order to reduce carbon emissions in line with government targets.

The buildings we design and construct today need to be of low carbon intensity or ideally 'carbon neutral' and must be adaptable for our future climate. There are different facets of the answer to the above question and these are listed below.

Social responsibility

Businesses are increasingly recognising the importance of green credentials as a key part of corporate responsibility reporting and maintaining reputation. By engaging in sustainable practices, businesses can meet their social obligations, and their shareholders' or stakeholders' requirements, and can create new growth and business opportunities.

Energy security is a major concern to the UK, with heavy reliance on importing energy from overseas. This, coupled with an increasing demand and reduction of supply, means that UK is at risk of not having control over its energy. Reduction of energy use can help mitigate this.

The cost of carbon emissions to the economy has been put at approximately $300/t according to the Stern Review (2006), and even taking into account the carbon reduction commitment (CRC) trading cost of £12/t, it shows the significant impact of carbon emissions on the wider economy.

Financial incentives and penalties

Meeting the CRC commitments and generally being more sustainable can incur a higher initial capital cost. However, there are a number of considerations that mean holistically the effect is not as financially unviable as it might first appear.

- ❖ **Offsets** may mean that sustainable concepts help save money elsewhere: better wall insulation also helps acoustic values; green roofs also help surface water run-off, support ecology and provide cooling, etc.

- ❖ There is also evidence that shows that an energy efficient and sustainable development **increases the value of asset** – rental rates can be increased, for exmaple, or homes sold at a premium.

- ❖ Renewable technologies can also now provide an income in the form of a **Feed-in Tariff (FiT)** – see *Green legislation*, page 393. The service provider will pay a tariff back to the owner of the renewable generation, and a renewable heat incentive is also being considered.

❖ **Tax relief** in the form of Enhanced Capital Allowances (ECAs) for some renewable energy enhancements may also be relevant. Specialist advice is needed for this.

❖ **Funding opportunities** – there is limited funding available for schemes that are energy efficient, although these are in the process of being phased out and have restrictions.

Therefore consideration beyond initial capital costs alone must also be made and more emphasis put on the analysis of life cycle costs (see *Life cycle costing*, page 121) together with the tangible and intangible investment for the life of an asset. Payback periods and life cycle costs can be a compelling argument when proposing sustainable design.

Altogether, more objective and alternative value assessments need to be considered to demonstrate the entire benefits of being sustainable.

Legislative impact

Notwithstanding any financial benefits, legislative requirements are being imposed on development through planning policies (such as PPS4; London Plan, etc.) and increasingly restrictive Building Regulations.

The most immediate regulation to be imposed on the property industry is the CRC energy saving scheme. This is being introduced in phases and commenced in 2010. It incorporates a carbon trading league table for those companies with a half-hourly energy demand of greater than 6,000mwh per annum. This will result in additional costs for all companies within the scheme and may either damage or enhance their CSR.

See also the CRC section on page 400.

Sustainability and risk management

A sustainable approach to development has also become an exercise in risk management and risk avoidance. For example, exposure to the high costs of rising fuel prices can be mitigated by taking the time to include sustainable design solutions at inception. Another example, in respect of planning applications, is a development which focuses on sustainable objectives thereby increasing its chances of gaining planning permission and minimising opportunities for stakeholder objections.

The current UK Government uses policies, regulations and legislation that penalise unsustainable practices and reward those who actively promote sustainability. Compliance with such policies, regulations and legislation mitigates and manages business risk, particularly with respect to prosecution for breach of regulations, public relations, business survival and cost exposure.

Effectively with the stick (legislation and policy, with ever-increasing targets) and the carrot (incentives such as tax relief) approach being employed by government, it is more financially advantageous to have a sustainable development than one that is not.

The environmental impact of construction activities and the built environment

Everyday modern activities within business or domestic life have a cumulative impact on the environment and therefore it is up to every individual or business to take responsibility and accountability for taking action to minimise the impact of human activity – small steps are important to the overall achievement.

The increase in landfill taxes, costs of hazardous waste disposal, the climate change levy and Building Regulations, for example, are designed to encourage more resource efficiency. This by implication will have an effect on the sustainability bottom line, and stimulate improvement in efficiencies (a virtuous circle).

Sustainability

The construction industry and the built environment have an important contribution to make in supporting long-term sustainability objectives associated with the effective management of:

- ❖ materials and natural resources;
- ❖ energy;
- ❖ water;
- ❖ emissions, effluents and waste;
- ❖ transport;
- ❖ ecology; and
- ❖ land use, urban form and design.

From client inception onwards, developments must be designed and procured to embrace all of the environmental, social and economic issues associated with immediate and long-term sustainability objectives.

Creating a sustainable built environment

The *Strategy for sustainable construction*, published in June 2008 by the UK Government in association with the Strategic Forum for Construction, illustrates that this joint industry and government strategy is based on a shared recognition of the need to deliver a radical change in the sustainability of the construction industry. See www.berr.gov.uk/files/file46535.pdf

The solutions to achieving sustainable objectives demand a holistic and often innovative approach. Many construction activities and buildings will not achieve total sustainability, as it will not always be practicably or feasibly possible. However, by demonstrating a positive commitment to environmental 'damage limitation', construction and property professionals can collectively contribute to providing a more sustainable built environment.

The following guiding principles should be followed to design for sustainable developments:

- ❖ Adopt the principles of the London Plan in terms of energy – Lean, Clean, Green – by making existing buildings more energy efficient (e.g. fabric, energy efficient M&E); using efficient energy delivery (e.g. CHP); and using renewables (e.g. solar panels).
- ❖ Recycle more in order to save the energy used to manufacture, transport and dispose of materials – even the materials from demolition on site.
- ❖ Physically orientate buildings to maximise their capacity to exploit solar energy.
- ❖ Utilise prefabricated components.
- ❖ Incorporate natural/sustainable/recyclable building materials where practical into construction.
- ❖ Procure low maintenance materials in order to reduce further the energy and resources used during the future life of the building.
- ❖ Use materials that do not emit harmful gases, radiation or dust.
- ❖ Recycle rainwater and grey water and specify water-efficient devices.
- ❖ Design buildings to be sympathetic with their local environment and encourage ecology and habitat restoration.
- ❖ Design to minimise waste generation and consider the long-term impacts of design decisions.
- ❖ Adopt 'just-in-time' ordering where possible to prevent the wastage of unused materials.

❖ Educate all designers, site operatives, senior management, end users and maintenance staff to enhance their understanding of sustainability, not only in the design and construction but also in the use of the asset.

❖ Consider low carbon construction and balance the carbon emission with actual 'embodied' carbon, i.e. that used in the manufacture, transportation and construction processes, for example, by procuring local materials, manufacturing and labour when practical.

❖ Consider 'Building for Life' (www.buildingforlife.org) and 'Lifetime homes' (www.lifetimehomes.org.uk) specifications for housing developments.

These guiding principles are by no means comprehensive. They simply provide a flavour of the scope that environmental sustainability might encompass. It is, however, important to consider the hidden environmental costs of recycling and reusing – travel to recycling facilities should also be factored in when considering overall carbon footprints.

There are tools and guidance from various organisations that will help define the objectives for sustainable development: Building Research Establishment (BRE), Homes and Communities Agency (HCA), Commission for Architecture and the Built Environment (CABE – disbanded but information is still accessible), Energy Saving Trust, Carbon Trust and WRAP.

The most common assessment tool is BREEAM (the Building Research Establishment Environmental Assessment Method). This can rate the sustainability impact of a development, particularly with regard to the environmental impact of a development, and is increasingly being championed through legislation and planning policy. See *Environmental labelling*, below.

Further information

Guidance on, tools for, and examples of, good practice sustainable development can be found at:

❖ www.berr.gov.uk/files/file46535.pdf

❖ www.sustainablecities.org.uk/good_practice

❖ www.cabe.org.uk/files/building-sustainable-communities.pdf

❖ www.buildingforlife.org/

❖ ww2.defra.gov.uk/environment/economy/sustainable/

❖ www.sd-commission.org.uk

❖ www.wrap.org.uk/construction/index.html

❖ www.carbontrust.co.uk

❖ www.energysavingtrust.org.uk

See also the handbook sections on *Green legislation* (page 393), *Environmental labelling* (below), *Code for Sustainable Homes* (page 412) and *Renewable and low carbon energy* (page 389).

Contributed by Cullum Alexander, cullum.alexander@watts.co.uk and Robert Burke, robert.burke@watts.co.uk

Environmental labelling

There are a number of different environmental labelling schemes used in the UK and internationally. The systems are normally promoted or developed by the Green Building Council of that region. Developers and designers can utilise these labelling systems for a range of reasons, including creation of better environments for people to work in, increased building efficiency, improved marketability, increased value and rentals and also as a benchmark for comparing buildings. On the whole they are voluntary but are increasingly being included in legislation or planning policy.

BREEAM

The Building Research Establishment Environmental Assessment Method (BREEAM) is the world's most widely used system for assessing, reviewing and improving a range of environmental impacts associated with buildings. BREEAM can be used on any type of building, both new and existing.

Since its launch in 1990, BREEAM has been increasingly accepted in the UK construction and property sectors as offering best practice in environmental design and management.

Buildings are assessed against performance criteria set by the BRE and awarded 'credits' based on their level of performance. The building's performance is then rated as pass, good, very good, excellent and outstanding. The outstanding rating was issued with the 2008 version of BREEAM.

BREEAM covers a range of building types, including:

- ❖ offices;
- ❖ homes (called *Code for Sustainable Homes*);
- ❖ industrial units;
- ❖ retail;
- ❖ education;
- ❖ courts;
- ❖ healthcare;
- ❖ prisons; and
- ❖ data centres.

In addition, there are also Bespoke, International and Gulf assessments to customise BREEAM for particular regions or multi-use buildings.

Note that for the residential sector BREEAM developed a system called EcoHomes which will be replaced shortly. For new build projects this was superseded by the *Code for Sustainable Homes* (CSH), see page 412.

A new BREEAM standard for domestic refurbishment is in the final stages of trial and has already been taken up by one local authority. The new method is designed to sit alongside CSH, providing a means of setting environmental requirements for refurbishment projects.

BREEAM In-Use assessment was introduced to the market on 5 June 2009. This allows an organisation to assess an existing asset, the management of an asset and the environmental performance of the organisation within the asset. The ratings are the same as the usual BREEAM assessment. This can lead to improvements in the environmental credentials of an asset, the building management or the organisation.

BREEAM is updated every year to ensure best practice and relevance to changing standards and regulations. The challenge to achieve the highest rating has increased as targets are being continually raised. Mandatory credits have also been introduced that require specific 'credit' to be gained in order to achieve a higher rating.

A BREEAM assessment is undertaken at the completion of the design stage and a certificate is then issued. The post-construction phase of the assessment is then undertaken in order to ensure that what was designed is actually built. On conclusion of the project and after practical completion, a post-construction certificate is awarded.

The BREEAM scheme requires a commitment to a number of areas that are reviewed by independent assessors who are trained and licensed by BRE.

These areas are:

- ❖ **Management**: overall policy, site management via the Considerate Constructors Scheme and procedural issues.

- ❖ **Health and well-being**: both internal and external issues affecting occupants' health and well-being.

- ❖ **Energy efficiency**: including operational energy and carbon dioxide issues. This is based on the EPC rating of a building.

- ❖ **Transport**: location-related factors, including amenities, public transport and provision of cycling facilities.

- ❖ **Water consumption**: efficiency and leak detection.

- ❖ **Materials**: environmental implications and life-cycle impact.

- ❖ **Waste**: associated with the construction process and recycling facilities within the building.

- ❖ **Land use**: regarding greenfield and brownfield sites.

- ❖ **Ecology**: including enhancement of the site as well as ecological value conservation.

- ❖ **Pollution**: of air, water and the local environment.

- ❖ **Innovation**.

To achieve an outstanding rating, the most cost-effective approach is to address the main issues at the earliest point of the design process with input from the full project design team. An interim design and post-construction prediction checklist is available to assist with this process.

The BRE have also implemented the accredited professional (AP) qualification that requires qualified assessors to attend an examination. Two additional innovation credits can be awarded if an AP is involved in the project from Stage C.

A BREEAM assessor can be used to coordinate and collate input from the team and to track the development of ideas. The assessor can also give advice about BREEAM to the entire project team at the start of the project. As the scheme progresses, the assessor can:

- ❖ provide specialist advice on the specification of products to achieve particular BREEAM credits;

- ❖ undertake preliminary BREEAM assessments to assess the predicted rating; and

- ❖ provide a sustainability report for submission for planning approval.

At completion of the post-construction element of the project, a certificate illustrating a final score and rating is issued by the BRE that can be used for marketing the associated asset.

Ratings are Good, Very Good, Excellent and Outstanding.

Further information

- ❖ www.breeam.org

LEED

Leadership in Energy and Environmental Design (LEED) is an American environmental system developed by the US Green Building Council. Whereas BREEAM is often tied into planning (or, in the case of the *Code for Sustainable Homes*, grant funding), LEED is a largely voluntary system. It is often seen as a competitor to BREEAM in regions such as the Gulf and India, where both systems are used. LEED is divided into different build categories similar to BREEAM:

- ❖ **Sustainable sites**: A broad category that covers using previously developed land; minimises a building's impact on ecosystems and waterways; encourages regionally appropriate landscaping;

rewards smart transportation choices; controls storm water run-off; and reduces erosion, light pollution, heat island effect and construction-related pollution.

❖ **Water efficiency**: Water reduction, inside and out.

❖ **Energy and atmosphere**: Reduction of energy use, and the use of renewable and clean sources of energy.

❖ **Materials and resources**: Encourages the selection of sustainable materials (embodied carbon) and reduction of waste as well as reuse and recycling.

❖ **Indoor environmental quality**: Improvement of indoor air as well as providing access to natural daylight and views, and improving acoustics.

❖ **Locations and linkages**: Transportation, access to open space, etc.

❖ **Awareness and education**: Education of the users to ensure that the building is used properly.

❖ **Innovation in design**: Bonus points for projects that use new and innovative technologies and strategies.

❖ **Regional priority**: Credits meeting regionally important issues/local priorities.

Ratings are Silver, Gold and Platinum.

Other systems

DGNB Certification System

The German Sustainable Building Certification was developed by the German Sustainable Building Council (DGNB) together with the Federal Ministry of Transport, Building, and Urban Affairs (BMVBS) to be used as a tool for the planning and evaluation of buildings. Six subjects affect the evaluation:

❖ ecology;

❖ economy;

❖ social-cultural and functional topics;

❖ techniques;

❖ processes; and

❖ location.

Ratings are Bronze, Silver, or Gold.

Green Star

This is an environmental labelling system developed by the Green Building Council of Australia, based on similar principles to both BREEAM and LEED. It is a voluntary system generally used in the Australasian region and South Africa. The nine categories included within all Green Star rating tools are:

❖ management;

❖ indoor environment quality;

❖ energy;

❖ transport;

❖ water;

❖ materials;

❖ land use and ecology;

❖ emissions; and

❖ innovation.

Similarly to BREEAM, these credits are scored and weighted. The environmental weighting factors vary across states and territories to reflect diverse environmental concerns across Australia. The ratings that can be achieved are 4, 5 and 6 star ratings.

For further information see: www.gbca.org.au/green-star/

IGBC Green Rating System

Indian Green Building Council (IGBC) has developed voluntary green building rating programmes (Homes, SEZ – special economic zones – and Factory). Rating programmes help projects to address all aspects related to environmental issues and to measure the performance of the building/project. The rating system evaluates certain credit points using a prescriptive approach and other credits on a performance-based approach.

LEED and BREEAM are also widely accepted labelling systems in India.

CASBEE

Comprehensive Assessment System for Building Environmental Efficiency (CASBEE) is a voluntary system in Japan, but is currently being included in planning policy in some regions. In contrast to the other systems, CASBEE looks at Q – Quality and performance (which evaluates improvement in living amenity for the building users, within the boundary of the building); and L – Loadings (which evaluates negative aspects of environmental impacts of the building).

The ratings that can be achieved are 3, 4 and 5 out of a maximum of 5.

For further information see: www.ibec.or.jp/CASBEE/english/index.htm

SKA

In 2005 Skansen, an interior construction company, commissioned a research project with RICS and AECOM which then developed into the Ska rating. Ska complements other labelling methods and labels 100% of the environmental performance related to the scope of fit-out projects, rather than being a whole building assessment, and is designed to rate and compare the environmental performance of fit-out projects for only office buildings in the UK. They are currently looking to develop this for other types of fit-out.

Ska comprises 99 good practice measures covering similar categories to the other labelling systems. As each fit-out project is unique, Ska Rating scores the project on basis only of those measures that are relevant to the project called 'Measures In Scope'. Typically between 30–60 measures are likely to apply to most projects, and they are ranked from 1 to 99, (1 is the highest and 99 the lowest) depending on the importance from a sustainability perspective. The project has to achieve a number of the highest-ranked Measures in Scope in order to rate, known as Gateway Measures.

The score is ranked in three thresholds, Gold, Silver and Bronze (75%, 50% or 25% respectively).

The Ska rating is assessed three times during the life cyle:

- ❖ during design/planning delivery;
- ❖ during construction; and
- ❖ finally with a post-occupancy assessment.

For further information see: www.ska-rating.com/

Labelling systems in development

Common Carbon Metric

The World Green Building Council has formed a partnership with the Sustainable Building Alliance and the UNEP Sustainable Building Construction Initiative to develop the Common Carbon Metric Framework (CCM). This is to establish a benchmark metric to enable comparative energy use across international portfolios and to help provide consistent measurement of carbon trading.

Code for Sustainable Buildings

The UK Green Building Council has advocated for a *Code for Sustainable Buildings* to provide a single framework for all new and existing non-domestic buildings. They set up a task force containing members of RIBA and representatives from prominent consultancies (such as Davis Langdon, Arup, Faber Maunsell, etc.).

This new framework would differ from the BRE models of *Code for Sustainable Homes* and BREEAM in a number of ways, namely:

❖ it would set an 'escalator' of targets, e.g. CO_2 emissions per m^2, but not the method of reaching them;

❖ it would look at a 'building MOT', i.e. reviewing the running and use of the building over its life cycle; and

❖ it would cover refurbishments.

A report by the task group was issued in March 2009 and a 'Code Working Group' is expected to form to develop the policy and guidance for the code, dependent on the outcome of further government consultation.

For further information see: www.ukgbc.org

Global Green Rating

A group of property developers and investors have tried developing a global 'Green Rating' and will look at energy use, carbon emissions, water use, waste generation, health and location close to public transport.

The scheme was launched in Spain in 2009 to try and develop a global benchmark that moves away from new build (which is the focus of a lot of labelling systems). It does however have a lot of competition from local, more established labelling systems and does not seem to be well utilised.

Contributed by Cullum Alexander, cullum.alexander@watts.co.uk

Code for Sustainable Homes

Driven by the wider requirements of the EU *Energy Performance of Buildings Directive*, the *Code for Sustainable Homes* (CSH) replaces previous EcoHomes requirements to become the single national standard to measure sustainability of **new** homes. Any residential refurbishments can be certified under Ecohomes XB (a voluntary scheme).

The *Code for Sustainable Homes* was launched on 13 December 2006 and since April 2007 it has completely replaced EcoHomes **for new build homes**. The most recent edition of the code was released in May 2009.

Although this code is produced by the Building Research Establishment (BRE), it is 'owned' by the Department for Communities and Local Government (DCLG) (in contrast to the other BREEAM systems), so the designation of how the credits are applied is dictated by DCLG.

The *Code for Sustainable Homes* can be seen as 'BREEAM Residential' under a different heading, the main difference being that the CSH has been adopted by the Homes and Communities Agency (HCA: www.homesandcommunities.co.uk) and is thus led by them rather than BRE. Under their National Affordable Housing Programme (NAHP) 2008/11, HCA are expected to require all **new** social and affordable housing developments to achieve Level 4 from April 2010. Currently it is proposed that all developments will have to achieve Level 6 by 2014 in order to have access to funding, although this is currently being debated while the definition of zero carbon is being clarified.

Assessments must be undertaken by a Licensed Code Assessor. Assessment involves a pre-assessment at the planning stage; and then formal assessments are made at the design and post-construction stages (which include a BRE audit), after which a certificate is issued.

Home Information Packs (HIPs) are still operational in Scotland (where they are called Home Reports), where a minimum of a nil-rated certificate is needed (HIPs were suspended in England and Wales in 2010).

It is advisable that a Code assessor is appointed early, to enable the design to be aligned with the aspirational code level. A Code assessor can be used to coordinate and collate input from the team and to track the development of ideas – see also BREEAM, page 408.

A list of qualified assessors can be obtained from BRE (see www.breeam.org)

How to score credits

Under the Code, each area or category is broken down into a number of 'issues'. Credits are awarded against these issues, and then a weighting is applied to those credits scored in each category (see the *Code categories* table later) to get the final code score (total number of points).

Code levels

The Code has six levels (see the following table).

Code levels		Total score
Level 1 (★)	above regulatory standards and a similar standard to BRE's Ecohomes PASS level and the Energy Saving Trust's (EST) Good Practice Standard for energy efficiency	36 points
Level 2 (★★)	a similar standard to BRE's EcoHomes GOOD level	48 points
Level 3 (★★★)	a *broadly* similar standard to BRE's EcoHomes VERY GOOD level and the EST's Best Practice Standard for energy efficiency	57 points
Level 4 (★★★★)	broadly set at current exemplary performance Code level 4 is a 44% improvement above Part L 2006 and 25% above Part L 2010	68 points
Level 5 (★★★★★)	based on exemplary performance with high standards of energy and water efficiency	84 points
Level 6 (★★★★★★)	aspirational standard based on zero carbon emissions for the dwelling and high performance across all environmental categories	90 points

The nine categories are detailed in the following *Code categories* table. It should be noted firstly that **energy, health, ecology,** and **management** get high weightings. Secondly, minimum standards must be met for **particular categories (denoted with an 'M' in the table)** just to achieve the minimum entry level. The table gives simplified descriptions, available credits for each issue, and the category weighting factor. The Technical Guide should be referred to for the detail (and the most up to date description), as new editions are constantly being issued. The latest edition, as at going to print, is November 2010, and it has tried to align the Code with Part L (2010).

Code categories

Code categories	Description	Available credits	Category weighting factor
Energy and CO$_2$ emissions			
Dwelling Emission Rate (M)	% improvement of the DER over TER given the SAP calculations	10	
Fabric energy efficiency (M)	to improve fabric energy efficiency performance	9	
Energy display devices	specification of equipment to display energy consumption data	2	
Drying space	where space with posts or fixings is provided for drying clothes – can be in the bathroom but NOT the kitchen	1	
Energy labelled white goods	either using A rated goods, or if not provided then information on what they mean and where to get them	2	
External lighting	amount of external lighting that is dedicated energy efficient fittings, including space and security lighting with timers or daylight switches	2	
LZC energy technologies	% reduction in total carbon emissions that results from using Low or Zero Carbon (LZC) energy technologies	2	
Cycle storage	adequately sized, safe, secure, convenient and weather-proof cycle storage is provided	2	
Home office	space and services in a room to be used effectively as a home office (can be part of another room except the kitchen)	1	
	Category total	31	36.4

Code categories	Description	Available credits	Category weighting factor
Water			
Indoor (potable) water use (M)	use reduction of the predicted potable water in litres/person/day – levels 3 and 4 have mandatory usage of 105l/p/day	5	
External water use	rainwater collection	1	
	Category total	6	9.0
Materials			
Environmental impact of materials (M)	three of the following key elements achieve a D rating or more from the *Green Guide to Specification*: ❖ roof; ❖ external walls; ❖ internal walls; ❖ upper and ground floors; and ❖ windows.	15	
Responsible sourcing of materials – basic building elements	80% of the assessed materials responsibly sourced; additionally, 100% of any timber in these elements must be legally sourced	6	
Responsible sourcing of materials – finishing elements	80% of the assessed materials responsibly sourced; additionally, 100% of any timber in these elements must be legally sourced	3	
	Category total	24	7.2
Surface water run-off			
Management of surface water run-off (M)	as a minimum, ensure that run-off rates and annual volumes of run-off post development will be no greater than the previous conditions for the site. 2 credits for using SUDS to the specifications.	2	
Flood risk	low probability of flooding, or levels of 600mm above flood levels	2	
	Category total	4	2.2
Waste			
Storage of waste (M)	either: all external containers provided under the relevant local authority/recycling schemes, or the minimum capacity of internal waste storage	4	

Sustainability

Code categories	Description	Available credits	Category weighting factor
Construction site waste management (M)	effective and appropriate management of construction site waste	3	
Composting	individual home composting facilities; or a communal or community composting service (within 30m)	1	
	Category total	8	6.4
Pollution			
Global warming potential (GWP) of insulants	**all** insulating materials in the elements of the dwelling avoid the use of substances that have a GWP of less than 5. Note: check the blowing agent	1	
NOx emissions	NOx emissions arising from the operation of space heating and hot water systems for each dwelling type	3	
	Category total	4	2.8
Health and well-being			
Daylighting	❖ kitchens to achieve minimum average daylight factor of at least 2%; ❖ all living rooms, dining rooms and studies (including any home office) must achieve a minimum average daylight factor of at least 1.5%; ❖ 80% of the working plane in kitchens, living rooms, dining rooms and studies (including any home office) must receive direct light from the sky.	3	
Sound insulation	sound insulation greater than Part E of Building Regulations	4	
Private space	outdoor space (private or semi-private) has been provided (specific requirements apply)	1	
Lifetime Homes (M – only to meet level 6)	all the principles of Lifetime Homes have been complied with	4	
	Category total	12	14.0

Code categories	Description	Available credits	Category weighting factor
Management			
Home user guide	a home user guide is available, it is also available in alternative accessible formats, and covers information relating to the site and its surroundings (see the checklists in the Code)	3	
Considerate Constructors Scheme (CCS)	meet best practice or above under CCS or similar scheme	2	
Construction site impacts	procedures to monitor CO_2, water, dust, noise, etc.	2	
Security	Architectural Liaison Officer (ALO) or Crime Prevention Design Adviser (CPDA) is consulted at the design stage and their recommendations are incorporated into the design of the dwelling (an actual Secured by Design Certificate is not required)	2	
	Category total	9	10.0
Ecology			
Ecological value of site	development site is confirmed as land of low ecological value by a qualified ecologist – must be done before any demolition occurs	1	
Ecological enhancement	developer adopts all key recommendations and 30% of additional recommendations of the ecologist	1	
Protection of ecological features	protect existing ecological features from substantial damage during the construction works	1	
Change in ecological value	minimise reductions in the ecological value of the site	4	
Building footprint	ratios of net internal floor area (NIFA): net internal ground floor area (NIGFA) to be met depending on mix of development	2	
	Category total	9	12.0
Total		107	100.0

Conclusion

It is hoped that the Code will offer a range of benefits, in terms of:

❖ the reduced environmental impact of new homes provided;

❖ to consumers, through lower fuel costs; and

❖ to house builders, as a mark of quality assurance.

Further information

For access to the Technical Guidance and other useful information go to:

❖ www.breeam.org/page.jsp?id=86

❖ www.communities.gov.uk/publications/planningandbuilding/
codeguide

❖ www.planningportal.gov.uk/buildingregulations/greenerbuildings/
sustainablehomes

Contributed by Cullum Alexander, cullum.alexander@watts.co.uk

Reused materials

There is widespread recognition that more needs to be done to reduce waste and to recycle or reuse redundant construction materials. By way of example, in 2009 London created some 9.7 million tonnes of construction and demolition waste, around 50% of which was recycled.

The Waste & Resources Action Programme (WRAP) is a major UK programme established by the government in 2000 as part of its waste strategy. WRAP's stated aim is to help the construction sector and its clients use materials more efficiently and to halve waste going to landfill by 2012. Current data shows a total increase of 28% of construction waste sent to landfill between 2008 and 2009, representing a fall from 3.1 million tonnes in 2008 to 2.2 million tonnes by the end of 2009.

Definition of recycled materials

Recycled materials can be defined as any materials that have been redirected from landfill. Primary materials are those with no recycled content – see *Environmental labels and declarations – Self-declared environmental claims* (Type II environmental labelling) (AMD 13493 – renumbered from BS ISO 14021:1999). Examples of recycled materials could include aggregates made from blast-furnace slag, or crushed concrete or brick liberated from a demolition project.

Definition of reused components

WRAP defines reclaimed (or reused) products and materials as those that have been taken from the waste stream and reused in their original form with minimal reprocessing. Materials such as whole bricks, slates or roof tiles would fall into this category.

Industry acceptance

There is a groundswell of opinion in favour of the use of recycled materials and reclaimed products. For example, in 2007, the Building Research Establishment's *Green Guide to Housing Specifications* included, as A+ rated materials:

❖ reclaimed timber floorboards;

❖ reclaimed bricks for internal partitions;

❖ reclaimed roofing slates; and

❖ reclaimed clay roof tiles.

Concerns over performance

While one might be tempted to believe that the case for recycled materials is the product of recent concerns for the environment, the reality is that for many years recycled materials, particularly aggregates, have been commonplace. For example, pulverised fuel ash and ground granular blast furnace slag have been covered by British Standards for at least 15 years.

Furthermore, very many construction products use a proportion of recycled materials in any event. Specifying a higher recycled content may mean the use of one manufacturer over another, but no loss in performance. In most cases, the standards and tests that apply to one material are exactly the same that apply to another material that uses a higher recycled content.

Drivers

The *Secure and Sustainable Buildings Act* 2004 has, among other things, extended the scope of the Building Regulations to cover the use of recycled and reused materials, and specifically includes a duty on the Secretary of State to report on the recycled content of buildings in England and Wales every two years – a measure intended to prevent the provisions from 'gathering dust on the shelf'.

The government collects a levy called Landfill Tax on every tonne of waste dumped in British landfill sites. The Landfill Tax Credit Scheme allows landfill operators to use 20% of the tax collected to promote more environmentally sustainable methods of waste management and environmental improvements. In any given project, 90% of the funding can come from the Landfill Tax Credit Scheme but the last 10% must come from another source.

A further measure to encourage sustainable practices is the Aggregates Levy. This levy reduces demand for primary aggregates by increasing their cost and makes the use of recycled and secondary materials more viable.

The Aggregates Levy Sustainability Fund uses some of the revenue from the Aggregates Levy to further address the environmental impacts associated with quarrying operations (noise, dust, visual intrusion, loss of amenity and damage to biodiversity).

Under Article 1 of the EC Framework Directive on waste (75/442/EEC – as amended by 91/156/EEC), waste is defined as any substance or object which the holder discards or intends or is required to discard. Regulation 1 of the *Waste Management Licensing Regulations* 1994 is the UK enactment of the Directive. It essentially requires that, other than where an exemption is prescribed, a waste management licence is required by anyone who deposits, recovers or disposes of household, commercial or industrial waste (the term 'controlled waste' is used to describe these types of waste). Part II of the *Environmental Protection Act* 1990 also deals with this subject.

Under the *Control of Pollution (Amendment) Act* 1989 and the *Controlled Waste (Registration of Carriers and Seizure of Vehicles) Regulations* 1991, anyone who, in the course of a business or in any other way for profit, transports controlled waste within Great Britain is required to register as a waste carrier. Similarly, someone who arranges for the disposal or recovery of waste but is not the holder of the waste (i.e. a broker) is required to register.

The above provisions could be seen as a barrier to the use of waste products for construction, although this should not necessarily be the case.

The Regulations do not apply to materials that do not fall under the definition of waste, although ascertaining whether or not waste is 'waste' can require some thought at an early stage. In particular, the following questions need to be addressed:

❖ Does the substance or object fall into one of the categories set out in Part II of Schedule 4 to the *Waste Management Licensing Regulations* 1994?

❖ If so, has it been discarded by its holder, do they have any intention of discarding it, or are they required to discard it?

Planning Policy Statement 1: *Delivering Sustainable Development* (PPS1) sets out the government's planning policies on the delivery of sustainable development through the planning system. One of the key policies is to ensure that sustainable development is pursued in an integrated manner, in line with the principles for sustainable development set out in the UK strategy. Regional planning bodies and local planning authorities should ensure that development plans promote outcomes in which environmental, economic and social objectives are achieved together over time. Development plans should consider the management of waste in ways that protect the environment and human health, including producing less waste and using it as a resource wherever possible.

Reclamation

The *Reclaimed and recycled construction materials handbook*, CIRIA (Construction Industry Research and Information Association) and DETR (Department of Environment, Transport and the Regions), in part 2, invites designers to consider the following questions:

❖ Which of the materials already on site (e.g. from buildings to be demolished) can be reclaimed or recycled for use in the new works?

❖ Can reclaimed or recycled materials from off site be used?

❖ How can the percentage of materials used in this project that will be reclaimed or recycled at the end of its life be maximised?

These questions will prompt a debate as to whether or not aiming for recycling or reclaiming is a sensible thing to do because, it may be perceived, the specification introduces additional risks into the construction process. Similarly, in order to design for recycling, component parts must be capable of being dismantled – and this in itself creates challenges. For example, conventional building orthodoxy dictates the use of Portland cement mortar in masonry construction. This effectively means that once laid, masonry units, whether they are bricks or blocks cannot be reclaimed. Portland cement prevents the clean dismantling of a wall and results in damage to the masonry during demolition. Conversely, if the masonry units are bedded in lime mortar (as they were 100 years ago) taking down and reclamation is perfectly feasible. Yet using lime mortar is something of a 'black art' to many engineers, specifiers and bricklayers – they are simply not trained to use it.

CIRIA advocates that a strategy towards using recycled or reclaimed materials should be the default position and not the alternative – such a move would be in line with the UK Government's stance on sustainability and waste management. However, this will not happen if the key decision-makers are not in tune with the concept, or if they lack the will to drive it through.

Are there any risks to health?

This is a difficult question to answer, but it could also apply equally to virgin products; there is no reason why recycled products need to be considered any differently – indeed in some circumstances, recycled products can actually perform better. Recycled carpets, for example, made from Polyethylene Therephthalate (PET), will release far less in the way of volatile organic compounds or formaldehyde than their virgin counterparts. Each case needs to be examined on its merits and a risk-assessment-based approach adopted. Where materials are being utilised for site works, sources of potential hazards are recognised and quantified, pathways identified along which the hazards may migrate through the environment, and receptors or targets on which any potentially hazardous substance(s) may impact are assessed.

Is there a sufficient local supply?

Sources such as WRAP and the National Green Specification have links to suppliers. On-site processing of waste concrete can yield a good supply of recycled aggregates, although authorisation will be needed from the local authority and the environmental impact of crushing operations will need to be considered. Care will be needed to ensure that the operations do not fall within the definition of controlled waste given earlier.

In May 2010, the London Waste and Recycling Board (LWARB) announced that it would fund £500,000 over three years to help set up a reuse centre in Croydon, South London, selling construction waste such as bricks and tiles. The centre is the first of its kind in the UK and is intended to divert over 3,500 tonnes of waste from landfill over five years.

Can the client be persuaded to accept the use of recycled or reclaimed material?

Can recycled materials be expected to perform as well as primary or virgin materials? Provided they are selected and specified properly and used in the way that the manufacturer intends, there should be no reason why they will fail to perform. As noted earlier, many materials are mainstream products, although quality in reclaimed material can be hard to control.

Is the selection of reclaimed/recycled material the best thing from an environmental point of view?

Some products contain high embodied energy as a result of remanufacturing processes or transport. Similarly, for example, the environmental consequences of crushing concrete in a congested city centre site might make the process unacceptable.

Can delivery/construction programmes be maintained?

For very many recycled materials, delivery schedules can be planned in advance – many products are mainstream (blocks, plasterboard, carpets, etc.) and are purchased in much the same way as virgin products. Difficulties can arise, however, in the supply of aggregates and products selected locally, particularly if the level of supply is likely to fluctuate.

Conclusion

By specifying materials that are either reclaimed or recycled, the overall value of recycled content in a building can be increased significantly and without there necessarily being any addition to cost. Reclamation of materials assists local economies and stimulates demand. But recycled materials are not new; they have been around for many years. All that needs to happen is a shift in awareness of what is available and the compelling arguments for taking greater care in specification and purchasing to ensure that the opportunities are met.

Further information

❖ WRAP (the Waste & Resources Action Programme): www.wrap.org.uk – advice on specifying recycled materials in house-building, construction, highways, estates management and other sectors.

❖ The *Reclaimed Building Products Guide*, freely downloadable from WRAP.

❖ Aggregain (WRAP): www.aggregain.org.uk – source of practical information on the use of recycled and secondary aggregates.

❖ BRE: www.bre.co.uk – BREEAM related assessment schemes and the *Green Guide to Specification*.

❖ Salvo: www.salvo.co.uk – Market place for reclaimed construction materials/products.

❖ National Green Specification: www.greenspec.co.uk – technical specifications, design and product information for sustainable construction.

❖ Sustainable Build: www.sustainablebuild.co.uk – impartial information and advice on sustainable development, building and using eco-friendly construction techiniques.

❖ The *Reclaimed and Recycled Construction Materials Handbook* – CIRIA.

❖ BioRegional: www.bioregional.com/about-us/sustainability-action-plan/ – an entrepreneurial charity which initiates and delivers practical solutions to sustainability.

Contributed by Trevor Rushton, trevor.rushton@watts.co.uk

Surveyors and sustainability

This section explains the practical implications for chartered surveyors who want to understand and embrace the principles of sustainable development. This will help to clarify the subject, highlight the changing duties of chartered surveyors, and develop knowledge. Surveyors have opportunities in many aspects of their daily roles to input and challenge opinions and decisions to create actively more sustainable developments. It is important that a surveyor's professional and personal limitations are also considered when proposing to improve developments in this way. Each differing profession is uniquely placed to contribute towards better sustainable communities.

RICS publishes key dedicated sustainability related guidance papers for RICS members. The *RICS Sustainability Policy* details the different areas of practice and the core principles of sustainable development.

There are three main professional groups that can impact on sustainability, each containing two or three key surveying practices.

The Land Group

❖ **Planning and development (P&D) surveyors**: P&D surveyors can influence every stage of planning and development to create more sustainable communities. P&D surveyors can assist public and private clients to protect the environment and regenerate areas by planning the use of land sustainably, as it is a fundamental natural resource. They can understand the impact the development could have on the natural built environment. Significant energy savings can also be made at the design stage through implementing positive forms of energy production. P&D surveyors can not only provide input in the physical aspects of a scheme but also in the social and environmental aspects. They should be aware of the government's heightened emphasis on design and quality within regeneration projects and their impact on climate, demographics, transport and sources of renewable energy.

❖ **Rural practice surveyors**: Their opportunity lies in the close links they have to landowners and the environment. They are involved at every stage of a development and can help to restore the natural and economic environment. Rural practice surveyors can provide advice to government bodies, local authorities and other interest groups on new and existing legislation. In order to give reasoned advice to clients, they will need to understand the costs involved in sustainable initiatives and payback periods. Areas of understanding would include protection and enhancement of biodiversity, land use/ecology, implications of flooding and drainage, cultural heritage, geology and soils, waste, and the potential for the introduction of renewable energy technologies.

❖ **Environmental surveyors**: Environmental surveyors are key in that their role requires them to consider the interaction of environmental issues in conjunction with land value. They survey and analyse data from contaminated land surveys and identify, record and monitor plants and/or animals in their natural environments, and they make recommendations to help preserve habitats and stimulate growth. Key tasks would be the application of life cycle costing and whole-life value analysis within their appraisals. They should have a consistent knowledge base of economic sustainability issues involving travel and transport, crime and security, health and well-being and Environmental Impact Assessments.

The Built Environment Group

❖ **Quantity surveyors and construction surveyors**: Specific areas for quantity surveyors to consider in sustainability would be life cycle costings, cost of alternative materials, renewable energy schemes, recycled content schemes, and ethical sourcing of materials and labour. Quantity and construction surveyors can help clients understand the value of sustainable developments, which will perform better economically and environmentally throughout the life cycle of the building. As part of their role due diligence must be performed at the initial stages to ensure all sustainability issues are reviewed at the development appraisal stage. Issues reviewed could be legal liabilities, and/or substantial cost that may affect decisions to invest, and the projected value of the development for rent or sale in the future.

❖ **Building surveyors**: Building surveyors can influence by the use of new legislation, e.g. Energy Performance Certificates, or simply by enhancing the character and quality of buildings. The promotion of sustainable options to clients as investments with estimated payback times and money-saving assets is important. Building surveyors also advise clients of new legislation which must be adhered to, to avoid prosecution and mitigate the environmental impact of buildings. Building surveyors can carry out inspections to assess if there are ecological features to be retained and protected during any potential works. Key details to note would be the locations of all relevant buildings, landscapes, local heritage and visual impacts, transport (existing and provision) and relevant social conditions.

❖ **Project manager surveyors**: Project managers can ensure issues such as energy use, water consumption, waste generation, biodiversity, travel and transport, and local skills are reviewed and considered. They can assist in setting requirements and adopting designs for assessments such as BREEAM or LEED.

The Property Group

❖ **Residential property surveyors**: Residential surveyors can advise both vendors and purchasers on energy efficiency and conservation within properties. They can also give practical suggestions on sustainable improvements to help energy ratings. Residential surveyors can provide advice at the design stage (for new build or extensions) through the choice of more sustainable materials, layout and specification. Potential sustainable factors to be considered are location, access to public transport, the level of energy efficiency of the property, potential hazardous substances in the vicinity, location of local space/amenity, and issues of noise, waste and other potential disturbances. Information collected is vital for landlords, tenants or potential buyers and includes, for example, likely running costs, energy efficiency and proximity to public transport.

❖ **Business property surveyors**: Business property surveyors can influence social, economic and environmental issues and advise owners and occupiers on commercial properties. Advice would include the management of properties (ensuring efficient disposal systems, particularly if a client produces high volumes of normal or hazardous waste), and also consideration of the infrastructure in relation to the site and how this could impact on the local community and the environment.

❖ **Valuation surveyors**: 'In accordance with International Valuation Standards, valuation surveyors are duty-bound to reflect the market's interpretation of the manner in which Sustainability is impacting on value – or price.' (*Surveying Sustainability: a short guide for the property professional*, RICS, 2007).

Valuation surveyors need to evaluate and understand the value of low-carbon buildings with lower operation costs, and their positive effect on environments. They should refer to the *RICS Valuation Standards* (the *Red Book*) for guidance. They should also ensure there is full disclosure of information relating to sustainability to ensure that all parties can make decisions with full knowledge.

Each group has many different roles within sustainable developments and these are reflected by the core principles drawn from the *RICS Sustainability Policy*:

❖ 'protection and enhancement of the natural environment;

❖ encouraging the sustainable use of resources;

❖ reduction of waste generation and the responsible disposal of waste;

❖ reduction of energy consumption;

❖ promotion of sustainable land use and transportation planning and management;

❖ promotion of sustainable design, development and construction practices, including whole-life costs and value; and

❖ promotion of community development and social inclusion.'

Extracts from the RICS Sustainability Policy are reproduced with permission from the RICS Land Group.

Chartered surveyors must meet client expectations to provide relevant appropriate and up to date advice on sustainable developments. The RICS guide *Surveying Sustainability; A Short Guide for the Property Professional*, which this section is drawn from, contains more in-depth detail for property surveyors under the above core principles. Surveyors have a clear role to play in promoting sustainability in their day-to-day work environments.

Further information

❖ *Sustainability and the RICS property lifecycle* (1st edition), RICS guidance note, 2009 (which provided source material for this section).

Contributed by Andrea Jutrzenka, andrea.jutrzenka@watts.co.uk

Knowledge management

Over the last 20 years 'knowledge management' has come to be recognised as a company asset alongside traditional assets such as land, labour and capital.

It is unique in its capacity to determine an organisation's (and even a nation's) competitive success – Japanese car manufacturing probably being one of the most recognisable of these successes.

Knowledge management begins with knowledge capture and this falls into two distinctive categories – soft techniques and hard techniques.

Soft techniques for knowledge capture

Soft techniques involve collaborative learning forums, such as project review meetings, value engineering and risk workshops. The knowledge generated then requires robust systems for capture, recording, storage and reuse.

Hard techniques for knowledge capture

Hard techniques include ICT systems, particularly intra and extranets and workflow/business process management (BPM) software.

Project extranets utilise client server technology and allow access using only a web browser. Company intranets are a robust system for the recording, storage and reuse of knowledge, facilitating ease of recovery and reuse of knowledge.

'Smart' technology

With the onset of smart or intelligent technology, capture, storage and retrieval of knowledge is today relatively easy to achieve. Building management systems and 'smarthomes' systems, once considered futuristic, have now become a reality and in some cases may even be standard installations.

Of the most recent smart technology inventions available quick response (QR) barcodes are probably seeing the fastest growth. These 'intelligent' 2D bar codes are capable of storing in excess of 7,000 bits of data. In comparison a standard bar code stores 22 bits of data. QR codes can be used for storing and transferring URL, text, numeric, image and even video data.

Using this technology, a building component part and even whole building information can be accessed via QR barcodes, enabling smart readers to access information pertaining to materials and methodologies used in any given situation. In effect this allows the building to describe the materials and processes used in its construction.

Why knowledge management is important

Managing organisational knowledge is important in the 21st century due to the vast volume of project data generated on a daily basis.

Direct benefits include:

- ❖ no 'reinventing the wheel';
- ❖ rapid problem solving;
- ❖ better and faster decision making;
- ❖ more innovation;
- ❖ less repetition of mistakes;
- ❖ lower dependence upon key individuals;
- ❖ competitive advantage; and
- ❖ less waste.

Sustainability

In practice most organisations will use a mixture of hard and soft techniques but often with very little strategy for capturing and storing the project knowledge generated.

Robust strategies should include:

❖ mentoring and coaching – assigning a mentor with adequate experience and expertise to facilitate knowledge transfer;

❖ collaborative software – applications designed to assist in developing and assisting team working (e.g. team calendars, discussion forums, etc.);

❖ development of Communities of Practice (CoPs) – teams and groups whom share common interests; and

❖ apprenticeships – the traditional method of transferring skills and knowledge.

Why organisations undertake knowledge management

The table below summarises the benefits of knowledge management.

Adaptability	❖ anticipate potential opportunities ❖ adapt to unanticipated changes ❖ responsiveness to new market demands ❖ learn faster than competitors.
Creativity	❖ innovate new products and services ❖ identify new business opportunities ❖ access and build on experience to fuel innovation.
Internal effectiveness	❖ staff retention ❖ capture expertise of personnel ❖ capture and share best practice ❖ streamline internal processes.
External effectiveness	❖ improve communication ❖ capture new information about the sector ❖ manage customer relationships ❖ enhance supply chain management ❖ improve strategic alliances.

Cross project knowledge management

In order to prevent 'reinventing the wheel', effective knowledge management captures project learning and stores it for reuse on subsequent projects.

It is important that construction specialists are involved at project conception stage in order to maximise accrued knowledge. This is related back to the client's objectives and requirements and helps to formulate a strategy for compliance with client business needs.

Successful knowledge transfer between projects is influenced by the method of capture (when and how).

Adopted systems for capture should:

❖ facilitate the reuse of collective learning by the individual firm and project team involved in delivery;

❖ provide knowledge which can be used at the operational and maintenance stages of the asset lifecycle; and

❖ involve members of the supply chain, irrespective of contractual arrangements for involvement.

Project reviews

Project review is recognised as the key procedure of the development cycle for knowledge capture.

It allows consolidation of project learning and assists in providing a shared understanding across the delivery team.

The RIBA plan of work (2010) mentions only review of project performance in use, while the CIOB *Code of Practice for Project Management for Construction and Development* (4th edition, 2009) contains post-project review as the ultimate stage for work, post completion and handover.

This methodology has come under some criticism from within the industry as many participants are involved only in the early stages of development and have moved on by the time completion is achieved. As such, project knowledge is at risk of being lost due to the time lapse involved.

Project reviews for knowledge capture should:

❖ contain a description and comment on the nature of the development and client objectives and requirements;

❖ detail the project organisation structure;

❖ highlight project milestones and key activities making note of any specific problems and solutions;

❖ detail any unusual developments and difficulties, and their solutions, noting the involvement of relevant parties;

❖ contain a summary of strengths, weaknesses and lessons learned; and

❖ detail variances to:
  – cost,
  – scheduling and programming,
  – technical competency of the team,
  – overall quality of the completed project,
  – health and safety,
  – sustainability requirements, including details of how these were implemented.

Contracts and knowledge management

The nature of the contract also influences knowledge capture. For example, design and build contracts require the contractor to be involved much earlier than traditional procurement routes. This leads to greater continuity of knowledge transfer across different stages of development.

Private Finance Initiative (PFI) takes this strategy further with contractor involvement at finance and life cycle stages.

Framework agreements have similarities to this in that the contractor and consultants are involved across projects for a longer term (typically five years). These arrangements allow the project team to maintain and improve continuity, increase organisational knowledge and consistently develop procedures and best practice.

Knowledge management as an asset

Company and organisational assets fall into one of two categories:

❖ tangible assets (such as buildings, IT equipment, etc.); and

❖ intangible assets (such as relationships, culture, reputation and knowledge management).

The distinction is easily made as tangible assets are finite resources and depreciate through use. Intangible assets, and in particular knowledge, grow through use and depreciate when not used. Knowledge can also be used by many people at the same time, in contrast to some tangible assets which are only able to be used singularly.

Contributed by David Massingham, david.massingham@watts.co.uk

Building information modelling

What is building information modelling (BIM)?

'BIM is described as being digital representation of physical and functional characteristics of a facility creating a shared knowledge resource for information about it forming a reliable basis for decisions during its lifecycle, from earliest conception to demolition'. (Source: *BIM in the UK*, NBS briefing January 2011, RIBA et al)

BIM needs to be viewed as more than a design process. BIM allows 3D, 4D (time) and 5D (cost) modelling to be incorporated into one virtual building model, facilitating design, feasibility testing and analysis by different parties on the same model at the same time – thus reducing the need for reproduction of design information and speeding up the design and feasibility functions.

The model also contains information about the construction and finishes of each element and is able to store information on the resources needed for construction, enabling accurate specification and programming to be produced. It is therefore more about the database of information than it is about the visual model itself.

Benefits of BIM are possibly not yet fully realised as changes in technology present greater opportunities on a constantly changing basis. However, some of the benefits which can be realised immediately include:

- ❖ improved design process;
- ❖ coordination of construction and specification information (with the possibility to link to national building specifications, dependent upon software package);
- ❖ incorporation of environmental analysis
- ❖ quicker design revision
- ❖ quantity take offs
- ❖ planning and resource allocation
- ❖ more efficient construction phasing, with less wastage; and
- ❖ links to facilities management for lifetime planning.

BIM software facilitates change tracking and conflict checks or component clashes, which are highlighted as changes to the model are carried out by each member of the design team. This allows a degree of feasibility and performance testing which in the past has taken months (or years) to complete. It also reduces information losses during transfer and errors created through human checking.

BIM requires greater and earlier interaction between the members of the whole supply chain and because of this traditional design methods are being challenged. It is thought that architects in particular will need to change their approach to the early stages of construction and adopt new methodologies for sharing information across the supply chain.

BIM software

Currently there is no one piece of software available to encompass all of the building functions, therefore various pieces of software will contribute to the BIM. It is essential that there is a common language between differing software packages. The Building Smart Organisation has developed a standard language known as IFC (Industry Foundation Classes), which is an evolving international standard (ISO 16739) for this purpose. (Source: BDONLINE.co.uk Monday 23 May 2011 Page 2)

BSI has produced a standard (ISO 29481-1) for the production of an Information Delivery Manual (IDM). The standard gives guidance for production and issuing of documents, specifying items such as naming, referencing, styling and sign off. Further information can be obtained at : www.bsigroup.com/standards

A BIM system no longer uses lines, shapes, volumes and text boxes to construct the building (2D or 3D). Instead it uses data sets to describe objects virtually, similarly to how they will be handled physically. This methodology facilitates full interoperability and integration which is the key to BIM.

Autodesk has a number of software packages available for BIM, some of these being: Buzzsaw, Vault, Revit Sharer and BIM 360. Further information can be obtained at http://usa.autodesk.com

BIM software such as REVIT by Autodesk and ArchiCAD by GRAPHISOFT are 'intelligent' software packages in that they are able recognise elements of the construction (such as walls ceilings, windows, etc.), therefore when changes are made to one element (e.g. windows) the model adjusts the openings in walls. Where this creates a conflict it will be easily identified and can be adjusted accordingly.

Implementation of BIM

In 2010 Paul Morrell, the government's chief construction adviser, announced that BIM would be incorporated on all public building projects by 2016. To achieve this the government commenced a rolling programme in the summer of 2011.

The industry has also seen an increase in adoption of BIM since the onset of the credit crunch, driven by the need for reduced costs, increased productivity and new ways of working. However there is a cost to implementing BIM systems, which include investment in hardware, software and staff training. Currently these are calculated to be £10,000 per 'seat'.

Careful consideration will need to be given when devising a strategy for adoption of BIM. Using a pilot project, which simulates real development, can mitigate expensive mistakes and allows the full use of support and training offered by software vendors.

Formulation of a strategy for implementation of BIM should consider the following:

❖ nomination of a senior person to champion BIM;

❖ selection of team members who are enthusiastic about BIM and are up for the challenge;

❖ identification of a training programme which complements organisational objectives;

❖ the level of support services offered by the software vendor;

❖ required changes to existing processes; and

❖ direct and indirect costs associated with implementation of BIM.

Drawbacks of BIM

The drawbacks of using BIM currently tend to revolve around the level of responsibility of the parties involved.

It is essential to establish who carries ultimate responsibility for the design created within the model. All parties are able to carry out changes to the model therefore it is also essential to ensure that changes can be tracked. Some software companies that sell packages claim to provide BIM as an 'add on' – such packages and companies need to be treated with extreme caution for the reasons mentioned above.

Construction contracts, possibly with the exception of PPC 2000 do not currently cater for multi-party arrangements. The usual bi-partite arrangements would need to be amended considerably to cater for BIM. However, there are currently two US documents which, as their terminology is not specifically US-orientated, would be adaptable for use with BIM projects.

Consensus DOCS 301 is a form of contract developed by contractors and puts BIM at the forefront of its recommendations with greater emphasis on cost, ownership and use of the BIM. Document E202 tends to be architectural and relies on construction phases and design development.

The future for BIM

BIM is not a new concept and it is already being effectively used on new build and refurbishment schemes with equal success. National surveys carried out in 2010 have indicated that many design practices are planning to implement BIM in the next three or four years, although the same surveys indicate that a large percentage of the construction industry was not aware of BIM at all.

In July 2011 the BIM industry working group issued the BIM working strategy paper which has been broadly accepted by Constructing Excellence (notwithstanding issues surrounding contractual arrangements for working with BIM).

Some concerns will inevitably surround the responsible parties and issues of liability until robust contractual arrangements can be resolved. It is hoped that this will happen with the next major revision of standard contract documents. At the time of going to print these were being reviewed by the BIM industry working group, in particular NEC 3, which is expected to be the first standard document to fully address BIM.

Further information is available at: www.constructingexcellence.org.uk and https://KTN.innovateuk.org

Contributed by David Massingham, david.massingham@watts.co.uk

Useful resources

The RICS Assessment of Professional Competence

The Assessment of Professional Competence (APC) is a route to professional membership of the Royal Institution of Chartered Surveyors (RICS). There are 21 APC pathways, which relate to land, property, construction and the environment.

Successfully completing the APC entitles RICS members to practice as qualified chartered surveyors. There are a number of routes to membership and details of these, the APC pathways and specific requirements are set out on the RICS website: www.rics.org/apc

What does it involve?

Candidates are required to complete a period of structured training, normally for a minimum of 23 months, although this depends upon the entry route. During this period they are allocated an APC Counsellor and Supervisor who will give them guidance on their training and day-to-day work.

The APC training is competency-based and candidates are required to demonstrate that they have the skills and abilities to satisfy specific competencies.

Assessment takes the form of a submission of a suitable project or instruction that the candidate has been working on and feels adequately demonstrates their experience to date and a professional interview known as the 'final assessment'. Candidates are required to make a presentation to a panel of RICS assessors and answer detailed questions relating to their work experience and wider issues.

RICS has produced a series of guides and templates to assist candidates, supervisors, counsellors and employers, all of which can be downloaded from the RICS website. In particular, the APC pathway guides provide essential advice on the competency requirements for relevant pathways.

Ten APC tips

1. Choose your employer wisely: Attempt to gauge a firm's commitment to graduate training by enquiring about the level of support and training offered. It is also essential to gain the correct spread of work experience during your training period to satisfy relevant competency requirements.

2. Get organised: The timing of your APC application and other submissions can be critical. For example, a delay in your enrolment could hold up your final assessment by six months. Clarify requirements and diarise key dates and milestones.

3. Carefully consider competency choice: You should do some research and set about gaining good advice in relation to competency choices from your employer and colleagues who have recently undertaken their APC. It is essential to ensure that there is a 'fit' with the range and nature of work you will be undertaking.

4. Get out and about: There is no substitute for quality one-to-one on-the-job training; so try to ensure that you make the most of shadowing opportunities from the outset of your training period. If your employer is multi-disciplinary try to gain experience with other disciplines, such as project management and quantity surveying, as this experience will broaden your knowledge thus aiding you in the final assessment.

5. Take ownership of your training: Make time to administer your APC paperwork and proactively set about identifying and planning your own training needs and work experience requirements. Your Supervisor and Counsellor should help with this.

6. Network and get advice: Join in with company activities, speak to colleagues about their experience of the APC, consult with your local RICS APC Doctor, and get involved with RICS MATRICS, the organisation for young chartered surveyors, trainees, graduates and friends you graduated with now working in the profession.

You will benefit from advice, broaden your perspective of the profession and, as importantly, have fun and make lifelong friendships.

7. Professional approach: Keeping abreast of current trends and hot topics is essential. Reading relevant property and industry magazines and keeping up to date with changes in legislation, etc. will help build your confidence as a rounded professional, along with providing you with hours to log for continuous professional development (CPD).

8. Personal development: You will need to develop personal skills during the course of your training period in preparation for the final assessment. Good time management, organisation and presentation skills are essential. These cannot be attained at the last minute.

9. Technical competence: Continually develop your technical ability. Be resourceful, grow interest in your subject area, attend seminars and undertake structured reading relevant to your workload.

10. Prepare for the final assessment: Allow plenty of time to prepare for the final assessment interview. Ask experienced colleagues to conduct a mock final assessment interview. Receive feedback, refine your presentation and repeat as necessary. Attempt to gain interview experience with other companies.

Contact details

Royal Institution of Chartered Surveyors (RICS)

> Website: www.rics.org/apc and www.rics.org/matrics
>
> Email: contactrics@rics.org
>
> Telephone: +44 (0)870 333 1600

Watts Group PLC

> Website: www.watts.co.uk/working-for-us/
>
> Email human resources: human.resources@watts.co.uk
>
> Telephone: +44 (0)20 7280 8000

Useful references

These guides are all available to download free on the RICS website:

- ❖ *APC candidates guide*;
- ❖ *APC/ATC requirements and competencies guide*;
- ❖ *APC guide for supervisors, counsellors and employers*;
- ❖ *APC Pathway guides*; and
- ❖ *Rules of Conduct*- Guidance note

The following guides are available for purchase at: www.ricsbooks.com

- ❖ *APC 2012: Your practical guide to success*, published 2011;
- ❖ *AssocRICS: Your practical guide to success*, published 2011; and
- ❖ *Supervisors' and counsellors' guide to the APC*, 3rd edition, published 2009.

Contributed by Robert Burke, robert.burke@watts.co.uk and Doug Vernon, doug.vernon@watts.co.uk

Conversion factors

Within the following table, to convert the units in column A into the equivalent in column B, multiply by the factor shown. To convert the units in column B into the equivalent in column A, divide by the factor shown.

Units in Column A	Factor	To give units in Column B
acres	0.404685642	hectares
acres	4046.8627	m^2
atmospheres (atm)	0.007348	ton/sq inch
atm	76	cm of mercury
atm	14.7	pounds/sq in.
atm	1,058	tons/sq ft
bars	10,200	kgm^{-2}
bars	2,089	pounds/sq ft
bars	14.5	pounds/sq in.
Btu	10.409	litre-atmosphere
Btu	1,054.8	joules
Btu	0.0002928	kWh
Btu/hr	0.2931	Watts (W)
cm	0.03281	feet
cm	0.3937	inches
cm	0.00001	km
cm	0.01	m
cm	10	mm
cm^2	0.001076	sq feet
cm^2	0.1550	sq inches
cm^2	0.0001	m^2
cm^2	100	mm^2
cm^2	0.0001196	sq yards
cm^3	0.0003531	cu feet
cm^3	0.06102	cu inches
cm^3	0.000001	m^3
cm^3	0.000001308	cu yards
cm^3	0.0002642	gallons (US liq.)
cm^3	0.001	litres
cm^3	0.002113	pints (US liq.)
cm^3	0.001057	quarts (US liq.)
cubic feet	28,320	cm^3
cubic feet	1,728	cu inches
cubic feet	0.02832	m^3
cubic feet	0.03704	cu yards
cubic feet	7.48052	gallons (US liq.)

Units in Column A	Factor	To give units in Column B
cubic feet	28.32	litres
cubic feet	59.84	pints (US liq.)
cubic feet	29.92	quarts (US liq.)
cubic inches	16.39	cm³
cubic inches	0.0005787	cu feet
cubic inches	0.00001639	m³
cubic inches	0.00002143	cu yards
cubic inches	0.004329	gallons (US liq.)
cubic inches	0.01639	litres
cubic inches	0.03463	pints (US liq.)
cubic inches	0.01732	quarts (US liq.)
cubic inches	28.38	bushels (dry)
cubic yards	764,600	cm³
cubic yards	27	cu feet
cubic yards	46,656	cu inches
cubic yards	0.7646	m³
cubic yards	202	gallons (US liq.)
cubic yards	764.6	litres
cubic yards	1,615.9	pints (US liq.)
cubic yards	807.9	quarts (US liq.)
cubic yards/min	0.45	cubic ft/sec
cubic yards/min	3.367	gallons/sec
cubic yards/min	12.74	litres/sec
days	86,400	seconds
drams	1.7718	grammes
drams	0.0625	ounces
feet	30.48	cm
feet	0.0003048	km
feet	0.3048	m
feet	0.0001645	miles (naut.)
feet	0.0001984	miles (stat.)
feet	304.8	mm
feet/sec	30.48	cm/sec
feet/sec	1.097	km/hr
feet/sec	0.5921	knots
feet/sec	18.29	m/min
feet/sec	0.6818	miles/hr
feet/sec	0.01136	miles/min
gallons	0.004951	cu yards
gallons	3.785	litres
gallons (liq. Br. Imp.)	1.20095	gallons (US liq.)

Units in Column A	Factor	To give units in Column B
gallons (US liq.)	0.83267	gallons (Br. Imp.)
gallons of water (US liq.)	8.3453	pounds of water
gallons of water (liq. Br. Imp.)	10.022	pounds of water
gallons/min (US liq.)	0.0002228	cu ft/sec
gallons/min (US liq.)	0.06308	litres/sec
gallons/min (US liq.)	8.0208	cu ft/hr
gallons/min (liq. Br. Imp.)	4.54609	litres/min
gallons/sec (US liq.)	0.8326725	gallons/sec (Br. Imp.)
grammes	0.001	kg
grammes	1,000	mg
grammes	0.03527	ounces (avdp)
grammes	0.03215	ounces (troy)
grammes	0.002205	pounds
hectares	2.471053816	acres
hectares	10,000	m^2
horsepower	33,000	foot-lbs/min
horsepower	550	foot-lbs/sec
horsepower	10/68	kg-calories/min
horsepower	0.7457	Kilowatts (kW)
horsepower	745.7	watts
inches	2.540	cm
inches	0.002540	m
inches	25.40	mm
joules	0.0009480	Btu
kg	1,000	grammes
kg	9.807	joules/metre (newtons)
kg	2.205	pounds
kgm^{-2}	0.00009678	atmospheres
kgm^{-2}	0.00009807	bars
kgm^{-2}	0.003281	feet of water
kgm^{-2}	0.002896	inches of mercury
kgm^{-2}	0.2048	pounds/sq ft
km	3,281	feet
km	39,370	inches
km	0.6214	miles
km/hr	27.78	cm/sec
km/hr	54.68	feet/min
km/hr	0.9113	feet/sec
km/hr	0.5396	knots
km/hr	16.67	m/min
km/hr	0.6214	miles/hr

Units in Column A	Factor	To give units in Column B
kWh	3,413	Btu
kw	56.92	Btu/min
kw	1,000	watts
litres	1,000	cm³
litres	0.03531	cu feet
litres	61.02	cu inches
litres	0.001	m³
litres	0.001308	cu yards
litres	0.2642	gallons (US liq.)
litres	2.113	pints (US liq.)
litres	1.057	quarts (US liq.)
m	0.0005396	miles (naut.)
m	0.0006214	miles (stat.)
m	1,000	mm
m	1.094	yards
m	3.2808	feet
m²	0.000247105	acres
m²	0.0001	hectares
m²	10.7639104	square feet
m³	1,000,000	cm³
m³	35.31	cu feet
m³	61,023	cu inches
m³	1.308	cu yards
m³	264.2	gallons (US liq.)
m³	1,000	litres
m³	2,113	pints (US liq.)
m³	1,057	quarts (US liq.)
metres per min (m/min)	1.667	cm/sec
m/min	3.281	feet/min
m/min	0.05468	feet/sec
m/min	0.06	km/hr
m/min	0.03238	knots
m/min	0.03728	miles/hr
m/sec	196.8	feet/min
m/sec	3.281	feet/sec
m/sec	3.6	km/hr
m/sec	0.06	km/min
m/sec	2.237	miles/hr
m/sec	0.03728	miles/min
miles (statute)	5,280	feet
miles (statute)	63,360	inches

Useful resources

Units in Column A	Factor	To give units in Column B
miles (statute)	1.609	km
miles (statute)	1,609	metres (m)
miles (statute)	0.868357	miles (nautical)
miles (statute)	1,760	yards
miles/hr	44.70	cm/sec
miles/hr	88	feet/min
miles/hr	1.467	feet/sec
miles/hr	1.609	km/hr
miles/hr	0.02682	km/min
miles/hr	0.8684	knots
miles/hr	26.82	m/min
miles/hr	0.1667	miles/min
ml	0.001	litres
mm	0.1	cm
mm	0.003281	feet
mm	0.03937	inches
mm	0.000001	km
mm	0.001	m
ounces	0.0625	pounds
ounces	0.9115	ounces (troy)
pounds/cu ft	0.01602	grammes/cm³
pounds/cu ft	16.02	kg/m⁻³
pounds/sq in.	703.1	kgm⁻²
pounds/sq in.	144	pounds/sq ft
quarts	0.9463	litres
square feet	0.00002296	acres
square feet	929	cm²
square feet	144	sq inches
square feet	0.0929	m²
square feet	0.1111	sq yards
watts	3.413	Btu/hr
watts	0.05688	Btu/min
watts	0.001341	horsepower
watts	0.00136	horsepower (metric)
watts	0.01433	kg-calories/min
watts	0.001	kilowatts

To convert temperature

$$°C = 5/9 \ (°F) - 32$$
$$°F = 9/5 \ (°C) + 32$$

Contributed by Trevor Rushton, trevor.rushton@watts.co.uk

Watts' publications

For further information on any of the following publications, please contact Watts' Marketing Department. T: +44 (0)20 7280 8000. Email: marketing@watts.co.uk

Watts website

watts.co.uk

The Watts website gives an overview of the business and includes information about our staff, services, sectors and expertise. The website also features the latest industry news and back issues of Watts' technical newsletter, the *Watts Bulletin*. The 'working for us' section contains detailed information for potential staff and graduates, including our latest vacancies.

Watts Bulletin

The *Watts Bulletin* is the technical companion to the *Watts Pocket Handbook*, regularly keeping its readership abreast of industry news. It covers a variety of topics, including environmental issues, health and safety, new materials and the latest techniques within the industry. It is distributed to selected clients and contacts by email.

Subscription is complimentary and available on request from Watts' Marketing Department or on the Watts website. Back copies of the Bulletin are also available on the Watts website. To register go to www.watts.co.uk/publications

Watts 2012

Watts 2012 is a comprehensive review of the business – the services we offer, how we deliver and why our people make the difference. The review outlines Watts' expertise in project management, technical due diligence and specialist consultancy services, as well as our experience across market sectors and, above all, our passion for buildings. Hard copy and PDF versions are available from Watts' Marketing Department.

An introduction to Watts…

The publication *An introduction to Watts* offers a general synopsis of the business, focusing on Watts' experience in various sectors using case study examples. Bespoke versions for each of Watts' local offices are available on request from Watts' Marketing Department.

Watts on Twitter

@Watts_Group

Followers of the Watts Twitter page will receive up-to-the-minute information about the business, our events and staff activites. The page also includes comment on industry news and issues from our experts, as well as links to the latest *Watts Bulletin* articles.

Watts on LinkedIn

Watts' LinkedIn company page allows members to connect with our staff and learn more about their experience in the property and construction industry. Members can also join the *Watts Bulletin* group, an open forum to discuss issues arising from bulletin articles.

See also RICS resources for RICS publications written by Watts' employees as authors.

Contributed by Kirsty Maclagan, kirsty.maclagan@watts.co.uk

RICS resources

www.isurv.com

Building value from knowledge

isurv is an online database of best practice guidance, providing expert commentary on surveying issues, RICS standards products, model letters, forms and a case law database. Continually updated, and with over 280 contributors (including a number from Watts), it is an ideal resource for surveyors and other built environment professionals.

For more information or to take out a free trial, please visit www.isurv.com

www.ricsbooks.com

Investigating defects in commercial and industrial buildings

Trevor Rushton, trevor.rushton@watts.co.uk

ISBN: 978 1 84219 441 6

Arranged by building element, this technical yet highly practical book follows a workflow structure mirroring the process of carrying out a survey of a commercial or industrial building.

Investigating hazardous and deleterious building materials

Trevor Rushton, trevor.rushton@watts.co.uk

ISBN: 978 1 84219 291 7

This book should be your first point of reference for practical guidance to the identification and treatment of problems associated with some types of building materials.

Residential building defects

Geoff Hunt

ISBN: 978 1 84219 508 6

A practical, no-nonsense, easily digestible guide, ideal for all building surveyors dealing with residential properties, whether graduates, sole practitioners or those working as part of a larger organisation.

Remedying damp

Ralph Burkinshaw

ISBN: 978 1 84219 305 1

This book provides the knowledge and tools to understand how to deal with damp problems in buildings, including practical help and advice in tackling the effects of damp and possible remediation action.

Index

Index

Index

Watts Group directory

Watts
Property and Construction Consultants

watts.co.uk

Belfast
Scottish Provident Building
7 Donegall Square West
Belfast BT1 6JH
T: +44 (0)28 9024 8222

Birmingham
Colmore Place, 39 Bennetts Hill
Birmingham B2 5SN
T: +44 (0)121 265 2310

Bristol
25 Marsh Street
Bristol BS1 4AQ
T: +44 (0)117 927 5800

Dublin
74 Fitzwilliam Lane
Dublin 2
T: +353 (0)1 703 8750

Edinburgh
86 George Street
Edinburgh EH2 3BU
T: +44 (0)131 226 9250

Glasgow
176 Bath Street
Glasgow G2 4HG
T: +44 (0)141 353 2211

The Hague
Baron de Coubertinlaan 39
2719 EN Zoetermeer
PO Box 7246
2701 AE Zoetermeer
T: +31 (0)79 361 88 91

Leeds
49a St Paul's Street
Leeds LS1 2TE
T: +44 (0)113 245 3555

London
1 Great Tower Street
London EC3R 5AA
T: +44 (0)20 7280 8000

Manchester
60 Fountain Street
Manchester M2 2FE
T: +44 (0)161 831 6180

Stockholm
Wallingatan 18
111 24 Stockholm
T: +46 (0)8 791 7300

European alliances
Watts has strategic alliances with several other firms throughout continental and
eastern Europe. For further information, please contact:
Mark Sherrell, Director
Tel: +49 30 345 0569 0

Watts.